Trust beyond Borders

CONTEMPORARY POLITICAL AND SOCIAL ISSUES

Alan Wolfe, Series Editor

Contemporary Political and Social Issues provides a forum in which social scientists and seasoned observers of the political scene use their expertise to comment on issues of contemporary importance in American politics, including immigration, affirmative action, religious conflict, gay rights, welfare reform, and globalization.

Trust beyond Borders

Immigration, the Welfare State, and Identity in Modern Societies

MARKUS M. L. CREPAZ

with a Foreword by Arend Lijphart

THE UNIVERSITY OF MICHIGAN PRESS
ANN ARBOR

Copyright © by the University of Michigan 2008
All rights reserved
Published in the United States of America by
The University of Michigan Press
Manufactured in the United States of America
∞ Printed on acid-free paper

2011   2010   2009   2008   4   3   2   1

A CIP catalog record for this book is available from the British Library.

Library of Congress Cataloging-in-Publication Data

Crepaz, Markus M. L., 1959–
    Trust beyond borders : immigration, the welfare state, and
    identity in modern societies / Markus M. L. Crepaz ; with a foreword
    by Arend Lijphart.
        p.   cm. — (Contemporary political and social issues)
    Includes bibliographical references and index.
    ISBN-13: 978-0-472-09976-4 (cloth : alk. paper)
    ISBN-10: 0-472-09976-0 (cloth : alk. paper)
    ISBN-13: 978-0-472-06976-7 (pbk. : alk. paper)
    ISBN-10: 0-472-06976-4 (pbk. : alk. paper)
    1. Welfare state.   2. Emigration and immigration—Government
policy.   3. Ethnicity—Economic aspects.   I. Title.
    JC479.C74   2007
    325'.1—dc22   2006103261

To Nicole and
the Austrian welfare state:
for nourishment, emotional and material

Foreword
The Resilience of the Welfare State

AREND LIJPHART

MARKUS CREPAZ'S *TRUST BEYOND BORDERS* is a highly significant contribution to comparative politics, which I'm sure will be welcomed with enthusiasm by the political science profession. In particular,
I admire his creative combination of the literatures on immigration and
the welfare state and the further link that he establishes with the concept
of interpersonal trust.

Crepaz's findings suggest a welcome optimism about the future of the
welfare state—one of the most important achievements of the industrialized democracies. There are numerous challenges to the viability of
modern welfare states, especially the increasing longevity of their populations—a favorable development the welfare state itself is at least partly
responsible for—and their low birthrates. But it is certainly good news
that the large-scale immigration into most of the advanced industrialized
countries in recent decades is not likely to lead to their demise.

It is tempting to extrapolate from the American experience of immigration-induced diversity to the European present and future. But the
fact that the United States has failed to develop a complete welfare state
probably has much more to do with the weakness of the political Left
and the absence of significant socialist and social-democratic parties. This
is the most frequently discussed aspect of "American exceptionalism."
My own work with Bernard Grofman and Matthew S. Shugart on
American democracy in comparative perspective finds that when we

compare the United States with 28 other contemporary democracies almost all of the principal attributes of American democracy—formal
governmental institutions, as well as political parties, elections and electoral systems, interest groups, and so on—are either unique or highly unusual. The United States is very clearly a *different* democracy. This does
not mean that it should not be included in comparative studies but that
we should be careful when drawing general lessons from the American
example. Such caution is especially important because political scientists
have analyzed American government and politics much more thoroughly than the political systems of other countries. Extremely important and useful knowledge has been accumulated in this way—but with
only limited generalizability beyond the American case.

Crepaz's conclusion that the continuation of the modern welfare state
is not fatally threatened by increasing ethnic diversity is completely persuasive. In addition to the arguments that he presents, one might consider indirect evidence from countries such as the Netherlands, Belgium,
and Austria (see especially Lijphart 1969, 1977). All three developed their
extensive welfare systems in the first 15 to 20 years after World War II.
During this period, their societies were deeply divided along religious,
ideological, and, in the Belgian case, linguistic lines—to such an extent
that it is correct to describe them as consisting of separate and mutually
antagonistic subsocieties. The societal cleavages were also so serious that
power-sharing institutions were needed to maintain the stability of their
democratic systems. What is significant is that their welfare states could
be developed in spite of these deep cleavages. The differences between
current immigrant and native populations may be even greater than the
older religious- ideological-linguistic divisions, but they are not different
in kind. Since welfare states could be instituted in spite of the older di-
versities, it is not unrealistic to expect that they could be maintained in
spite of the new ones as well.

Finally, *Trust beyond Borders* makes the important point that political institutions are capable of generating trust. This is in line with the general
assumption of the so-called new institutionalism, that political structures
can and do influence political cultures. It is worth pointing out that the
early behaviorists did not really argue the opposite. For instance, in their
major behavioral work *The Civic Culture,* Gabriel A. Almond and Sidney
Verba wrote that structural and cultural phenomena are variables in "a
complex, multidirectional system of causality" instead of merely a one-
way impact of culture on structure (1963, 35). The new institutionalist lit-

erature has been gradually assembling the evidence needed to prove this thesis. Crepaz now adds another impressive piece of evidence: the welfare state has nurtured a broad sense of moral community originally designed to bridge class conflict but now having similar effects in nurturing attitudes among natives that are less hostile to immigrants. Just as the welfare state was able to bridge class conflicts, it can now bridge conflicts between natives and newcomers.

Contents

Figures

Tables

Preface and Acknowledgments

In the spring of 2004, visiting Vienna, the capital of my homeland Austria, my wife and I found ourselves one Saturday morning in one of the magnificent market squares, where a rainbow of people made of different races, religions, languages, and any other conceivable difference were offering their wares. This bazaar of humanity struck me unawares. I had visited Vienna many times before the end of the cold war. In those days, it was not unusual to encounter the occasional guest worker from Turkey or Yugoslavia, but the iron curtain brutally kept East and West apart. On that spring morning, however, reveling in the cacophony of voices, I realized that Vienna is reclaiming its function of bridging the cultures of East and West.

Yet, as I was partaking in this multicultural mélange, I couldn't help but ask: what is the nature of this amalgamation of peoples? Do they combine like milk added to coffee and thereby create something new or is this mix more like a tossed salad, which is quite colorful yet each vegetable is clearly visible and distinct in color, shape, and taste? My highly unscientific observations on that morning led me to conclude that it is more likely the latter. If that is in fact the case, I wondered: will Austrians, or for that matter any natives in modern welfare states, continue to fund the welfare state with their taxes if they perceive that the recipients of their sacrifices are increasingly people who are quite different from themselves?

Fortunately, I had the support of many individuals and organizations in my attempt to answer these questions. I am deeply indebted to my colleague and friend Christopher S. Allen at the University of Georgia for reading my manuscript in most remarkable detail. While he was unsparing in his criticism, his comments were always incisive and insightful and were conveyed with a civility becoming of a New Englander. The advice of Keith Banting and Will Kymlicka, both at Queens University in Canada, was invaluable and greatly appreciated. Gary P. Freeman at the University of Texas at Austin and Jack Citrin at the University of California, Berkeley, read various chapters of my manuscript and provided very helpful suggestions. Christian Joppke, from the International University in Bremen, Germany, graciously provided his assessment of my manuscript, which helped improve it in critical ways. The detailed comments of two anonymous reviewers were fair and appropriate and led to the incorporation of many of their suggestions into the final volume. I would like to thank Jim Reische, the acquisitions editor for political science at the University of Michigan Press, who helped me navigate the treacherous sandbars and rocks that lurk in the deeps of the book-publishing business.

This book also benefited from an intense conversation with Eric Uslaner of the University of Maryland, during a break at the 2005 annual meetings of the American Political Science Association in Washington, DC, personifying that social trust is an activity long before it becomes an academic topic. At that same conference, Evan S. Lieberman of Princeton University masterfully discussed my paper, which comprises one chapter of this book. I am glad I took good notes as they proved to be most useful in resolving some of the problems he identified. Bo Rothstein of the University of Göteborg and Sven Steinmo of the European Union Institute in Florence provided valuable comments on different parts of the manuscript.

I thank Tom McNulty from the Department of Sociology at the University of Georgia for help with the multilevel analysis. I am also indebted to two of "my" graduate students: Regan Damron, who assisted me with great patience in data management; and Lichao He for expert research assistance. Few academics are lucky enough to have a fellow political scientist as a neighbor. The conversations Eugene Miller, Professor Emeritus at the University of Georgia, and I shared in our backyards about cosmopolitanism and what the boundaries of morality should be proved most enlightening. While it is true that we also talked, at times, about how to best install our respective fishponds, our conversations improved parts of the manuscript in critical ways.

The graduate students in my seminar on social capital in the spring of 2005 deserve special recognition as we collectively explored issues of trust, ethnic heterogeneity, and the role of the state in fostering social capital. Many of their ideas found their way into my manuscript. The

Center for the Study of Global Issues (GLOBIS), directed by Han S. Park, gave me an opportunity to present some of my preliminary findings and sparked a most creative discussion, which gave birth to some ideas that are reflected in this book.

Most important, I would like to thank my wife Nicole for sharing her sheer talent with me. A gifted researcher in her own right, we spent hours together debating various aspects of my research, ranging from problems of causal inference to potential endogeneity problems in my models, what the meaning of empirical results might be, and many other such issues. She was the toughest of my critics, lavish in her praise yet unsparing in her criticism. Although there were times when it appeared that I was married to my computer, she kept nudging me on. Yet, despite her expert knowledge, I could not have written this book without her loving support. Her intellectual yin is perfectly balanced with her emotional yang, and I benefited from both. Most critically, she was the one insisting I write this book after we shared our impressions on the happenings in that Viennese marketplace one spring morning.

Finally, I would not be writing a preface and acknowledgments for any book were it not for the Austrian welfare state. This institution allowed me to attend the University of Salzburg, in Austria, in the early and mid-1980s. While I would move on to other institutions in other countries, the four years at the University of Salzburg offered me the chance of my life to discover my passion for the social sciences and the privilege of thinking, reading, and writing about esoteric topics without having to worry about my material constraints of life. In that sense I am indebted to the Austrian taxpayers, whose contributions allowed me to steer my life in directions that otherwise would not have been conceivable. Ultimately this was possible because I belong to an exclusive club: the club of Austrian citizens. I know from personal experience that citizenship matters because I greatly benefited from membership in a society that cares about the welfare of others.

Athens, Georgia
March 2006

CHAPTER 1

Introduction

"I want to be a millionaire" was the sentence the U.S. immigration official asked me to write. I scribbled it on a piece of paper and handed it over to the representative of the state, who studiously compared my production with the sentence that appeared on her computer screen. She approvingly noticed that I spelled *millionaire* correctly, with a double *l,* and with the rest of the sentence in order also the official proclaimed that I had passed the English writing test in addition to the U.S. history and government test. Despite the many hours of waiting on that day in overcrowded and overheated rooms, I had to ask: "What would have happened if I had misspelled that sentence?" The official, with a stern look on her face, told me that there would have been another sentence prepared for me: Asking what that sentence would have been, she responded: "I want a new car."

It would be tantalizing, although ultimately futile, to speculate what motivated those who either constructed those sentences or chose them to be used to test the writing skills of immigrants. And yet, is the message they convey accidental?[1] It is possible, of course, that a phrase such as "life, liberty, and the pursuit of happiness" was not chosen because the sentence in which it occurs is very long and *happiness* is difficult to spell (it does contain two *p*'s *and* two *s*'s after all), but I suspect that some immigration officials believe the material aspirations in the sentences I was asked to write speak more to the hopes and dreams of potential immigrants than do the arguably nobler motives contained in the world-famous phrase. Reenforcing these aspirations by making immigrants write their most important sentences in life, some officials may think, brings them one step closer to becoming "like us."

The concept of being like us implies the existence of its dialectical negation: "like them." No other marker embodies this dichotomy more powerfully than citizenship: being a citizen means to be endowed with a repertoire of rights and obligations that is not, by definition, available to outsiders. A legal wall separates those in the "in-group" from those in the "out-group." But citizenship is not only a legal but also a cultural concept, as any observer of European soccer matches can attest. References to wars fought long ago, chauvinist shouts, and nationalist stereotypes fly just as high as the fireworks and fists with which fans sometimes engage each other.

Just as dramatic, and oftentimes much more tragic, are the encounters between strangers in today's modern societies. Since 1965, the United States has been experiencing its third massive wave of immigration, and in Europe labor migration since the mid-1950s has drastically altered the ethnic, racial, linguistic, and religious diversity of these societies, making them significantly more diverse than they used to be. Immigration, both voluntary and involuntary, raises thorny issues of "belonging" as the relative homogeneity of West European societies gives way to a richer mosaic of cultures and identities.

The question of "who belongs" becomes critical when distributional issues arise. Societal homogeneity, according to many observers, is crucial because the sacrifice to give up part of your income is more easily made if the benefits go to someone who looks and behaves like you. In order for the welfare state to function, so the argument goes, there must be a certain amount of fellow feeling, a caring about other people's life chances and a sense of belonging to a community of fate.

Arguments that base the development and continuing viability of the welfare state on racial, ethnic, religious, or linguistic categories are not new, although few observers have made these connections explicit in the past. Recently, however, there has been a flurry of interest in the impact of such "essentialist," primordial concepts on one of the most important institutions in the modern polity: the welfare state. Intriguingly, this literature highlights the American experience and the combined roles of decentralized institutions and primordial categories as inhibitors for the development of a more complete American welfare state. When applied to the European context, such arguments typically end with dire proclamations such as this one from one of the keenest observers of matters of race, ethnicity, and the welfare state, Nathan Glazer (1998, 17): "[W]hat will happen to European social benefits as they are seen to go disproportionately to immigrants . . . and to fellow citizens different in religion and race[?]. . . . One may well see a withdrawal in European countries from the most advanced frontier of social policy . . . because these are seen as programs for 'others'."

The purpose of this book is to examine the validity of this extrapolation from the American to the European context and to probe whether such an "Americanization of the European welfare state" is indeed occurring as a result of immigration-induced diversity. This is a complex question and requires the examination of three streams of literature that are rarely linked: the literature on the welfare state, immigration, and interpersonal trust.

The welfare state and immigration are said to be connected through the primordial argument I have outlined, which is embodied in the classic phrase by T. H. Marshall (1950, 24), who averred that the foundation of citizenship "requires a direct sense of community membership based on loyalty to a civilization which is a common possession." In other words, it is easier to part with a fraction of your income in the form of taxes if the recipients of public assistance look and behave like you. Consequently, a basic ingredient for the establishment of a welfare state is a certain level of social homogeneity, or so many observers argue.

The relationships between trust and the welfare state, on the other hand, are more complex. Trust is the foundation on which the extractive capacity of the welfare state is built. When it comes to paying taxes, interpersonal trust is crucial. If you trust others to pay their fair share, then you will be more likely to do it too. In turn, empirical analyses have shown that more extensive welfare states tend to generate higher levels of interpersonal trust. This raises the difficult question of causality. This book ultimately argues that institutions precede trust and have the capacity to generate it.

Finally, trust and immigration are also related in a complex fashion and ultimately depend on whether one thinks of trust as either a "trait" (enduring and unchanging) or a "state" (rapidly changing, adjusting to environmental stimuli). If trust is a trait, the perspective taken in this book, the more "trusting" societies are the less they perceive immigrants as "others" and the more they are willing to embrace them and treat them as part of the community. This lessens widespread prejudice and hatred, reduces the impact of radical right-wing parties, and allows governments to create more "rational" policies without having to appease a radical right wing for reasons of political expediency. If trust is thought of as a state, increasing diversity will undermine it, which in turn will hollow out the sense of community and adversely affect support for the welfare state. Thus, treating trust as a trait has very different hypothesized effects on welfare support compared to treating trust as a state.

In combining these literatures of the welfare state, immigration, and trust, this research heeds the urgent call by Wayne Cornelius and Mark Rosenblum (2005, 6), who implore political scientists not to neglect immigration studies. They detect a curious lacuna of immigration studies in the field of political science, observing that "even as political scientists devote increasing attention to a range of related issues—trade policy, the welfare state, ethnicity, and nationalism—political science lags behind other social sciences in research on international population movements."

It is indeed puzzling why there has been relative inattention by political scientists to matters relating to population movements. The consequences are so massive and widespread that they affect many aspects of daily politics. Governments in modern societies are struggling to find solutions to the intractable consequences of immigration. In the spring of 2004, the Netherlands expelled 26,000 unsuccessful asylum seekers, the Italian navy was intercepting migrants and refugees in the Mediterranean and returning them to Libya, radical right-wing parties were agitating on the basis of *Ausländer raus* and winning votes and seats in the German *Bundesländer,* Great Britain had moved to the top of the European "xenophobes' league" as the Conservative Party was exploiting such sentiments in preparation for the general elections in 2005 (*Economist,* December 11, 2004, 51), and in the United States armed private citizens, whom President Bush called "vigilantes," were patrolling the Arizona-Mexico border because they did not trust the governments' commitment to do its job. In the fall of 2004 the gruesome assassination of filmmaker Theo van Gogh by a radical Muslim led to a spate of church and mosque burnings. Van Gogh argued that Muslims are "backward" and that the Netherlands should put a stop to immigration. The Dutch minister of immigration, Rita Verdonk, spoke of the "breakdown of the social fabric" as a result of growing ethnic enclaves and the increasing unwillingness of the immigrants to mix with the natives. There are parts of the Swedish town of Malmø where ambulance drivers refuse to go without a police escort for fear of being attacked. Almost 40 percent of the residents of this town of 250,000 are foreign born, most of them recently arrived Muslim refugees, and over 50 percent of them are unemployed. Rather than mixing with the Swedish population, they are increasingly living in a "parallel society."While in 2003 only a few of the 6 to 10 year old girls residing in the high-density housing project of Rosengård, located southeast of Malmø, were wearing head scarves, 80 percent were covering their heads by 2005 (Caldwell 2005). In other parts of the world, refugees squeeze into the wheel wells of jets, where they freeze to death and fall out of the sky when the airplanes extend their landing gear, and dozens of Chinese immigrants expired in a shipping container in Dover, England, in a desperate search for a better life. Most important, immigration raises the crucial question of national identity. As societies become more diverse, one question invariably arises: who is my brother?

While some see migration as a challenge, others see it as a solution to the problem of the demographic shifts occurring in welfare states. Modern societies are experiencing an increasing "graying" of their populations as a result of voluntarily declining fertility. Almost all public pension systems are based on a "generational contract" in which the young, active working population pays social security, which is used to support people in retirement. However, as the demographic bulge of the baby boomers is working its way toward their golden years, fewer and fewer young, active workers are there to support them, leading to a frantic search for solutions such as extending retirement ages, increasing the minimal amount of active working years necessary to be eligible for retirement, attempts at "privatizing" social security (in the United States), and generally increasing the number of hours worked per week (Wilensky 1975; Kotlikoff and Burns 2004; Brittan 1998). Of course, low fertility is not only a problem for pension systems; it is a problem for the welfare state in general since only "productive members of society" pay the taxes with which the welfare state is financed in addition to the direct relationship between economic and population growth.

Taking the Federal Republic of Germany as an example, the numbers are staggering. According to estimates by the Federal Statistical Office of Germany (Statistisches Bundesamt), by the year 2050 the German population will have shrunk to the level of 1963. This scenario assumes an average fertility rate of 1.4 children per woman, increases in life expectancy, *and* an inflow of 200,000 immigrants per year. During the last thirty years Germany's population shrank by 5.5 million, almost as many people as emigrated from Germany to the United States between 1815 and 1914. After the fall of the Berlin Wall, former East German *Länder* experienced a population implosion. The average fertility per woman dropped to .77 the lowest rate ever measured in any country in this world. The consequences: the closing of schools and factories and collapsing infrastructures. Standard & Poor's lowered the credit rating of the *Land* of Saxony explicitly on the basis of lack of population growth, which the company considers crucial for economic growth.

Is immigration the solution to the problem of the welfare state? While this is not the focus of this book, a preliminary analysis suggests that it is not. As indicated, even with an influx of 200,000 immigrants a year Germany's population will still shrink. Estimates suggest that immigration would have to rise to 300,000 per year by 2020 and to half a million per year by 2050 just to keep Germany's population at the current level (Klingholz 2004). It is highly unlikely that the German or any other European polity would find such levels of immigration acceptable. In addition, while immigrants are generally young and have high fertility rates, by the time the first and second generation comes around, fertility rates tend to adjust to the host society's rate. In addition, such large numbers of immigrants would find less of a need to integrate, producing "ethnic enclaves" and "parallel societies" and potentially increasing social conflicts. This is a problem not only for Germany but for many other industrialized societies also. Immigration is not the silver bullet that can stop Germany's decline in population. The solutions are not easy to come by, yet the options are clearly defined: Germans can have more babies, extend the pension age, work more hours, pay higher taxes, accept lower pensions, or adopt a combination of these. But it is obvious that most Germans and many other Europeans do not find any of these options attractive.

A RESEARCH PUZZLE

The primordial argument is a formidable contender for the continued viability of the welfare state. Most observers take a pessimistic view, arguing that ultimately blood is thicker than water. If welfare states do not manage to control immigration, people will disengage from willingly contributing funds that are believed to be going disproportionately to "strangers." This point has been made most forcefully by Gary Freeman (1986, 61–62), who argued that, "There can be no doubt that migration has been little short of a disaster . . . [for] immigration has tended to erode the more general normative consensus on which the welfare state was built."

Of course, a second policy option, closing off a country's borders, is possible, but for most European societies this is not really an option. Most of these societies have in fact managed to control the immigration of unskilled laborers since 1974 and today allow only qualified workers entry visas or "green cards." Despite these efforts, immigration as a result of family unification has continued, complemented by asylum seekers and refugees. International norms and human rights conventions, to which many European countries have signed on, have made it very difficult to exclude asylum seekers and family members who want to join their families in a European country. Thus, for both legal and humanitarian reasons modern societies find it challenging to close off their borders.[2]

In addition, the 2004 European Union (EU) enlargement, which added eight Eastern European countries (the Czech Republic, Estonia, Hungary, Latvia, Lithuania, Poland, Slovenia, and Slovakia) and two Mediterranean islands (Malta and Cyprus), meant that over 75 million people now have unhindered access to the rest of the union, significantly increasing diversity in Europe. Furthermore, in October 2005 membership talks between the EU and Turkey began, and, while it may take a long time for Turkey to become a member, serious reservations have been voiced about the cultural incompatibility between Turkey, with its overwhelmingly Muslim population, and the rest of the union. With the horrific attacks on September 11, 2001, the brutal killing of Theo van Gogh in the Netherlands by a radical Muslim, and the growing Islamophobia in Europe since the early 1990s triggered by the increasing immigration of Muslims into relatively homogeneous European nations, many observers argue that European citizens will find it very difficult to accept Turkey as a partner in the EU on cultural grounds. One example of the cultural chasm separating Turkish and Western cultures can be found in the "honor killings" that have occurred in Berlin, where over a period of four months six Turkish women were murdered by their own family members, mostly their brothers or husbands, because they wanted to end a relationship with their Turkish partners; refused to wear the traditional *hijab,* the Muslim head scarf; or, the ultimate shame, decided to adopt a Western lifestyle.[3] And as of this writing (February 2006) over thirty people have been killed in demonstrations over cartoons depicting the prophet Muhammad. These cartoons, one of which depicted Muhammad's turban as a bomb with a burning fuse, were originally published in a Danish newspaper four months before widespread demonstrations and protests erupted in almost every Muslim country with arson attacks on Western embassies and a Pakistani cleric offering a million-dollar reward for anyone who killed the cartoonist (El-Deeb 2006).

Such sad events make the primordial argument appear to be a persuasive one. If it is indeed true that the welfare state requires a certain level of cultural commonality, through which redistribution can be achieved, it seems unlikely that European publics will want to continue funding the welfare state when they perceive that their taxes are received by people who are thoroughly different from themselves.

Yet not everybody shares such a bleak outlook. On the basis of empirical observations, one eminent welfare state scholar, Peter Taylor-Gooby, came to the conclusion that, "All the survey evidence indicates that as society becomes more diverse, support for public spending on core state services increases" (*Newsweek,* May 3, 2004). This observation is not compatible with much of the literature, which claims that support for the European welfare state will erode as a result of increasing diversity. Resolving these contradictory claims is what this book attempts to do.

When Freeman speaks of "consensus" and Taylor-Gooby of "support," they are both referring to public perceptions. It is ultimately perceptions about immigrants and their effect on the national economy and culture that shape politics in liberal democratic societies. The central reason why this study focuses on public opinion surveys is the fact that public reactions to immigration, multiculturalism policies, or support for the welfare state manifest themselves early in public opinion, long before aggregate data on public expenditures indicate such a link. Public opinion functions as an early warning system providing basic guideposts as to what effects various policies might have. To be sure, politics does not always follow public opinion, and that is probably a good thing. But in a democracy whose legitimacy is based on popular sovereignty politicians who ignore public opinion do so at their peril.

THEORY AND RESEARCH QUESTIONS

This book confronts the primordial claim that the biggest threat to the welfare state originates in the attitudes of natives who see a disproportionate amount of social benefits going to people who are different from themselves. This, so the argument goes, undermines the sense of a shared fate, and as the collective community begins to crumble so does the readiness to support "strangers" with one's contributions. As a result, maintaining the welfare state becomes untenable. This is an argument that unfolds over time. Unfortunately, pollsters have not consistently queried publics across time in all industrialized democracies. Some questions have been asked in one wave but not in another or have been posed in one country but not in another. Whenever possible, this book attempts to tell the story over time, but some of the empirical analysis will have to be based on cross-national comparisons.

This project is not directly concerned with the welfare uptake of immigrants and its effects on the viability of the welfare state, although in the country-specific sections on the United States, Germany, and Sweden that issue invariably raises its head. However, the bigger challenge arises from the possibility that large parts of the *dominant* society "detach" or "withdraw" from the welfare state as this would have most dramatic consequences for income inequality, class relations, government stability, electoral politics, the arrangements between unions and employers' organizations, social peace, strikes and lockouts, and most other conceivable outcomes. According to some observers, it was basically this very process that undermined the development of a more solid welfare state in the United States. The question this book attempts to answer is whether immigration-driven diversity will undermine the willingness of natives to continue funding the welfare state.

The central thesis of this book is that extrapolating from the American experience is problematic for the following reason: the primordial challenge to the European welfare state is unfolding at a time when it has *reached maturity,* as opposed to the American experience in which diversity hampered the development of a more comprehensive welfare state *from the beginning.* In Europe, diversity impinges on established, comprehensive welfare states, leading to two different trajectories. First, as a result of the impact of unions and social democratic parties, which pushed for the development of a welfare state, a significant constituency has developed that is very supportive of public provision. Second, interpersonal trust levels are higher in more extensive welfare states precisely because they developed relatively undisturbed by diversity for many decades. Both of these trajectories combine to create a different policy-making environment compared to that of the United States. As a result, it is not intuitive to believe that Europe should suffer the same fate as the United States as far as diversity's effects on the welfare state are concerned.

Moreover, the causal arrow points not only from perceptions of foreigners to the public's willingness to continue funding the welfare state.

The welfare state itself has a material force that affects the perceptions of people and their levels of trust. Universal welfare states should soften the impact of immigration on the perceptions of natives, as well as establishing higher levels of trust than in residual systems of public provision. As such, institutions are not simply reflections of the conditions that gave rise to them, a view favored particularly by economists. They are "sticky," and even as conditions change they tend to continue having their intended effects, thereby changing the matrix of public inputs, political outputs, and outcomes. Is it possible that the welfare state functions as a trust-generating device that makes natives more willing to embrace foreigners and thus avoid the "Americanization" of the European welfare state?

In addition, governments are not passive bystanders as the drama of encounters with strangers continues. They are active shapers of this interaction through the creation of policies on immigration (who is allowed entry) and immigrants (the integration of immigrants once they have arrived). These policies have had marked effects on public perceptions of foreigners and natives alike. For instance, on January 1, 2000, Germany underwent a historic turn, moving from jus sanguinis to jus soli, thereby thoroughly changing the meaning of German identity. Also, multiculturalism policies have been devised with the intent to allow immigrants to continue their lives in relative cultural autonomy. Do incorporation and multiculturalism policies make a difference for nativist resentment and prejudice?

Much of this research focuses on a strata of society where if there is any "detachment" from the welfare state visible it should manifest itself in a group that is sometimes referred to as *Modernisierungsverlierer* or losers in the process of modernization. These are people who are mostly industrial workers with relatively low education and incomes, who may have had a bout with unemployment, and who more often than not live in precarious economic circumstances. These vulnerable sectors of society are most threatened by immigration and as a result should express the strongest anti-immigrant sentiments. It stands to reason that any detachment, or "disengagement," from the welfare state as a result of a perception that benefits go to immigrants should be visible in such groups. As obvious as this sounds, there exists an equally plausible alternative hypothesis: there is no reason why such vulnerable sectors of society should withdraw from the welfare state simply because immigration is increasing. If anything, such groups should favor maintaining the welfare state precisely because the state provides a safety net. Rather than withdrawing from the welfare state, public opinion in such exposed strata should indicate continued support for the welfare state on the one hand and strict limits on immigration on the other.

PLAN OF THE BOOK

The spatial parameters of this book encompass the developed societies of Europe, North America, and the antipodes. The unit of analysis is individual-level attitudes across 17 nations: Australia, Austria, Belgium, Canada, Denmark, Finland, France, Germany, Italy, Ireland, the Netherlands, New Zealand, Norway, Sweden, Switzerland, the United Kingdom, and the United States. Unfortunately, since some question items were not polled in every country, it is not always possible to report findings for all 17 countries. In some cases, results were obtained on attitudes tapped in only 11 countries, producing an N of around 12,000. The temporal parameters encompass the attitudes and changes in them from 1980 to 2000 as manifested in the four waves of the World Values Survey (WVS). In a few cases, data were aggregated to the national level and some econometric analyses used multilevel, hierarchical modeling combining both aggregate and individual-level data.

Four large-scale multinational surveys were used to tap individual attitudes: those of the World Values Survey (Inglehart et al. 2004), one of the oldest and largest multinational public opinion surveys, the fourth wave of which has recently become available. The first wave of this survey was conducted in 1981, the second in 1991, the third in 1995, and the fourth in 1999–2001. The second major data source was the European Social Survey (ESS), the newest among large-scale multinational European surveys, whose fieldwork was completed in the fall of 2002. It contains a battery of over 50 items directly connected to issues of immigration. The third main data source is the International Social Survey Program (ISSP), a large-scale international survey that contains different themes in addition to a set of standard question items. Finally, various waves of the Eurobarometer (EB) series were employed to tap attitudes on welfare support, immigration, and other related items.

Before delving into the empirical matter, chapter 2 examines the primordial claim in detail, highlighting how economists, anthropologists, ethologists, political scientists, historians, and others have connected categorical differences to the willingness to engage in collective sacrifices.

This chapter also qualifies these arguments and highlights the constructed nature of such assertions. In addition, the role of political institutions and policies is underscored as one reason why some societies are more willing to redistribute incomes from the rich to the poor.

Chapter 3 maps the various degrees of "nativist resentment" and "welfare chauvinism" in modern societies. It establishes the profile of people who should be most affected by immigration and introduces a crucial difference between the "demand" for welfare provisions and the "supply" of welfare through willingness to pay taxes. Statistical analyses find striking differences between the demand for welfare and the willingness to supply it by paying taxes among people who harbor nativist resentments.

Chapter 4 introduces "trust" as a mediating factor between the perceptions of foreigners and the public's readiness to continue supporting the welfare state. The burgeoning literature on trust is sorted and analyzed. The general trust measure is found to be inadequate to capture the complex dynamic between natives and their encounters with strangers. This book refines the measure of trust and develops three subtypes: universal trust, primordial trust, and what is termed "anomie." These three forms of trust prove to be surprisingly strong predictors of how natives react to foreigners and their support, or lack thereof, of the welfare state.

A further examination of the origins of trust and the institutional effects of different types of welfare states is conducted in chapter 5. This chapter reverses the causal arrow—this time going from institutional design to public attitudes—and shows how different types of welfare regimes affect not only attitudes about the welfare state but also trust.

Chapter 6 moves to the realm of policies and examines whether the type of incorporation regime and multiculturalism policies matter in the public's attitudes with regard to nativist resentment, welfare chauvinism, and welfare state support. This chapter also introduces a relatively new methodology to political scientists: multilevel, hierarchical modeling, which allows us to examine the effects of national-level policies on individual-level attitudes.

Finally, chapter 7 adds historical depth and more nuance to these questions by comparing the cases of Germany, Sweden, and the United States. Relatively more space is given to the case of Germany since this country has undergone the most dramatic changes in its immigration policy and has very recently significantly cut welfare expenditures. The thicker description in all three cases highlights the similarities in the challenges these nations face, and yet there are different policy trajectories observable as a result of their different institutional architectures.

Debates on immigration often lead to emotional flare-ups precisely because the issue is so fundamental to the identity of individuals and nations. Governments, political parties, and civil society must take the concerns of the public seriously but resist the temptation to jump on the anti-immigrant bandwagon for electoral reasons and enforce the public's often misguided opinions about immigration by engaging in fiery populist rhetoric. Neither should such groups do the opposite: branding those who favor more immigration controls as "racists."

Those with the power to define must inform and educate while they play a central role in the construction of the host society's identity. Education is the enemy of ignorance: it increases tolerance and instills a sense of empathy for the life situation of "others." It is precisely this concern for others that has made the welfare state work in the past and will continue to make it work in the future. One of the central findings of this book is that in the face of immigration, people who only trust their own primordial group do indeed withdraw from funding the welfare state, while those with the capacity to trust strangers are willing to continue supporting the welfare state with their taxes. This book demonstrates how and why people who have an extended sense of community and moral responsibility are not withdrawing from the provision of social insurance. The welfare state is safe among those whose trust reaches beyond borders.

CHAPTER 2

A Primordial Challenge to the Welfare State?

It's just obvious that you can't have free immigration and
a welfare state.
—Milton Friedman

This fellow was quite black from head to foot, a clear proof
that what he said was quite stupid.
—Immanuel Kant

THE HISTORY OF THE WELFARE STATE is a history of political economy within fixed national borders. By the end of the nineteenth century and the beginning of the twentieth, nations had been made, sometimes through processes of federation, as in the case of Belgium, but mostly as a result of wars in which ethnicities had "sorted themselves" or "were sorted into" their respective state vessels, creating relatively homogeneous societies in which the concepts of nation and state largely coincided. In the memorable words of Charles Tilly (1975, 42): "War made the state and the state made war," creating the "necessary condition for free institutions, that the boundaries of governments should coincide in the main with those of nationalities" (Mill 1968, 312).

At the same time states were being created externally, they were being created internally, for the only other challenge comparable to the one without was the one within. The forces that threatened the viability of the state from within were of course the various communist and socialist movements of the late nineteenth century and the early twentieth. The nation builder's answer to that internal challenge was the development of the welfare state.

Bridging the class divide was the original purpose of the welfare state in the late nineteenth and early twentieth centuries, as conceived by one of its foremost practitioners, Otto von Bismarck. Bismarck noted in 1881, when he put his proposals for social insurance before the Reichstag, that: "Whoever has a pension for his old age is far more content and far easier to handle than one who has no such prospect. Look at the difference between a private servant and a servant in the Chancellery or at court: the latter will put up with much more, because he has a pension to look forward to" (quoted in Taylor 1955, 203). Bismarck hoped that the introduction of social insurance would squash the socialists on the one hand and resolve *die soziale Frage* on the other. In the middle of the twentieth century, T. H. Marshall (1950) made it very clear that "class abatement" was still the main purpose of the welfare state, although for him equal citizenship rights were also the first step toward the establishment of a sense of solidarity and community among members of society. While social amelioration was a central purpose of the creation of the welfare state, its origins and development are rarely seen in the larger context of European nation building in the nineteenth and early twentieth centuries (Esping-Andersen 2002) in which the warfare and welfare state were closely intertwined.

It is no small wonder then that some contemporary analysts of the welfare state focus on its political economy, taking as a constant the autonomy and sovereignty of the units they are examining. This explains why the contemporary literature on the "challenges" or "crises" or "pressures" on the welfare state by political scientists has been rather narrowly focused. Part 1 of an outstanding collection of essays entitled *The New Politics of the Welfare State,* edited by Paul Pierson (2001b), does not contain a single reference to growing social heterogeneity, immigration, or diversity as a potential challenger to the welfare state. Rather, the "usual suspects" that challenge the welfare state are identified as "globalization" (Schwartz 2001), "deindustrialization" (Iverson 2001), or "postindustrialism" (Pierson 2001b). Others have argued that demographic shifts leading to the "graying" of modern societies will seriously undermine the capacity of welfare states to continue their levels of social protection (Wilensky 1975; Brittan 1998; Kotlikoff and Burns 2004). There is a venerable literature on the "moral challenges" to the welfare state, arguing that the very existence of the paternalistic state leads to a withering of the natural bonds of family and friendship (Habermas 1987; Taylor 1987). Other highly respected volumes on the limits of the welfare state

have also curiously overlooked the challenge to the welfare state posed
by increasing, immigration-driven diversity (Swank 2002; Hicks 1999).

All of these arguments have increased our understanding of the dynamics of welfare states immeasurably, and the points have been made
with great effectiveness by their protagonists. Perhaps it is because political scientists are afflicted more than others with thinking of sovereign
states as "natural" units in which things happen and where values are au-
thoritatively allocated that little attention has been paid to forces that
cross boundaries.

As a result, so far most political scientists have curiously overlooked a
potentially formidable challenger to the viability of the welfare state:
increasing social heterogeneity as a result of massive immigration into
Europe and the United States during the last two decades. With the exception of John D. Stephens's work (1980), which recognizes the corrosive effects of ethnic, linguistic, and religious diversity on the effectiveness of the organization of labor, much of the welfare state literature has
remained silent on the impact of such categorical factors. Among the
flood of books and articles written about the "crises" of the welfare state,
particularly since the "stagflation" period of the mid-1970s, few political
scientists have associated immigration-driven increases in social heterogeneity with attitudes about the welfare state. Early warnings about this
potential conflict issued by Gunnar Myrdal (1960) and Harold Wilensky
and Charles Lebeaux (1965) remained largely unheeded.

In this chapter the claims of a new strand of challenges to the welfare
state are assessed. Although it is true that some observers indicated early
on that growing social heterogeneity could present serious challenges to
the welfare state, these calls have become louder as diversity in Western
Europe and in the United States has dramatically increased as a result of
massive immigration over the last four decades (Myrdal 1960; Wilensky
1965). This challenge is of a different kind than any other challenge to the
welfare state that came before: this challenge is primordial. Immigration
has brought together peoples of such different ethnic, racial, and religious
identities that it may question the viability of the welfare state as we know
it. Immigration is about a transition in the basic ingredients of what gives
meaning to the terms *identity* and *community*. Before the logic of the primordial argument is examined, it will be necessary to gather the threads,
weave them into a tapestry, and present what is sometimes called the
"politics of difference" and its relevance to the welfare state literature. This
tapestry will tell the story of how economists, sociologists, political theo-

rists, psychologists, ethologists, and a few political scientists have analyzed the divisive powers of these categorical differences and their effects on welfare states, the functioning of democracy, the problem of order, and the cement that bonds the elements of society.

This story may appear to be rather grim at first, as these primordial categories seem immutable. However, this is not the first time that societies have encountered these challenges. After all, people have been in motion since the beginning of their time and in many cases have managed to peacefully coexist despite categorical differences that are not as immutable as some have claimed. In fact, a lot of integration has been going on: concentrating on the sore spots leaves one with a distorted view. Moreover, most of this literature treats the welfare state as the effect and social heterogeneity as the cause. There is no reason to believe that an obverse relationship may exist: the very presence of the welfare state, particularly in its universalist fashion, might prove to be an integrating force, diminishing the economic differences between the natives and the newcomers. It is argued that what appears to be immutable, even such things as race and ethnicity, are not givens. They are themselves constructions created by those who have the power to define. Despite the sad, tragic, and undeniable history of racial, religious, and ethnic persecution, this argument is good news for it opens a space in which change is conceivable.

PRIMORDIAL CONSTRUCTIONS AND
CONSTRUCTING PRIMORDIALISM

Social thinkers such as Karl Marx and Max Weber believed that ethnic conflicts will become a relic of the past. According to Marx, class will come to dominate the relations between people. They will be linked to each other on the basis of their positions in the process of production and not based on blood ties or ethnicity. In short, class will become the sole organizing principle in capitalist systems. Max Weber saw a somewhat different process at work. He argued that as the process of rationality and modernization unfolds the old community-oriented relationships will decline. Only in places where "rationally regulated action is not widespread" will such forms of social organization remain viable (1968, 389).

Robert Park, a sociologist at the University of Chicago, argued that global factors such as trade, migration, new communications technologies, and even the cinema would bring about a vast interpenetration of peoples. According to Park, writing in 1926, these forces, which today are usually referred to as globalization, would integrate peoples with one another, "leading ultimately to universal participation in a common life and culture." Park believed that the forces of history would create a global melting pot. "If America was once in any exclusive sense the melting pot of races, it is no longer. The melting pot is the world" (Park 1926, quoted in Cornell and Hartmann 1998, 6). Gunnar Myrdal argued in a similar fashion: as a result of industrialization, increased social and geographical mobility, secularization, and "intensified intellectual communication, folkways and mores have been gradually breaking down. . . . The more instinctive, less questioned norms of behavior of the old society generally lost their hold upon the mass of the people" (Myrdal 1960, 33). The idea that increased contact between different members of the human family will decrease the salience of their differences was thus shared by Park as well as Myrdal. At the individual level, in a book entitled *The Nature of Prejudice* the eminent social psychologist Gordon W. Allport established the "contact hypothesis," claiming that intergroup contact reduces social prejudice (Allport 1954).

In addition, as many former colonies became independent after World War II there were high hopes that these countries would quickly modernize. Secularism, economic rationality, modern lifestyles, expanded education, urbanization, efficient production methods, and new forms of communication would forge a new, modern identity that would undermine kinship, blood ties, and traditional cultures (Lipset 1960; Parsons 1951; Huntington 1968; Deutsch 1963).

It was not to be. Instead of declining, racial and ethnic differences have been resurgent, often with devastating consequences, certainly during the period of the Third Reich and again in the last two decades of the twentieth century. The concept of the "clash of civilizations" (Huntington 1996) has now become commonplace. In the words of Donald Horowitz (1985, xi): "Ethnicity is at the center of politics in country after country, a potent source of challenges to the cohesion of states and of international tension. . . . [It] has fought and bled and burned its way into public and scholarly consciousness."

Why has there been such a resurgence of ethnic conflict since the end of the cold war? The cold war helped foster cohesion within each of the two broad worldviews, albeit enforced through military intervention on the part of the Soviets to keep its Eastern European comrades in line and also on the part of the United States, which intervened in many Latin

American and Middle Eastern countries to ensure that pro-Western governments either stayed in power or came to power. Ethnic affirmation and mobilization was of secondary importance compared to the potential for nuclear annihilation, whose avoidance was clearly the higher-order goal. However, once the higher-order goal of avoiding mutual annihilation disappeared with the collapse of the Soviet empire, ethnic conflicts began to stir, revealing a boiling brew of ethnic hatreds where battles that were either lost or won hundreds of years ago suddenly took on new meaning. In the ensuing scramble to forge new nations, leaders used primordial attachments as a central mobilizing principle. As a result, academic interest in ethnic conflict was renewed and essentialist, primordial arguments, once believed to be dead, began to stir again.

Thomas Spira (1999, 499), in his encyclopedia entitled *Nationalism and Ethnicity Terminologies,* defines *primordialist view* as: "The belief that race and ethnicity are fundamental, ascriptive, and immediate identities, i.e., that ethnic boundaries are given, reflecting ancient, cultural and perhaps genetic differences in the origins of peoples." One of the first scholars who used the term *primordial* was Edward Shils (1957, 142), who, in an autobiographical essay of sorts, was struck by the strength of family attachments: "As one thought about the strengths and tensions in family attachments, it became apparent that the attachment was not merely to the other family members as a person, but as a possessor of certain especially 'significant relational' qualities, which could only be described as primordial. . . . It [the attachment to another member of one's kinship group] is because a certain ineffable significance is attributed to the tie of blood."

The eminent cultural anthropologist Clifford Geertz (1963, 109) defines *primordial attachment* as follows.

By a primordial attachment is meant one that stems from the "givens"—or, more precisely, as culture is inevitably involved in such matters, the assumed "givens"—of social existence: immediate contiguity and kin connection mainly, but beyond them the givenness that stems from being born into a particular religious community, speaking a particular language, or even a dialect of a language, and following particular social practices. These congruities of blood, speech, custom, and so on, are seen to have an ineffable, and at times, overpowering, coerciveness in and of themselves.

In this often quoted definition of the term, Geertz seems to struggle with the immutability and fixity of the primordial story. His qualifiers "culture is inevitably involved in such matters" and "are seen to have" indicate that he himself is not completely convinced that these "givens" are in fact givens rather than creations.

It is most remarkable that in the same edited volume in which Geertz's celebrated essay "The Integrative Revolution" first appeared, McKim Marriott (1963, 29), predating Benedict Anderson's famous *Imagined Communities* by 20 years, made the following statement.

> Modern means of communication have been gradually transform-
> ing the cultures of many nations for a century, generally without
> having been made the instruments of international policy. But the
> availability of such means of communication also open up new po-
> tentialities for the *manipulation of culture.* The possibility of educat-
> ing their citizens to a newly chosen way of life, of *mobilizing them
> in support of deliberately cultivated values,* of representing them to the
> world according to a *consciously created image*—all these are open to
> the elites of the new states, either in actuality or in prospect. (em-
> phasis added)

This view is diametrically opposed to the primordial one, for it argues that it is not so much ethnic identity that gives meaning to human beings but rather human beings that give meaning to ethnic identity. Indeed, studies of sociologists and anthropologists are replete with examples of how ethnic, and racial, identity is politically constructed.[1]

Examples abound. Stephan Thernstrom (2004, 57) reports on an article in the 1999 *Yale Law Journal* that asks "Are Asians Black?" and answers the question in the affirmative.[2] Stephen Cornell and Douglas Hartmann (1998) explore the process of "racialization" that occurred when Chinese immigrants began to appear in the early 1870s in the Mississippi Delta. By that time, a behavioral etiquette had been established in terms of how whites treated blacks and vice versa. However, with the arrival of the Chinese this etiquette proved insufficient. The question became: what race are the Chinese? Obviously, they were not white, but they could easily be considered black, which is what they became. "They were racialized as Black, assigned the same status as Blacks, and as a consequence experienced essentially similar day-to-day treatment at the hands of Whites" (Cornell and Hartmann 1998, 116).

Originally, the Chinese saw themselves as sojourners, staying in the Mississippi Delta for only a certain amount of time. As they became economically successful, they had increasing reasons to remain in the United States. Over time, they actively began to change their behavior, which included reducing their contacts with the black community (and particularly reducing intermarriage with blacks), decorating their stores to look more like those of the white community, setting up their own Baptist churches and missions, organizing social clubs, and even establishing Chinese cemeteries so as to not be buried with blacks. By the early 1950s, the Chinese had succeeded in jettisoning their "black" status and were increasingly accepted, not as whites but not as blacks either. By that time, most white schools had opened their doors to Chinese American children (Cornell and Hartmann 1998, 119). For blacks, *Brown v. Board of Education* (1954) was just around the corner, but actual integration would not occur for decades. At the beginning of the second millennium, many wonder whether "separate but equal" might not have been better for blacks than desegregation given the "voluntary" segregation observable in America today.

This account of the reconstruction of the Chinese "race" from black to white suggests that race is not immutable, fixed, biological, natural, or rooted in history. It suggests that it is more a matter of how strongly a minority groups asserts itself and the degree to which this "ethnic reorganization" is acceptable to the native majority (Cornell and Hartmann 1998). If primordial attributes are indeed givens, enduring, and set in stone, they are not supposed to change, yet evidence abounds that attests to the fact that identities are circumstantial, situational, fluid, and constructed on a daily basis. Ethnicity and race matter only if those who want to make them count do so, be that the members of minorities themselves or native majorities. "Races, like ethnic groups are not established by some set of natural forces but are products of human perception and classification. They are social constructs. . . . The characteristics [such as skin color, hair type, stature, and others] that are the basis of the categories [race and ethnicity], however, have no inherent significance. We give them meaning, and in the process, we create races" (1998, 23, 24).

Nathan Glazer and Daniel P. Moynihan (1970, x1), in their famous *Beyond the Melting Pot*, powerfully made that point when they argued that, "For just as a 'nigger' can be made by treating him like a 'nigger', and calling him a 'nigger', just as a black man can be made by educating to a new, proud, black image—and this education is carried on in words and images, as well as in deeds—so can racists be made, by calling them racists and treating them like racists."

One of the intriguing findings of the Glazer and Moynihan volume is that oftentimes ethnic leaders and elites used their cultural groups as focal points for mobilization and as constituencies as they were competing against other ethnic groups for resources, power, and influence, particularly when the appeal of class as a focal point for mobilization seemed to be waning. In the last pages of their book they make the following argument: "Social and political institutions do not merely respond to ethnic interests; a great number of institutions exist for the specific purpose of serving ethnic interests. This in turn, tends to perpetuate them. In many ways, the atmosphere of New York City is hospitable to ethnic groupings: it recognizes them, and rewards them, and to that extent encourages them" (Glazer and Moynihan 1970, 310).

This means that ethnic identity can be created either by members of the ethnic groups themselves, who gain advantages from official recognition, or by the authorities, who establish institutions to respond to the special interests of ethnic groups. As a consequence, ethnic mobilization may also occur among those groups that are not officially recognized, potentially creating conflicts between ethnic groups that might have not occurred if official recognition of others had not been granted.[3]

It is intriguing that just when ethnicity is making a comeback and the headlines in the newspapers speak of suicide bombers, ethnic cleansing, genocide, racial profiling, glass ceilings, and discrimination along every conceivable human difference a "constructivist" view of ethnicity has developed that questions its primordial character. Of course, there is no contradiction between the gruesome deeds committed in the name of "culture" or "ethnicity" and the constructivist approach, which denies that there is anything ineffable, immutable, fixed, or genetic about these horrific acts. A constructivist understanding can quite easily explain conflicts based on ethnicity, blood ties, or culture and would argue that, while these categories are not in and of themselves "good" or "bad" or the causes of anything, combined with agency that mobilizes groups based on these primordial categories they can become highly militant, peaceful, or anything in between.

Thus, it is "beliefs about" ethnicity, blood ties, and culture that have the potential for both unimaginable cruelty and self-sacrificial humanitarianism. Beliefs about ethnicity, blood ties, or culture can be created and are contextual, fluid, constructed, imagined, invented, asserted, situational, and circumstantial, leading some observers to claim that "primordial identity is itself an intellectual construction" (Doyle 2002, 15).[4]

Consider, for example, the creation of the American nation. On what basis is the American identity constructed? If racial, ethnic, religious, and linguistic homogeneity is necessary for the development of a "common" identity, America was very poorly endowed with these crucial building blocks. Given the disparate backgrounds of the settlers in terms of religion, ethnicity, language, and common history, the building materials for the American nation-building process were sparse and frail. The attempt to explain American nation building from a primordial perspective is doomed from the start (Doyle 2002). But what America did have, as Gunnar Myrdal so powerfully stated, was an "American Creed," by which he meant "the cement in the structure of this great and disparate nation."

Today it is widely agreed that American identity rests on political principles such as liberty, equality, private property, individualism, human rights, and the rule of law, not on any claim that Americans are or were a distinctive people. These political principles developed in opposition to increasingly restrictive British policies, which were interpreted for the colonists by American revolutionaries such as Thomas Paine, who argued that America could become a "laboratory for enlightenment ideas" and a "workshop for liberty." The very term *founding fathers* suggests the deliberate making of a new nation. American identity grew out of opposition to British rule, and, lacking racial, historical and ethnic bonds, "American nationalism had to be invented, and quickly in the maelstrom of war" (Doyle 2002, 20).[5]

In Samuel Huntington's recent book *Who Are We?* he modifies this widely held view and argues that America was not always seen as a nation of immigrants. Rather, he claims, America was a settler nation first and a nation of immigrants second. The settlers brought with them the "Christian religion, Protestant values and moralism, a work ethic, the English language, British traditions of law, justice, and the limits of government power, and a legacy of European art, literature, philosophy, and music" (Huntington 2004, 40). He poses the rhetorical question: "[W]ould America be the America it is today if in the seventeenth and eighteenth centuries it had been settled not by British Protestants but by French, Spanish, or Portuguese Catholics? The answer is no. It would not be America; it would be Quebec, Mexico, or Brazil" (59).

If it is true that the origins of the American Creed lie in an Anglo-European culture, where did the notion of America as a nation of

immigrants come from? Huntington (2004, 38) suspects that it originated in 1938 when President Franklin D. Roosevelt reminded the
Daughters of the American Revolution: "Remember, remember always,
that all of us, and you and I especially, are descended from immigrants
and revolutionists."

Nothing illustrates better the malleability and fluidity of identity construction than this metamorphosis of American identity, which until the
middle of the eighteenth century was based on ethnicity, religion, race,
and culture. The American Creed developed as a means to distinguish
the American settlers from the British once the relationship between the
settlers and their British government began to decline. America needed
to develop its own identity vis-à-vis its British counterpart and in so
doing constructed the American Creed. And today Huntington worries
that the creed itself is under attack as a result of multiculturalism and diversity. It is no small wonder that Huntington (2004, 22) believes: "Identities are, overwhelmingly, constructed. People make their identity, under
varying degrees of pressure, inducements, and freedom."

Some Europeans also attempted to build nations on the basis of creedal
principles rather than primordial differences. For instance, Giuseppe
Mazzini attempted to build an Italian nation on the Enlightenment
principles that could unite people divided by ethnic and linguistic differences. The "constructive" aspect of nation building is nowhere clearer
to be seen than in Massimo D'Azeglio's famous quote: "Now that we
have made Italy, we need to make Italians."[6] In France, too, the powerful
republican principles on which the French Revolution was built not
only destroyed the ancien régime but forged a new nation based on the
principles of brotherhood, liberty, and equality, transcending primordial
differences. In stark contrast to Italy and France stands the German experience, in which nation builders time and again, and sometimes with
disastrous consequences, have appealed to the ethnic character (*völkisch*)
of German identity.

The overwhelming evidence that identities can be shaped and created, often enough by political entrepreneurs of hate, speaks to the
poverty of primordialism as an organizing principle of social relations.
There is nothing inevitable, logical, or natural about categorical differences such as race, religion, and ethnicity. Such differences by themselves
do not explain social or political outcomes. But such differences do become important when they are mobilized by demagogues, leaders of
radical parties, or false prophets on the fringes of religious fundamental-

ism. One of the most telling facts about the power of constructing identities is represented in the case of German unification. By all accounts, there were no differences in race or ethnicity in Germany before it was divided into East and West. Yet after reunification it was observed that "Germans from the former East Germany are treated as a different ethnic group in the west" (Sassen 1999, xvi).

Because of the particular German legacy, racial conflicts, spurred on by entrepreneurs of hate, are viewed with special concern and caution. The two German Christian parties, the Christlich Demokratische Union (CDU) and Christlich Soziale Union (CSU), both of which are conservative, played the "xenophobia" card for political gain shortly after the fall of the Berlin Wall. Normally, it is not surprising to see radical right-wing parties, such as the Republikaner in Germany, engaging in xenophobic rhetoric and complaining about *Überfremdung* (overforeignerization), but even the "old," established parties make use of xenophobia when they believe such a strategy can help them win votes, sometimes with catastrophic consequences, as was the case in the first few years of Germany's unification.

Shortly after the fall of the wall in late 1989 and early 1990 West Germans welcomed streams of East Germans and Poles into their homeland and immigration and asylum was a nonissue. West Germans stood at the checkpoints and personally greeted the East Germans as they flowed into West Germany. However, by 1991 the number of immigrants and asylum seekers greatly increased, the sensationalist German tabloid *Bild-Zeitung* and the Christian parties "worked hand in hand in denouncing the asylum seekers" (Thraenhardt 1997, 195) in the German city-state of Bremen. The CDU and CSU announced that they would campaign on the basis of immigration and asylum issues, hoping to brand their main opponent, the Social Democratic Party (SPD), as weak on immigration issues. The CDU's secretary general, Volker Rühe, went so far as to claim that, "Every additional asylum seeker is an SPD asylum seeker" (Wüst, 1995, 99). An unintended consequence of this strategy was the radicalization not only of the Christian parties but also of the right-wing Republikaner party (Thraenhardt 1997) as the number of asylum seekers rose from 250,000 in 1991 to 450,000 in 1992. It is no accident that the deadly and appalling arson attacks against immigrants, mostly Turks, in Rostock in August 1992 and in Mölln in November 1992 occurred soon after the CDU/CSU, an established party, made xenophobia *salonfähig* (widely acceptable).[7] The motive given for the arson attack was *Ausländerhass* (hatred of foreigners).

Identity, nationhood, and the attendant concept of citizenship were the result of bloody confrontations in the past that provided the legends out of which national identities were constructed. History is written by historians, and while victory has a hundred fathers and defeat is an orphan even orphans have legends. One such legend, the infamous *Dolch-stosslegende* (stab in the back legend), maintained that the German army was never really defeated in World War I. Rather, it was the incompetent leadership of civilians that was responsible for the German defeat. This legend kept the myth of the almighty German army alive, and Hitler was able to exploit this unbroken tradition of German militarism, ultimately leading the world into the abyss of World War II. While the origins of such legends are imagined, their consequences are real.

Constructivism takes primordialism and adds a healthy dose of agency to it. Beliefs about race, ethnicity, and other differences are the material out of which either war or peace can be sculpted. The crucial question is: who are the sculptors? In the few cases examined here, sometimes it is the government of the nation-state and in other cases political parties, politicians, the military, party activists, all forms of the media, members of the minority groups themselves, lobbyists, philanthropists and misanthropists, intellectuals, pundits, commentators, educators, corporate leaders, literati, artists, musicians, academics, and purveyors of popular culture. In other words, anybody who leaves a public trace shapes the collective identity.

In Alberto Alesina and Nathan Glaeser's recent book, race accounts for about 50 percent of the reasons why the American welfare state is smaller than the European, the other 50 percent being explained by different institutions. They argue that "taxpayers will automatically be more supportive when payments go to people who physically and socially resemble themselves." Realizing that this presents a rather grim outlook, they formulate another, "more nuanced view, which . . . is that racial hatred is endogenous and often created by entrepreneurial politicians. . . . According to this view, human beings are genetically endowed with an ability to hate, but the targets of their hatred are situational and can be readily manipulated" (Alesina and Glaeser 2004, 136).

While this statement would make many a constructivist cringe, Alesina and Glaeser describe at length how redistribution in the United States from the rich to the poor by the Populist Party in the 1890s became "racialized." Even though the populists were particularly strong in the impoverished South, conservative forces continued to be successful in blocking redistributive politics by appealing to racial hatred and effectively dividing the populist movement. Similarly, it was the civil rights movement in the mid–1960s and the adverse reaction of southerners to Lyndon B. Johnson's idea of a "great society" that cemented the hold of the Republican Party on the South.

In a fascinating yet deeply disturbing book, an evolutionary biologist, Frank K. Salter (2004), from the Max Planck Institute in Andechs, Germany, brings together a host of ethologists and "behavioral ecologists," including Pierre L. van den Berghe, and Irenäus Eibl-Eibesfeldt, arguing for a theory of "ethnic nepotism." This theory basically argues that close kin will be favored over more distant kin. This approach is applied to modern, diverse welfare states and comes to the conclusion that the more diverse societies become the less caring they are (Sanderson 2004).

While the power of primordial attachments cannot be denied, applying "sociobiologically informed social policy" to the development of welfare states is an analytical overstretch. These "sociobiological" approaches overemphasize the *bio-* to the detriment of the *socio-*. The application of evolutionary theory to the development of welfare states has serious drawbacks. First, much of this biological approach does not acknowledge that any of these so-called primordial differences are constructed or gives the issue short shrift. Second, the essentialist rhetoric of these Darwinian approaches sees the causal arrow going from individual to group to society and does not, and cannot, entertain the possibility that it could go the other way. The capacity to shape their lives is significantly greater among humans than among animals. Third, the political implications of the use of Darwinian methods are politically suspect: by highlighting differences among groups of people, they justify ethnocentrism, which inevitably leads to group conflict. In a paradoxical way, those committed to a sociobiological approach based on primordial characteristics are handmaidens in the *construction* of a divisive ideology to be used by the entrepreneurs of hate, who will utilize it to further their own dubious political goals.

This raises a very important question concerning the political responsibility not just of researchers but of anybody who is active in public affairs. The media in particular carry a very high burden of responsibility since they have the capacity to shape in large measure the degree to which social issues are widely perceived. In terms of the way welfare issues are perceived, Martin Gilens (1999) specifically identifies the media as the culprit in spreading stereotypes about the connections between race and welfare, writing that "the overly racialized images of poverty and the association of blacks with the least sympathetic subgroups of the poor reflect news professionals' own racial stereotypes" (6).

Categorical differences among people have received a new impetus since 9/11. It would be a grave mistake to belittle the capacity of such categories to spread hatred for they represent the raw material out of which catastrophic events can be shaped. But clay contained in the soil does not a clay pot make. Categorical differences per se do not make people hate each other. It is the sentiments that are constructed on the basis of these categorical differences that have the capacity to be turned into unimaginable tragedy. The old saw that says "You can't make something out of nothing" certainly applies in the processes of nation making, race, and ethnicity. The "something"—that is, the shaping of people's identity—depends on subconsciously held, latent beliefs. However, those beliefs are not objective facts, givens, or absolute truths but are themselves conceptions or misconceptions of events whose origins are often lost in the mists (or myths) of time. They are enactments of battles, interpretations of stories, renderings of heroes, depictions of villains, narratives in children's books, legends of bravery, and the irresistible myth of ones' own bravery and the other's vileness. What actually happened in the past is far less important than how it is remembered. When it comes to remembering or forgetting one's past, it is far easier to give in to wishful thinking than to deal with perhaps painful historical facts. Thus legends are born.

It is often traumatic experiences that create a sense of identity—and it does not matter whether one is the victor or the almost vanquished. The United States did not have a strong sense of an American identity until the beginning of the Revolutionary War, which brought the various ethnic groups in America together against a common enemy. Similarly, in Europe the identities of the French, English, Dutch, Spanish, Swedes, Prussians, Germans, and Italians were forged in the crucible of war. In the words of Alan Wolfe, "Behind every citizen is a graveyard" (quoted in Goodhart 2004).

Nationalism even transcended the class struggle. Lenin's disappointment is well known when he learned that German and French workers had fired at each other at the outbreak of World War I. To Lenin's dismay, nationalism proved stronger than class consciousness. On the day of the declaration of war against Serbia, the Austrian socialist newspaper *Arbeiter Zeitung* declared, "Zeigt, dass auch die Männer des Klassenkampfes bis zum letzten Atemzug zu ihren Fahnen stehen" (Show that also the men of the class struggle, until their last breath, stand on the side of their flag).

Even intellectuals were seduced by the fever of war. War, like few other events, has the capacity to bring together people of most disparate origins. Consider Sigmund Freud, the founder of psychoanalysis, who shouted jubilantly on the day of the declaration of war against Serbia, "Ich fühle mich zum ersten Mal als Österreicher" (This is the first time I feel that I am Austrian). This is most remarkable since in 1914 Austria was a *Vielvölkerstaat,* a multinational state, that encompassed a multitude of peoples, religions, cultures, and ethnic backgrounds. To what part of this multinational Austria Freud was referring only he knew.[8] For Freud, the state took precedence over the nation.

External wars represent a common threat that makes people move closer together even in multinational societies. It is rather tragic that it takes wars to establish a fellow feeling among people, a feeling that if it existed in peace might make war less necessary. War has a way of uniting people by representing a higher-order threat and at the same time a higher-order goal that can overcome social chasms. In times of war, terrorist attacks, or natural disasters, the fragmenting effects of social heterogeneity are muted, while in times of peace social heterogeneity tends to have a centrifugal effect, tearing society apart even when the members find themselves on the same side of the class struggle.

As a result, historical narratives are the product of those who invent them. They can lay dormant and remain relatively benign or can be awakened and potentially used for sinister ends. For human suffering to occur in catastrophic proportions, as in the case of the Holocaust or the genocide in Rwanda, invention must be followed by action. The historical narrative is the necessary condition; action is the sufficient condition. That sufficient condition lies within the purview of agents who deliberately act in order to achieve particular outcomes. These agents often make masterful use of the media to spread their message, such as Hitler, who commissioned Leni Riefenstahl's film *Triumph des Willens,* or the Hutu government, which allowed a hate radio station in Rwanda to daily call on Hutus to kill Tutsis "like rats, until there are no Tutsis left."

Constructivism can also work in the opposite direction. Ethnic identities can be constructed so as to become benign. A prime example is German nationalism, which viewed much of Europe, particularly its Eastern neighbors, as inferior and as a result to be there for the taking. Today this worldview has changed, resulting in a tolerant, nonaggressive

Germany without any inclinations to dominate other countries. Similar reorientations have occurred in nations such as Italy, which today sees itself very much as a responsible member of the family of European nations.

Constructivism and primordialism are not opposites; rather they are complementary. Many protagonists of the constructivist approach underestimate the power of latent primordial sentiments. A sculptor can only shape if there is putty or clay there in the first place. The shaping represents a willed, deliberate act independent of the raw material. It is thus not the raw material itself but the totality of the shaper's will that determines the final form. Construction of identity is thus an ongoing process driven by the active shaping of an existing yet constantly changing corpus of narratives. The purpose of the flag, statues, national or religious holidays, street names, monuments, anthems, postage stamps, and the names of federal buildings, airports, and tall ships is simultaneously the invocation and manifestation of the common narrative. Ernest Renan, in his unforgettable phrase, called this continual creation and re-creation of national identity the "daily plebiscite."

It appears that constructivism has won the day. In the words of Chandra Kanchan, "[I]t is now virtually impossible to find a social scientist who openly defends a primordialist position" (2001, 8). And Rogers Brubaker (2004, 3) has confidently announced that "constructivism has become the epitome of academic respectability, even orthodoxy. It is not that the notion of social construction is wrong; it is rather that it is today too obviously right, too familiar, too readily taken for granted." It may be true that there is a consensus among many social scientists about the constructed nature of identity, but for most people identity is the opposite of constructed; it is real. They tend to unconsciously reify this concept as something that is immutable and stable and has unity, internal harmony, and an unquestionable core. While infinitely contestable, in periods of national crisis this ordinary use of identity can harden to such a degree that public criticism of one's national identity may meet fierce resistance, as was seen in the immediate aftermath of the horrific attacks on 9/11 when the vaunted American "culture of dissent" drowned in a sea of Old Glory.

When it comes to identity, most people do not want to concern themselves with the intellectual question of whether their gut feelings are constructed or not. In the perception of ordinary people, they are who they are. They are not wracked with self-doubt and do not engage in introspection as to why they may have the identity they have. This is partly because lack of such reflection is comforting and provides people with certainty, with a perhaps distorted understanding of the world around them yet nevertheless, in their view, a firm sense of who they are. Social scientists may be constructivist, but most citizens are not.

Ronald Grigor Suny, a sociologist at the University of Chicago and Armenian by descent, learned this the hard way. He tells the story about what happens when "constructivists," such as himself, encounter people endowed with great certainty about their identity (Suny 2001). He was invited to a conference in 1997 at the American University of Armenia in Erevan, and he was asked to speak on the topic "prospects for regional integration." The thrust of his talk was to question the usefulness of ethnonationalism by suggesting a more constructivist understanding of nationness. He argued that "nations are congealed histories. They are made up of stories that people tell about their past and thereby determine who they are. Histories in turn are based on memories organized into narratives" (2001, 863). He made other, similar statements. He described the reaction to his talk as "explosive." He reports that leaflets were distributed the next day, and newspapers and radio broadcasts attacked his speech. Hostile questions were directed to him at the conference, and he was accused of being an agent of the oil companies. When angry crowds surrounded him as he was leaving the hall, he required security guards, who whisked him to safety. Personal attacks on his speech and him as a person continued, and a year later a book appeared in Erevan denouncing Western scholarship and particularly his own work.

There is no denying that people's identities are constructed. However, that does not mean that their identities can be shaped and reshaped throughout their lifetimes. Some sociologists believe that the "formative" years of the socialization process are the most crucial ones for the development of an individual, but once a person has reached adulthood the effect of socializing institutions such as family and schools wane. Is there a similar process at work in constructing one's identity? Once somebody's identity is formed, how easy is it to reconstruct it? Steven Van-Evera, one of the few self-avowed primordialists, argues that ethnic identities, once formed, are very difficult to reconstruct, particularly in societies that have achieved mass literacy and when violent conflicts among ethnic groups have occurred (VanEvera 2001).

This view suggests that ethnic identity is "stickier" than many constructivists assume. More directly related to the topic in this book, it may be that natives, particularly those who precariously live on the margins of society, view immigrants as a direct threat to their well-being. As a result, they may perceive increasing diversity as a crumbling of community and may retreat from their willingness to fund the welfare state as they believe that more of their taxes go to people who are different from themselves. The next section examines the nexus between community and the willingness of natives to continue funding the welfare state in the face of increasing diversity.

Funding the Welfare State: Is Blood Thicker Than Water?

In order for the welfare state to function, so the argument goes, it is necessary that the person in need shares similar primordial characteristics with you. Some of the most fervent defenders of a primordialist view are Frank Salter and his team of political ethologists at the Max Planck Institute. They attempted to experimentally test the theory of "ethnic nepotism" (van den Berghe 1981), which claims that almsgiving should be greater within ethnic groups than between them. In order to test this claim they observed almsgiving among three different ethnic groups on Russian trains. The groups were ethnic Russians, Moldavians, and Gypsies. They found that Russian riders gave more alms to Russians than to Moldavians and Gypsies, thus concluding that altruism is more pronounced within than between ethnic groups, leading the authors to assert that this evidence confirms the theory of ethnic nepotism (Butovskaya et al. 2000; Salter 2004).

Although Salter and his team push the sociobiological argument farther than any other observers, Gunnar Myrdal also opined on the effects of social heterogeneity on the viability of the welfare state. Myrdal contended that for the welfare state to flourish "intensive popular participation in civic life on all levels" is necessary. He identifies the United States as lacking in civic life because "until comparatively recently, [the United States] has had much immigration which in its later stages brought in peoples from national cultures rather different from the old stock. In spite of the very rapid advances made towards national integration, heterogeneous elements still linger everywhere in the population, and with them remnants of separatistic allegiances" (Myrdal 1960, 54). Interestingly, Myrdal also observed that as a result of "high mobility in America," by which he means physical not social mobility, a more closely knit national community will develop, which will favor the development of a more vibrant polity (55).

A similar argument was made more than thirty years ago by Harold Wilensky (1975, 53) in his classic *The Welfare State and Equality,* in which he addressed the challenge of social heterogeneity in hypothesis form: "Social heterogeneity and internal cleavages. Hypothesis: No pattern will be visible because of the contradictory pressures of minority groups." Wilensky could not make any predictions as to the effects of social heterogeneity but he realized that "a wider civic virtue cannot fully flourish when ties to minority groups are strong, for racial, ethnic-linguistic, and religious cleavages block meaningful participation in less parochial voluntary associations and encourage separatist allegiances; further, minority groups sometimes create welfare and education services of their own, thereby subverting public expenditures." He argued for further "intensive investigation" of these issues in order to disentangle the various cross-pressures on the welfare state as a function of increased social heterogeneity (53).

Despite his call for further investigation of the effects of social heterogeneity on the viability of the welfare state, political scientists have remained mostly silent on these issues. However, they have not escaped the attention of economists, sociologists, social and political theorists, social psychologists, and social policy observers. In the mental maps of economists, states are an obstacle to the logical unfolding of market forces. Thus, economists have a more amorphous view of the world, and they were quicker on the uptake in recognizing that immigration and its attendant increases in diversity might be a problem for mature welfare states. The first economist to model discrimination was the economist Gary Becker, winner of the 1992 Nobel Prize, who argued that there is an inverse relationship between the level of discrimination and the level of competition that exists in an industry. Becker, in *The Economics of Discrimination* (1957), pointed out that if an employer refuses to hire a productive worker simply because of his or her skin color that employer loses out on a valuable opportunity. As a result, discrimination backfires, leaving the discriminator worse off than if no discrimination had occurred. Thus, he concluded that economics could be a great leveler if it were not for the stubbornness of racism.

More recently, much of the empirical work on the connections between social heterogeneity and extent of the welfare state has been conducted by the economist Alberto Alesina. He, together with Reza Baqir and William Easterly (1999), examined U.S. cities, metropolitan areas, and urban counties and found that shares of spending on productive public goods are inversely related to ethnic fragmentation in the respective area. Similar findings are reported by Alesina and LaFerrara (1999), who argue that participation in civic organizations is adversely affected by diversity. In another piece, Alesina, Edward Glaeser, and Bruce Sacerdote (2001, 1) find that the reason why European countries are much more generous to the poor is because "racial animosity in the US makes redistribution to the poor, who are disproportionately black, unappealing to many voters." Alesina and Glaeser (2004) argue that racial diversity is negatively related to public generosity. People are more likely to support welfare if they see it received by people of their own race but are less supportive if they see it received by people of another race.

Peter Lindert, also an economist, makes a similar argument, although it comes from the opposite direction. He argues that the more "social affinity" there is the more willing people are to pay higher taxes to fund social protection schemes. "The more a middle-income voter looks at the likely recipients of public aid and says, 'that could be me' (or my daughter, or my whole family), the greater that voter's willingness to vote for taxes and fund such aid." He goes on to explain that such social affinity would be fostered by ethnic homogeneity between middle class voters and the perceived recipients. However, "ethnic divisions would create suspicions that taxpayer's money would be turned over to 'them'" (Lindert 2004, 187). Race and ethnicity also seem to drive public policy outcomes. Rodney E. Hero and Caroline J. Tolbert (1996) find that lower education and public policy outcomes in the states of the United States are driven by ethnic and racial diversity, and Therese McCarty (1993) finds that ethnic diversity discourages transfer payments by central governments.

It is not surprising that social heterogeneity has also attracted the interest of social psychologists. The dynamics of racial prejudice were investigated by Gordon W. Allport (1954), who argued that prejudice will subside the more contact there is between members of different races. This important claim has not received the widespread interest it deserves since this and other studies do find evidence that the more contact there is between immigrants and natives the less nativist resentment such natives harbor.

The social psychologist Henri Tajfel studied the phenomenon of in-group favoritism as a way of exploring out-group hostility (Tajfel 1981).

Tajfel's (1982) social identity theory assumes that human beings are motivated to positively evaluate their own groups in order to increase their self-esteem. This means elevating the status of your in-group and stereotyping the members of an out-group on the basis of race, religion, language, nationality, or any other difference that exists between the two groups. Any threat to the in-group from the outside, be it military, social, or otherwise, will result in heightened in-group bias.

The simple act of assigning different group names to otherwise identical individuals can lead to in- and out-group bias. The famous Robbers Cave experiment illustrates this issue very clearly. In the summer of 1954, a small group of eleven-year-old boys, all white, well-adjusted, and from middle-class backgrounds and all strangers to one another arrived at a camp at Robbers Cave State Park in Oklahoma. For about a week this group took part in the normal activities of a summer camp. They gave themselves a name, which was printed on their T-shirts and caps.

The boys were under the assumption that they were the only ones at the camp. However, after about a week they found out that there was another group present, with another name, and that sports tournaments had been arranged between them. Finally, the "Rattlers" and the "Eagles" met and competed against each other in baseball, football, treasure hunts, tug-of-war, and other events. When the boys were asked their opinions of each other, they described themselves as "tough," "brave," and "friendly" and members of the other group as "sneaky," "stinkers," and "smart alecks." After having thoroughly polarized the two groups, the experimenters tried to bring them together again by proclaiming positive things about both groups and arranging meets between them under noncompetitive conditions. None of these strategies worked. Ultimately, the experimenters arranged for the camp truck to break down, necessitating the help of both groups to pull it up a steep hill. "These activities worked like a charm. Negative perceptions dissipated as did the fighting. By the end of camp, the two groups liked each other so much, that they insisted on traveling home on the same bus" (Brehm and Kassin 1990, 169–71). Cooperation was thus achieved by establishing a higher-order goal whose achievement necessitated the transcendence of in- and out-group biases.

This intriguing finding has serious implications for policies promoting affirmative action and multiculturalism. In such policies the state is called on to explicitly recognize different groups and grant them specific support. Judging from the findings of the social psychology literature, the effects of such "singling out" might be a heightened awareness of differences, particularly among those who are not specifically recognized as belonging to a "minority" group, as opposed to assisting in integrating and reducing conflicts driven by social heterogeneity.

Categorizations matter. This was also the finding of Charles Tilly (1998, 7) when he attempted to map the phenomena that give rise to "durable inequality." He found that "large significant inequalities in advantages among human beings correspond mainly to categorical differences." The categorical differences Tilly had in mind were "female/male, aristocrat/plebeian, citizen/foreigner and more complex classifications based on religious affiliation, ethnic origin or race" (6). A similar argument is made by Dennis Wrong (1994, 159), who argued that "groups differentiated by religion, ethnicity, occupation, locality, political ideology-group conflict in overt or covert form, is endemic to societies characterized by social heterogeneity, a high degree of internal differentiation, and social inequalities among large groups or social aggregates."

Political theorists echo some of these findings. David Miller (2000, 30), a proponent of the idea that nations should remain the enduring form of social organization, claims that "it is essential to national identity that the people who compose the nation are believed to share certain traits that mark them off from other peoples." Michael Walzer (1983, 38) argues that immigrants "experience a tension between love of place and the discomforts of a particular place. While some of them leave their homes and become foreigners in new lands, others stay where they are and resent the foreigners in their own land. Their members will organize and defend the local politics and culture against strangers. Historically, neighborhoods have turned into closed and parochial communities whenever the state was open."

With that statement, Walzer summarizes succinctly the question of this chapter: will increased immigration lead to a "closing" of the dominant community, that is, to a reduced willingness among the natives to fund the welfare state? In different words, but in the same vein, David Goodhart posed the following question in the liberal British magazine *Prospect*: "Too diverse? Is Britain becoming too diverse to sustain the mutual obligations behind a good society and the welfare state?" Predictably, this set off a firestorm among intellectuals in Britain, as well as the United States. It is worth citing Goodhart (2004) at length.

Thinking about the conflict between solidarity and diversity is another way of asking a question as old as human society itself: who is my brother? With whom do I share mutual obligations? The traditional conservative Burkean view is that our affinities ripple out from our families and localities, to the nation and not very far beyond. That view is pitted against a liberal universalist one which sees us in some sense obligated to all human beings from Bolton to Burundi an idea associated with left-wing internationalism. . . . In any case, Burkeans claim to have common sense on their side. They argue that we feel more comfortable with, and are readier to share with, and sacrifice for, those with whom we have shared histories and similar values. To put it bluntly—most of us prefer our own kind.

This piece drew many measured and not so measured responses from a whole range of commentators, from serious academics to thinly veiled racists, in what became briefly known on the Internet as the "Goodhart debate." Goodhart raises a crucial issue: on what basis should people obey the law, make sacrifices, assist others, and have social relations? Does national identity not presuppose an identity of some older, deeper kind? Will people accept the legitimacy of the state only if such a deeper, more fundamental form of identity exists or is at least imagined? Whose interests should the state take into consideration?

These questions have become central in the age of the modern state. In prestate empires and kingdoms, such questions had no relevance as people were the objects rather than the subjects of rule. However, since in modern states it is "We, the people" who decide collectively, it is crucial to know "who we are" (Huntington 2004). In a democracy, people not only decide collectively, but they also deliberate collectively. The communitarian Charles Taylor has argued that such deliberation "implies a degree of cohesion. To some extent, the members must know one another, listen to one another and understand one another. If they are not acquainted, or if they cannot really understand one another, how can they engage in joint deliberation?" (Taylor 2003, 21).

Social heterogeneity appears to be a powerful thread that runs through the fabric of societies in the minds of most influential theorists. Speaking about the conditions under which democracy can flourish, John Stuart Mill (1991, 310) argued that, "Free institutions are next to impossible in a country made up by different nationalities. Among a people without fellow-feeling, especially if they read and speak different languages, the united public opinion, necessary for the working of representative government cannot exist."

Mill (1968, 307) was particularly explicit in his emphasis on a common past in understanding the concept of nationality.

> A portion of mankind may be said to constitute a Nationality if they are united among themselves by common sympathies, which do not exist between them and any others—which make them co-operate with each other more willingly than with other people. . . . This feeling of nationality may have been generated by various causes. Sometimes it is the effect of identity of race and descent. Community of language, and community of religion, greatly contribute to it. Geographical limits are one of its causes. But the strongest of all is identity of political antecedents; the possession of a national history, and consequent community of recollections; collective pride and humiliation, pleasure and regret, connected with the same incidents in the past.

Mill follows this statement immediately with a qualifier, indicating that these "circumstances" are not necessarily sufficient by themselves and citing Switzerland, which has a strong sentiment of nationality, even though the various cantons are of "different races, different languages and different religions" (308). Still, his argument is that a national identity is stronger if it is built on a "community of recollections."

This community of recollections was severely fractured when unionists in the United States attempted to mobilize the working class. The ethnic diversity of immigrants proved to be so corrosive to establishing unions and socialist parties that it became one of the core answers to the famous question: why is there no socialism in the United States? (Sombart 1976). It is the very absence of a tightly organized socialist party that explains the relative "backwardness" of the American welfare state.[9] When it came to organizing labor, blood proved to be thicker than water. In the absence of strong socialist parties, few countries managed to develop a sizable welfare state.

Different waves of immigrants of varying nationalities and religions entering the United States created an extraordinarily diverse labor force. Socialists appealed to workers along class lines while Democrats and Republicans exploited ethnic differences in appealing to members (Lipset and Marks 2000). The craft unions in the American Federation of Labor (AFL) were organized along ethnic lines, which aggravated the problems faced by the socialists, particularly after the 1890s when the largest streams of newcomers were no longer the "old immigrants," British, Germans, and Northern Europeans who were skilled and assimilated rather quickly into the larger society, but immigrants from Southern and Eastern Europe, who had fewer skills, spoke poor English, and were discriminated against by the earlier immigrants, who blended more easily with the native-born whites (Lipset and Marks 2000).

In addition, the immigrants themselves were ideologically quite distinct. The most radical immigrants were the Germans, who brought with them experiences of the failed democratic revolutions of 1848 and the persecution of socialists under Bismarck. In addition, they had first-hand experience with the strains of industrial production. On the other hand, many immigrants were actually quite conservative and ready to absorb the reigning ideology of their new homeland. Because many found life to be much better in the New World than in their old homelands, they, "with the enthusiasm of converts, praised the Republic and the material blessings it offered" (Hanson 1964, 96). Moreover, given the sectarian, fundamentalist character of the Socialist party, many Catholic immigrants could not find an ideological home in it. In the words of Seymour M. Lipset and Gary Marks: "Vigorous Catholic opposition to socialism can hardly be exaggerated as a reason for the failure of the Socialist party" (Lipset and Marks 2000, 154). Finally, even the socialists succumbed to racism and agitated for the restriction of immigration to Northern Europeans and the exclusion of Catholics, American Negroes, and Southern and Eastern Europeans (Lipset and Marks 2000). Obviously, the American experience in labor organizing was very different from the European. Precisely because European nations were relatively homogeneous was it possible for "class" to become a salient issue. Only on the basis of ethnic homogeneity was it possible that class could become a powerful vector in European politics—a vector that ultimately pointed in the direction of the welfare state.

While bridging the class divide was certainly the main purpose of the welfare state, it appears that race may have spurred the development of the welfare state in Europe while it had the opposite effect in the United States. The development of the welfare state occurred during the "age of empire" (Hobsbawm 1987). The creation and expansion of the welfare

state in the nineteenth and twentieth centuries in Europe were under-
pinned by citizens' sense of community and social solidarity toward each
other at home while at the same time the welfare state builders were
busy creating and running empires abroad. The creation of empires and
welfare states occurred simultaneously: by extending social rights at
home, nation builders completed the circle of full citizenship vis-à-vis
the "subjects" abroad. In the British, German, and French colonies, the
subjects of rule were starkly outside this privileged group of citizens.
Racial differences may have even accelerated the creation of welfare
states in Europe precisely because the imperial subjects were not part of
the homeland, thus making it relatively easy to exclude them. Race and
location overlapped, for both the citizens and the subjects of rule. The
whites lived in France, Great Britain, or Germany while their subjects
lived in far-flung places around the world. This clear separation facilitated drawing the line between those who were eligible and those who
were not, those who could be tied to the state via social protection and
those who could be excluded. "The politics of welfare state building,"
argues Robert C. Liberman (2002, 108) "the construction of a means of
social solidarity at home, was connected to the process of race based distinctions between national citizens and colonial subjects across national
boundaries." Today many erstwhile subjects of former British and French
colonies are immigrating to France and the United Kingdom, making
both countries very diverse. But these immigrants enter countries whose
welfare systems were originally built for their national white populations
not with the colonial subjects in mind.

In the United States, the logic was different because whites and blacks
were not so neatly separated as in the European colonies. From the very
beginning, blacks and whites shared the same physical space, creating a
heterogeneous society where the "imperative of uniting whites against
blacks produced an approach to welfare policy that was necessarily ex-
clusionary and decentralizing rather then inclusionary and national"
(Liberman 2002, 110).

In the European context, the basic premise on which the state "can extract large sums of money in tax and pay it out in benefits is that most
people think the recipients are people like themselves, facing difficulties
that they themselves could face" (David Willets, MP, quoted in Goodhart
2004). This organicist notion of the welfare state was founded on widely
held concepts of community and feelings of mutual obligation toward
fellow citizens.

Gary Freeman has powerfully articulated the dynamics between in-group and out-group, natives and immigrants, and the connection to the welfare state, writing that "immigration has tended to erode the more general normative consensus on which the welfare state is built. Welfare benefits are now for the first time associated in the public mind with a visible and subordinate minority. . . . When the welfare state is seen as something for 'them' paid by 'us,' its days as a consensual solution to societal problems are numbered" (1986, 62).

Reflecting on this tapestry we have woven, it appears that academics in many different fields, policymakers, and intellectuals display a strong belief in the essentialist rhetoric of primordialism. Of course, the power of race and ethnicity as a central organizing principle cannot be denied. Too many pages in history are stained with the blood of those who have been victimized simply because they were different, making the message of our quilt, so far, rather grim and unsettling. Thus, it is now time to take a closer look at the primordialist argument and assess whether it is indeed such an unchangeable essence.

MITIGATING FACTORS: FROM PRIMORDIALISM TO COSMOPOLITANISM?

Before the question of whether primordial sentiments represent a challenge to the welfare state is answered, a few more observations are in order. This section makes four points that provide further context to the primordial/constructivist debate. First, in much of the primordial literature the argument proceeds from a "given" difference to outcomes, treating the primordial categories as causes and various outcomes, such as the welfare state, war, genocide, or political stability, as effects. This is unwarranted. It may very well be that the welfare state as a means of statecraft may have integrative capacities, reversing the causal arrow. This argument will be further pursued empirically in more detail in chapter 5. Second, despite recurrent and predictable nativist claims that "this new group of immigrants is not assimilable," the reality is that there has been a massive amount of integration going on. Third, there is an unquestioned assumption that diversity has to have deleterious effects on the well-being of a nation. Finally, while primordialism may strike a chord among many people, as a result of globalization and the awareness that many central problems, such as global environmental issues, can only be solved globally, an old approach in political thought has been revived, one that goes under the label "cosmopolitanism." This approach specifically asks whether we should have more of a duty toward our immediate in-group, our region, or even our nation as opposed to the "distant other." Cosmopolitanism tends to argue that we have an equal duty to all human beings, with little room for partiality. This claims stands in direct opposition to the primordial one detailed earlier.[10]

First, in the preceding narrative, the causal story either goes directly from social heterogeneity to outcomes or views social heterogeneity as leading to the creation of institutions that respond to the needs of members of minority groups by attaching material benefits to their status and thereby cementing or even strengthening their identity. Thus, viewed from this angle, institutions are endogenous to the conditions that give rise to them.

However, institutions are not simply a reflection of societal conditions; rather, they have the capacity to affect outcomes on a wide range of issues. The burgeoning literature over the last two decades labeled, "neoinstitutionalism" has convincingly shown that different political institutions have systematically different effects on a variety of outcomes (Lijphart 1999; Katzenstein 1985; Rothstein 1998; Tsebelis 2002, and many others; Steinmo, Thelen, and Longstreth 1992; Crepaz 2002), giving credence to Montesquieu's alleged observation that "in the beginning, men make institutions, but, with the passage of time, institutions make men."

Achieving social harmony in many European countries was no small feat and can clearly be attributed to the development of social protection schemes built up in times of economic expansion after World War II. Can the integrative logic of the welfare state also be applied to groups such as "guest workers," who inhabit the state but are not citizens, or minorities, who request recognition of, and support for, their status? So far it has been argued that the causal arrow goes from diversity to a purportedly impotent welfare state. Could it be the opposite? A welfare state that, qua welfare production, facilitates integration of foreigners?

This raises the issue of institutional design, which we will examine in more detail in chapter 5. Just as identity can be used to construct institutions specifically designed to meet the needs of minorities, as shown by Glazer and Moynihan (1970), so we will argue that institutions can shape the success of integration by establishing programs such as reading, writing, and citizenship courses for immigrants; by allowing immigrants who are not yet citizens to vote in local elections; and by helping immigrants find a job. In terms of welfare state regimes, could it be that the more inclusive and universal political institutions are the more difficult it is to identify the "other"? As a result, might this blunt nativist reactions against immigrants?

Just as the welfare state bridged the class conflict and bound citizens together on the basis of national policies, so it should have an integrative capacity, particularly in a centralized state. Examining Sweden, Staffan Kumlin (2002) has found that the actual experiences of citizens with means-tested forms of welfare provision have undermined trust and reduced support for the political system while experiences with universal forms of welfare provision have had opposite effect. Once foreigners become citizens, it may be that universal forms of welfare provision will hasten their integration into society while means-tested forms will continue to stigmatize them as the foreigner, which will hamper their integration and perhaps undermine support for the political system. Thus, there may be a causal arrow going from the type of welfare regime to a citizen's perception of newcomers and his or her willingness to continue funding the welfare state.

The argument that "Europe's new immigrant based heterogeneity may eventually push the continent toward more American levels of redistribution" (Alesina and Glaeser 2004) is problematic. While it is the purpose of this book to ascertain the viability of the welfare state in the eyes of the European and American publics as they are confronted with unprecedented immigration, a market-conforming American welfare state in Europe is unlikely for two reasons. First, immigration impinges on European societies with political institutions that differ greatly from those of the United States. There is a well-established literature that highlights the institutional aspects of welfare state developments (Flora and Heidenheimer 1981; Rimlinger 1971; Mommsen 1981; Wilensky 1975). The two most important institutional differences between the United States and most European countries are proportional representation and centralization of political power. Proportional representation allowed socialist parties to gain access to the political process, which they used to push a prowelfare agenda. Centralization, on the other hand, gives reformers more power, facilitates political and policy coordination, and provides fewer veto points to block reformist legislation (Noble 1997). In the United States, courts played a particularly obstructionist role in stifling the creation of a European-style welfare state. Theda Skocpol describes the United States as "court dominated," a state where in the first twenty years of the twentieth century about 300 labor laws were struck down and judges "invoked constitutional prohibitions against special, or class legislation" (1992, 255).[11] On the other hand, courts played a very limited role in the creation or obstruction of European welfare states. Proportional representation and political centralization are two of the reasons why European welfare states provide much more universal incorporation and robust protection of their citizens than their American counterpart does. Once these political institutions were in place, they allowed the development of generous welfare states, "decommodifying" large parts of society and irreversibly tying them to the state and severely limiting the options of the welfare state in dealing with increased demands as a result of immigration. It is much more difficult for welfare states with a social democratic tradition to deny welfare benefits to newcomers than it is for states without such a tradition and very weak, decentralized welfare institutions. James Hollifield (2000, 110) highlights the differing immigration control strategies.

> In countries like the USA which have no social democratic tradition and a weak welfare state, the first strategy for internal control is likely to be a roll back of social rights, i.e. the restriction of *positive freedom*. Conversely, in countries like Sweden and Germany which have a strong social democratic tradition, social rights are likely to be preserved for all members of society, denizens, as well as citizens; and the preferred strategy for control will be external control of borders, strict regulation of labor markets, and limits on negative freedom. (emphasis in original)

Another reason why Americanization of the European welfare state is unlikely is also path dependent. As a result of many decades in operation, welfare states, particularly the Scandinavian ones, have developed high levels of trust. As a result, nativist resentment that could push these states to exclude immigrants from public welfare are likely to be muted. This topic is developed in detail in chapter 5.

Second, despite the seeming potency of the primordial argument, there has been and still is a massive amount of integration going on, a fact often overlooked by those who favor the primordialist account. Some of the founders of the American nation, particularly John Jay and Alexander Hamilton, believed that only immigrants of British descent would be able to extend the idea of American republicanism (Bischoff

2002).[12] With every new wave of immigrants from different nations or religions, new prejudices were voiced, all of them eerily similar regardless of whether they were cast against the Germans, Scandinavians, or Catholics. In the late 1840s and early 1850s, the Irish were the target of nativists. In 1882, Congress passed the Chinese Exclusion Act, which set a quota on the number of Chinese immigrants admitted each year. This law remained on the books until 1943. In the 1880s, a new group of immigrants reached American shores: Southern and Eastern Europeans, many of them from the Middle East and in terms of religion encompassing many Jews; Catholics; Russian, Greek, and other Orthodox Christians; and a few Moslems and Buddhists. This led to a new wave of anti-immigrant resentment.

Yet today Germans, Irish, Italians, Greeks, Catholics, Jews, Buddhists, Russians, Chinese, and many others have been basically integrated into American society. This has been a remarkable achievement compared to the racist and nativist claims heard at the time of their arrivals, and it was not supposed to happen according to the proponents of primordial sentiments.

Similarly, the once intense hatred between French and Germans, fanned by the two costliest wars in human history, has given way to friendship between these two nations, which have become the locomotives behind European integration. Despite all the talk about the top-down approach of the European Union and the "democratic deficit," the nations of Europe, which were ravaged by World War II just over 60 years ago, have come together to create the biggest internal market in the history of mankind. Cold war propaganda machines in both the United States and the Soviet Union for almost half a century engaged in establishing the "other" as the enemy, only to find that when the Soviet empire ended with a whimper Russian immigrants to the United States were welcomed with open arms.

Herbert Gans (2004) argues that, even though "ethnicity is a hearty plant," eventually assimilation will run its course, "as intermarriage creates a population so multi-ethnic that its ethnic options run out." He believes that race will prove more resistant to assimilation since "skin color has consequences for economic and social assimilation." Still, according to Gans, "in the longer run, and if all goes well racially, all Americans may have brown skins one day—just the right color to survive global warming" (44).

Similarly, Stephan Thernstrom (2004) makes the point that about 58

million Americans answered "German" to the 2000 census question
"What is your ancestry or ethnic origin?" making it the largest ancestry
group in the United States. He goes on to say, "These days we hear constant references to the Hispanic or Latino 'community', to Hispanic 'issues', and 'concerns', to Hispanic 'leaders'. Why is there nary a word
about the far more numerous German-American 'community', German
'issues', or the German 'vote'? . . . The answer is obvious. . . . There was
a German ethnic group once, a huge and powerful one. But it has van-
ished in the melting pot" (Thernstrom 2004, 52).[13]

Saskia Sassen (2004), in an Internet response to Goodhart's "Too Diverse?" article reminds us that if we take a longer time frame into account, "we can see that integration happened." Nathan Glazer, allowing
for the possibility of multiple identities, the ones of the old country and
a growing American identity, concludes that "eventually, today's immigrants, like their predecessors a century ago, will most likely become
Americans" (Glazer 2004, 73).

Third, let us briefly examine the seemingly unquestioned assumption
in all primordialist accounts that diversity is detrimental to the well-
being of a society. One of the best-known writers of the mid–nineteenth
century, Ralph Waldo Emerson, very perceptively likened the coming
together of different peoples in America to the "smelting pot of the dark
ages" in Europe, where before the invention of states there was indeed a
remarkable mixing of peoples, which he considered responsible for the
"vigor of the new Europe" (quoted in Bischoff 2002, 73).

> I hate the narrowness of the Native American Party. . . . It is pre-
> cisely opposite to true wisdom. . . . In this continent—asylum of all
> the nations—the energy of the Irish, Swedes, Poles, and Cossack,
> all the European tribes—of the Africans, and the Polynesians, will
> construct a new race, a new religion, a new state, a new literature,
> which will be vigorous as the new Europe which came out of the
> smelting pot of the dark ages.

Thomas Nichols, a physician from New England, examined the issue
of diversity from a genetic angle. He argued that as a result of diversity
"man, like other animals, is improved and brought to its highest perfec-
tion by an intermingling of the blood and qualities of other races. . . .
The great physiological reason why Americans are superior to other nations is freedom, intelligence, and enterprise, is because that they are the

offspring of the greatest intermingling of races . . ." (quoted in Bischoff 2002, 84).

This undeniable advantage of genetic diversity was not lost on the heir to the throne of the Austro-Hungarian Empire, Archduke Franz Ferdinand, whose assassination sparked World War I. It is well known that the Hapsburg rulers used "strategic" marriages to members of the same house to expand or cement their empire. The archduke complained about the shallowness of the Hapsburg gene pool: "Bei uns sind Mann und Frau immer zwanzigmal meiteinander verwandt. Das Resultat ist das von den Kindern die Hälfte Trottel oder Epileptiker sind" (Among us [the Hapsburgs] husbands and wives are always related with each other twenty times over. The result is that half of the children are either idiots or epileptics) (Lackner 2004, 36). Speaking about the advantages of the "admixture" of races, John Stuart Mill (1968, 314) also believed that diversity is a positive rather than negative attribute of society.

> Whatever really tends to the admixture of nationalities, and the blending of their attributes and peculiarities in a common union, is a benefit to the human race. Not by extinguishing types, of which, in these cases, sufficient examples are sure to remain, but by softening their extreme forms, and filling up the intervals between them. The united people, like a crossed breed of animals (but in still greater degree, because the influences in operation are moral as well as physical), inherits the special aptitudes and excellencies of all its progenitors, protected by the admixture from being exaggerated into the neighboring vices.

One of the most eloquent and consequential arguments praising the virtues of diversity occurred during the debate over the founding of the American Republic. James Madison urged the creation of a federal state since he did not trust "pure democracies," which consisted of "a small number of citizens, who assemble and administer the government in person." He argued that by making the body politic larger and more diverse the chances that any given "faction" would dominate the political agenda would be reduced. For Madison, diversity meant an "extended republic." With a large territory and a significant population, social diversity in the new nation would be ensured and the chance that the government would become oppressive would be reduced, particularly when combined with a system of political "checks and balances."

From that perspective diversity is desirable because it ensures political fragmentation, which in turn prevents the accumulation of excessive political power (Madison, Federalist #10).

In 1924, the United States passed the National Origins Act, which established rather generous immigration quotas for Western and Northern Europeans but dramatically reduced the quotas for Southern and Eastern Europeans, who were seen as "less desirable." For many Asian nations, there were no quotas at all, which meant total exclusion. These quota laws were in effect until 1965, although they were severely criticized by Presidents Harry Truman and John F. Kennedy. Referring to the quota laws, Truman said, "The idea behind this discriminatory policy was, to put it boldly, that Americans with English or Irish names were better people and better citizens than Americans with Italian or Greek or Polish names . . . [and] such a concept is utterly unworthy of our traditions and our ideals" (quoted in Bischoff 2002, 77). When President Lyndon B. Johnson signed the 1965 immigration law abolishing quotas, he said, "Our beautiful America was built by a nation of strangers. From a hundred different places or more, they have poured forth . . . joining and blending in one mighty and irresistible tide. The land flourished because it was fed from so many sources—because it was nourished by so many cultures and traditions and peoples" (quoted in Bischoff 2002, 127).

Finally, a fascinating stream of literature has reemerged recently with roots in ancient Greece. It takes dead aim at the question of what the radius of our moral commitment should be. This revived school of thought is called "cosmopolitanism." As the name implies, it suggests that as a result of technological development, increases in trade, immigration, international terrorism and crime, foreign direct investments, global environmental challenges, diseases that cross borders, and similar phenomena loosely associated with what we call "globalization" a more extended form of the "moral community" is necessary. Much of this literature is connected to the work of Peter Singer (2004), Martha Nussbaum (1996), Steven Vertovec and Robin Cohen (2002), Tan (2004), and others.

While some of the literature is animated by a functionalist logic, that is, the need for global institutions to deal with global challenges such as the environment, its more intriguing aspects are found among those who examine the degree of moral obligation necessary for solving global problems. Martha Nussbaum, for example, highlights the limits of patriotism by arguing that defining oneself in national terms first is "morally questionable" since national identity is a "morally irrelevant characteristic." According to her, it is more important to recognize that interactions should center on the "human problems of people in particular concrete situations" as opposed problems arising as a result of varying identities (Nussbaum 1996, 5).

But it is not just the "nation-state" that is in an uneasy relationship with cosmopolitanism. Even more tightly drawn circles of identity are increasingly in conflict with cosmopolitan ideals. Stuart Hall (2003, 26), drawing on the work of Jeremy Waldron (1992), argues:

> It is not that we are without culture but we are drawing on the traces and residues of many cultural systems, of many ethical systems—and that is precisely what cosmopolitanism means. It means the ability to stand outside of having one's life written and scripted by any one community, whether that is a faith, or tradition, or religion or a culture—whatever it might be and to draw selectively on a variety of discursive meanings.

Thus, cosmopolitanism requires an ability to step beyond one's own identity, to recognize that the world is made up of different groups, none of which can claim superiority over any other. This requires a "moral universalism" that emphasizes the similarities rather than the differences in humanity. The question is: on what "universal values" could such a global ethics be built? Sissela Bok argues that there are indeed a certain set of basic values that can be found across all ethnic, racial, national, and other boundaries. These values include "some form of positive duties regarding mutual support, loyalty, and reciprocity." A second category includes the negative duty to refrain from harmful actions such as "'force and fraud', violence, and deceit," and a third group includes "norms of at least rudimentary and procedural justice ... such as the bearing of false witness" (Bok 2002, 13–16). On the basis of these common values, Bok argues that "Cultural diversity can and should be honored, but only within the context of respect for common values" (24).

Cosmopolitanism stands in stark contrast to the primordial view and appears overly idealistic. It may be that this "imagined humanity" is built on too thin a foundation, that is, there is not enough shared history, shared experiences, on which to construct an identity that commands allegiances comparable to the force of family, tribe, or regional affiliation. Yet chapter 4 finds strong empirical evidence in the attitudes of some respondents that hints of the existence of such mind-sets. There is a stable fraction of about 27 percent of respondents who in the fourth wave of the World Values Survey in 2000 indicated either very much or much "concern for the living conditions of humankind." More detailed empirical analysis will show that they indeed demonstrate much social trust, favor redistribution, and are willing to continue funding the welfare state despite increased immigration.

The purpose of this short exposé was to highlight four things. First, contrary to the claims of primordialists, there is much more integration going on than the primordial theory predicts. Second, the short accounts presented here show that diversity need not be detrimental to the well-being of a society. Third, primordial categories do not solely dominate political outcomes. Rather they are mediated by institutions that can either reinforce these categories or weaken them. This is particularly crucial in European countries, where the welfare state was solidly established *before* massive immigration occurred. Depending on how social protection is organized, it can have either inclusive effects, in which case nativist resentment toward foreigners will be blunted, or exclusive effects, in which case natives' willingness to continue to fund the welfare state may be undermined or there may be strong public pressures to shut the door on further immigration. Finally, primordial views are increasingly challenged by cosmopolitanism, which is diametrically opposed to narrow conceptions of identity. This revived approach is a direct outgrowth of the realization that increasingly we live in one world, with global interactions producing global problems that can only be solved on a global scale.

The welfare state has weathered many crises, and its death has been proclaimed many times prematurely. Some believe that the primordial impulses are more of a challenge to the welfare state if the state favors multiculturalist policies, that is, policies that recognize and heighten group differences. Some nations, such as the Netherlands and Sweden until the late 1990s, have pursued such policies and today appear to have abandoned them in favor of more integrationist policies designed to establish a common culture. A strategy of assimilation and integration of minorities will allow the state "to focus on social disadvantage as the main fulcrum around which politics should be organized" (Wolfe and Klausen 1997, 254). On the other hand, strong emphasis on group differences weakens the state's capacity to redistribute incomes precisely because nativist resentments can more easily be triggered by multiculturalism. This line of argument is more thoroughly explored in chapter 6.

It is also a challenge because the media, which bear a large responsibility for the attitudes of people, have simply become less responsible. As Gilens's work shows, skewed depictions by the media of blacks as lazy and undeserving have shaped whites' perceptions of welfare to such an extent that "welfare bashing" can always be counted on as a popular strategy in American politics.[14]

It is a quixotic undertaking to write off the power of primordial sentiments. Understanding, however, that there is nothing "given," "genetic," or "natural" about such sentiments and that such sentiments are the products of teaching, daily reproduction, and repetition is revealing because it opens the space of discourse about the human condition from the inevitable to the possible and allows for the realization that human agency is capable of both noble and ignoble deeds. Is primordialism a challenge to the welfare state? The answer, given within the context of this literature review, has to remain a contingent one: yes, but only if we, as citizens, allow it to be. The next chapter uses public opinion data to gauge the effects of anti-immigrant attitudes on public perceptions of the welfare state.

CHAPTER 3

The Politics of Resentment
Xenophobia and the Welfare State

Prejudices, it is well known, are most difficult to eradicate
from the heart whose soil has never been loosened
or fertilized by education; they grow there,
firm as weeds among rocks.
—Charlotte Brontë

WITH THE ESTABLISHMENT OF THE MODERN welfare state, the status of "citizen" came to define those who are eligible for social protection and those who are not. As a result, this sharp distinction, which significantly affects the life chances of many of its inhabitants, represents the hard border that distinguishes those who belong to the community from "others." In other words, citizenship means a sharp delineation of who is part of that community and outsiders. Ever since the invention of modern states, governments have sought to control exit and entry (immigration policy proper) and thus the distribution of life chances to those within it. Citizenship is granted in almost all countries either on the basis of *Blutrecht* ("blood right" by parental nationality) or jus sanguinis (as in Austria, Belgium, Denmark, Finland, Germany until 2000, Ireland, and Portugal) or on the basis of jus soli, which means by birthplace and is practiced in Belgium, France, Greece, Italy, Luxembourg, the Netherlands, Spain, the United Kingdom, and the United States (Lahav 2004).

But citizenship is not just a legal concept; it is also a cultural concept. The previous chapter detailed the various concepts of how John Stuart Mill's "fellow feeling" or T. H. Marshall's "direct sense of community membership" flow into the construction of a group united by a sense of

52

shared identity. And newcomers, at least in the first two waves of immigration in the United States and from the 1960s to the 1980s in Europe, were expected to assimilate (immigrant policy proper) and become indistinguishable from the natives save for physical differences.

In reality, the congruence between *ethnos* and *demos* is not that neat. In many Western countries, particularly in Germany, foreigners, mostly Turkish *Gastarbeiter,* have lived among Germans for generations without being able to become German citizens but still being eligible for the protections of the German welfare state. This is possible because of the remarkably liberal German *Grundgesetz* (Basic Law), which extends social protections even to noncitizens as long as they have entered Germany legally while at the same time "denying them the reality of immigration" (Joppke 1999, 9). Thus, this sharp distinction between citizen and noncitizen does not exist in many European countries. Instead, "there is continuum of rights attached to membership of a state rather than the sharp distinction between citizen and non-citizen" (Leyton-Henry 1990, 188). Best known is Tomas Hammar's term *denizen,* which denotes immigrants who are enjoying all, or most, of the social rights of citizens without actually being citizens (Hammar 1990). Virginie Guiraudon (1998) notes that in Western Europe the famous Marshallian order of the granting of rights from civil to political and finally to social rights has been reversed as far as the last two rights are concerned. Many immigrants enjoy social rights (i.e., welfare benefits) before they become citizens. It is also true that many foreign nationals are allowed to vote in local or regional elections in most European countries (Waldrauch 2003). Guiraudon's explanation for this reversal is somewhat conspiratorial: such rights are granted so as to stave off major political action on the part of immigrants before right-wing parties and the media begin to influence public opinion to such an extent that the government's maneuvering room is seriously constrained (Guiraudon 1998).[1]

Welfare bashing and stigmatizing minorities as receivers of "undeserving welfare benefits" have been a political strategy in the United States ever since the progressive populist movement in the nineteenth century was split by the race-based tactics of the Republicans. Similarly, in Europe the radical Right has mobilized its support by claiming that immigrants are abusing the welfare state, that they are taking out more than they are putting in, and that they are living a cushy life at the expense of the hardworking natives. It is precisely because immigrants are eligible to receive welfare benefits that the conflicts with native majorities are heightened.

According to Guiraudon, "[T]here are now about 13 million third country nationals legally residing in the European Union who enjoy the same
social rights as nationals in their country of legal residence" (2002, 129).

Even if they did not receive any welfare benefits it is likely that there
would be some hostility toward immigrants, but it might be more
muted. However, resentment toward and hatred of newcomers are intensified when cultural barriers combine with a diffuse sense that natives
not only have to live with the other but also have to pay for him or her,
that is, when the perception of poverty is reinforced with otherness. This
is a potent brew, and it gets particular traction in economic tough times
and among people who are already rather marginalized, uneducated, and
on the verge of losing their jobs. Christopher T. Husbands (1998)
showed that "political racism" increases when the number of immigrants
appears to pass a certain threshold.

Under such adverse conditions, it is easy for populists and demagogues
to exploit latent anti-immigrant emotions to gain support for their causes
by blaming the newcomers (Gibson 2002; Betz 1994; Betz and Immerfall
1998; Schain, Zolberg, and Hossay 2002). In the American context, the
know-nothings achieved remarkable success with their anti-Irish and
anti-Catholic rhetoric in the nineteenth century. More recently, the exploitation of hostility toward immigrants by racist political entrepreneurs
has become a mainstay of radical right-wing parties such as the Lega Nord
in Italy, the Front National (FN) in France, and the Freiheitliche Partei
Österreichs (FPÖ, the Liberal Party of Austria), which has been the junior
member of a ruling coalition with the Austrian Conservative Party from
2000 to 2005, when the party broke apart with the FPÖ going into opposition and the BZÖ (Bündnis Zukunft Österreich) remaining part of
the coalition. In the Netherlands, Pim Fortuyn's party gained strong support based on his anti-Islamic stance before he was assassinated and Filip
Dewinter of the Belgian Vlaams Blok urged his supporters to "stop the
Islamic invasion." The Vlaams Blok, which campaigned on the basis of
forcible repatriation of immigrants, was banned by Belgium's appeal's
court on November 9, 2004, on the basis of violating antiracism laws. It
had become the most popular party in Flanders, with over 26 percent
support in opinion polls (Economist 2004, 56). It is not inconceivable that
this drastic ban on the Vlaams Blok in Belgium was a response to the
murder of Theo van Gogh in the Netherlands and is seen as a measure intended to prevent the escalation of violence between the immigrants and
local communities.

The United States has its share of politicians and writers who bemoan the fact that most immigrants are not of European stock anymore and claim that uncontrolled immigration is undermining the American identity, which will result in "Americans no more" (Geyer 1996), an "Alien Nation" (Brimelow 1995), the "Disuniting of America" (Schlesinger 1998), and ultimately to the "Death of the West" (Buchanan 2002).

The leaders of the European radical right-wing parties are rather outspoken about the way they see the impact of immigration on the welfare state. Jean Marie LePen stated in 1992 that "there are simply too many immigrants, and they make who knows how many children whom they send into the streets and then claim welfare" (quoted in Alesina and Glaeser 2004, 176). Jörg Haider's FPÖ embarked on a rather promarket, Darwinian, neoliberal economic course, which is not compatible with the idea of the public provision of social protection. Referring to the rather generous Austrian welfare state, he claimed that his party could "no longer support a system in which some citizens had to pay more and more taxes with their hard earned money to allow others to have a good time in the hammock of the welfare state" (Haider, quoted in Betz 1994, 113, 114). A master of shrewd rhetoric, Haider knows how to incite nativist resentment by cloaking xenophobic messages behind relatively moderate language. Thus, he exclaimed in one of his speeches, "We have not led wars in past centuries against the Turks so that they now fill our school classes."[2] Similarly, the Swiss Automobile Party, classified by Hans Georg Betz (1994) as a radical, right-wing, populist party, also called for a cutback of the welfare state, arguing that the social safety net "must not become a hammock for those who don't want to make an effort" and work (quoted in Betz 1994, 115).

Empirical work conducted by Jorgen Goul Anderson and Tor Bjorklund (2002) examining attitudes on welfare provision and cuts in social spending by voters of the Progress Party in Norway and Denmark indicated support for cutting back the welfare state. Alesina and Glaeser (2004, 181) conclude their chapter on race and redistribution with an ominous comment: "As Europe has become more diverse, Europeans have increasingly been susceptible to exactly the same form of racist, antiwelfare demagoguery that worked so well in the United States. We shall see whether the generous European welfare state can really survive in a heterogeneous society." Herbert Kitschelt (1995, 258–59) also worries about whether a multicultural welfare state is "predicated on ethnic homogeneity or at least plural ethnic stability of a country . . . and will the multiculturalization of still by and large homogeneous or ethnically stable Western Europe lead to a decline of the welfare state?" There is no shortage of such comments in both the popular press and academic outlets.

This literature review makes it clear that if there is any crumbling in the foundation of the welfare state the cracks should be visible in those strata of the native society that are the most threatened by immigration: lower-class, blue-collar workers who perceive direct competition, correctly or incorrectly, from immigrants and who openly express their sentiments in public opinion surveys. They see themselves in competition with immigrants over public resources that allow immigrants to catch up with them quickly, leading to feelings of relative deprivation among the natives and fueling even more resentment against the newcomers. That is why this chapter examines nativist sentiments and the degree to which such groups do or do not support the welfare state.

What exactly is the connection between those who harbor such resentments and their attitudes about the welfare state? Rarely is this connection convincingly theorized. The next section will explore the causal links between diversity and the welfare state and will offer empirical tests based on analyses of public opinion surveys.

THEORIZING DIVERSITY AND THE WELFARE STATE

One of the most perceptive analyses of the connection between diversity and the welfare state has been provided by Alan Wolfe and Jytte Klausen (1997). They see the welfare state as being challenged not only from "above," as a result of globalization, but also from "below," meaning that the more identity groups request official recognition the more frail the community becomes, undermining the very capacity of the state to produce redistributive policies. They identify

> a difficult dilemma for identity groups: they can choose to strengthen the group and in the process, to weaken the state (whose purpose, presumably, is to provide enhanced benefits back to the group) or they can choose to strengthen the state, thereby expanding benefits to members of the group, but only by weakening the formal political claims of the group as a group. (Wolfe and Klausen 1997, 247)

While their overall message is in defense of the welfare state, they also share a concern that official recognition of identity groups leads to so frail a community that the extractive and redistributive capacity of the state becomes questionable. They do believe that the modern welfare state is robust and can absorb "mild forms of identity politics . . . as long as there are well-understood principles of assimilation and accommodation." However, "if claims for recognition on behalf of those groups weaken government, such groups may be accorded symbolic equality without government provisions to back them up—a Pyrrhic victory indeed" (Wolfe and Klausen 1997, 242). For Wolfe and Klausen, redistribution is prior to recognition; in fact, recognition of identity groups is ineffective without active government support.

However, another outcome may also be plausible. Jan Colijn, a bookkeeper from the northern Dutch town of Groningen, observing the burned out churches and mosques, remarked that "the generous Dutch social welfare system had allowed Muslim immigrants to isolate themselves. Because of that trend, there is a kind of Muslim fascism emerging here" (Smith 2004). He makes a very perceptive point, which is that precisely because immigrants are included in social protection they have less of an incentive to integrate into Dutch society. The more the state decommodifies their lives the less reason they have to actively pursue relations with the Dutch in terms of finding jobs or becoming part of a team on a job site that consists of Dutch and perhaps other multinational individuals. Mohammed Bouyeri was receiving unemployment benefits when he assassinated van Gogh. Could the state in fact be subsidizing isolation and prevent a mingling that, over time, might separate newcomers from natives even more?

Is it conceivable that strengthening the state may not lead to a weakening of immigrant groups' identity but to a form of isolation precisely because the welfare state takes care of their physical needs but by doing so precludes the need for integration? As an unintended consequence, welfare state support may isolate minorities and thereby undermine the establishment of a sense of "fellow feeling" because mixing with native majorities at the workplace, for example, becomes less necessary. Decommodification may lead to isolation precisely because the welfare state ensures basic survival without having to resort to a more personal form of assistance. Isolation is heightened if the receivers of social assistance are also racially, religiously, or ethnically diverse. Juergen Habermas (1987) has argued that an active welfare state undermines even settled, homogeneous communities. Is it conceivable that the welfare state heightens isolation because it obviates the need to seek more personal, community-based forms of help based on family and friendship? It is certainly true that these forms of social support are precisely what immigrants are lacking, but it is also true that relying on public support lessens the need for immigrants to establish relations with natives, creating ghettoes, which, once established, make integration even more difficult and add to nativist resentment. Government checks may help them to survive, but they also foster isolation not integration. On the other hand, much of the liberal multiculturalism literature makes precisely the point that integration is not what some identity groups seek (Kymlicka 2001). They seek recognition. But does recognition not mean separation? We will investigate that issue more closely in chapter 6.

The observation that many immigrants live in "parallel societies," disconnected from the natives, was not lost on the Dutch minister for immigration and integration, Rita Verdonk. In a speech delivered on June 30, 2004, she declared that "almost all EU member states are currently dealing with similar difficulties with regards to integration [of immigrants]: segregation of the housing market, educational and economic disadvantage among minority groups; social and religious tension, and a resultant breakdown in the social fabric" (Verdonk, June 30, 2004).[3]

A parliamentary report released in early 2004 concluded that "the country's 30-year experiment in tolerant multiculturalism had been a failure, and has resulted in poor schools, violence, and ethnic ghettoes that shun intermarriage with the Dutch" (*London Daily Telegraph,* February 19, 2004). Ghettoization is particularly unsettling in large cities where the number of immigrants has crossed certain thresholds. For example, the Dutch city of Rotterdam is now inhabited by more than 50 percent non-Dutch residents. Most of them are eligible for welfare support, which might "disintegrate" them from Dutch society in addition to attracting the wrath of the native majorities.

The intriguing question is: why should this wrath manifest itself in the desire of natives to cut back on their welfare programs? The very identity and electoral survival of a number of European parties are directly connected to the constituencies that support the welfare state (Swank 2002). Rather, the first reaction against immigrants by native majorities should be to restrict immigration rather than cutting back on welfare benefits, from which natives themselves profit. The most intriguing work and explicitly theoretical framework establishing why native majorities should "retreat" from the welfare state are provided by Keith Banting. It is worth quoting him at length as to why native majorities, which he sees as more important in terms of their effect on the welfare state than the immigrants themselves, should become less willing to fund the welfare state.

> Minority challenges to mainstream culture, in the form of demands for affirmative action . . . may generate a backlash amongst traditional supporters of the welfare state, dividing pro-welfare coalitions. Alternatively, majorities may simply withdraw support from programmes that channel resources to communities they do not recognize as their own, by denying benefits to newcomers, reducing programmes that disproportionately serve minorities, or restricting social programmes in general. This danger is presumably heightened when income inequality and cultural difference are highly correlated, when the poor are mostly minorities and the minorities are mostly poor. In these circumstances, dominant groups may abandon the idea of a set of wider obligations and quietly disengage, psychologically and perhaps even physically, from the wider society, shifting their allegiance to more conservative political philosophies and parties. (Banting 2002, 15, 16)

Banting's hypotheses on the effects of diversity on the welfare state are some of the most detailed in this literature. His hypotheses regarding the claim that native majorities should call for a reduction in, or perhaps even the elimination of, immigrant-specific entitlements are rather intuitive; however, his claim that "dominant groups may abandon the idea of a set of wider obligations and may quietly disengage" is problematic for three reasons.

First, immigration-driven diversity is impinging on mature welfare states in Europe, unlike the situation in the United States, where the development of the welfare state was at least partly hampered by race. For this reason different reactions by majorities to increased immigration are to be expected. Welfare state policies in Europe are firmly entrenched within particular national political institutions, as well as within the political culture of a nation. Wolfe and Klausen (1997, 236) suggest precisely such a path-dependent argument: "Once the modern welfare state was created, there was no going back." In the traditional social democratic welfare states of Scandinavia and even in Catholic/corporatist welfare states such as Germany and Austria, it is highly unlikely that widespread detachments from social provisions will occur. In these states, the welfare state enjoys widespread support from the civil society partly because it is universal in character, thus making it very difficult to exclude some groups and not others.

Second, in countries with centralized political institutions it is difficult for anti-immigrant populist sentiments to bubble to the top and begin to affect public policy outcomes. Rather than cutting back on welfare services, which would conflict with widely held views on equality, such societies would be expected to tighten control over immigration and to even repatriate aliens and asylum seekers. These trends are clearly visible in the Netherlands and Italy. In February of 2004, the Dutch government pushed through legislation that provided for the expulsion of more than 26,000 asylum seekers, including Afghans, Somalis, and Chechens who face civil wars upon arrival in their countries of origin. Under the new law, the first of its kind in Europe, children reared in the Netherlands and settled refugees with stable jobs will be uprooted and deported as the government attempts to clear a years-old asylum backlog in one "clean sweep." If they are not expelled, said a spokesperson, "they will become illegal immigrants without any right to benefits." The Dutch government provides free flights home and a repatriation cash bonus after a two-month stint in a deportation center (*London Daily Telegraph,* February 19, 2004). New asylum applications in the Netherlands have fallen steeply from 43,560 in 2000 to an estimated 10,000 in 2004. Still, there are concerns that as a result of continued immigration, mostly through family reunification, Dutch society is losing its identity.

Similarly, the Italian government forcefully returned over 2,000 African migrants who had gathered on the small island of Lampedusa and were planning to continue their journey north. They were returned in military aircraft to Libya, which has become a major staging ground for human traffickers smuggling Africans into Europe (Silvia Poggioli, National Public Radio, October 13, 2004).

Third, those most directly affected by immigration are generally members of the working class and people with little education. As a result, globalization, as well as "deindustrialization," that is, the shift from an industry-based, Fordist production structure to a more decentralized, service-oriented, postindustrial structure, has exposed blue-collar workers more than any other stratum, not only in terms of jobs but also in terms of values and lifestyles. This stratum of society has often been referred to as *Modernisierungsverlierer* (the losers in the process of modernization, who react to these structural changes by blaming the newcomers for unemployment, rising crime, housing shortages, or other things) (Swank and Betz 2003; Husbands 2002; Givens 2002). While members of this group tend to support radical right-wing parties that agitate for tougher immigration laws or expulsion of illegal aliens and cutbacks of welfare benefits for "them," it is not intuitive why they should want to retreat from a generous system that sends them the unemployment checks, allows them to live in state-subsidized apartments, protects them with sickness benefits, and ensures that they will receive their pensions. In tough economic times, as in Germany in 2004 and 2005 when the government introduced new labor market reforms, known as HARTZ IV (named after Peter Hartz, an executive at the German car company Volkswagen), intended to ultimately cut back the welfare state, the fight over tight public resources between newcomers and natives can only get more bitter. In hard times the first reaction of the dominant society should be to exclude "others" from participating in the welfare state rather than widespread detachment of the dominant group from the welfare state. This could clearly be seen in the unsettling successes of two radical right-wing parties, the National Democratic Party of Germany (NPD) and the German People's Union (DVU) in the eastern German states of Saxony and Brandenburg in the fall of 2004. The secret of the success of these two parties was that they agitated against cutbacks in the German welfare state contained in the proposals of HARTZ IV. Much of the initial support for these parties came from those living under the most precarious economic conditions, those who were most hostile to foreigners, and those who believed that only they had a rightful claim to social benefits. Radical right-wing parties came to the defense of the welfare state, drawing support from formerly social democratic voters. Diversity in this case did not manifest itself in a "retreat" from the welfare state by the dominant society but rather in the demand that foreigners be prohibited from using the benefits of the welfare state. The paradox of all of this is that there are relatively few foreigners in the eastern states of Germany in the first place.

On the other hand, widespread detachment from the welfare state is not inconceivable in residual welfare states with strong laissez-faire political cultures, where social benefits are targeted rather than means tested and political institutions are decentralized (e.g., when they allow for referenda). Attempts to roll back the welfare state should be strongest

in institutional environments where politics is closest to the people and
less of a concern where politics is more removed from the people.

In particular, when constitutions allow for referenda the monopoly
over policy-making by governmental elites is greatly undermined. Referenda have a way of bringing to the forefront issues that elites would
rather not confront. Immigration is precisely such an issue, one for
which there seems to be a remarkable disconnect between public and
elite opinion. "The most striking feature of immigration politics in democratic states," writes Gary Freeman (1998, 88), "is the persistent gap between the policies of governments and the preferences of mass publics."
However, when devices of direct democracy are used, such as referenda,
particularly if they are uncontrolled and antihegemonic,[4] dealing with
immigration issues, as in the United States (in the form of propositions
at the state level) or Switzerland, the public will can seldom be denied.
Clever timing of extending rights to immigrants and the venues that are
used to push these through the political process also help explain the disconnect between liberal, elitist, pro-immigrant policies and the reac-
tionary, anti-immigrant feelings of the public (Guiraudon 2002).

Given these categorizations, we should expect to see more attempts to
roll back welfare benefits in the United States, where native populations
are certainly trying to separate themselves from the immigrants by imposing limits on immigrants' cultural autonomy, citizenship status, or entitlements. Cases abound. The most recent case is that of a referendum, Proposition 200, in the state of Arizona, in which immigration was a central
issue during the 2004 presidential campaign. This referendum, which
passed by a wide margin, called for Arizonans to show proof of citizenship
when registering to vote and evidence of legal status when seeking "public services." It is not exactly clear what "public services" meant in the
proposition, but presumably they would include such items as immuniza-
tions, treatment of diseases such as tuberculosis, family-planning services,
HIV treatments, hospitalizations, and so on.[5] Another well-known case
was the passage of Proposition 187 on November 8, 1994, which denied
public services and education to children of illegal aliens in California.
Eventually this proposition was seen to contradict the constitutional principles established in *Plyler v. Doe,* which itself was a reaction to attempts
by the state of Texas to deny public education to children of illegal aliens.

Political institutions that decentralize power through means such as
federalism and referenda tend to narrow the gap between people's beliefs
and actual policy-making. It is well known that Switzerland makes wide-

spread use of referenda. On September 26, 2004, voters in Switzerland rejected a proposal to automatically extend citizenship to third-generation foreign nationals and children born in Switzerland. The current rules require immigrants to wait at least 12 years before they are eligible to apply for naturalization, which includes complex procedures such as Swiss inspectors who visit the applicants' homes in order to check whether their cleanliness is up to Swiss standards. Proponents of the ballot proposal charged that failure to pass it "would undermine what it means to be Swiss" (*International Herald Tribune,* September 27, 2004). "We don't want Switzerland to be a doorway for all and sundry," said Maria Angela Guyot, an official of the Swiss People's Party (*International Herald Tribune,* September 27, 2004). Nikad Hrustic, a Bosnian who has lived in Switzerland since 1992, said he was deeply disappointed: "This makes us feel we are not wanted here" (*Boston Herald,* September 28, 2004). The next section examines the effects of nativist resentment on people's attitudes toward redistribution and the welfare state in general.

MAPPING NATIVIST RESENTMENT

Before delving into quantitative analyses that are almost exclusively based on public opinion surveys, a word of caution about the use of such surveys is necessary. "Public opinion" according to James Fishkin (1995), is the "voice of the people." And yet, as in real life, one has to be careful what people say. There are problems with the wording of questions (Kangas 1997) and the temperamental nature of public opinion, as well as the reliability of the answers. The danger in public opinion research is systematic measurement error as a result of interviewer effects,[6] question order effects,[7] halo effects,[8] and "social desirability bias," which occurs when respondents give answers corresponding to what they believe the most widely held norms are rather than expressing what they truly feel about issues. These effects and biases can call the reliability of this kind of research into question. In the words of V. O. Key, "To speak with precision of public opinion is not unlike coming to grips with the Holy Ghost" (quoted in Papadakis 1992, 21).

Much of the literature that uses public opinion polls takes public opinion as the "popular will"; in other words, public opinion is prior to public policy, which is supposed to reflect, ultimately, public opinion. However, "Public opinion is not a genuine 'will of the citizens', it only tells how people have responded to the questions asked" (Forma 1999).

One of the most contested issues is the degree to which public opinion actually impacts public policy. Some observers have found that public opinion does impact public policy (Whiteley 1981; Monroe 1979;
Erikson 1976), while others, such as Harold Wilensky (1981) and Murray Edelman (1977), disagree. They believe that public opinion can be
selectively created by politicians so that in fact it is public policy that
drives public opinion rather than the other way around.

For the answers in a public opinion poll to be valid, it is assumed that
the respondents must have a certain level of information about the questions they have answered. This assumption is not always fulfilled, particularly when complex issues, such as the welfare state, are involved. Some
critics of public opinion go so far as to claim that citizens are not capable
of forming opinions about issues on the political agenda, that their answers to pollsters are simply "meaningless doorstep opinions" (Converse
1964) or even that "Public opinion does not exist" (Bourdieu 1979).
Using well-established, tested, and multiple data sets can alleviate some,
though not all, of the problems critics have raised. In such surveys, it is
highly likely that there is more signal than noise in the data. Gallya Lahav
(2004, 16) reminds us that "Analysis of attitudes is critical to understanding today's Europe of changing boundaries. This is especially important
in the case of immigration. . . ."

Thus, while the tone of the voices heard throughout this book should
be enjoyed with caution, they deserve to be taken seriously as they may
function like the canaries in the coal mines, indicating tendencies, shifts,
and directions in the public mood long before they manifest themselves
in aggregate data. Particularly with regard to immigration issues, public
opinion tends to be rather xenophobic. Elites tend to neglect, sometimes
justifiably, the oftentimes blatant racist messages contained in some opinion polls. Elites' more liberal stance on immigration and multiculturalism
is an important counterweight to the public's often unfounded fear of
foreigners, which is driven by ignorance, prejudice, and stereotypes.[9]
However, there are cases in which turning a blind eye, perhaps driven by
"political correctness," may be counterproductive.

A case in point is the Netherlands, whose admirable tradition of tolerance has morphed into a sclerotic and rigid form of political correctness
in which elites have either avoided or belittled the need for a frank dia-
logue about the challenges of immigration and multiculturalism. The political discourse has become so elitist and detached from the sentiments
of the people that the two groups find it difficult to communicate with
each other (Westerloo 2004). Pim Fortuyn's political fortunes rose mete-

orically in 2001–2 based on his anti-Muslim rhetoric and claims that the "boat is full." However, his anti-immigrant party fell apart very quickly after he was murdered by an animal rights activist in 2002. The murder of Theo van Gogh on November 2, 2004, drastically changed the public discourse in the Netherlands. Francis Fukuyama has argued that "Europeans are threatened internally by radical Islam in a much more severe way than Americans are in terms of their external threat." According to Fukuyama, Europeans have hitherto been deterred from debating the threat by a "stifling political correctness" (*Economist,* November 27, 2004, 56). The consequences of this murder and the ensuing arson attacks on mosques and churches have led to a freer and unadulterated public discourse about the limits of immigration and immigrant policy not only in the Netherlands but in many other societies with significant Muslim populations, including France, Germany, Britain, and Belgium. It appears that elites are beginning to take public opinion in matters of immigration policy more seriously. Ultimately, in a democracy "vox populi" cannot be denied. "Top down governance has its limits. Where officials ultimately must win a verdict in the people's court, public opinion both constrains public policy and has the potential to reshape it" (Citrin and Sides 2004).

With these caveats in mind, the following pages examine the connection between attitudes about immigrants and support for the welfare state. According to Banting (2000), the true challenge to the welfare state originates not with the immigrants themselves but with the reactions of native majorities to them.

It is useful to introduce two related yet different concepts: "nativist resentment" and "welfare chauvinism." The former can be defined as rejection of foreigners based on their differences in appearance, race, religion, and lifestyle. This concept captures the "cultural" dimension, including diffuse fears of the other (e.g., many natives believe that many immigrants are criminals and rapists and threaten the identity of locals). Welfare chauvinism can be defined as "the fear among groups in the native population (and settled immigrants) that certain new immigrant groups take away jobs, housing, and social services" (Faist 1994, 440). In other words, this definition captures the "economic" dimension, including fears that immigrants create native unemployment, abuse the welfare state, cheat on their taxes, and do not pull their own weight.

There are many public opinion polls tapping nativist resentment and welfare chauvinism in various countries, but few track such sentiments over time. Public opinion surveys are notoriously sensitive to particular events, so examining attitudes over time gives a better representation of attitudes than one poll taken immediately after an arson attack or hate-inspired murder. One of them is the World Values Survey, for which there are now four waves available (1981–82, 1990–91, 1995–97, and 2000–2001). In the United Kingdom, Germany, the United States, Norway, Sweden, and Finland the WVS asked the following question in each wave: "On this list are various groups of people. Could you please sort out any that you would not like to have as neighbors?" One of the groups respondents could indicate was "immigrants/foreign workers." Other groups included "people with a criminal record," "political extremists," "heavy drinkers," "emotionally unstable people," "drug addicts," and "homosexuals." In the fourth wave, the types of groups were expanded. Interviewers recorded respondents' answers in terms of whether they did or did not mention a particular group.[10]

Figure 3.1 shows the percentage of people who did not want immigrants as neighbors in the six countries for which uninterrupted time series are available. A few countries stand out. Swedes have the fewest problems with immigrants as neighbors. Germany started out as the country with the highest resentment in the early 1980s, but that figure dropped around the time of unification and dropped even more during the mid-1990s in the wake of many arson attacks on immigrants, which mobilized the main parties to engage in extensive governmental efforts to curb racism and xenophobia. These programs appear to have been of limited success, as in the 2000–2001 survey xenophobia climbed again. At the beginning of the new millennium the United Kingdom registered the greatest resentment of foreigners, followed by Finland, Germany, the United States, Norway, and Sweden. This corresponds to a Eurobarometer finding in early 2004 in which 41 percent of Britons see immigration as one of the two biggest problems faced by the nation, leading to the wry remark by the *Economist* that Britain "has risen to the top of the European xenophobes' league" (*Economist,* December 11, 2004, 51).

Other surveys also paint a relatively bleak picture in terms of how native majorities perceive immigrants. Another survey that captures citizen's attitudes on nativist resentment and welfare chauvinism over time is administered by the International Social Survey Program (ISSP). The ISSP has recently (spring 2006) released its second National Identity module with fieldwork done in 2003 complementing its earlier module with fieldwork conducted in 1995. This allows the establishment of a trend, albeit a very short one, as to how respondents' attitudes have changed between 1995 and 2003. The ISSP continues to poll "West" and "East" Germany separately, which is very useful as these two areas are

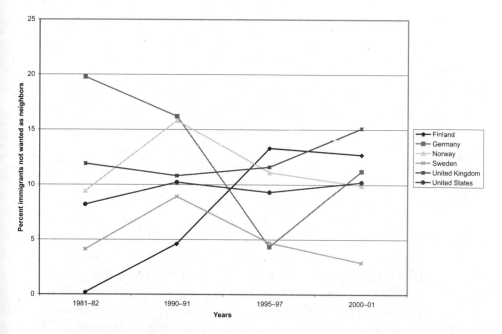

Fig. 3.1. Nativist resentment in six countries over four time points. (Data from World Values Surveys.)

still characterized by significant differences in economic development and political culture. Table 3.1 highlights the changes as to whether respondents believe that immigrants increase crime, and whether immigration should be reduced.

Inspection of the item "immigrants increase crime" paints a rather bleak picture: in 8 of the 11 countries for which two observations over time were available, the number of people who believe that immigrants increase crime has risen and has been reduced only in West Germany, Sweden, and the United States. The countries with particularly strong increases in this sentiment are Ireland, East Germany, Great Britain, and Norway.

Overwhelming majorities favor reductions in immigration in both time periods. However, it is intriguing to note the countries that experienced major shifts in public opinion. Australian respondents appear to have become the most welcoming: in 1995, 61 percent of Australians believed that immigration should be reduced, but by 2003 a minority of 39 percent shared this sentiment, indicating a 22 percentage drop. Other significant reductions occurred in Canada, West Germany, New Zealand, Sweden, and the United States. With the exception of West Germany and Sweden, all the countries that experienced significant drops in the belief that immigration should be reduced are traditional immigration countries.

Table 3.2 examines two other items over time. The first taps the most "classic" example of "welfare chauvinism," the attitude that immigrants take jobs away from the natives, and the second explores the respondents' beliefs of whether immigrants are generally good for the economy. Despite a general increase in the salience of immigration issues from 1995 to 2003, in 7 out of 11 countries fewer people in 2003 thought that immigrants take jobs away than in 1995. The most significant decrease in the sentiment occurred in Canada (−37 percent), Austria (−17 percent), and Sweden (−8 percent). The most massive increases in this belief are observable in West Germany and in Ireland. Again, the traditional immigration countries Australia, Canada, New Zealand, and the United States have all experienced a decline in the public's belief that immigrants take jobs away.

Finally, when examining the public's belief as to whether immigrants are good for the economy, a similar picture emerges. In the traditional immigration countries, the change from 1995 to 2003 is characterized by increases in the attitudes that immigrants are good for the economy,

TABLE 3.1. Attitudes about Crime and Whether Immigration Should Be Reduced from 1995 to 2003 (percent responding)

Country	Immigrants Increase Crime			Immigration Should Be Reduced		
	1995	2003	Δ	1995	2003	Δ
Austria	63	69	5	56	61	5
Australia	31	35	4	61	39	−22
Canada	20	27	7	43	32	−11
Germany (West)	68	63	−5	79	70	−9
Germany (East)	54	68	14	76	78	2
Great Britain	26	40	14	68	78	12
Ireland	13	38	25	22	59	37
New Zealand	24	30	6	62	57	−5
Norway	69	79	10	66	71	6
Sweden	59	57	−2	69	58	−11
United States	33	27	−7	64	56	−8

Source: International Social Survey Program (ISSP). National Identity (Module I and II). *Zentralarchiv für Europäische Sozialforschung,* Köln, Germany.
Question items
"Immigrants increase crime": There are different opinions about immigrants from other countries living in [COUNTRY]. How much do you agree or disagree with each of the following statements? Immigrants increase crime rates. (Entries in table reflect the sum of those who either strongly agreed or agreed with the statement).
"Immigration should be reduced": Do you think the number of immigrants to [COUNTRY] nowadays should be . . . (Entries in the table reflect the sum of those who have indicated that immigrants should be reduced "a little" and "a lot").

with only Canada showing no variation: Australia (+6 percent), New Zealand (+9 percent), and the United States (+11 percent). On the other hand, both polls of Germany and particularly Ireland have seen dramatic declines in the beliefs that immigrants are good for the economy. In 2003, in absolute terms, only in Australia (70 percent), Canada (63 percent), and New Zealand (59 percent) is there a majority of respondents who believe that immigrants are good for the economy. In all other countries, not even half of respondents share these sentiments.

One of the most methodologically advanced surveys in terms of the sampling, crafting, and testing of the questionnaires is the new European Social Survey. Pippa Norris (2004, 9) argues that this survey "will come to be regarded as the Rolls-Royce of cross-national surveys" and will "provide a model that other cross-national survey researchers will seek to emulate." Its first edition includes a battery of 58 questions on immigration and immigrants and presents a fount of information. Four items have been selected to demonstrate the distribution of what might be called nativist resentment, although there are undoubtedly many more that could have been chosen.

TABLE 3.2. Attitudes on Whether Immigrants Take Jobs Away and Whether They Are Good for the Economy from 1995 to 2003 (percent responding)

Country	Immigrants Take Away Jobs			Immigrants Good for Country		
	1995	2003	Δ	1995	2003	Δ
Austria	57	40	−17	43	38	−5
Australia	26	25	−1	64	70	6
Canada	64	27	−37	63	63	0
Germany (West)	26	39	13	39	29	−10
Germany (East)	53	58	5	32	22	−10
Great Britain	50	45	−5	17	22	5
Ireland	38	45	7	56	40	−16
New Zealand	40	35	−5	50	59	9
Norway	20	15	5	13	30	17
Sweden	16	8	−8	27	44	17
United States	48	43	−5	34	45	11

Source: International Social Survey Program (ISSP). National Identity (Module I and II). *Zentralarchiv für Europäische Sozialforschung*, Köln, Germany.
Question items
"Immigrants take jobs away" question: There are different opinions about immigrants from other countries living in [COUNTRY]. How much do you agree or disagree with each of the following statements? Immigrants take jobs away from people who were born in [COUNTRY].
"Immigrants are generally good for the economy" question: There are different opinions about immigrants from other countries living in [COUNTRY]. How much do you agree or disagree with each of the following statements? Immigrants are generally good for [COUNTRY's] economy (All entries in table 3.2. reflect the sum of those who indicated "strongly agree" and "agree").

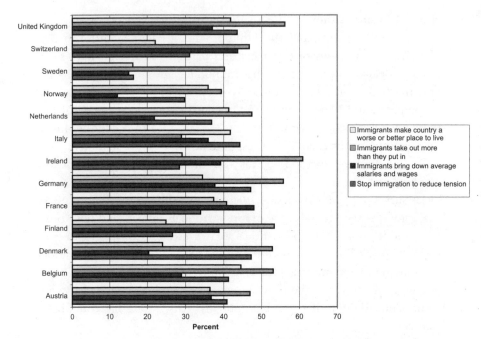

Fig. 3.2. Nativist resentment and welfare chauvinism in European societies. (Data from European Social Survey 2002.) (Note: The precise wording of the questions was (1) Immigrants make country a worse or better place to live. [0 = worse place to live, 10 = better place to live; the numbers reflect the cumulative percentages from answer categories 0–4]; (2) Taxes and services: immigrants take out more than they put in or less [0 = generally take out more, 10 = generally put in more; the numbers reflect the cumulative percentages from answer categories 0–4]; (3) Average wages/salaries are generally brought down by immigrants. [The numbers represent the cumulative percentages of those who "strongly agreed" and "agreed" with this statement]; (4) If a country wants to reduce tension, it should stop immigration. [The numbers represent the cumulative percentages of those who "strongly agreed" and "agreed" with this statement].)

Figure 3.2 shows that large segments of European societies display xenophobic and anti-immigrant tendencies. What is particularly interesting is that the longest bars in every country reflect native majorities' beliefs that immigrants are not paying their fair share and are taking out more in terms of taxes and services than they put in, in other words, that they are abusing the welfare state. This seems to be the leading concern in 11 out of 13 modern societies compared to the other three questions posed.

It is precisely this welfare chauvinism that motivates many radical right-wing parties and is theorized to be one of the core reasons why large swaths of native majorities should withdraw from the societywide

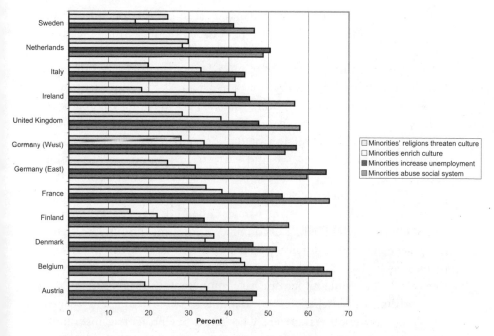

Fig. 3.3. Public opinion about the impact of immigrants on host society's culture and economy. (Data from Eurobarometer (53) 2000.) (Note: The exact wording for the questions were as follows. "For each of the following opinions, please tell me whether you tend to agree or tend to disagree: (1) the religious practices from people of these minority groups threaten our way of life; (2) people from these minority groups are enriching the cultural life of [country]; (3) the presence of people from these minority groups increases unemployment in [country]; (4) people from these minority groups abuse the system of social benefits." The answer options were (a) tend to agree or (b) tend to disagree. The percentage shown is those who indicated "agree.")

schemes of social protection (Banting 2000). This is a particular concern in Sweden, which shows relatively low levels of anti-immigrant sentiments with the exception of question 2, tapping the Swedes' concerns about the sustainability of the welfare state. The Danish and Finnish publics display similar concerns about the viability of the welfare state, and, somewhat surprisingly, the Irish public does as well.

A similar picture emerges when the Eurobarometer surveys are used. As a result of rising xenophobia, the Commission of the European Union issued three special Eurobarometer reports in 1993–94 (Eurobarometer 40), 1997 (Eurobarometer 47.1), and 2000 (Eurobarometer 53). Figure 3.3 compares four responses, two capturing "cultural" concerns and two capturing economic concerns, using Eurobarometer 53, conducted in 2000.

Close inspection of figure 3.3 demonstrates that the longest bars are again the economic ones, those that refer to minorities abusing the social system and increasing unemployment. The cultural issues—whether immigrants enrich the lives of natives and whether their religions threaten the native culture—are clearly not perceived to be as important by as many respondents. Thus, economic issues appear to trump cultural ones.

It is commonsensical to assume that nativist resentment and welfare chauvinism may be a function of the amount of immigration taking place. Indeed, in figure 3.4, we find a statistically significant relationship between the percentage of the foreign population (OECD Sopemi Reports, Trends in International Migration) and concerns about immigrants (measured as "who you would rather not have as neighbors," WVS, all four waves) for 12 EU countries at four time points. The higher the percentage of the foreign population the higher is nativist resentment, operationalized in this case as the percentage of people who indicated that they would rather not have immigrants as neighbors.

According to Kitschelt (1995), Banting (2000), Alesina and Glaeser (2004), and many others, citizens who harbor resentment against immigrants should be the first ones to "disengage" from the welfare state. Thus, at the aggregate level we should expect to see a negative association between the average percentage of people who resent immigrants and social expenditures. Figure 3.5 displays the results of a bivariate regression analysis based on 16 countries at four time points each. The countries are Australia, Austria, Belgium, Canada, Denmark, Finland, France, Germany, Italy, Ireland, the Netherlands, Norway, Sweden, Switzerland, the United Kingdom, and the United States. The four time periods are the same ones used in the WVS survey. The independent variable, average percentage of people who would rather not have immigrants as neighbors, is taken from the four waves of the World Values Survey and covers roughly the periods 1980–81, 1990–91, 1995–96, and 2000–2001 for a total of 64 observations.[11]

Both models were estimated using the Huber/White sandwich estimator of variance. Essentially, this method treats all observations within one time cluster as dependent but between clusters as independent. In other words, the four observations over time per country are treated as not independent of each other, while the clusters of countries themselves are treated as independent observations.

The results are exactly *not* what was predicted. Instead of nativist resentment having a depressing effect on social expenditures, the opposite

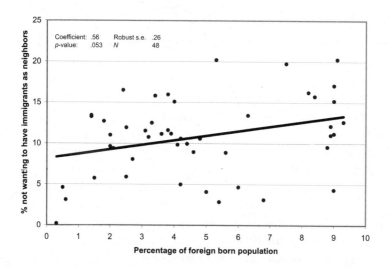

Fig. 3.4. Relationship between percentage of foreign-born population and percentage of people who do not want immigrants as neighbors. (Data from World Values Survey [all four waves]; OECD, *Trends in International Migration*.)

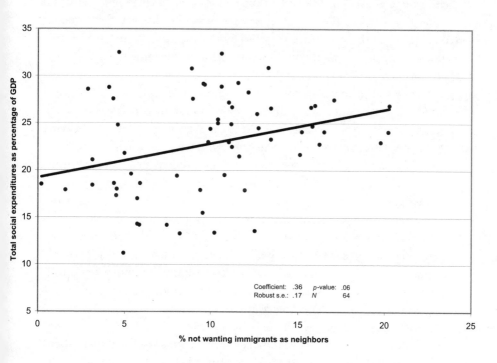

Fig. 3.5. Relationship between percentage of respondents not wanting immigrants as neighbors and total social expenditures. (Data from World Values Survey [all four waves]; OECD, Social Expenditure Database, 2004.)

is the case. The more people harbor nativist resentments, the higher welfare expenditures are. While this result is statistically significant at the .1 level (p-value .06), it explains only about 10 percent of the variation in social expenditures, the dependent variable. Still, it does not correspond with many of those who argue that immigration is the death knell of the welfare state. Of course, it could also be that public opinion does not matter or that it takes a long time for public opinion to become so influential that it begins to shape public policy. The latter argument is somewhat weak because the data cover a period of about 20 years (from 1981–82 to 2000–2001), a period in which much immigration has taken place.

Most likely the answer lies in the hypothesis spelled out earlier: people who harbor nativist resentment are exactly the ones to want to protect the welfare state since they need it more than many others do. Compared to other citizens, they tend to be poorer, less educated, and more threatened by unemployment, and as a result they should jealously defend all forms of social protection. The members of this group of *Modernisierungsverlierer* have been laid off or *wegrationalisiert* (downsized), and some live a rather precarious existence. Why should they favor cuts in welfare when the state plays a vital role in supporting them? They should be jealously defending the welfare state while at the same time displaying hostility toward "others."

Conceived in this way, hostility between natives and foreigners originates as a competition for scarce public resources in which natives claim first rights. Since the welfare state leads to a leveling of minimum living standards, native majorities are encountering feelings of relative deprivation compared to immigrants. The welfare state reduces the socioeconomic difference between them, unsettling many natives. They are asking themselves, "How is it possible that foreigners are making a living, partly supported by the welfare state, that is almost as good as mine, even though they have only come here recently, can barely speak the language, work dirty jobs, and live in squalor, while I have been paying taxes for years? Besides, I am a citizen and member of this cultural community, and they are not!" Such sentiments, however, should not undermine people's general support of the welfare state as they still want to partake of it as recipients of public welfare. It is hardly conceivable that such groups will detach from the welfare state and seek private solutions for their social protection from the vagaries of the market. However, it might affect citizens' willingness to pay their fair share; for example, it could undermine the extractive capacity of the state by encouraging natives to cheat on their taxes while continuing to support the redistributive function of the welfare state. This will be further examined in chapter 4. Their reaction should be support for reducing entitlements for immigrants or restricting immigration, not a wholesale withdrawal from the public provision of social welfare. Precisely this pattern was visible in the recent elections in the former East German *Länder* of Brandenburg and Saxony, where radical right-wing parties campaigned on a platform protecting the welfare state for citizens but not for foreigners. Similarly, at the beginning of 2004 the British government began restricting benefits to immigrants who have been in Britain for at least two years (*Economist* 2004), and in Austria in November 2004 a coalition between the conservative Austrian People's Party (ÖVP) and the liberal FPÖ abolished family assistance (*Familienbeihilfe*) to refugees (*Der Standard,* November 19, 2004).

Before examining in detail the effects of nativist resentment on welfare state attitudes a sociodemographic profile of people who harbor xenophobic tendencies must be established, for it is precisely this group that should show the first signs of an erosion of public support for the welfare state. In the spirit of Karl Deutsch, who famously declared that truth lies at the confluence of different streams of evidence, three databases, the ESS, ISSP, and WVS, will be examined. Table 3.3 shows the demographic profile of people with anti-immigrant attitudes.

Table 3.3 paints an intriguing picture of the attitudes of native majorities about newcomers. Strikingly, females and people with more education display significantly less nativist resentment than males and respondents with less education. In addition, the older people are the more negative attitudes they harbor against immigrants. This association holds up in all three surveys.

It is also expected that people in more precarious economic circumstances will display adverse sentiments. In the ESS survey, the attitude "feeling about household's income nowadays" allowed four answer options ranging from "living comfortably on present income" to "very difficult on present income." Those who struggle on a daily basis to make ends meet believe that it is better if everyone shares the same customs and traditions, indicating little tolerance for the divergent lifestyles of immigrants.

As expected, those who have friends in the immigrant community (the question is: "Do you have any friends who have come to live in [the country] from another country?") are much more tolerant and don't believe that immigrants should absorb the customs and traditions of the home country. This is evidence for Gordon Allport's (1954) "contact hypothesis," which argues that as different groups of people get to know each other better their resentment of each other, fueled by their other-ness, will disappear. A similar argument was made by Gunnar Myrdal (1960).

Examining the responses in the ISSP survey, the variable "church at-tendance" is striking: the less people attend church the more they dis-agree with the statement that immigrants increase crime. Presumably, the more "postmodern," tolerant, and liberal people are, characterized by lower church attendance, the less xenophobia they display compared to those who attend church regularly (Inglehart 1997).

TABLE 3.3.   Demographic Profile of Nativist Resentment

	Sharing Same Customs and Traditions (ESS)[a]	Crime (ISSP)[b]	No Immigrants as Neighbors (WVS)[c]
Age	−.008 (.002)★★★	−.0043 (.002)★	1.01 (.001)★★★
Female	.12 (.019)★★★	.14 (.04)★★★	.68 (.096)★★★
Education	.12 (.015)★★★	.22 (.028)★★★	.84 (.06)★★
Feeling about household income	−.085 (.022)★★★		
Income			.96 (.02)★
Church attendance		−.071 (.038)★	
Immigrants as friends	.22 (.019)★★★		
Nationalism			1.23 (.13)★★
Constant	2.40	2.08	
N	24,966	15,340	12,373
R^2	.10	.09	.05 (pseudo R^2)

Source: European Social Survey 2002; International Social Survey Program 1995; World Values Survey 1981/82, 1990/91, 1995/96.

Note: Robust standard errors in parentheses. Entries for the WVS are the odds ratios of logit estimates since the dependent variable is dichotomous. Entries larger than one are positive and smaller than one are negative. All relevant weights are applied. STATA, version 8.0, does not allow the application of weights in connection with logit commands. Thus, the third column shows the unweighted odds ratios.

The interpretation of the odds ratios is straightforward. For example, in this table, the odds ratio for "female" is .68. The odds ratio is less than 1, so the effect of "female" is negative and .68 means that a female is 32 percent less likely (100 − 68) to indicate nativist resentment than is a male.

★$p < .1$; ★★$p < .05$; ★★★$p < .01$.

[a]The specific question in the ESS is as follows: "It is better for a country if almost everyone shares the same customs and traditions." The answer options are (1) strongly agree, (2) agree, (3) neither agree nor disagree, (4) disagree, (5) strongly disagree.

[b]The question in the ISSP survey is as follows: "There are different opinions about immigrants from other countries living in [respondent's country]. (By immigrants we mean people who come to settle in [respondent's country].) How much do you agree or disagree with the following statement: "Immigrants increase crime rates." The same fivefold classification applies as in the ESS survey with 1 indicating strong agreement and 5 strong disagreement.

[c]The WVS survey asked the familiar question: "On this list are various groups of people. Could you please sort out any that you would not like to have as neighbors." Respondents who did not mention "immigrants/foreign workers" were coded 0; those who mentioned them were coded 1.

Two results of particular interest are contained in the third column of table 3.3, which presents the results of the WVS survey on the "neighbors" question. First, the survey found that the higher the income the less people indicated that they did not want immigrants as neighbors. This may be so because more highly paid people do not experience the competition for jobs from immigrants that low-paid respondents feel. The second interesting result is the association between the respondent's degree of national pride and not wanting immigrants as neighbors. The question was: "How proud are you to be . . ."? The stronger the pride in his or her nation the less the respondent wanted immigrants as neighbors.[12]

These results offer a profile of those who harbor nativist resentments. A forensic detective would describe the profile as an older male with low education and income in a precarious economic situation who shows strong nationalism, goes to church often, and has no immigrant friends. It is no small wonder that such people feel threatened by immigrants.

When immigrants begin to make use of unemployment benefits, housing support, health services, or sickness payments for which many are eligible, feelings of relative deprivation among locals arise. But does this relative deprivation lead to a withdrawal of large parts of the population from the welfare state? Again, any indication that such a connection exists should come from this group of people, which is the one most threatened by immigrants. Such groups may feel cheated by the welfare state insofar as it helps to support not only them but also newcomers, who have paid into the system very little and yet are "taking advantage" of it while the natives have supported public provision for years. Two reactions are plausible. First, if natives believe that they have to pay for social provision that goes to "foreigners," which helps them achieve almost the same living standards as the natives, they may indeed "abandon the idea of a set of wider obligations" (Banting 2000, 16) and retreat from publicly funded forms of social provision. Second, it is plausible that those who already live precariously should jealously guard and protect the welfare state. As Harold Wilensky (2002, 652) observed: "Even the lawless skinheads in Germany identify their biggest worry as *Zukunftssicherheit,* or 'future security'." Thus, it may be counterintuitive to expect that the radical Right is withdrawing from the welfare state. The next section will empirically estimate the effect of nativist resentment on support for the welfare state at the individual level.

THE PEOPLE'S VOICE AND THE DEMAND FOR
SOCIAL WELFARE

Few fields in political science are as thoroughly examined as the welfare state. Despite this level of maturity, using public opinion polls in gauging people's reactions to welfare state issues has not been that prevalent, although there are certainly some studies in this field that prove the exception to the rule (Papadakis 1992; Gelissen 2002; Svallfors and Taylor-Gooby 1999; Svallfors 1997; Coughlin 1980; Taylor-Gooby 1985). In addition, there is a massive five-volume set, *Beliefs in Government,* funded by the European Science Foundation, which, as the moniker suggests, relies on public opinion research to tap those beliefs. All of five volumes were published in 1995 by Oxford University Press (Klingemann and Fuchs 1995; Niedermayer and Sinnot 1995; Borre and Scarborough 1995; Deth and Scarborough 1995; Kaase and Newton 1995).

Economists have also investigated the effect of diversity on redistribution. Alesina and LaFerrara (1999) find that group formation and political participation are reduced in heterogeneous societies. Dora L. Costa and Matthew E. Kahn (2002, 3), reviewing the recent economic literature on diversity, come to the conclusion that "Over the last five years, at least 15 different empirical economic papers have studied the consequences of community heterogeneity, and all of these studies have the same punch line: heterogeneity reduces civic engagement." In their own study, they come to the conclusion that, "Not only is participation and expenditure lower in more diverse settings, but so is trust." James Poterba (1997) and Amy Harris et al. (2001) report evidence of a "Florida effect" in states' public school expenditures. In Florida, the average taxpayer is a white senior citizen while the typical public school student is Hispanic. The authors found that in an environment of such diversity there is less support for public school expenditures than in states where the students and the taxpayers share the same ethnicity. Erzo Luttmer (2001), using data from the General Social Survey, finds that redistribution is higher when the recipients are from the same social group. Claudia Goldin and Lawrence Katz (1999) find that educational expenditures in the U.S. states can best be predicted by ethnic, racial, and religious diversity. Examining the effects of ethnic diversity in African countries, William Easterly and Ross Levine (1997) concluded that high government deficits, political instability, less schooling, and reduced support for public goods and general rent seeking are connected to greater ethnic diversity.

In addition to the two competing hypotheses concerning whether people with anti-immigrant attitudes either favor or disfavor redistribution, there are other groups identifiable that should display systematic attitudes about the welfare state. Harold Wilensky (1975) argued three decades ago that the "middle mass," that is, the young, well-educated, dynamic, and postindustrial groups in society, should be the ones abdicating their reliance on the welfare state, leading to a welfare state "backlash." These groups represent economic individualists who "perceive no benefits from the welfare state" (Pettersen 1995, 200).

The important work on the rise of postmaterialism by Ronald Inglehart comes to similar conclusions. As a result of the scarcity and socialization hypothesis, once material scarcity is replaced with abundance and generations grow up in relative affluence, support for a system principally designed to ensure material provision should fade. Material goals have declined as the postwar recessions have become distant memories (Inglehart 1990). Even so, it is not clear that postmaterialist attitudes run counter to welfare state policies. Edeltraud Roller (1995, 172), emphasizing the "equality" dimension of welfare state goals, argues that "expectations about materialist equality policies such as redistribution should decline, while, at the same time, expectations about postmaterial equality policies should increase." Certainly, the welfare state created the conditions under which postmaterialist values could eventually develop. "Paradoxically, this crisis [of the welfare state] does not reflect the failure of the welfare state so much as the fact that it has succeeded in alleviating those problems it can most readily solve," argues Inglehart (1997, 239) "and thereby helped pave the way for new types of problems to become central." Since the welfare state was prior to postmaterialism which unfolded in the wake of economic security, we would expect that postmaterialism is negatively associated with attitudes on the welfare state.

Finally, the most obvious supporters of the welfare state should be members of the working class. This logic certainly applies in the European context in which "class" is strongly associated with welfare state support (Esping-Andersen 1990; Korpi 1983), with the working class clearly favoring the welfare state (Svallfors 1997). However, in the United States this is not the case. One of the enduring puzzles is why the poor in the United States do not favor more redistribution. Part of the answer lies in the widespread conception that poverty is of one's own making and not a function of the "system." In a society based on widely held perceptions of rapid social mobility, no matter how far-fetched

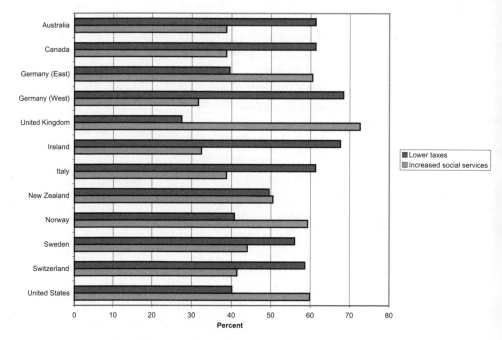

Fig. 3.6.   National preferences for lower taxes vis-à-vis higher social expenditures.
(Data from International Social Survey Program [ISSP] 1996, The Role of Government, module III.)

(Jäntti et al. 2006), why should the poor push for higher taxes on the rich
if they believe they will be there one day? (Alesina, Glaeser, and Sacerdote 2001; Alesina and Glaeser 2004). *Newsweek* (March 1, 2004) quoted
Benjamin Barber as saying: "The Clinton insight was not 'Don't argue
for equality', it was 'Don't bash the rich.' You're closing off people's
dreams." Or, in the memorable words of Nicos Poulantzas: "People do
not cut off the ladder on which they hope to climb one day."

Before we examine individual-level data, let us take a look at Figure
3.6, which taps the national "tastes" for redistribution. The 1996 ISSP, The
Role of Government III module, asked the probably most appropriate
question tapping support for the welfare state: "If the government had a
choice between reducing taxes or spending more on social services, which
do you think it should do? (We mean all taxes together, including wage
deductions, income tax, tax on goods and services and all the rest). Please
tick one box only: 1. Reduce taxes, even if it means spending less on social
services; 2. Spend more on social services even if this means higher taxes."

The reason why this is one of the most appropriate questions is because it captures the zero sum nature of taxes versus social expenditures

by making it explicit to the interviewee that more social services require higher taxes and lowering taxes will mean fewer social services. There are still "baseline comparability problems," that is, the respondents in each society responded in a tax/social services environment that is idiosyncratic to specific countries. In other words, Swedes already have a rather high marginal tax rate and relatively generous social services, that is, their tax baseline is higher than, say, the baseline in Great Britain, so it is not surprising that a majority wants lower taxes rather than more social services. On the other hand, Norwegian respondents, who, like the Swedes, are protected from the vagaries of the market, indicate an even greater desire for social services even if this means higher taxes.

Still, figure 3.6 contains some very surprising results. One of them is that a significant majority of British want to increase social services even if it means higher taxes. Comparison between the two Germany's is also remarkable: the former East Germany, which was used to forty years of a planned economy, has a majority of people saying they want more social services while in market-oriented West Germany the opposite is the case. More remarkable still are the preferences of American respondents. One of the most intriguing findings is that almost 60 percent want more social services even if this means higher taxes, while 40 percent want lower taxes even if this means fewer social services—almost exactly the same profile as the former East Germany! This does not fit at all with the perception of the American public as being generally averse to the welfare state, preferring tax cuts to social services.

In order to examine the effect of nativist resentment on the welfare state the European Social Survey 2002 was used. The following question tapping support for the welfare state was selected: "Using this card please say to which extent you agree or disagree with each of the following statements: the government should take measures to reduce differences in income levels." The answer options followed a fivefold scale and ranged from 1 = agree strongly to 5 = disagree strongly.

Table 3.4 shows two models that are very similar, with the main difference being that two different independent variables were used to gauge the effect of attitudes on immigrants. The variables of interest, "average salaries are brought down by immigrants" and "immigrants take jobs away," both of which can be thought of as welfare chauvinism by those who agree with these statements, show a positive effect on the statement that government should reduce income differences. In other words, the more respondents display anti-immigrant attitudes the more they support the redistributive function of the welfare state, exactly the opposite of what many observers have argued. People who harbor xenophobic tendencies, rather than detaching from the welfare state, are seeking help from it! These relationships did not become significant until unemployment was controlled for. Particularly in the first model, people who have been unemployed in the past not unexpectedly demonstrate support for the welfare state. In the second model, the sign for unemployment is in the correct direction, but it is not significant.

The more educated and the higher the income, however, the less people show support for the welfare state, giving credence to Wilensky's

TABLE 3.4.   Multiple Regression Analysis of the Impact of Nativist Resentment on Welfare State Support

	Government Should Take Measures to Reduce Income Differences	
	Model 1	Model 2
Average salaries are brought down by immigrants	−.06 (.016)★★★	
Immigrants take jobs away		−.025 (.01)★★
Age	−.000006 (.001)	.001 (.001)
Education	.08 (.01)★★★	.08 (.015)★★★
Income	.06 (.013)★★★	.07 (.014)★★★
Female	−.18 (.02)★★★	−.19 (.036)★★★
Strong concern for nature and environment	−.09 (.016)★★★	−.07 (.023)★★
Ever been unemployed (3 months or more)?	−.12 (.033)★★★	
Long-term unemployed (12 months or more)?		−.033 (.03)
Self-placement on left/right scale	.1 (.013)★★★	.09 (.014)★★★
Constant	1.4 (.14)★★★	1.3 (.17)★★★
N	17,311	4,201
R^2	.11	.095

Source: European Social Survey 2002.

Note: Robust standard errors in parentheses. Two-tailed tests.

★★★$p < .01$; ★★$p < .05$.

Question items

The precise wording for "average salaries are brought down by immigrants" was as follows: "Average wages and salaries are generally brought down by people coming to live and work here." The answer options were recoded so that 1 = disagree strongly and 5 = agree strongly.

"Immigrants take jobs away" is captured with the following item: "Using this card, would you say that people who come to live here generally take jobs away from workers in [country] or generally help to create new jobs?" Answer options: 10 = take jobs away; 0 = create new jobs (recoded).

The "care for nature and environment" variable was captured with the following question: "Now I will briefly describe some people. Please listen to each description and tell me how much each person is or is not like you. He/she strongly believes that people should care for nature. Looking after the environment is important to him/her." The sixfold answer options ranged from 6 = very much like me to 1 = not like me at all and are also recoded.

"Ever been unemployed" is captured as follows: "Have you ever been unemployed and seeking work for a period of more than three months?" The dichotomous answer options were 0 = no; 1 = yes (recoded).

Long-term unemployed: "Has any of these periods of unemployment and work seeking lasted for twelve months or more?" 0 = no; 1 = yes (recoded).

"middle mass," which refuses to support the welfare state. The obverse is also true: people who hold racist sentiments, who tend to be poor and less educated, are supporters of the welfare state. Most remarkable is the gender gap. Females are clearly in favor of government redistribution! Age has no impact on welfare state support, but the Left-Right orientation has; as might be expected, the more a person places oneself toward the right end of the ideological scale the more he/she disagrees with the statement that the government should reduce differences in income levels.

In terms of Ronald Inglehart's hypothesis of value change, it was argued above that the welfare state helped produce the conditions under which postmaterialism was able to develop and thus represented a prior stage in the process of postmodernization. Consequently, a negative association between postmaterialism and support for the welfare state was expected. However, the opposite is the case: the findings indicate that the more postmaterial people are the more they favor the welfare state! Overall, given the high number of observations, the R^2s of .11 and almost .1 are rather impressive.

To round out this chapter, one more data set, the fourth wave of the World Values Survey, will be examined along similar lines. This triangulation of pursuing the same questions using different data should increase the confidence that the results are not just a fluke of a particular data set, time period, or choice of variables.

This time, instead of relying on just one question item, we take advantage of principal component factor analysis, which is, in essence, a data reduction technique. Factor analysis examines the degree to which different items in a survey cohere or capture similar concepts. The advantage of such a data-reducing technique is that it helps a researcher to identify the commonalities among different question items that otherwise would not be readily apparent. With this technique, a researcher can construct a deeper yet wider concept that does not depend on responses to just one question item. The rotated factor loadings identify which items display commonalities and, put together, make up a new, "latent construct," which is in essence a new name for a variable consisting of the combined items. Cronbach's alpha measures how well a set of items measures a single, unidimensional, latent construct. It ranges from 0 to 1 with .7 or higher considered to be "acceptable" (Nunnaly 1978).

The variable nativist resentment is derived from the well-known "neighbors" question: "On this list are various groups of people. Could you please sort out any that you would not like to have as neighbors?"[13] In the fourth wave of the WVS, respondents are given a list containing

13 different groups of people. The choice of the respondents is dichotomous, that is, the interviewer records whether the respondents mention
or do not mention any of these groups as ones they would not like to
have as neighbors. For our 18-country OECD data set, respondents
could indicate the following groups they would not like to have as
neighbors: people with a criminal record, people of a different race,
heavy drinkers, emotionally unstable people, Muslims, immigrants,
people with AIDS, drug addicts, homosexuals, Jews, evangelists, people
of a different religion, and Gypsies.[14] Of those 13 items, people with
AIDS, homosexuals, and evangelists are excluded, as they do not load
highly on any of the three factors. After conducting a principal component factor analysis of the remaining 10 items, three factors emerged
clearly.

Table 3.5 shows three groups of factors of varying strength emerging
among the 10 items. The first group (in bold type) is what we will call
nativist resentment and consists of the following groups that people do
not want to have as neighbors: people of a different race, immigrants,
Muslims, and Jews. The second, weaker group (underlined) may be called
"crime and drugs"; that is, the respondents do not want people with a
criminal record, emotionally unstable people, heavy drinkers, or drug
addicts as neighbors. The third group (in italics) is a "political extremist"

TABLE 3.5.   **Principal Component Factor Analysis (varimax rotation) of Preference
for Types of Neighbors**

	Nativist Resentment	Crime and Drugs	Political Extremists
People of a different race	**.82**	.08	−.07
Immigrants	**.82**	.10	−.06
Muslims	**.77**	.13	−.10
Jews	**.75**	.05	−.10
People with a criminal record	.25	.63	−.02
Emotionally unstable people	.26	.56	−.07
Heavy drinkers	.08	.66	−.23
Drug addicts	.02	.75	−.09
Left-wing extremists	.18	.14	−.85
Right-wing extremists	.01	.03	−.90
Cronbach's alpha	.83	.62	.72
N	min: 18,076	min: 23,661	min: 14,945
	max: 23,664	max: 23,664	max: 14,945

Source: World Values Survey 2000.

Question item: "On this list are various groups of people. Could you please sort out any that you would not
like to have as neighbors?"

cluster in which people do not want left- or right-wing political extremists as neighbors.

Thus, the central variable, "nativist resentment," consists of those respondents who have indicated that they do not want these four kinds of people as neighbors: (1) people of a different race, (2) immigrants, (3) Muslims, (4) Jews. Across 16 countries and with an N of 18,075, about 20 percent of respondents indicated that they did not want at least one of these groups as neighbors. On average, almost 9 percent indicated that they did not want people of a different race as neighbors, over 17 percent indicated that they did not want Muslims as neighbors, over 11 percent indicated that they did not want immigrants as neighbors, and 7.7 percent indicated that they did not want Jews as neighbors.

There is, of course, tremendous variation within industrialized countries along the elements of what we call nativist resentment. The extent of this variation is revealed in table 3.6.

Of the four groups, Muslims is the one natives least prefer to have as neighbors, followed by immigrants, people of a different race, and Jews. The fieldwork for this survey was completed before 9/11 and the "sum-

TABLE 3.6. Percentage of Respondents Who Indicated Groups They Did Not Want as Neighbors

	Different Race	Immigrants	Muslims	Jews
Australia	5	4.7	n.a.	n.a.
Austria	8.5	14.5	18	9.7
Belgium	16	18.7	25	12.5
Canada	4	4.7	7	4.1
Denmark	8	11.9	19.5	2.5
Finland	14	14.6	23	9
France	10	13.8	19.2	6.3
Germany	6.3	12.4	14.3	7.3
Ireland	14	14.3	17	13
Italy	18	19.8	20.8	15
Netherlands	5.25	5.3	14	1.7
New Zealand	3	5.7	n.a.	n.a.
Norway	8.9	11	24	n.a.
Sweden	2.6	3	10	2.2
Switzerland	9.4	11.6	21.6	n.a.
United Kingdom	10.1	18	16.4	6.6
United States	8.8	11.3	12.3	10
Average	8.9	11.5	17.5	7.7

Source: World Values Survey 2000.

Note: n.a. = not available.

mer of discontent" in Great Britain, which witnessed widespread racial violence (in the United States the fieldwork for wave 4 of the WVS was conducted between November 19, 1999, and September 25, 2000, and in Great Britain during October and November of 1999). It is safe to assume that 9/11, the British race riots of 2001, the terrorist attacks in London of July 2005, the war on terrorism, the political murders of Fortuyn and van Gogh in the Netherlands, and the ensuing racial conflicts have only exacerbated the prejudices and negative stereotypes of the public.

Using this latent construct of "nativist resentment" consisting of these four groups of people, how will such attitudes affect people's willingness to support the welfare state? We have already seen that, using ESS data, there existed an unexpectedly positive relationship between those who harbored nativist resentments and those who supported the welfare state. This is unexpected because many of the new radical right-wing parties have a neoliberal, promarket orientation, suggesting a turn away from supporting social protection themes (Betz 1994). Alesina and Glaeser (2004, 175) make a similar point when they note that "these ruling coalitions," a reference to the radical right-wing parties that are part of governing coalitions in Austria and the Netherlands, "have also, not incidentally, been committed to rolling back the European welfare state. Europe's new immigrant-based heterogeneity may eventually push the continent toward more American levels of redistribution."

Using the fourth wave of the WVS, I selected two question items to capture "support for the welfare state." First, "In order to be considered 'just' what should a society provide: please tell me for each statement whether it is important or unimportant to you. 1 means very important, 5 means not important at all: society should provide, eliminating inequalities." The welfare state cannot, of course, "eliminate" inequalities completely, but its task is in essence to reduce differences in life chances through publicly provided social protections; to assist those who have been laid off, injured on the job, or fallen ill; and to help provide for people in their old age. This may be considered the socioeconomic security function of the welfare state while policies intended to reduce income inequalities may be called the equality function of the welfare state (Roller 1995).

The second question used to capture "support for the welfare state" is: "Now I'd like you to tell me your views on various issues. How would you place your views on this scale? 1 means you agree completely with the statement on the left, 10 means you completely agree with the statement on the right, and if your views fall somewhere in between, you can choose any number in between: 1 People should take more responsibility to provide for themselves. 10 The government should take more responsibility to ensure that everyone is provided for."

This question taps the degree to which people are willing to allow the government some control over their lives. Presumably, those who think that government should take more responsibility would favor the welfare state since the welfare state manifests itself in the lives of most people in the form of social security checks, food stamps, reduced housing costs, or unemployment benefits. If respondents think that people should take more responsibility for themselves, it is reasonable to assume that they are not in favor of the welfare state. They may be in favor of private provision of security but most likely not of the welfare "state."

Table 3.7 demonstrates that in both models nativist resentment reveals itself to have a positive effect on welfare state support. In model 1, the positive coefficient of nativist resentment indicates that the more people harbor nativist resentment the more they believe that government should take more responsibility for seeing that everyone is cared for while in the second model higher nativist resentment is negatively related, that is, respondents harboring more nativist resentment believe that it is important for society to eliminate inequalities. In both models, the more respondents

TABLE 3.7. Multiple Regression Analysis of the Impact of Nativist Resentment on Welfare State Support

	People/Goverment Should Take Responsibility	Society Should Eliminate Inequalities
Nativist resentment	.56 (.13)***	−.12 (.05)**
Female	.18 (.05)***	−.04 (.04)
Income	−.19 (.04)***	.036 (.037)
Age	−.007 (.001)***	−.002 (.0009)**
Education	−.027 (.24)	.067 (.012)***
Postmaterialism (Inglehart's 4-item scale)	.028 (.067)	.038 (.034)
Self-placement on left/right scale	−.19 (.03)***	.14 (.025)***
Unemployed	.21 (.07)**	−.13 (.78)
Constant	5.9 (.22)***	1.5 (.16)***
N	11,961	9,478
R^2	.04	.085

Source: World Values Survey 2000.
Note: Robust standard errors in parentheses. Two-tailed tests.
***$p < .01$; **$p < .05$.

place themselves on the political Right the less they show support for the welfare state. In model 1, females and the unemployed favor the welfare state while people with higher incomes and older people disfavor it. In model 2, more educated people disfavor the welfare state while older people think it is important for society to eliminate inequalities. In neither model did postmaterialism make any difference.

The evidence from the ESS and the WVS demonstrates a surprising result: those groups of respondents whose livelihood is threatened most by immigrants, and show it by clearly being xenophobic, also demonstrate support for the redistributive role of the welfare state rather than withdrawing from it! Immigration-driven diversity does not appear to reduce the demand for welfare, as has been claimed by so many observers. The "Americanization of the European welfare state" has not occurred yet, at least not in terms of the demand for welfare by those who feel the most threatened by immigration.

THE PEOPLE'S VOICE AND THE SUPPLY OF SOCIAL WELFARE

The outcomes reported here are certainly intriguing, yet a more basic question looms very large: how would it be possible for individuals, in the words of Banting (2000, 16), to "abandon the idea of a set of wider obligations and quietly disengage, psychologically and perhaps even physically, from the wider society" as a result of increasing diversity? What mechanisms could be applied by those who feel threatened by immigration? It is hard to believe that those groups would suddenly argue that they do not want further support from the welfare state as a result of increasing diversity. However, there is another mechanism at their disposal, one that goes to the heart of the viability of the welfare state.

The welfare state and individuals intersect at two points: first, when an individual claims welfare benefits; and, second, and when an individual pays taxes. Extraction through taxation and redistribution are among the most crucial functions of the welfare state. This is the nexus that connects individuals to the state in its coldest form. It is individual compliance with the law that ensures that the state will collect sufficient revenues, which are then channeled into various programs of public provision. This is the *locus classicus* where citizens and the state meet and where individuals in modern societies must comply to a sufficient degree by paying their "fair share" for the maintenance of the state as such. This is what is meant by "the supply of social welfare" in the title of this section. Many fringe groups dissatisfied with national policies have resorted to tax revolts, realizing that the Achilles' heel of government is the degree to which it can or cannot extract revenues.

A prime example is Mogens Glistrup, the founder of the radical right-wing Progressive Party in Denmark in the early 1970s. Glistrup's popularity was driven by the claim that no one should have to pay more taxes than he or she wants, and he even compared tax evaders to the Danish groups that resisted German occupation during World War II. There is a close connection among radical right-wing ideology, a Darwinian understanding of laissez-faire economics, and tax revolts (Andersen and Bjorklund 2000).

While not paying one's taxes is of course illegal, it highlights the degree to which individuals see themselves as part of a larger community or see themselves as detached, atomized, and unencumbered by social rights and obligations. Those who have a wider view of the moral community, that is, a community that includes persons who are different from themselves, most likely are not put off by the presence of newcomers and continue funding the welfare state by truthfully declaring their taxes.

Conversely, people who feel that they are in competition with foreigners for scarce public goods may be more inclined to cheat on their taxes and claim public benefits for which they are not eligible. Such respondents may feel disenchanted with the authorities insofar as they may blame them for the presence of immigrants. People in a precarious economic situation may feel that by cheating the state they can get back what they perceive is rightfully theirs. They may perceive cheating on taxes to be a form of silent protest against an elitist policy that brings "foreigners" into their country who threaten their survival. People who hold nativist resentments are expected to be less law abiding because they have a more fractured view of society, that is, those who believe that as society is becoming more diverse the cement that attaches them to society is crumbling. In the presence of foreigners who also are eligible to draw on welfare benefits they may not see themselves as part of a "community of fate" any longer and as a result do not see what they are paying in taxes as their "fair" share.

The fourth wave of WVS asked a series of question items tapping what might be called "obeying the law." The precise wording is as follows: "Please tell me for each of the following statements whether you think it can always be justified, never be justified or something in between using this card: 1. Claiming government benefits to which you are not entitled. 2. Cheating on taxes if you have a chance. 3. Someone accepting a bribe in the course of their duties." (The range of all three items is: 1 = never justifiable, 10 = always justifiable). The three questions tie individual attitudes to the welfare state. If people believe that it is justifiable to claim benefits to which they are not entitled or cheat on taxes if they have a chance, such attitudes would indeed endanger the viability of continued social protection and would call the welfare state project into serious question. The question on bribery is also included as it taps in a general way the degree to which people take license with the law.

The findings in table 3.8 reveal intriguing results. Most important, while controlling for a whole host of sociodemographic and other variables, the results indicate that people who display nativist resentment have fewer scruples about claiming welfare benefits to which they are not entitled, tend to cheat on their taxes, and have a rather cavalier attitude about taking bribes.

This is a central finding so far in this project because it means that, in-

TABLE 3.8.　Multiple Regression Results of Nativist Resentment on Three Central Features of the Welfare State in 11 Modern Societies

	Claiming Benefits	Cheating on Taxes	Bribery
Nativist resentment	.33 (.12)**	.92 (.17)***	.31 (.09)***
Life satisfaction	−.073 (.03)***	−.09 (.02)***	−.05 (.014)***
Age	−.021 (.001)***	−.022 (.002)***	−.01 (.001)***
Female	−.16 (.03)***	−.41 (.06)***	−.16 (.03)***
Income	−.034 (.039)	−.0006 (.05)	−.006 (.03)
Education	−.048 (.018)**	.004 (.03)	−.017 (.014)
Unemployed	.3 (.08)***	−.011 (.08)	.05 (.06)
Stable relationship	−.13 (.04)***	−.05 (.05)	−.08 (.035)*
Self-placement on left/right scale	−.04 (.018)*	.028 (.025)	.015 (.01)
Nationalism	−.09 (.07)	−.26 (.07)***	−.096 (.012)***
Constant	4.07 (.45)***	4.28 (.04)***	2.6 (.26)***
N	9,737	9,749	9,769
R^2	.05	.063	.03

Source: World Values Survey 2000.

Note: Robust standard errors in parentheses. Two-tailed tests.

*p < .1; **p < .05; ***p < .01.

Question items

The exact wording for life satisfaction is "All things considered, how satisfied are you with your life these days?" 1 = dissatisfied; 10 = satisfied.

Stable relationship: "Whether you are married or not: do you live in a stable relationship with a partner?" 0 = no; 1 = yes.

Nationalism: "How proud are you to be [nationality]?" 1 = not at all proud; 4 = very proud (recoded).

deed, sentiments stirred up as a result of diversity manifest themselves in attitudes that are detrimental to the basic principles on which the welfare state is built: it appears that the willingness on the part of the public that harbors nativist resentment to fund the welfare state is seriously compromised! The highly significant positive coefficients indicate that people with nativist resentments have fewer qualms about cheating on their taxes, taking bribes, and claiming welfare benefits to which they are not entitled.

As far as control variables are concerned, in all three models the older people are the more they are satisfied with their lives and females are "model citizens" insofar as such respondents tend to believe that neither one of the three behaviors is ever justified. Income does not show any significant relationship in the three models. In the "claiming welfare benefits" model, people with higher education do not believe that it is ever justified to claim government benefits to which they are not entitled, as do people who are on the right side of the political spectrum and those who are more integrated into society, that is, those who live in a stable relationship. However, those that are currently unemployed have fewer qualms about engaging in such behavior.

The effect of the "nationalism" variable is particularly interesting. The highly significant and positive outcome means that the more proud people are of their nation the less they think that cheating on taxes is justifiable, while the less proud they are the more they find that proposition acceptable. Bribery overall shows a very similar relationship to the tax model, with nationalist feelings representing a strong barrier to the slippery slope of accepting bribes. The same is true of a respondent being firmly ensconced in a stable relationship, which also appears to make people more virtuous.

The implications of the findings in this chapter are powerful. The argument was that the strata of society that are the first to exhibit attitudes detrimental to the welfare state should contain those who feel they are the most threatened by immigration. In terms of demand for welfare, that proved to be false. In the accounts presented here, there is no indication that such persons are retreating from the welfare state. The opposite seems to be the case. They are jealously guarding their privileges as citizens. They may be disturbed by the leveling effect of the welfare state, which puts immigrants rather quickly in the vicinity of the same rung of standard of living as the natives, but that does not make them retreat from the publicly funded forms of social protection. They are demanding what they believe they are entitled to as a result of being a citizen.

What is more disturbing, however, is that people who disdain diversity as a result of immigration are retreating from their duty to pay their taxes,[15] undermining the foundation on which the welfare state project is built. This finding demonstrates that when it comes to the supply side of the welfare state, that is, citizens paying their fair share, people afraid of diversity withdraw their support while at the same time continuing to demand services. Thus, the thesis that nativist resentment will undermine the welfare state is only true as far as the supply side is concerned. When it comes to receiving goodies from the welfare state, people with anti-immigrant attitudes are not shy to take them but retreat from doing their part when it comes to paying for them.

It is heartening and revealing to see the strong negative effect of education on xenophobia. Much of xenophobia is about prejudice and stereotypes, and, as with many such concepts, these are constructed. Education, which is also a form of construction, is shown to be a counterweight to these primordial fears, as well as a ray of hope, for it demonstrates that the roots of primordial sentiments grow most prolifically in an environment of ignorance. The observation that higher education leads to less xenophobia demolishes the essentialist, primordial claim that categorical differences must separate individuals from each other and creates space for the possibility that education can reduce hatred between humans of different races, religions, or ethnic backgrounds even further.

If enough citizens are beginning to be concerned about immigration and are displaying a similar reluctance to pay their fair share, the European model of the welfare state may indeed be in danger. While aggregate data do not indicate major retrenchment in European welfare states (Pierson 2001), studying attitudes about the demand and supply of welfare may function like an early warning system that could provide indications about the degree to which mass publics are willing to continue funding the welfare state in the face of unprecedented immigration. The results, at least up to this point, are not encouraging, as they support much of the literature that argues that diversity leads to lower redistribution. Does that mean that European welfare states will undergo a slow and inevitable decline, driven by immigration, until they begin to look like the American "residual" welfare state? The answer is "no," and the next chapter examines why this is the case.

CHAPTER 4

Trust in Diverse Societies

You may be deceived if you trust too much, but you will
live in torment if you don't trust enough.
—Frank Crane

THE FORAY INTO THE ORIGINS OF primordial attachments suggested that there is a direct relationship between diversity and outcomes
such as the extent of the welfare state, societal order, or the quality of
democracy. However, this chapter argues that the picture is more com-
plicated and introduces "trust" as an intermediary between diversity and
support for the welfare state.

Trust is important because it is impossible to regulate every aspect of
human interaction on the basis of legal codes, an observation that Émile
Durkheim made over 100 years ago when he stated that "a contract is not
sufficient unto itself, but is possible only thanks to a regulation of the
contract which is originally social" (1964 [1893], 215). Even though
Durkheim stressed terms such as *morality* rather than *trust,* it is clear that
there is a strong affinity between these two concepts. The economic
world and its contracts unfold within a framework of social norms and
morality without which "incoherent chaos" would reign in the economic
world (Durkheim, quoted in Giddens 1971, 69). Niklas Luhman (1988,
103) argued similarly when he explained that "A system, economic, legal,
or political, requires trust as an input condition. Without trust, it cannot
stimulate supportive activities in situations of uncertainty and risk."

Trust "lubricates" social interaction, solves collective action problems,
and reduces transaction costs. Economists have unearthed most intriguing
evidence indicating that more trusting societies have higher economic
growth rates (Knack and Keefer 1997; Zak and Knack 2001). Alesina and

LaFerrara (2001) find that income and education are strongly correlated with trust. Alesina and LaFerrara (2002, 207) conclude that "individuals who express stronger feelings against racial integration trust relatively less the more racially heterogeneous the community is."

Robert D. Putnam (1993) of course, has argued that social capital, of which trust is a significant element, would make "democracy work" in northern Italy. The eighteenth-century Italian political economist Antonio Genovesi (1731–79) highlighted the role trust played in the establishment of commerce. Genovesi distinguished between *fede privata* and *fede pubblica,* the first meaning private trust originating in the family and kin group and the second meaning public trust, encompassing wider strata of society. Only by "surrendering their instinctive habits of distrust" were members of such societies able to establish a "commercial society" (Pagden 1988, 130).

In *Bowling Alone* Putnam (2000) claims that social capital leads to lower crime rates, better health and well-being, and a whole host of other positive outcomes. Finally, the importance of trust becomes apparent to anybody whose trust in others has been disappointed. Trust, in other words, is a societal resource that allows people to achieve outcomes and engage with each other in interactions that make all of them better off than they would be if they did not trust each other. Gary Miller (2001) argues that trust reduces moral hazard and can make organizations more efficient.

Nevertheless, the temptation to shirk one's duty is powerful, particularly if the good to be provided is public in nature. One such public good is the welfare state, "where citizens must trust each other to both take part as contributors and not take advantage as beneficiaries. Trust is aided by identification with fellow citizens. Identification with fellow citizens is easiest in ethnically and culturally homogeneous societies" (Soroka, Banting, and Johnston 2002, 2). In this account, it is not diversity per se that leads to reduced welfare support, but trust may be reduced as a result of diversity, and this reduced trust may be responsible for lower welfare state support. Thus, trust subtly slips between diversity as cause and welfare state support as an effect. Trust is enhanced when individuals share certain basic tracers such as race, ethnicity, religion, or language. Conversely, one might argue that the temptations to cheat and shirk one's duties are enlarged in the provision of public goods when such categorical differences exist.

European countries have been rather homogeneous and have experienced diversity as a result of immigration only since the mid-1950s. What happens if diversity impinges on societies with relatively high trust levels such as the Scandinavian countries? Since diversity has never been an element in the experience of these societies, the contact with "others" may have very different trajectories than in the American case since in the Scandinavian context high trust levels have already been attained.

Because immigration and diversity occurred later in Europe, it had time to establish a cohesive culture of trust that, once established, should better able to deal differently with impending increases in diversity than is a society, such as the United States, that experienced diversity from the beginning. This opens policy paths for European countries, partic-ularly the Scandinavian ones, that were closed for the United States be-cause diversity had already eroded trust to such a degree that wide-spread support for the welfare state never developed.

The case is different for European countries: immigration happened later, and societies had a chance to establish trust while they were still relatively homogeneous. Immigration impinged and is impinging on European societies, some but not all with higher trust levels than those in the United States, and as a result the adverse consequences of diversity should be deflected or refracted by the differences in trust levels, allow-ing policy options for at least some European countries that are simply not available for the United States.

Thus, in the high-trust countries in Europe diversity should show a different trajectory as it impinges on given levels of trust than in the United States. Consequently, it is in fact not intuitive to argue that the high-trust European countries will follow eventually the same pattern as the United States in their welfare state development, as some do under the banner of "the Americanization of the European welfare state" (Freeman 1986; Alesina and Glaeser, 2004) because the conditions under which diversity impacts Europe are different from conditions in the United States. Could it be that diversity impacts the high trust societies in Europe that the adverse effects of heterogeneity are avoided and the people continue to pay taxes and do not abuse the welfare state despite the presence of diversity?

This book argues that trust matters by refracting, reducing, or blunt-ing nativist resentment. Thus, trust mediates the effect of nativist resent-ment on welfare state support. This argument is different from that of Soroka and Banting (2002), which tests the claim that increasing diver-sity leads to a hollowing out of trust, which should lead to a reduction in welfare state support. For the case of Canada, however, they do not find that reduced trust adversely affects welfare state support. Rather, diversity should interact with given levels of trust in systematic ways. My research assumes that trust is relatively enduring and unchanging, and it is treated throughout this book as a "trait" rather than a "state."

The argument on the connection between rising diversity, trust, and welfare state attitudes is as follows: as diversity increases, it impinges on relatively unchanging and enduring levels of trust, which in turn affects attitudes about the welfare state. It is argued that natives' reaction to immigrants will be more muted among "high trusters" than "low trusters." But before going any farther it is important to examine the peculiar term *truster* in more detail. Depending on the usage of this term, very different connotations and logics ensue.

Is Trust a State or a Trait?

The theory laid out earlier requires further clarification, particularly as to the role of trust, as formerly rather homogeneous societies are becoming more diverse. There are two ways of thinking about the interactions among diversity, trust, and the public's willingness to continue funding the welfare state. One can think of trust as either a "state" or a "trait." Much of the trust literature uses the term *trusters* without making the conceptual implications transparent. In social psychology *trait* is defined as "enduring features of the way individuals function" as opposed to *states,* which refers to "momentary states of structures and processes at a certain moment in time under certain external conditions" (Magnusson 1990, 206). The implications of this difference for the understanding of trust as a result of increasing diversity are significant.

For instance, Soroka, Banting, and Johnston argue that for the welfare state to function "citizens must trust each other to both take part as contributors and not take advantage as beneficiaries. Trust is aided by identification with fellow citizens. Identification with fellow citizens is easiest in ethnically and culturally homogeneous societies" (2002, 2). In this account, it is not diversity per se that leads to reduced welfare support; rather, trust is reduced as a result of diversity, and this reduced trust may be responsible for lower welfare state support. Trust is enhanced when individuals share certain basic tracers such as race, ethnicity, religion, or language. In other words, understanding trust to be a state means being able to treat it as a dependent variable that is a function of the degree of diversity in society. Putnam (2002, 415) seems to be taking that position when he states that "the problem of inequality in access to social capital is greatly exacerbated in socially heterogeneous communities. . . . It appears that ethnic heterogeneity and high rates of immigration are part of the story. If so, then the rapid increase in ethnic immigration in most OECD countries in recent decades may pose important challenges to both the quantity and the social distribution of social capital in all our countries." Alesina and LaFerrara (2002, 207) also understand trust to be a state when they conclude that "individuals who express stronger feelings against racial integration trust relatively less the more racially heterogeneous the community is."

Conversely, one can think of trust as a trait, that is, it is enduring and unchanging. If that is the case, then diversity, by definition, should not be able to affect trust and trust can be taken as an independent variable explaining the public's willingness to continue funding the welfare state. If trust is understood to be a trait, then more "trusting" societies should perceive immigrants less as others and be more willing to embrace them and treat them as part of the community. In other words, for any given reason, some societies are either more or less trusting and increasing diversity does not significantly affect trust levels in these societies. This means that in "high-trusting" societies we should expect to see less widespread prejudice against and hatred of foreigners while "low-trusting" societies should suffer more from nativist resentment as a result of increasing diversity. Thus, treating trust as a trait has very different hypothesized effects on welfare support compared to treating trust as a state. If trust is a state, then the causal story goes as follows: diversity affects trust, which affects nativist resentment, which in turn affects the public's willingness to support the welfare state. If trust is a trait, diversity will *not* affect trust (while they differ from country to country, levels of trust are nation specific and may be driven by differences in institutions, experiences of nation building, differences in policies, or many other reasons). This allows trust to be taken as an independent variable, as a bulwark that should systematically mediate and blunt the effects of diversity rather than being influenced by it.

Economists have unearthed most intriguing evidence indicating that more trusting societies have higher economic growth rates (Knack and Keefer 1997; Zak and Knack 2001). Slemrod and Katuscak (2002) find that trusting attitudes positively affect income. Schwabish, Smeeding, and Osberg (2003) find that trusting societies are more willing to share economic resources with others not so fortunate. Two political scientists, Scholz and Lubell (1998) find that trust significantly increases the likelihood of tax compliance. All of these cases use trust as a trait of course.

The crucial question is which perspective of trust is the "correct" one. Three arguments should make the case for trust as a trait: first, the stability of trust levels over time despite immigration; second, evidence that trust is "learned not earned," in the words of Eric Uslaner (Uslaner 2002, 77), suggesting that once trust has jelled into values it remains rather stable; third, the literature on trust and social capital, at least some of which seems to suggest that it takes a long time for trust to develop.

To determine whether trust is a trait or a state it is necessary to empirically examine levels of trust over time to see how stable or unstable such levels are. Figure 4.1 demonstrates the dynamics of trust in selected countries. It was decided not to use the International Social Survey Program 1998 data point on the trust question since this point was consistently higher across all countries than the WVS or European Social Survey results, perhaps as a result of a different sampling method or other unknown reasons.

Figure 4.1 indicates relative stability over time in the levels of trust, particularly since the 1996 WVS data point. The main differences are between sets of countries rather than dramatic changes over time within countries, although there are undeniable fluctuations across time within countries. Sweden, Norway, and the Netherlands show relatively stable and high levels of trust, and Germany, the United Kingdom, and France also show relatively stable and lower levels of trust, with the United States taking up a middle position. The Scandinavian countries are particularly interesting since they show very high trust levels while at the same time becoming more diverse as a result of immigration with no deterioration in their trust levels. Similarly, Germany even shows a slight increase in trust in 1996 in the wake of massive immigration to this country. The Netherlands is also a very intriguing case in which trust in fact increased despite heavy immigration. Thus, if immigration-driven diversity increases and trust stays relatively constant, diversity cannot be the cause of trust. These findings are similar to Uslaner's (2002, 252), who discovered that "trust varies over time, but is rather stable across individuals and particularly across countries."

Second, the eminent psychologist Erik Erikson argues that trust originates in the early infantile experience, particularly in the mother-child relationship (Erikson 1963). Uslaner also argues that generalized trust,

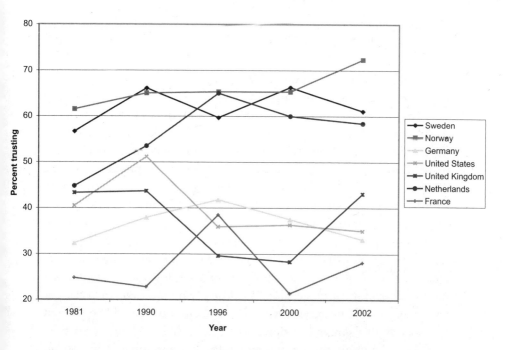

Fig. 4.1. Trust over time for selected countries. (Data from World Values Survey, various waves; European Social Survey 2002; and, for the United States, General Social Survey 2002. Question item: "Generally speaking, do you think that most people can be trusted or that you can't be too careful?")

that is, trust in people in general, not specific trust in your car mechanic, for instance, is learned very early in life. "Generalized trust stems from an optimistic view of the world that we initially learn from our parents. . . . Generalized trust reflects our outlook on the world and is stable over time" (Uslaner 2002, 77). Thus, the stability of generalized trust is found in the process of socialization. In other words, nativist resentment is endogenous to the trust levels in a given society. As immigrants arrive in different countries they impinge on their host societies with a given level of trust. The respondents in our surveys reflect the attitudes of native majorities that have spent nearly all their lives in their countries. If it is true that trust finds its origins in the optimistic outlook of an individual and the early socialization process in which trust became instilled, it would be hard to imagine that trust would be suddenly undermined with the arrival of newcomers in the host society. Uslaner (2002, 241) examines this issue specifically and comes to the conclusion that "overall, ethnic diversity does not shape trust."

Third, much of the literature avows that trust takes a long time to develop and once in existence has its own material force. Probably the best-known work of this kind is Robert Putnam's *Making Democracy Work* (1993). In it, he argues that trust originated in medieval northern Italy amid the bustling trading towns with relative horizontal equality while southern Italy was characterized by more traditional, hierarchical, feudal structures. According to Putnam, it took northern Italy almost a thousand years to develop the trust levels necessary to "make democracy work." Thus, the capacity to trust among citizens is the product of events that unfolded over the *longue durée,* giving credence to the argument that trust has relatively low volatility. Fukuyama (1995) and Banfield (1958) have similarly argued that a society's trust is a function of its historical experience.

For these reasons it is more persuasive to believe that nativist resentment is affected by the given trust level in a society. If a society consists mostly of primordial trusters, that is, people who are alike, then nativist resentment should be accentuated. The same emotions should be blunted in a society that consists of universal trusters, that is, people who trust strangers. As a result, this chapter argues for a dispositional view of trust, that is, the belief that trust is a trait rather than a state. Consequently, this chapter does not intend to search for the roots of different levels of trust; rather it takes levels of trust and examines their impact on nativist resentment and the public's willingness to continue funding the welfare state.

The "General Torrent of Social Life"— Making Sense of Trust

Matters of social capital and trust exploded onto the field of political science following the appearance of Robert Putnam's *Making Democracy Work* (1993), which explained the varying functioning of regional governments in Italy in terms of the presence or absence of "social capital." While Putnam's book certainly was not the first one to raise social capital as an issue, it popularized the concept at a time when comparative politics, and political science in general, became highly influenced by the rational choice approach. Social capital and trust are intuitively understood, although there are serious disagreements as to what these concepts mean. In putting a "human face" on the explanation of many social phenomena that researchers try to understand, it resonates with many of them. Nevertheless, due to disagreements over definitions, competing claims about causal arrows, proliferating types of trust, and varying interpretations of the meaning of data, the debate about social capital and trust has grown into such a thicket that it is all too easy to lose one's way, and even if one manages to stay the course one is bound to emerge scratched up, bloody, and mad.

There is, however, no disagreement that much of the concern about declining community originated with the wrenching processes of industrialization and modernization in the eighteenth and nineteenth centuries. It is no accident that many of the pioneers of social capital, such as Alexis de Tocqueville (1994), Ferdinand Tönnies (1988), Émile Durkheim (1893), and Max Weber (1978), viewed this "great transformation" as the pivotal point at which morality and community became subordinated to the efficiency of capitalist production, the atomizing tendency of liberalism, and the rationality of administration.

Durkheim attempted to countersteer these atomizing tendencies, believing that corporatist groups would create new meaning in an increasingly detached and unencumbered society. In *The Division of Labor in Society* (1893), he contended that:

> The absence of all corporative institutions creates . . . a void whose importance is difficult to exaggerate. . . . A nation can be maintained only if, between the state and the individual, there is intercalated a whole series of secondary groups near enough to the individuals to attract them strongly in their sphere of action and drag them, in this way, into the general torrent of social life. (28)

According to Robert Putnam (1993, 167), "Social capital . . . refers to features of social organizations such as trust, norms and networks, that can improve the efficiency of society by facilitating coordinated actions." For Putnam, trust arises from two related sources: "norms of reciprocity and networks of civic engagement" (171). Putnam considers the basis of collaboration in the civic community to be "not legal, but moral. The sanction for violating it is not penal but exclusion from the network of solidarity and cooperation. Norms and expectations play an important role" (183). In order to support this point, Putnam enlists the help of Michael Thompson, Richard Ellis, and Aaron Wildavsky (1990, 2), who in their book on political culture made the following claim: "Ways of life are made viable by classifying certain behaviors as worthy of praise and

others as undesirable, or even unthinkable." Putnam, immediately following this quote, states: "A conception of one's role and obligations as
a citizen, coupled with a commitment to political equality, is the cultural
cement of the civic community" (1993, 183).

What becomes clear from these definitions is that throughout his
book Putnam is speaking about interpersonal relationships in a relatively
homogeneous society. Few political scientists have systematically examined the issue of social capital and trust in diverse societies. Jack Knight's
(2001) contribution in the second of the Russell Sage Foundation's
"trust books" (2001) is the exception that proves the rule, together with
the work of John F. Helliwell, Stuart Soroka, and Richard Johnston
(2005). Collaboration in a civic society based on moral principles requires basic agreement on what these moral principles are—a difficult
task for newcomers. Particularly Thompson's et al.'s advice is not that
useful for immigrants since their "ways of life" are quite different from
those of the natives. It is certainly more difficult for a foreigner to de-
code local social norms in order to engage in "behaviors that are worthy
of praise" than it is for a native. Similarly, Putnam uses the qualifier *citizen*
when he speaks about one's role and obligations in the civic community.
Applied to the 7.3 million legal foreigners (year 2001) who are not German citizens, Putnam's dictum would leave them out in the cold without
a "conception of one's role in society" since they are not members of
that society.

As immigrants arrive, they encounter natives with a given "amount"
and "type" of social capital or trust. Depending on what type of trust or
social capital is present, the natives' reactions to the newcomers should
be different. A particularly useful typology is Putnam's distinction between "bonding" and "bridging" social capital. A society based on bonding social capital connects people on the basis of race, ethnicity, age, gender, social class, religion, and so on while bridging social capital refers to
"social networks that bring together people who are unlike one another" (Putnam 2002, 11). While the bonding type of social capital is
important for one's identity, one must not overly romanticize this concept for it can easily be used to mobilize people for rather sinister ends.
German skinheads, the Italian Mafia, and the Ku Klux Klan (KKK) in
the southern United States possess much bonding social capital but little
bridging social capital or, as Putnam put it so persuasively, "[B]onding
without bridging equals Bosnia" (12).

This distinction between bonding and bridging social capital is particularly relevant for this project for two reasons. First, the bonding aspect is closely connected to what was termed "primordial sentiments" in chapter 2, where it was found that the more networks are based on primordial sentiments the more difficult it is to cooperate with those who are unlike us. On the other hand, the more networks are based on bridging social capital the more easily immigrants should be accepted as part of the civic community. More specifically, the more social capital of the bonding type there is the more adverse natives' reactions to immigrants should be, while the more social capital of the bridging type there is the less adverse natives' reactions to immigrants should be.

Both types of social capital, bonding and bridging, are based on networks. In fact, in his 2002 book Putnam seems to have removed trust from his original triad of "trust, norms and networks" (the cornerstones of his 1993 definition) and placed more emphasis on "networks and norms of reciprocity." In his 2002 definition, he describes "social networks and the associated norms of reciprocity as social capital" (8). In fact, the term *trust* appears only twice in his introduction to the 2002 edited volume, once in connection with the KKK and once in connection with the ways in which the state might be able to instill trust.

This is highlighted because trust may not be thought of as arising out of networks but may in fact be a general value orientation that develops independent of the existence of networks. In Putnam's account, trust emanates from joining the civic community with its multitude of fraternal societies, gun clubs, soccer clubs, bowling leagues, birdwatcher groups, choirs, and other such organizations. Interaction in these in-groups instills trust, which spills over into the wider society and helps cement a civic community. The sequence runs from an individual joining an in-group; as a result of like-minded interaction developing trust; and eventually, through a spillover mechanism, developing the capacity to trust those not in the in-group (i.e., generalized trusting).

This spillover from in-group trust to generalized trust is little understood. Dietlind Stolle (2001, 205) emphasizes the importance of generalized trust and asks: how can "the trust that we obviously build for people we know well . . . be extended and used for the development of generalized trust, or trust for people we do not know well?" This is precisely the central issue in our question since natives can be expected to know very little about immigrant societies and their cultures and vice versa. Stolle reaches an unsettling verdict: apparently, joining an association only has positive effects for the members, with very little, if any, generalized trust created in the wider society, a finding Stolle desribed as "disturbing . . . for social capital theory" (233).

Absent primordial bonds or shared associational interests, on what basis can trust be built? Is it possible that it can be built purely on the basis of pursuing one's individual interests in terms of rational market exchanges? One of the best-known accounts of such an approach is Russell Hardin's (2001, 3) concept of trust as "encapsulated interest." He defines it as follows.

> In modal trust relationships, the trusted party has an incentive to be trustworthy, an incentive grounded in the value of maintaining the relationship into the future. That is, my trust of you is encapsulated in your interest in fulfilling the trust. . . . Although one might object superficially to bringing interests into trusting relationships, such as those between close relatives or friends, they are clearly there much, and perhaps, most of the time. Indeed, the whole point for many other trusting relationships is likely to be interests.

In this account, trust is not a matter of involvement in social networks. Trust, so the argument goes, evolves out of a mutual calculus of parties intended to maximize their interests. Interaction is prompted by expectations that the other will engage in predictable exchanges that benefit both parties. Trust in this case is similar to the "leap of faith" in the classic prisoner's dilemma game, in which one player decides to "cooperate" even though there is a chance that he or she will reap the "sucker's payoff" if the other player defects. Although that leap of faith can be explained in many different ways, such as the creation of institutions, the rule of law, tradition, religion, or culture, in Hardin's account it is explained purely on the basis of "interests," with moral principles playing no significant role.

It was precisely this utilitarian view against which Émile Durkheim reacted in his *Division of Labor* (1893). According to him, a society would disintegrate within a short period of time if individuals pursued only their narrow self-interest. He writes: "There is nothing less constant than interest. Today it unites me to you; tomorrow it will make me your enemy" (quoted in Giddens 1971, 77). Wilhelm Roepke (1960, 91) echoes Durkheim: "The market economy is not everything. It must find its place in a higher order of things which is not ruled by supply and demand, free prices and competition. . . . Man can wholly fulfill his nature only by freely becoming part of a community and having a sense of solidarity with it. Otherwise, he leads a miserable existence, and he knows it." Community on the basis of interest alone seems to be skating on thin ice.

Hardin's utilitarian view is not shared by everybody. Some scholars allow various levels of morality to flow into the definition of *trust,* thus establishing a conception of communal trust (Blackburn 1998; Tyler 1998; Pettit 1998; Peel 1998; Braithwaite 1998; Messick and Kramer 2001) in juxtaposition to the utilitarian view of trust (Hardin 1998; Levi 1998; Bianco 1998; Whiting 1998; Jennings 1998).

Recently, yet another view of trust has emerged, one that deviates drastically from both Hardin's and Putnam's views. This view is particularly relevant for this project and is connected to the work of Eric M. Uslaner, who argues for a dispositional view of trust. According to him, it is not really surprising that we trust people we know well because they are in the same club as we are or that we trust (or do not trust) people with whom we had past exchanges. In Uslaner's (2002, xi) poignant words, "[T]here really is nothing remarkable about trusting my wife." For Uslaner, the moral foundation of trust means "that we must do more than simply cooperate with others we know are trustworthy. We must have positive views of strangers, of people who are different from ourselves and *presume that they are trustworthy.* . . . Trust solves bigger problems than getting people to hang out with people like themselves. It connects us to people with whom *we don't hang out*" (2, 3; italics in original).

Further criticism against the Hardinian notion of encapsulated trust based on interest and utilitarian calculus is leveled by Jonathan Mercer. He declares that, "Rationalists drain the psychology from trust by turning it into a consequence of incentives." He continues, "Emphasizing incentives as the basis for trust eliminates both the need for trust and the opportunity to trust. If trust depends on external evidence, transparency, iteration, or incentives, then trust adds nothing to the explanation" (Mercer 2005, 95). Mercer emphasizes the impact of emotion as the central ingredient for trust and claims that "trust without emotion implies an expectation of trustworthiness based on incentives; trust adds nothing if incentives explain cooperation" (99). If it is a matter of information, signaling, reputation, and interests that determines whether people trust or not, trust itself drops out of the equation as an explanatory factor.

Piotr Sztompka (1999) argues similarly. He identifies three dimenions of trust, the first of which is trust as a relationship between two parties engaged in an exchange in which each partner is driven by rational calculations very similar to the ones Russell Hardin describes. However, Sztompka's second dimension of trust, which he calls "trust as a personality disposition" is a "quality of the truster, rather than of the relationship between a truster and a trustee," and is the product of "successful socialization in the intimate, caring climate of healthy families. This propensity to trust may later be enhanced by happy life experiences with well-placed, mutual, reciprocated trust" (Sztompka 1999, 65). This second dimension of trust, according to Sztompka, is "independent of any rational considerations." He goes on to claim that "neglect of such psychological biases toward or against trust reduces the ability to rational choice theory . . . to deal adequately with trust" (66).

This dispositional view of trust represents a marked departure from the basic assumption, shared by Putnam, Hardin, and many others, that trust can only develop when people know each other. Uslaner's moral conception of trust is dispositional; people generally have it or they do not. The question item that is employed by many surveys tapping trust is worded: "Generally speaking, do you think that most people can be trusted or that you can't be too careful?" Based on this question, how does trust vary across OECD countries? Figure 4.2 displays average trust in 16 OECD nations using the standard trust survey question as measured in the four waves of the World Values Survey (WVS). Each data point represents the average of four WVS observations.[1] It places the Scandinavian countries (Norway, Sweden, Denmark, and Finland) at the top and the United Kingdom, Austria, Belgium, and France at the bottom of the trust scale. The degree to which trust unfolds in different countries *over time* was indicated in figure 4.1.

Uslaner's conception of trust is particularly useful for this project since it examines the impact of immigration on relatively homogeneous societies. Beginning in the late 1950s, when the very first Italian guest workers arrived in Central Europe, followed by Turkish and Yugoslavian guest workers in the 1960s, Europeans have come face to face with people from different cultures, religions, and ethnic backgrounds. This book argues that initial trust levels are decisive in the way foreigners experience discrimination.

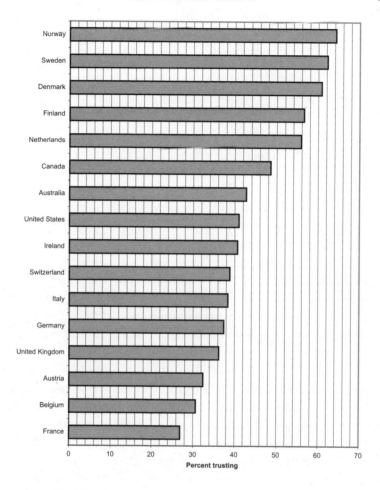

Fig. 4.2.   Average trust in 16 OECD nations (1981–2001)

If some societies have more generalized trust (i.e., a basic predisposition to trust strangers), then this should manifest itself in less xenophobia and nativist resentment. Moreover, more generalized trust should also lead to more support for the welfare state since trust is required for the welfare state to function (Soroka, Banting, and Johnston 2002; Uslaner 2002). Also, generalized trusters should be more law-abiding than particularized trusters, particularly when it comes to two central elements of individual behavior as far as the welfare state is concerned: not abusing the welfare state by claiming benefits for which they are not eligible and cheating on taxes. These two behaviors represent the precise nexus between trust and the welfare state. In the next section, we will put these claims to the test.

TRUSTING STRANGERS AND ITS CONSEQUENCES: INDIVIDUAL-LEVEL EVIDENCE

Uslaner (2002, 26, 27) explains the difference between generalized and particularized trust as follows.

> *The central idea distinguishing generalized from particularized trust is how inclusive your moral community is.* When you only trust your own kind, your moral community is rather restricted. And you are likely to extend trust only to people you think you know. So particularized trusters rely heavily upon their experiences . . . or stereotypes that they believe to be founded in knowledge in deciding whom to trust. But they are not agnostic about strangers. Particularized trusters assume that people unlike themselves are *not* part of their moral community, and thus may have values that are hostile to their own. (italics in original)

People who are particularized trusters share many of the primordial sentiments highlighted in chapter 1. They should react adversely to the presence of newcomers, particularly if these newcomers are "visible minorities." Particularized trusters are "bonders" (Putnam 2002), have "thick" trust (Williams 1988), or have what Mark S. Granovetter (1973) termed "strong ties." In other words, they have a very strong sense of in-group versus out-group. They are ready and willing to cooperate with others, as long as the others are like themselves. Kinship relations and ethnic, religious, racial and national identifications are crucial for particularized trusters, who tend to prefer, as David Goodhart put it, "their own kind." As a consequence, particularized trusters are expected to display a higher degree of nativist resentment than generalized trusters, who are willing to trust strangers.

Uslaner (2002, 27) argues that generalized trust is "well captured" in the standard survey question "Generally speaking, do you think that most people can be trusted or that you can't be too careful in dealing with people?" The first part of this question ("do you think that most people can be trusted") may capture the concept of generalized trust. It is not obvious, however, that "you can't be too careful" should mean particularized trust.

With the recent availability of the fourth wave of the WVS, it is possible to construct an improved measure of these two types of trust. The fourth wave of the World Values Survey (2000–2001) asked a series of intriguing questions about the respondent's "concern about the living conditions" of different groups. If it is true that the width of the moral community captures the range from generalized to particularized trust, the following item, asked in the WVS (fourth wave) will allow us to better discriminate between generalized and particularized trust. The following question was asked.

"To what extent do you feel concerned about the living conditions of the following groups?"

a. Your immediate family
b. People in your neighborhood
c. The people of the region you live in
d. Your fellow countrymen
e. Europeans
f. Humankind

While this question certainly deals with "concern about the living conditions" of different groups, it taps the range of the width of the moral community of each respondent. The absence or presence of such concerns captures the concepts of primordial and universal trust quite well. The two measures of trust, primordial and universal, are not necessarily opposites. They highlight different dimensions of trust, those being able to trust only people who are like themselves (primordial trusters) and those with the ability to trust strangers (universal trusters). These two groups certainly differ in terms of how far they extend trust, yet they still trust. Primordial trusters do trust, even though their range of trust is extended only to people who are like themselves.

After conducting a principal component factor analysis, factors that are termed "primordial trust" and "universal trust" stood out very clearly (see table 4.1).

In the table, the three highest rotated factor loadings of the first factor are the items in bold type and the two highest rotated factor loadings of the second factor are the underlined items. The item "people of the region you live in" loaded high on both constructs and was thus removed from the overall analysis. Cronbach's alpha measures how well a set of items measures a single unidimensional latent construct. Cronbach's alpha, which measures the scale reliability coefficient, is .8324 for the first factor and .71 for the second factor, indicating that there is strong internal coherence across these three and two items, respectively. Although Cronbach's alpha of .71 for primordial trust is barely inside the acceptable range, it is actually quite high given that this construct consists of only two items. Generally, Cronbach's alpha increases with the number of items analyzed. Overall, this principal component factor analysis indicates that there are two clearly identifiable groups reflecting two separate latent constructs.

Across 11 countries (Austria, Belgium, Denmark, Finland, France, Germany, Ireland, Italy, the Netherlands, Sweden, and the United Kingdom in 1999–2001 when the fieldwork for the fourth wave of the WVS was done) and for almost 15,000 survey participants, table 4.1 shows that there are indeed two kinds of respondents: those that are concerned about their immediate environment (family and neighborhood) and those that are concerned about a wider community (the nation, Europeans, and humankind). Since the first type of trusters connect with people who are like themselves, we call them "primordial trusters." As the second type demonstrated a capacity to trust people in the wider community, including humankind, we call them "universal trusters." The main difference between our typology and the standard trust question is that I have given a more precise meaning to "primordial" and "universal" trust than is contained in the standard trust question. These two forms

TABLE 4.1.   Principal Component Factor Analysis of Types of Trust (varimax rotation)

Item	Universal Trust	Primordial Trust
Humankind	.87961	−.03988
Europeans	.86620	.23619
Fellow countrymen	.77819	.41825
Immediate family	.03054	.90199
People in neighborhood	.32679	.79897
Cronbach's alpha	.8324	.71
N	14,798	14,920

Source: World Values Survey 2000.

Note: Eleven countries were included: Austria, Belgium, Denmark, Finland, France, Germany, Ireland, Italy, the Netherlands, Sweden, and the United Kingdom.

Question item: "To what extent do you feel concerned about the living conditions of the following groups?"

of trust, primordial and universal, are distinctly different from trust derived from the standard trust question.[2]

The opposite of universal trust is anomie, not primordial trust. As already mentioned, people with primordial trust do trust. But their radius of trust is much smaller than the radius of universal trusters. There are people, however, who do not seem to trust anybody. Fortunately, there is an item in the fourth wave of the WVS that captures what might be called "anomic" attitudes: The question is: "Can you tell me your opinion on the following statement: People should stick to their own affairs." Respondents had five choices in answering this question: strongly agree, agree, neither agree nor disagree, disagree, and strongly disagree. Those who answered this question in the affirmative are not necessarily "nontrusters"; they may simply think that people should not be nosy or meddle in the affairs of others or they may even take this to mean the inviolability of one's person. Interestingly, however, it turns out that there is a darker dimension to those who answered this question in the affirmative. People who overwhelmingly think that people "should stick to their own affairs" show highly antisocial behavior, high nativist resentment, and very low levels of trust. Logit analysis shows that anomie has a very strong negative effect on the standardized trust question (odds ratio .74, standard error .01, z-test -20.91).

As a result, this sizable group of respondents (44 percent) are termed "anomic." This anomic group does not see itself as part of any collectivity. Its members appear to be at sea, atomized, detached, and unencumbered by the rituals and obligations of communal life. Their concerns for others stop on the fringes of their own egos. In the words of Émile Durkheim: "Man is the more vulnerable to self-destruction the more he is detached from any collectivity, that is to say, the more he lives as an egoist" (1961, 113, from: Moral Education). Thus, this item not only captures a dimension of "privacy" but also a much darker dimension, revealing the absence of community and the inability to trust anybody.

What Is Universal Trust?

Before empirically examining the question of the impact of different forms of trust on various attitudes, the important issue of validity needs to be tackled. Can we really say that the measure "concern with the living conditions of fellow countrymen, Europeans, and humankind" captures the concept of universal trust or is it in fact closer to the concept of community? These questions of validity often arise when principal component analyses or other, similar, data-reducing operations are applied and when the researcher creates a new variable by christening a bundle of latent concepts that share certain commonalities. The purpose of this section is to compare the concept of universal trust, as operationalized earlier, with the concept of community.

A brief excursion into the lives of the residents of the Italian village of Montegrano circa 1955, as told by Edward Banfield (1958) in his classic *The Moral Basis of a Backward Society,* a pioneering study of trust or the lack thereof, will help make the case that universal trust and community are at least close cousins.

The villagers of Montegrano were only concerned about the living conditions within the very narrow orbit of their own families. For the Montegranesi, life was a daily battle against abject poverty without the time for any concern for the living conditions of others in equally dire straits. The people in this impoverished village, rather than helping others, who as a result might "get ahead," preferred not to help others so that they would all be at least equally worse off. Despite the widespread poverty under which almost all the Montegranesi suffered, "public-spiritedness" was absent and some villagers "find the idea of public-spiritedness unintelligible" (Banfield 1958, 18). Banfield reports the encounter of an interviewer who explained to a young teacher that a public-spirited person is one who acts for the welfare of the whole community rather than himself alone. The teacher said, "No one in town is animated by a desire to do good for all of the population. Even if sometimes there is someone apparently animated by this desire, in reality he is interested in his own welfare and he does his own business." Another teacher indicated that not only was public-spiritedness lacking but many people wanted to prevent others from getting ahead. "Truly, I have found no one who interests himself in the general welfare. On the contrary, I know there is a tremendous envy of either money or intelligence" (18, 19).

Lack of trust and lack of concern for others were intimately intertwined in Montegrano. "Successful self government depends, among other things, upon the possibility of concerting the behavior of large numbers of people in matters of public *concern*" (7; emphasis added). Lack of concern for the living conditions of others and lack of trust went hand in hand in Montegrano. And because the Montegranesi did not trust others they were not concerned with the living conditions of others, which of course did not engender in others any concern about their living conditions.

It is here that the concepts of trust, community, and solidarity really begin to merge. The item used to construct the universal trust measure asked about the respondent's "concern about the living conditions" of various groups of people at varying distances from the respondent. If people show concern about the living conditions of others, this may easily be termed "solidarity." Similar ideas are echoed in the Responsive Communitarian Platform, a text created by academicians and social thinkers in 1990 which proclaims that members of a community not only have a duty to provide for themselves but also to provide "for the material and moral well-being of others. This . . . means the constant self awareness that no one of us is an island unaffected by the fate of others." Robert Bellah notes that, "Solidarity points to the fact that we become who we are through our relationships—that reciprocity, loyalty, and shared commitment to the good are defining features of a fully human life" (Bellah 1998, 18).

If we are interested in the "fate of others" and if it is the relationships that we have with others, it becomes very difficult to clearly separate universal trust from community. After all, it is hardly conceivable that a community could exist without trust, that trust could develop without community, and that for both "concern about the living conditions" of others is a fundamental precondition, as Bellah so powerfully states. Empirical analyses also conclude that social trust is a feature of the most basic level of community (Newton 1999). Eric Uslaner specifically connects an understanding of "social solidarity," which is very close to the concept of "concern with the living conditions" of others employed, by explicitly stating that, "Trust, after all, reflects a sense of social solidarity" (2003, 3).

Solidarity, which in the wake of the French Revolution was known as fraternity, became a thoroughly modern concept as it developed in tandem with the welfare state. Universal trusters are people who, as a result of socialization, have "overstepped the narrow barriers of face to face communities, and command moral duties vis-à-vis aliens, in the last instance, vis-à-vis all human beings" (Preuss 1999, 283). It is a sort of unconditional solidarity, that is, not a solidarity that arises out of a realization that only with the assistance of others can a particular goal be achieved. It is an "altruistic" solidarity, defined as "solidarity that is

understood as a commitment towards the disadvantaged which motivates individuals to render altruistic assistance" (Voland 1999, 158), and
thus it is directly opposed to the concept of "cooperative solidarity"
understood to be a means to an end and, according to Eckart Voland,
representing the "direct pursuit of selfish interests" (158).

Trust means you have to care about others; if you don't, you think the
whole world is against you, which is precisely what Banfield described
in his "amoral familism"—a lack of concern for anybody but your own
family. "The world being what it is, all those who stand outside of the
small circle of the family are at least potential competitors and therefore
also potential enemies" (Banfield 1958, 116).

The measure of primordial trust captures the degree to which people
are concerned with their own in-group and less, or not at all, with their
out-group. If you don't care or are not concerned about the living
conditions of the members of your out-group, you most likely do not
trust them. On the other hand, there are people who are universal
trusters, that is, people who are concerned about the living conditions of
groups that are unlike them; it is likely that they trust them more than if
they did not show any concern.

Claus Offe and Susanne Fuchs (2002, 190) describe "attention,"
which is, in their view, one of three central ingredients of social capital.
It is very closely related to the concept of universal trust, defined as
concern for the living conditions of others, and it is worth quoting at
length.

> Attention refers to a set of thoughts and opinions concerning social
> and political life. When we monitor what is going on or how others
> are doing, or are attentive to collective conditions, we display atten-
> tion of this kind. Attention . . . focuses upon the material well-being,
> moral conduct, personal development, esthetic qualities, and other
> features of the conditions of life of some collectivity . . . who are
> considered fellow citizens and are perceived as belonging to a
> shared political community. (190)

While "attention" is certainly a close cousin to "concern with the living conditions" of diffuse groups of people, the latter concept is perhaps
an even stronger one, as it seems to go beyond just "monitoring" and
paying attention to what is going on somewhere else. *Concern* suggests a
deeper, personal involvement with distant groups of people, which are

seen nevertheless to share a common humanity. Would it be unusual for people with such an empathic capacity to also extend unconditional trust to strangers? Not at all. After all, a "democratic community . . . applies to groups of any size, and ultimately to the world as a community" (Bellah 1998, 19). It is not difficult to see the similarities between what is called universal trust and the term *cosmopolitanism* as it is used in chapter 2. In fact, one of the central concepts of cosmopolitanism is to be able to treat "distant others" with the same concern as people who are closer to one's own primordial group.

A prosperous existence cannot be achieved on the basis of primordial trust alone, as Banfield so powerfully states. It seems paradoxical, but only if one is willing to go out on a limb, to make oneself vulnerable to exploitation, can one reap the largest fruits. This means trusting people you do not know. Sticking with your family and kin will keep you mired in parochial familiarity with few opportunities. Max Weber made a similar point when he determined the reason why China never experienced the economic growth of the West. According to Weber, in China, "the fetters of the kinship group were never shattered" and it took precisely, "the great achievements of the ethical religions, above all the asceticist sects of Protestantism . . . to shatter the fetters of the kin" (Weber, quoted in Pagden 1988, 139). Victor Nee and Jimy Sanders (2001) report that Asian immigrants coming to the United States and finding jobs either with members of their extended families who are already settled or with employers who are of the same ethnic group tend to be more exploited and have to work harder and for less money than those who arrived with more financial and human capital and found jobs with employers outside their ethnic groups. Those who relied on ethnic social capital did worse than those who relied on human or financial capital. Just like the compelling story told by Banfield, relying on close-knit familial ties limits economic opportunities and leads to a meager existence.

For primordial trusters, trusting one's in-group and being concerned about its living conditions go hand in hand while the opposite, having no or low trust in out-groups and showing low concern for them, also go hand in hand. The range from your immediate family to humankind captures the distinction between primordial and universal trust insofar as the wider the community becomes we should expect to see a decrease in primordial trust and an increase in universal trust. As the groups widen, the less likely it is that somebody will personally know others, that they will become more diverse, and that the moral community will become less and less inclusive. Thus, for primordial trusters trust declines in proportion to their distance from the group for which they express concern about their living conditions. Conversely, among universal trusters we should expect people's trust in others to remain rather inelastic as the community widens.

As opposed to the more rational account of trust understood as a facilitator of exchanges, trust understood as "concern with the living conditions" of others does not imply any returns or favors for displaying concern about others. Universal trust is altruistic in nature. This does not mean gullibility, however. It is a kind of trust that starts out with cooperation as the first move and is capable of adjustment. Unreciprocated trust will reduce cooperation with that party, but it will not, or will only in small increments, shade the view of the universal truster of other people. The reason why universal trusters' experiences with others are rarely frustrated is precisely because they are universal trusters. Trust begets trust; distrust begets distrust. People who trust others will be trusted; people who do not trust others will not be trusted. Trust is a two-way street; it requires trusting (seen from the first-person point of view) and being trusted or seen as trustworthy (seen from the second-person point of view).

Universal trust means a genuine, authentic interest and fraternity with people transcending the boundaries of otherness. Universal trust means forging bonds of equal strength with all of humanity, not just with kith and kin. This fraternity is not limited to the traditional markers of identity and does not ask for anything in return. In other words, universal trust is not conditional on others' performance or behavior. I agree with Adam B. Seligman (1997, 44), who argues that trust "is a form of belief that carries within it something unconditional and irreducible. . . . [T]he unconditionality of trust is first and foremost an unconditionality in respect to alter's response."

Jane Mansbridge (1999) develops a "moralized" version of trust, which she calls "altruistic trust," that is also very closely related to our concept of universal trust. People who show "concern with the living conditions of your fellow countrymen, Europeans, and humankind" are likely to also trust these strangers, to "give them the benefit of the doubt." "I will call trust 'altruistic', explains Mansbridge, "when it results from empathy or from a principle intended to benefit others, or uphold an ideal that usually benefits others" (1999, 291). It does not require an incredible stretch of the imagination to argue that concern for the living conditions of strangers is similar to empathy and closely connected to solidarity, which in turn is based on trust.

FORMS OF TRUST AND THEIR EFFECT ON NATIVIST RESENTMENT

As was explained earlier, primordial trusters are expected to show a higher degree of nativist resentment than universal trusters and "anomic" respondents to display the highest degree of nativist resentment. It is now time to examine the effects of different forms of trust, primordial and universal, and anomie on nativist resentment.[3] "Nativist resentment," a dichotomous variable, is the same latent construct as was developed earlier. The wording for the variable "concern for immigrants" is: "To what extent do you feel concerned about the living conditions of immigrants in your country?" The answer options on a fivefold scale are: 1 = very much to 5 = none at all.

Table 4.2 demonstrates some remarkable results. One of the central predictors of nativist resentment are those who agree that it is "better to stick to themselves," an attitude termed anomie. Primordial trust does not show any significant effect on nativist resentment, although it is very close to being significant (if a one-tailed test were applied, it would be significant at the .1 level, indicating that people with primordial trust show higher nativist resentment). However, when it comes to "concern for immigrants" primordial trusters do show significant concern. Most interesting is the effect of universal trust on nativist resentment, as well as concern for immigrants: in both models, universal trusters show significantly less nativist resentment and high concern for immigrants.

Again, older people and those who place themselves on the right end of the political scale show significantly higher levels of nativist resentment. In terms of gender, a clear pattern is occurring: females show significantly weaker anti–immigrant attitudes.

The more postmaterial respondents are the less they display xenophobic attitudes, a finding that is consistent with Inglehart's (1997) results. Somewhat disturbing is the finding that the less educated people are, and the less interested they are in politics, the stronger their xenophobic attitudes in both models. However, this is consistent with the findings in chapter 3, which established a very similar profile for xenophobes. Finally, in the "concern for immigrants" model, people in whose life God is very important show higher concern for the living conditions of immigrants. The R^2 of .27 in the second model is remarkable given that the number of observations is almost 8,000, indicating a relatively good fit for the model.

Table 4.2 shows that not all forms of trust are created equal. There are clearly differences in the way people's different forms of trust inform their attitudes about foreigners. Thus, the conceptual differences in trust laid out earlier manifest themselves also in empirical differences. Table 4.3 examines additional instances of how the different forms of trust dampen xenophobic attitudes.

The results in table 4.3 demonstrate very clearly the different effects of anomie, primordial, and universal trust. Across all three models there are statistically significant differences between the two types of trust and

TABLE 4.2. Forms of Trust and Their Effects on Nativist Resentment (logit estimation) and Concern for Immigrants (multiple regression)

	Nativist Resentment	Concern for Immigrants
Anomie	1.21 (.025)★★★	.046 (.016)★★
Primordial trust	1.1 (.07)	−.09 (.024)★★★
Universal trust	.82 (.041)★★★	−.43 (.024)★★★
Age	1.01 (.003)★★★	.0015 (.0009)
Education	.88 (.013)★★★	−.038 (.008)★★★
Income	.88 (.013)	−.037 (.008)
Female	.69 (.055)★★★	−.057 (.036)
Self-placement on left/right scale	1.17 (.013)★★★	.065 (.009)★★★
Postmaterialism (4-item scale)	.73 (.07)★★★	−.12 (.033)★★★
Unemployed	1.05 (.04)	−.012 (.014)
Nationalism	.93 (.07)	−.015 (.014)
Interested in politics	1.19 (.053)★★★	.07 (.026)★★
Importance of God in life	.98 (.015)	−.035 (.008)★★★
Constant		4.7 (.17)★★★
N	7,872	7,965
Pseudo R^2	.054	
R^2		.27

Source: World Values Survey 2000.

Note: Robust standard errors. Two-tailed tests. The population weight is included but not shown. The nativist resentment model is a logit model, and the entries are odds ratios (odds ratios > 1 = a positive effect; < 1 = a negative effect).

★★★$p < .001$; ★★$p < .01$; ★$p < .05$.

Question items

The exact wording for the "nationalism" variable is as follows: "How proud are you to be [nationality]?" 1 = not at all proud; 4 = very proud.

For the "interested in politics" variable: "How interested would you say you are in politics?" 1 = very intrested; 4 = not at all interested.

For the "importance of God in life" variable: "How important is God in your life?" 1 = not at all; 10 = very important.

anomie. In the first model, universal trusters significantly disagree that jobs should be given to locals over immigrants while primordial trusters favor discrimination against immigrants. The same observation, in even starker terms, applies to those people who believe that it is better to "stick to one's own affairs." Older people and those on the political Right also favor employers giving jobs to locals rather than immigrants. However, the opposite is true for more highly educated people and post-materialists.

In terms of model 2, universal trusters do not support a ban on immigrants coming to work in the host country while primordial trusters tend to favor a more restrictive policy. This is even more the case for people who are high on anomie. A very similar picture emerges with the control variables. Older people, males, and people who place themselves on the political Right favor a restrictive immigration policy while more highly educated people and postmaterialists favor a more open immigration policy.

Model 3 captures the degree to which natives would allow multiculturalism to flourish. Again, the negative sign for universal trusters indicates that they favor immigrants maintaining their distinct customs and

TABLE 4.3. Forms of Trust and Their Effects on Various Attitudes about Immigrants (logit and ordered logit estimations)

	Model 1	Model 2	Model 3
Universal trust	.22 (.03)***	−.36 (.028)***	−.38 (.031)***
Primordial trust	−.14 (.028)***	.074 (.024)***	.15 (.027)***
Anomie	−.26 (.021)***	.088 (.017)***	.091 (.02)***
Age	−.009 (.001)***	.0023 (.0013)*	.009 (.001)***
Education	.22 (.013)***	−.1 (.01)***	−.08 (.012)***
Income	.01 (.032)	−.025 (.027)	.04 (.031)
Female	−.037 (.049)	−.09 (.04)**	−.08 (.048)*
Political self-placement	−.17 (.013)***	.12 (.01)***	.11 (.012)***
Postmaterialism (4 items)	.54 (.042)***	−.46 (.034)***	−.37 (.04)***
N	8,298	9,193	8,514
Pseudo R^2	.14	.05	.06

Source: World Values Survey 2000.

Model 1: "When jobs are scarce employers should give priority to [respective nation] people over immigrants." The answer options were (a) agree, (b) disagree, (c) neither (the answer option "neither" was recoded as missing data). Model 2: "How about people from other countries coming here to work? Which one of the following do you think the government should do? (a) Let anyone come who wants to (b) Let people come as long as there are jobs available (c) Place strict limits on the amount of foreigners who can come here. (d) Prohibit people coming here from other countries." Model 3: "Which of these statements is nearest to your opinion? (a) immigrants should maintain distinct customs and traditions, (b) take over the customs of the country."

***$p < .001$; **$p < .01$; *$p < .05$.

traditions while primordial trusters would have them absorb the customs of the host country. Those who say it is "better to stick to one's own affairs" also favor immigrants taking on the traditions and customs of the host country. Again, older people, males, and those on the right of the political spectrum favor assimilation while the more educated people and the postmaterialists are more tolerant of immigrants' customs and traditions and would allow them to practice them.

FORMS OF TRUST AND THEIR EFFECTS ON THE WELFARE STATE

Let us now look at the degree to which universal trust affects welfare state support. In the fourth wave of the WVS, there are three questions that tap support for the welfare state. The first question is: "In order to be considered just, what should a society provide? Please tell me for each statement whether it is important or unimportant to you. 1) Society provide: eliminating inequalities. 2) Society provide: basic needs for all." For each of the two statements the respondents' answer choices were in the range from very important = 1 to not at all important = 5. For the third model, "government should provide," the exact wording of the question item is: "Now I'd like you to tell me your views on various issues. How would you place your views on this scale? 1 means you agree completely with the statement on the left, 10 means you completely agree with the statement on the right, and if your views fall somewhere in between, you can choose any number in between: 1 People should take more responsibility to provide for themselves. 10 The government should take more responsibility to ensure that everyone is provided for."

Table 4.4 provides strong evidence that universal trusters favor redistribution. In all three models, respondents high on universal trust indicated that they favor society eliminating inequalities and ensuring that everybody's basic needs are satisfied and that it is governments' responsibility to see that everyone is taken care of. Generally, people who are satisfied with their lives and older people do not favor redistribution with the exception of "eliminating inequalities," which older people support. Females, again, strongly believe that the government should ensure that everybody is provided for. People with higher incomes and education generally do not tend to support the welfare state, while people who are unemployed, understandably, favor it. Very consistently, the farther people place themselves on the political Right the less they support

TABLE 4.4.   Multiple Regressions of the Effects of Universal Trust on Welfare
State Attitudes

	Eliminate Inequalities	Basic Needs for All	Government Should Provide
Universal trust	−.19 (.038)***	−.09 (.018)***	.14 (.045)**
Life satisfaction	.042 (.02)**	−.002 (.011)	−.075 (.031)**
Age	−.0024 (.0009)*	.0025 (.008)***	−.006 (.002)***
Female	−.04 (.4)	−.037 (.026)	.2 (.054)***
Income	.03 (.037)	.001 (.002)	−.19 (.05)***
Education	.074 (.013)***	−.008 (.008)	−.05 (.23)*
Unemployed	−.11 (.07)	−.08 (.045)	.21 (.07)***
Self-placement on left/right scale	.13 (.02)***	.039 (.007)***	−.17 (.036)***
Postmaterialism	.067 (.033)*	−.006 (.027)	−.045 (.081)
Constant	1.6 (.18)***	1.6 (.15)***	6.2 (.4)***
N	9,448	9,470	9,435
R^2	.1	.03	.04

Source: World Values Survey 2000.

Note: Robust standard errors. Two-tailed tests. The equilibrium weights are included but not shown. Ten countries (Austria, Belgium, Denmark, Finland, France, Germany, Ireland, Italy, the Netherlands, Sweden).

***$p < .001$; **$p < .01$; *$p < .05$.

welfare programs. Many of these findings echo the results described in chapter 2 with the additional insight that universal trust matters in terms of people's attitudes toward redistribution.

Why should universal trusters support social welfare programs? People who have concern for others, even people they do not personally know, demonstrate a strong sense of solidarity, as laid out earlier. Universal trusters are endowed with empathy and concern for people unlike themselves. People with such a thoroughly moralized and global concept of universal trust show strong support for the welfare state, while disaffected, unencumbered, atomistic, and detached individuals show a strong aversion to redistribution. Primordial trusters, who have a limited sense of loyalty and trust, are either indifferent to social welfare or tend to withdraw from it.

EXCURSION: CONFIDENCE IN INSTITUTIONS

In addition to universal and primordial trust, there is another form of trust that might be termed political trust or confidence in institutions.[4] At first blush, political trust should be a very different concept than social trust. After all, one represents relations between individuals and institutions while the other represents relations between individuals. Niklas

Luhman (1988, 102) argued for a very strict separation of these two terms: "Trust remains vital in interpersonal relations, but participation in functional systems like the economy or politics is no longer a matter of personal relations. It requires confidence, but not trust." Also Kenneth Newton (1999, 185) reminds his readers that "the term 'trust' must always be qualified by the terms 'social' or 'political'."

This section examines whether confidence in government and primordial and universal trust are related and is mostly geared toward testing whether the three forms of personal trust vary systematically with trust in political institutions. Thus, the point of this section is mostly to test the validity of the empirical separation among primordial trust, universal trust, and anomie. If the theoretical bases of these three concepts are valid, support for different kinds of institutions, domestic or international, should vary systematically with different kinds of trust and anomie.

It seems intuitive that if governments do not "deliver the goods" and "voting the rascals out" does not seem to make any difference, citizens will become more cynical and grumpy.[5] If a state, such as Poland, finally manages to deliver the goods after a gut-wrenching transition from communism to capitalism, trust in government may emerge. "After the drabness and grayness of socialist city landscapes, [and] the misery of the 'queuing society,' . . . shopping, dining out, driving fast cars, foreign trips, plentiful entertainment and leisure are the newly discovered pleasures that raise the general mood of satisfaction and optimism. And this provides a fertile ground for trust" (Sztompka 1999, 187). However, this may just be a very short-lived state of happiness, as demonstrated by some of the even richer European countries or particularly the United States, where material abundance occurs in tandem with a general sense of civic malaise. Similarly, there was initially a tremendous elation when the first waves of East Germans discovered and enjoyed the material abundance of West Berlin and West Germany. However, this materially induced happiness did not last very long, and identity issues of the *Ossis* (citizens of former East Germany) and the desire to be treated equally very quickly crowded out the short-lived material binge.

Kenneth Newton and Pippa Norris (2000, 53) claim that "an erosion of confidence in the major institutions of society . . . is a far more serious threat to democracy than a loss of trust in other citizens." Such an erosion of political trust, or confidence in political institutions, can lead to skepticism, disillusionment, and general discontent with the machinery of government (Dalton 2004).[6] Inglehart (1999, 236) has argued that postmodernization makes governing "more difficult than it used to be: the tendency to idealize authority that characterized societies of scarcity has given way to the more critical and demanding publics of postmodern societies. Authority figures and hierarchical institutions are subjected to more searching scrutiny than they once were." Still, as the self-explanatory title of his contribution suggests, Inglehart maintains that while modern publics are becoming more disrespectful of political authority support for democracy is increasing (Inglehart 1999). In an incisive volume, J. S. Nye, P. D. Zelikow, and D. C. King argue that confidence in government will affect "the willingness of the public to provide such crucial resources as tax dollars, the willingness of bright young people to go into government, and voluntary compliance with laws" (Nye 1997, 4).

Newton and Norris (2000) and Newton (1999) find only a weak connection between these two forms of trust while Dalton (2004) finds a strong connection. While they use the standard "trust" question, this analysis will use the more meaningful distinction between universal and primordial trust. The focus is on institutions of government such as "confidence in Parliament," rather than "government" or "politicians," which captures the agency part of a representative democracy.

Since the focus is on political institutions rather than political actors, there can be no conditional relationship between universal trusters and an institution since presumably the institution itself is inhabited by different political actors, who may favor some constituencies over others, but the institution itself is politically neutral. The legitimacy that derives from such an institution is procedural in nature, not performative. In other words, the legitimacy of "Parliament" does not depend on which party is in power but on a broad consensus that the maintenance of that institution itself is a necessary part of the democratic flow of power. What is important however, particularly in the context of European democracies, is that parliaments are institutions that are relatively distant from the public as opposed to, say, the Congress of the United States, where, as a result of weak parties and an individualized form of representation, policy-making is much more fragmented but also more local.

As a result, primordial trusters should favor more local forms of representation, which are more congruent with the width of their moral community. They ask what is in it for them, what can they get out of it, rather than what, or even why, they should put anything into a distant institution that affects them only tangentially. Universal trusters, on the other hand, should be more willing to give what in German is called a *Vertrauensvorschuss,* or "trust advance," to institutions that operate at a higher level and produce nationwide policies. This is because universal trusters' sense of ethical commitment transcends the boundaries of their own identity and extends beyond their immediate in-group. They see institutions operating at the distant federal level to be designed to represent everybody, not just their own immediate interests.

The causal arrows are notoriously difficult to pin down in such analyses. It is quite plausible that the causal mechanism goes from institutions to the establishment of trust (Rothstein 2004) or that trust leads to the establishment of less corrupt, more trustworthy institutions (Uslaner 2004; Putnam 2000). A third option is that they determine each other in some kind of endogenous relation (della-Porta 2000). A fourth option may be that there is no relationship between the two. One remarkable development is taking place in Sweden, where confidence in institutions is declining while at the same time interpersonal trust remains very high (Katzenstein 2000; Holmberg 1999). This suggests that there is no connection between social trust and confidence in governments. On the other hand, the pathbreaking work of Tom Tyler (1998) points again toward social trust as the cause of confidence in government. It is not possible to address all of these different issues in this book. The point of this excursion is simply to demonstrate whether the different types of trust,

TABLE 4.5.   Ordered Logit Estimates of the Impact of Various Forms of Trust on National and International Institutions

	Confidence In			
	Parliament	**EU**	**NATO**	**UN**
Universal trust	1.3 (.07)★★★	1.4 (.1)★★★	1.3 (.05)★★★	1.4 (.08)★★★
Primordial trust	.94 (.06)	1.1 (.07)	.88 (.06)★	.94 (.07)
Anomie	.94 (.03)★★	.99 (.05)	.96 (.04)	.9 (.02)★★
N	9,919	9,684	7,192	9,662

Source: World Values Survey 2000, 2001.

Note: Robust standard errors in parentheses. Two-tailed tests. All of these models control for age, income, female, education, and self-placement on left/right scale. However, for reasons of space they are not shown.

Question item: "I am going to name a number of organizations. For each one, could you tell me how much confidence you have in them: is it a great deal of confidence, quite a lot of confidence, not very much confidence, or none at all?" (1 = none at all; 4 = a great deal of confidence). The polarity of the answer options was reversed by recoding. Numbers represent odds ratios (higher than 1 means a positive effect of the independent variable on the dependent variable; lower than 1 means a negative effect on the dependent variable).

primordial, universal, and anomic, have systematically different effects on confidence in political institutions situated in national or international contexts.

Unfortunately, no survey I know of has asked questions in terms of confidence in local institutions, but there are questions that tap respondents' confidence in the European Union, the North Atlantic Treaty Organization (NATO), and the United Nations (UN). If there were questions about trust in local institutions, we would hypothesize that primordial trusters should demonstrate support for such institutions. However, questions about national and even supranational institutions are available, and it is expected that universal trusters should show confidence in international institutions while little or no confidence in such institutions should be displayed by primordial trusters. Table 4.5 shows the association at the individual level among three forms of trust (universal, primordial, and anomie) and confidence in Parliament, the EU, NATO, and the UN. All of the models controlled for age, gender, income, education, and self-placement on the left/right political scale. For reasons of space, only the trust variables are shown.

Table 4.5 shows that there is a clear difference between the various forms of trust. Universal trust strongly and significantly affects confidence in all institutions, the national Parliament, the EU, NATO, and the UN. Primordial trust tends to negatively affect these institutions (with the exception of EU), although the only significant effect is on NATO, while anomie, those people who believe that it is better to stick to one's own affairs, also shows strong negative effects on confidence in national parliaments and the United Nations. No significant effects were found on the EU and NATO. Universal trust and confidence in government, and in institutions that extend beyond national boundaries such as the EU, NATO, and the UN, are significantly associated with each other. Again, while it is difficult to argue which causes which, this finding clearly demonstrates that not all forms of trust are created equal. Universal trust, primordial trust, and particularly anomie have significantly different effects.

Trust and the Supply of Welfare

Chapter 3 demonstrated that the crucial nexus between the welfare state and an individual is the degree to which people are willing to pay their "fair share" in the form of taxes, to "obey the law" by not claiming welfare benefits to which they are not entitled, and to not engage in bribery.

In the absence of legal or moral constraints, evading taxes is the rational strategy. In terms of outcomes, the best outcome for any individual is that he or she does not pay taxes but everyone else does. All the public goods will be provided, and the lack of the individual's contribution will not significantly reduce the stock of public goods. The second-best outcome is that everyone pays taxes. The third-best outcome is that nobody pays taxes. Clearly, the worst outcome is that our individual is the only one paying taxes, thus reaping the sucker's payoff.[7]

Friedrich Schneider and Dominik H. Enste (2003, 37) estimate that the shadow economy (i.e., any economic activity that goes unreported and thus never finds its way into the state's coffers) accounts for about 12 percent of the gross national product (GNP) of OECD countries, with Italy being by far the country with the highest estimates of tax evasion (35 percent of GDP). In Africa, estimates of tax evasion are 44 percent, in Latin America 39 percent, and in Asia about 35 percent. In the United States, the Internal Revenue Service (IRS) estimates that in the tax year 1992 91.7 percent of income that should have been reported was in fact reported, even though audit rates fell from around 5 percent in the 1960s to below 1 percent in the 1990s (Scholz 1998). It is rather puzzling, particularly given the logic of the free-rider problem, why so many people in fact do pay their taxes.

Trust becomes relevant at this intersection between the welfare state and individual behavior. If people claim welfare benefits for which they are not eligible, or if they cheat on their taxes at increasing levels, this could have far-reaching consequences for the welfare state. One of the central findings of Scholz and Lubell (1998) was that if people in the United States thought other citizens would pay their fair share of taxes then they would pay too. Similarly, people will not claim welfare benefits to which they are not entitled unless they believe that others will do the same. One of the most puzzling findings of experimental psychologists, political scientists, and sociologists is that when people are put into prisoner's dilemma situations, in which defection is the "rational" outcome, cooperation occurs more often than the rationality axiom would predict (Axelrod 1984; Bendor and Swistak 1997; Orbell and Dawes 1991), producing a pattern of behavior that is "better than rational" (Cosmides and Tooby 1994).

How do anomie and primordial and universal trust fit into this rationalist account? The difference between primordial and universal trust is the "radius" of concern about others. For primordial trusters solidarity only encompasses their families and neighborhoods, while for universal trusters it includes the nation, Europe, and ultimately humankind (as originally operationalized in the WVS fourth wave). It was argued earlier that universal trust is a form of social solidarity that involves a certain amount of concern about and responsibility for the living conditions of strangers, even of people who are not part of one's own country. This wide-ranging solidarity tends to lead to an understanding that "we are all in the same boat," and universal trusters see no contradiction in dutifully paying their taxes even though the benefits go to people they will never meet. Universal trusters do not ask for specific things in return when they pay their taxes. For primordial trusters, since they are only concerned about their immediate families and neighborhoods, tax evasion becomes "the rational thing to do" since they do not see themselves as part of a larger community. They know that many of their taxes go to people other than their immediate family clans and even to people of very different races, religions, or ethnic backgrounds. Hence, they feel a much weaker bond, making them think twice whether they should pay their "fair" share. Banfield tells us that in Montegrano the widespread assumption was: "It is taken for granted that all those who can cheat on taxes will do so" (1958, 92). Since their concerns and solidarity with the rest of society are much more limited, they do not see it as imperative to do their societal duty since "society" for them is a relatively closed circle.[8]

Our measure of anomie (i.e., those people who believe that it is "better to stick to one's own affairs" should also negatively affect taxpaying, welfare benefit claiming, and bribery. A young schoolteacher in Montegrano said that even if he could prove that bribery was going on in his school he would do nothing. "You are likely to be made a martyr. It takes courage to do it. There are so many more dishonest people than honest ones that they can gang up on you . . . twist the facts so that you appear to be the guilty one. Remember Christ and the Pharisees" (Banfield 1958, 88). Societal attitudes such as these have corroding effects on the fabric of society.

Nowhere are trust and the welfare state more closely connected than at the moment when taxpayers either honestly or dishonestly declare his or her taxes. If the taxpayer is a primordial truster, the "state" or even the "nation" may be too removed a concept to instill a sense of solidarity strong enough to induce the individual to honestly pay his or her share. However, for a person with universal attitudes of trust, and thus an expanded view of the moral community, such a taxpayer should be more willing to pay his or her fair share.

The fourth wave of the WVS asked questions precisely geared toward issues of tax evasion, claiming welfare benefits, and attitudes about bribery. Table 4.6 indicates the results of multiple regression analysis with robust standard errors.

A close look at table 4.6 reveals that people with higher nativist resentments have fewer scruples when it comes to cheating on taxes and claiming welfare benefits for which they are not entitled. They also think that bribery as more justifiable compared to the views of people with less nativist resentment. Primordial trusters (people who trust only members of their in-group) do not indicate significant attitudes in any direction. What was termed anomie (respondents who believe it is "better to stick to one's own affairs") indicate particularly strong asocial tendencies with regard to all three variables (the beliefs that tax evasion, claiming benefits for which they are not eligible, and accepting bribes are justifiable). On the other hand, as predicted, universal trusters (people endowed with attitudes of social solidarity and concern for others) clearly are more law-abiding and do not believe that tax evasion and bribery are justifiable.

TABLE 4.6. Correlates of Tax Evasion, Illegal Claiming of Social Benefits, and Bribery

	Tax Evasion	Claiming Benefits	Bribery
Nativist resentment	1.45 (.38)***	.74 (.41)*	.56 (.15)***
Universal trust	−.16 (.05)***	−.035 (.06)	−.08 (.035)**
Nativist resentment × universal trust	−.27 (.1)**	−.11 (.12)	−.12 (.04)**
Primordial trust	.08 (.07)	.036 (.08)	.09 (.06)
Anomie	.13 (.03)***	.14 (.04)***	.073 (.037)*
Life satisfaction	−.09 (.016)***	−.06 (.03)**	−.04 (.013)***
Age	−.02 (.002)***	−.02 (.001)***	−.012 (.002)***
Education	.003 (.02)	−.04 (.017)**	−.012 (.009)
Income	−.035 (.032)	−.11 (.03)***	−.05 (.03)
Female	−.32 (.05)***	−.09 (.024)***	−.18 (.03)***
Self-placement on political scale	.04 (.04)	−.06 (.026)	.024 (.017)
N	9,909	9,897	9,927
R^2	.06	.05	.03

Source: World Values Survey 2000.

Note: Robust standard errors in parentheses. Appropriate weights are included but not shown. One-tailed tests. The questions were as follows: "Please tell me for the following statements whether it can be always justified, never be justified, or something in between: (1) Cheating on taxes if you have a chance; (2) claiming government benefits to which you are not entitled; (3) someone accepting a bribe in the course of their duties." Range 1–10 (1 = never justifiable; 10 = always justifiable).

The strongest of all predictors across the three models is age. Older people clearly are the most law-abiding and believe that tax evasion, claiming illegal government benefits, and taking bribes are never justifiable. Similarly, females are clearly more law-abiding than males. In terms of life satisfaction, the more people are satisfied with their lives the more law-abiding they are. Somewhat surprisingly, education showed only a weak negative effect on illegal government benefits, meaning that more highly educated people believe that is not justifiable to claim government benefits for which they are not eligible. There is no relationship among education, tax evasion, and accepting bribes. Income proved to be strongly and significantly related to not accepting illegal government benefits. In terms of self-placement on the political scale, the only impact is on claiming illegal government benefits, that is, the more people place themselves on the right of the political scale the more they think it is not justifiable to accept government benefits for which they are not eligible.

The implications of these findings are far-reaching. Without a certain level of willingness on the part of the populace to pay their taxes and be truthful in claiming only welfare benefits for which they are eligible, the welfare state would collapse. The state, conceived as a coercive agent that imposes costs on those who do not comply with their obligations as citizens, is effective only to a certain degree. The transaction costs of monitoring everybody would soon outstrip the additional revenues collected.

Thus, universal trust matters greatly. At its core, universal trust carries a sense of republican virtue, an understanding that supporting the larger community is more important and satisfying than the pursuit of narrow-minded, parochial interests. Universal trusters are integrated individuals; they see themselves as part and parcel of a larger community. It is precisely this attitude on which an encompassing welfare state can be built. Universal trusters, people who are endowed with a sense of social solidarity and concern for others beyond their immediate families and neighborhoods, however, clearly believe that it is their duty to pay their share in taxes and do not believe that bribery is justifiable. Universal trusters understand that living in a community means making sacrifices and that despite these sacrifices the whole is greater than the sum of its parts. In the words of Durkheim (1893, 228), "Men cannot live together without acknowledging, and consequently making mutual sacrifices, without tying themselves to one another with strong, durable bonds." These findings demonstrate that sacrifices such as paying one's taxes are made more willingly if individuals believe they are part of a community and that the community will profit as a whole from their sacrifices. The central ingredient, it seems, for the willingness to engage in such sacrifices is universal trust.

On the other hand, primordial trust and anomie are too weak to command sufficient solidarity to compel people to pay their taxes and not to claim illegal government benefits. It is perhaps not surprising that people whose views of their moral communities are restricted to their families and neighborhoods trust faraway capitals less with their tax money than do individuals who see themselves as part of a larger community. Primordialists demand more from the state but are willing to give less. Universalists, however, are willing to give more and ask for less. Primordial trust creates a cozy but limited and ultimately dysfunctional society at a time when national borders are becoming increasingly porous, when whole continents are becoming integrated, as with the European Union, and when modern forms of information, transportation, and communications technologies are connecting people in this world like never before.

Table 4.6 also indicates a statistically significant interaction term between nativist resentment and universal trust. Interaction terms are very useful in determining the extent to which the effect of one explanatory variable on the outcome variable depends on the level of another explanatory variable. Figures 4.3 and 4.4 show that the effect of nativist resentment on tax evasion and bribery is significantly blunted depending on the level of universal trust. I have argued that immigration-driven nativist resentment will be either blunted or heightened depending on whether individuals are more or less trusting. Figures 4.3 and 4.4 indicate that universal trust can significantly affect the impact of nativist resentment on tax evasion and bribery.

Figure 4.3 plots the interaction effects between nativist resentment and tax evasion for different levels of universal trust. What the graph clearly shows is that in individuals with high universal trust the effects of nativist resentment on tax evasion are significantly reduced. At high levels of nativist resentment, high universal trust (defined as the mean trust plus one standard deviation of trust) can reduce the effect of nativist resentment on tax evasion by almost 10 percent (from around 5 to 4.1 on a 10-point scale) compared to individuals with low trust (defined as the mean trust minus one standard deviation of trust).

Similarly, in figure 4.4 a statistically significant interaction effect is visible between nativist resentment and bribery depending on the

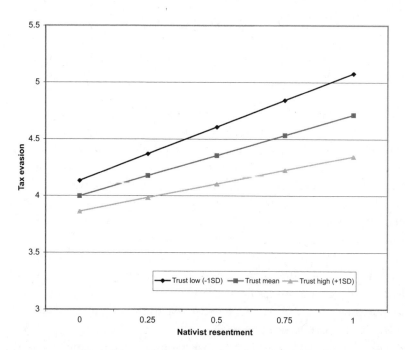

Fig. 4.3.   Interaction effects between nativist resentment and tax evasion given different levels of universal trust

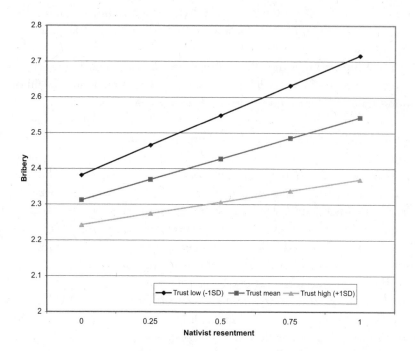

Fig. 4.4.   Interaction effects between nativist resentment and bribery given different levels of universal trust

levels of trust. Individuals with high universal trust again depress the effect of nativist resentment on bribery while low trust heightens these effects.

The graphs showing the interaction effects highlight two central findings. First, people with prejudices against foreigners have a cavalier attitude about paying their taxes, potentially endangering the viability of the welfare state. Second, universal trust matters because it significantly reduces this very cavalier attitude about paying taxes. However, while universal trust manages to significantly *reduce* the slope of the interaction effect, it fails to *reverse* the slope. Nevertheless, the graphs show that for the welfare state to work a sense of universal trust is crucial. Universal trust means an expansive sense of solidarity, a sense of extended community that transcends one's own racial, religious, and ethnic identity. Not only do such fraternal attitudes favor the welfare state, but they also reduce the corrosive effects of nativist resentment on the welfare state and attitudes about corruption in general.

This chapter has demonstrated that anomie is incompatible with the maintenance of a welfare state. This is a significant finding, particularly if it is viewed against the background of a growing individualism in modern societies. These findings indicate that if such trends continue there will be very little support for the communal provision of social protection in the future.

Most interesting is the effect of primordial trust on paying taxes. Primordial trusters (i.e., people who trust only their families and neighborhoods) are indifferent on the issue of doing their part to make the welfare state possible. This is a surprising result because it shows that not even primordial attitudes are powerful enough to command allegiance to large redistributive arrangements such as the welfare state. This stands in stark contrast to the many authors cited in chapter 2 who have claimed that "fellow feeling" or a "that could be me" attitude is necessary in order to maintain the welfare state. This research shows that local, or even national, perceptions of "we" are no longer sufficient. This may be because self-interested attitudes are beginning to slowly but surely dissolve the cement of society. Anomie is eating into national cohesion, fraying the ties that bind. These results show that even perceptions of a national moral community are no longer sufficient for the welfare state to function. Paradoxically, it requires a level of "trust without borders" to instill the kind of selfless attitudes necessary to engage in large national forms of societal redistribution. Only those with a truly "universal" orientation can still muster the unselfish attitude that is necessary to support a redistributive national welfare state.

Chapters 3 and 4 have provided a "bottom-up" explanation of how individual traits affect the demand and supply for welfare. They have demonstrated that immigration-driven diversity has frayed the social fabric of society insofar as those segments that are most affected by immigration tend to reject supplying the welfare state by paying their fair share while at the same time demanding continued protection. Concurrently, levels of trust have significant impacts on the degree to which individuals continue funding the welfare state. People endowed with universal trust favor continued support of the welfare state and dampen the adverse effects of nativist resentment on the further provision of social welfare.

In the next chapter, we take a "top-down" approach. Is it possible that differences in welfare regimes can affect people's attitudes about the welfare state? Does it matter for individual attitudes whether the regime is based on "universal" or "means-tested" concepts? It is also very suspicious that the highest interpersonal trust is found in Scandinavian societies, which are also the ones with the most developed welfare states. Perhaps the solution to this riddle lies in the institutional setup of welfare state regimes. In other words, the next chapter asks: depending on the form of the welfare regime, does it have an integrative or disintegrative effect? After all, the great achievement of the welfare state was to bridge class conflict and establish social harmony. At the danger of anthropomorphizing the welfare state, instead of it being an innocent bystander to which immigration and diversity "happens" maybe it plays an active role in the process of integrating newcomers.

Enjoying the rights and privileges of social citizenship, albeit not national citizenship, may also have an integrative function and a role in alleviating the pressures of diversity. After all, T. H. Marshall (1950, 28) also argued that "The components of a civilized and cultured life, formerly the monopoly of the few, were brought progressively within reach of the many, who were thereby encouraged to stretch out their hands towards those that still eluded their grasp" (1950, 28). Thus, enjoying the fruits of social citizenship instilled and reinforced a sense of a common fate that doused the fires of the class struggle, but can it also douse the fires of racial and ethnic diversity?

CHAPTER 5

Welfare State Regimes as a Regimen for Building Trust?

Contextualizing Attitudes

> I now understand that my welfare is only possible if
> I acknowledge my unity with all the people of the
> world without exception.
> —Leo Tolstoy

A CENTRAL FINDING IN THE LAST CHAPTER was that at the individual level people with high universal trust supported the welfare state more than people with high primordial trust. In addition, the effects of nativist resentment on welfare state support were significantly mediated by universal trust. This section reverses the causal arrow and investigates to what extent welfare state regimes can affect individual attitudes. The questions are the following. Why is it that some countries have more trust than others? Is it conceivable that the differences in trust levels, even at the individual level, can be explained by the different welfare regimes? To take Esping-Andersen's famous three-part division of "welfare worlds," would it make a difference for individual attitudes about trust, the welfare state, and nativist resentment whether the respondent lives in a social democratic, Catholic/corporatist, or liberal/residual welfare state? This chapter "contextualizes" trust and searches for its roots in the different types of welfare state regimes.

Claiming that "primordial" sentiments can be affected by the type of welfare regime is of course antithetical to its very concept. The term *primordial* suggests that group characteristics are prior to and constitutive of any form of social organization. As shown in chapter 2, primordialists have consistently argued that categorical similarities are what gives meaning to individuals and groups and more extended forms of social organization, such as states, are only possible on the basis of such group similarities. Ethnic nepotism theory argues that when it comes to establishing extensive welfare states with relatively high marginal taxes such sacrifices are easier to make if the beneficiaries of such redistribution share similar categorical traits (Salter 2004).

However, the findings so far indicate opposite outcomes: there is evidence that primordial trusters are xenophobic and favor less redistribution compared to universal trusters, who are not only less xenophobic but also more supportive of the welfare state. Biology may be destiny in the animal kingdom but not among *Homo sapiens.* The essentialist primordial proposition has a difficult time explaining the existence of universal trust, that is, why some people trust strangers who are unlike them in every respect and even trust them with their tax money.

Another view, quite similar to the sociobiologically inspired one and propounded by economists, is that political institutions are essentially "endogenous," that is, constitutional structures such as the electoral system, bicameralism, or federalism are simply reflections of the conditions that gave rise to them (Alesina and Glaeser 2004). Such a view is an essentially reflexive, static, and ultimately tautological one that does not give credence to the possibility that political institutions, once created, take on lives of their own and sometimes work as intended by the creators and sometimes not. Institutions tend to be "sticky," and, even though at some point in time there may have been a strong congruence between initial conditions and the function of institutions, societies often change while institutions do not, making a mockery of the notion of the endogeneity of institutions.

Viewed from the perspective of political scientists, the economists' concept of endogeneity of political institutions is fundamentally flawed. Empirically, there are many examples of highly divided societies that against all odds have managed not only to survive but to thrive and establish extensive welfare states that by all accounts have succeeded in equalizing the life chances of their citizens and, partly for that reason, to enjoy widespread legitimacy. Cases in point are the Netherlands, which is divided along socioeconomic and religious lines (Catholics vs. Protestants), and Belgium, which is also split along socioeconomic, religious (liberals vs. Catholics), and cultural/ethnic lines, as exemplified by the Dutch-speaking Flemings in the north and the French-speaking Walloons in the south, with a German-speaking minority in eastern Belgium. Another prime example of a highly "pillarized" society is Austria during the interwar years and even today. Adam Wandruszka (1954, 290) spoke of the "natural or god-given three part division of Austria's social structure," by which he had in mind the divisions among the conservative, socialist, and nationalist *Lager* (camps). Stein Rokkan (1977, 567) also described Austria as having one of the highest levels of *verzuiling* (pillarization). To be sure, there were no "racial" differences, but class and political and religious cleavages were enough to plunge Austria into a bloody civil war in 1934, from which it emerged with a fascist government, was absorbed into the Third Reich, and was occupied for 10 years. All three countries however, managed to establish very generous welfare states as measured by Esping-Andersen's (1990, 52) still widely used decommodification scores, which are only exceeded by those of Denmark, Norway, and Sweden. In addition, they established, despite being highly divided, harmonious relations among their *Lagers* after World War II, an outcome not predicted if the endogeneity thesis is to be taken seriously.

The great contribution of political scientists such as Arend Lijphart (1968), Jürg Steiner (1970), Gerhard Lehmbruch (1967), Douglas Rae (1967) and many "neoinstitutionalists" was to demonstrate that through "electoral engineering" it is possible to achieve social harmony, even in highly divided societies, by establishing inclusive political institutions. So-called consociational political institutions based on veto powers, proportional representation, segmental autonomy, and grand coalitions allow minorities a place at the table and as a result are able to accommodate their differences peacefully. Institutions, once created, not only reflect the conditions that gave rise to them but take on their own independent, material force. This is the very essence of the concept of "constitutional engineering," in which the causal arrow originates in the constitutional structure and points toward social, economic, and other outcomes. Arend Lijphart (1999, 252) is certainly convinced of that, as he states in his autobiographical "academic life story": "The 1990s, and in all probability the early years of the twenty-first century, are the era of democratization but also of severe ethnic conflict. . . . Questions of democratic institutional design . . . are of such crucial importance . . . that they are likely to demand most of my professional energies—both as a political researcher as well as a constitutional engineer—for many years to come."

Only by granting institutions their independent material force can the puzzle of achieving social harmony be explained despite the persistence of deep social cleavages. The fact that such power-sharing institutions were created despite such deep-seated societal divisions is not consistent with the endogeneity hypothesis. Neither is it consistent with the fact that many such conflicts have in fact abated, making some of these institutions superfluous, yet they still exist and exert their expected influence. The institutions of corporatism and consociational democracy are still visible today despite some premature claims by some that they have become a victim of their own success. Given the resurgence of ethnic conflicts driven by immigration-induced diversity, such consociational or consensus institutions (Lijphart 1999) may well experience a renaissance in the coming decades.

The welfare state is also an institution, though perhaps not as "primary" an institution as, say, the electoral system or parliamentarism or bicameralism. It may be useful to think of the welfare state as a "secondary" institution that developed as a result of political movements that shaped particular formal constitutional structures such as proportional representation, which in turn helped establish and expand the welfare state. Once created, the welfare state can become an instrument of establishing and constructing identities. Patrick Ireland (2004, 25, 26), who examined the effect of the welfare state on the integration of immigrants in Europe, says that, "Institutions and policies have the power to shape ethnic relations, and it follows, offer hope of solving the challenges associated with immigration." In a similar vein, Anne L. Schneider and Helen Ingram (1997, 200) point out that the design of the welfare state "is an important independent variable that shapes citizens' orientations."

To be sure, in most cases nations made the welfare state. However, the welfare state can also make a nation, as recalled by Keith Banting (1999), who describes the incorporation of Newfoundland into Canada in 1949. One of the most attractive features of joining Canada for Newfoundlanders was the much more extensive social protection afforded by the more generous Canadian welfare state—a feature leaders in Newfoundland who led the campaign for union with Canada never grew tired of stressing. It turned out that the referendum about joining Canada was very close (52 percent favored accession), and the Canadian government wondered how long it would take before the Newfoundlanders would begin to feel like Canadians. Canadian officials believed that Newfoundlanders would be more quickly integrated the more they felt they were treated like members of any other Canadian province, "and they worked hard to ensure that family allowances and unemployment benefits were paid on time in the first month after union" (Banting 1999, 112). This turned out to be a highly effective strategy, and as the checks spread across the new province, "Canada's newest citizens in the remotest reaches of the province received the first visible signs that they were now Canadians. . . . [T]he federal social programs were the most recognized feature of the union with Canada, and they gave the process instant credibility" (R. Blake 1994, quoted in Banting 1999, 113). This is a powerful example of the capacity of the welfare state to "make Canadians" and integrate initially separate regions by tying the fates of disparate people to the fate of the country as a whole.

Thus, historically the overarching task of the welfare state was not only to integrate "classes," as in the Marshallian conception, but also to integrate territories with diverse ethnic populations. Bismarck was keenly aware of the diversity of the German Reich, which extended from Alsace-Lorraine to East Prussia and from the Rhineland to Silesia. Not only would various forms of social protection help reduce class differences, but centralized control over these forms of social protection would establish some loyalty among different ethnic groups and provide a modicum of legitimacy to the empire.

In a similar functionalist way, Durkheim sought refuge in a corporatist state since according to him societies had already lost their *conscience collective* and were increasingly becoming anomic. Corporatist institutions could reestablish group norms and help create a sense of identity and solidarity, which had been undermined by the division of labor. Peter Flora and Arnold J. Heidenheimer (1981, 24), reflecting on Durkheim's understanding of the welfare state, conclude that "the welfare state may be understood to *create* a new kind of solidarity in highly differentiated societies" (emphasis added).

Richard Henry Tawney also understood the welfare state to have an integrative capacity, particularly against the background of World War II, as interpreted by Graham J. Room. The collective commitment to a more egalitarian society, in Room's interpretation of Tawney, "could secure popular acquiescence . . . which would involve citizens as a collective force for social transformation." Out of this international conflict, "engendered by unprincipled capitalism, would come the reordering of society as morally just and hence socially cohesive" (Room 1981, 410). Tawney, very much like Durkheim, argued that the state plays an active role in the promotion of a principled order which is "*planned . . .* to em-

phasize and strengthen . . . the common humanity which unites men"
(Tawney 1969. Quoted in Room 1981, 410. Emphasis added).

Another pioneer of the modern welfare state, Richard Titmuss, also
was convinced that the welfare state could engender social integration.
One of his most influential contributions is his work on the stigmatization that comes with means-tested, or targeted, systems of welfare provision, leading to a destructive self-fulfilling prophecy. "If men are
treated as a burden to others—if this is the role expected of them—then,
in time, they will behave as a burden" (Titmuss 1968, 26). Aside from the
psychological damage that comes with the inhumane treatment of being
singled out as a supplicant, this very process undermines the development of a collective, egalitarian, organic society. Consequently, Titmuss
favored the establishment of universal social policies not based on need
but as a universal right of citizens, thereby helping to establish a vibrant,
cohesive, and egalitarian society (Reisman 2001).[1]

According to Titmuss, universal social policies not only avoid stigmatization but actually help integrate societies. "Race hatred can result
from denial of participation, from felt exclusion. Welfare services make
non-white people feel at home. . . . Ethnic integration is fostered by the
absence of formal barriers to access to all . . . on a universalistic basis"
(Titmuss 1965, 355). Social policy, for Titmuss, was more than helping
people in need; it was a way of establishing a universal sense of belonging, of highlighting the common humanity. "Welfare," according to him,
"can make a positive contribution . . . to the social ethic of human equality" (355).[2]

Although the United States is often regarded as a welfare "laggard,"
there is one program that enjoys overarching support, which is Social
Security. The genius of Social Security is precisely its universal character:
everybody who pays into it will get something out of it, binding cohorts
together on the basis of a "generational contract."[3] Social Security benefits have been understood "as returns for the 'contributions'—not just
of taxes, but also of work that employed Americans make over a lifetime"
(Skocpol 1997, 102). The universal character of the Social Security Act
of 1935 was powerfully described by its creator, Franklin D. Roosevelt:
"In this future of ours, it is of first importance that we yield not to the
sympathy which we would extend to a single group or class by special
legislation for that group or class, but that we should extend assistance
to all groups and all classes who in an emergency need the helping hand
of their Government" (quoted in Skocpol 1997, 104).

Today the countries with the most universalistic welfare states are the Scandinavian countries, particularly Sweden, Norway, and Denmark, not the United States or the United Kingdom, the country with which Titmuss was most concerned. The Scandinavian countries are, intriguingly, also the ones with the highest levels of trust, as shown in chapter 4, figure 4.2. This raises the complex question of cause and effect. Are the high trust levels in these three countries a function of their being the most universalistic welfare states or is it the universal welfare state that leads to these high levels of trust? Robert Putnam's well-known argument is rooted in associational, member-based activity, out of which trust emerges (Putnam 1993, 2000). However, Putnam (2002, 414) also argues that most of the evidence in his 2002 edited volume, *Democracies in Flux,* "appears to support the opposite view: that the welfare state has helped to sustain social capital rather than eroding it."[4] In a similar vein, Peter Hall (2002, 55), examining social capital in Britain, observes that "governments can have a substantial impact on levels of social capital."

This chapter examines the effects of different welfare regimes not only on trust but also on levels of welfare chauvinism. If it is indeed the case that universal welfare regimes can establish a sense of belonging and make a contribution to the "social ethic of human equality," can this Titmussian vision be extended to the integration of foreigners also? Is the politics of identity more benign in comprehensive welfare systems compared to needs-based ones? In other words, does it make a difference for trust, and for public perceptions of immigrants and welfare chauvinism, whether the system of welfare provision is means tested or universal?

WORLDS OF WELFARE AND WORLDS OF TRUST

No scholarly work attempting to classify welfare regimes has had more of an impact than Gøsta Esping-Andersen's *The Three Worlds of Welfare Capitalism* (1990). Only a little over one and a half decades old, it has already become a classic. Numerous scholars have relied on his threefold typology of welfare states: the conservative, liberal, and social democratic. The conservative welfare state is founded on a strong etatist, corporatist, and catholic tradition, and eligibility is based on prior contributions paid over the recipient's own working life. Esping-Andersen's cases that fit this ideal type are those of Italy, Japan, France, Germany, Finland, and Switzerland. These countries produce a fair degree of decommodification, defined as "the degree to which they permit people to make their living standards independent of pure market forces" (1990, 3). The second, liberal cluster embodies the primacy of the market and individualist principles. This group, which includes Australia, the United States, New Zealand, Canada, Ireland, and the United Kingdom, is characterized by low levels of decommodification. There is little redistribution of income, and welfare schemes are mostly based on means tests. The third group encompasses countries with a strong tradition of social democracy, resulting in generous universal and highly distributive benefits that do not depend on prior contributions. Predictably, this cluster yields the highest decommodification scores and includes Austria, Belgium, Denmark, the Netherlands, Norway, and Sweden (Esping-Andersen 1990).

Esping-Andersen is also very explicit in terms of the degree of "comprehensiveness" of welfare provision among the three clusters. The etatist model is best identified by the degree to which social insurance is "differentiated and segmented into distinct occupational and status based programs," while in liberal welfare states the "relative salience of means testing" is relevant. In social-democratic welfare states, the "relevant measure is clearly a degree of universalism" (1990, 69).

Since the publication of *The Three Worlds of Welfare Capitalism,* there have been many modifications, extensions, and additions to Esping-Andersen's classification. For example, Stephan Leibfried (1992) developed four types of welfare regimes: Anglo-Saxon, Bismarck, Scandinavian, and Latin Rim (1992). Francis G. Castles and Deborah Mitchell (1993) also identified four types: Liberal, Conservative, Non-right Hegemony, and Radical. Walter Korpi and Joakim Palme (1998) found five types: Basic Security, Corporatist, Encompassing, Targeted, and Voluntary State Subsidized. Many other authors have developed different classifications. John Gelissen (2002) provides a detailed overview of these different types. While many of these variations on Esping-Andersen's typology are quite insightful, they have not been helpful in establishing a broad consensus on what constitutes different clusters of welfare regimes.

Anybody who establishes classifications is easy prey for critics. Although *Three Worlds* received wide acclaim, some critics argued that its classification has theoretical and methodological shortcomings (Lessenich and Ostner 1998) while others described the scoring for the decommodification index as too impressionistic. In addition to lively debates about "extensions" and "placements" of different countries in Esping-Andersen's scheme, the recent release of Lyle Scruggs's new welfare state entitlements data set (2004), in which he updated, extended, and reanalyzed the original Esping-Andersen data questions Esping-Andersen's findings. By relying on the same characteristics as the original decommodification index, Scruggs and Allen found a "very different ordering and clustering of countries. Based on our analysis, the previous results misclassified eight of eighteen, or almost half, of the cases" (Scruggs and Allen 2004, 2a). In addition, the authors question whether there is such a thing as distinct clusters or "worlds of welfare." They find little consistent correlation among the elements of decommodification such as unemployment benefits or sick pay or pension benefits across countries. In other words, one country may have high unemployment benefits but low sick pay and average pension protection while another may have high pension protection, low unemployment benefits, and medium sick pay. In other words, the overall "package" of decommodification is too fragmented among its various elements to allow us to speak of a consistent triptych of welfare regimes. In addition, the Scruggs index is available on an annual basis from 1971 to 2002 for the original 18 countries in *Three Worlds*. Since the dependent variables in the following analysis are public attitudes in 2002, the decommodification scores for the year 2000 are shown.

Table 5.1 shows Esping-Andersen's levels of decommodification; the updated and reanalyzed Scruggs scores of decommodification; and, for comparative purposes, the total public social expenditures in percentage of GDP per country. An association between the index based on programmatic rules and actual expenditures should be expected. This is not to say that expenditures should equal the index that captures dimensions such as eligibility rules and restrictions on entitlements, levels of income replacement, the range of entitlements, and so on. In fact, Esping-Andersen was very explicit in arguing that in order to capture the degree to which states decommodify individuals, public expenditure measures are not valid since they can seriously distort the picture. Esping-Andersen himself gave the best-known example when he discussed unemployment insurance in the United Kingdom. While the Thatcher government in the United Kingdom was making major programmatic cuts in earnings-related unemployment and sickness benefits, spending on unemployment rose because the number of people depending on benefits grew faster than the programmatic entitlements were cut. As a result, by examining expenditures only, one might come to the incorrect conclusion that Prime Minister Margaret Thatcher expanded welfare benefits, when in reality welfare programs were phased out (Esping-Andersen 1990). Nevertheless, it is instructive to see programmatic scores and actual measures of total social expenditures displayed side by side.

Even though the Scruggs and Esping-Andersen measures were developed 20 years apart, and despite the corrections made by Scruggs, the correlation coefficient between the two measures is .9, meaning that, in terms of *their direction,* they are very strongly related. However, dividing the 17 countries into Esping-Andersen's triptych by ordering them according to the Scruggs results leads to shifts of some countries into different categories. Table 5.1 shows that using Scruggs's data and the year 2000 as a reference point, Canada moves from the liberal to the conservative/corporatist cluster and Italy drops from the conservative/corporatist cluster into the liberal one. Austria and Germany trade places: Austria drops from the social democratic into the conservative/corporatist cluster, while Germany moves the opposite way. Finally, Switzerland drops from the conservative/corporatist to the liberal cluster. Table 5.1

TABLE 5.1.   Scores for Decommodification (Scruggs index and Esping-Andersen index), Total Social Public Expenditures as Percentage of GDP, and Percentage of Foreign-Born Population

	Decommodification, 2000 (Scruggs 2004)	Decommodification, 1980 (Esping-Andersen 1990)	Social Expenditures as Percentage of GDP	Foreign Population (%)
Australia	18.16	13.0	18.6	23.6
Austria	28.65	31.1	26.0	9.3
Belgium	30.87	32.4	26.7	8.4
Canada	25.80	22.0	17.3	18.2
Denmark	34.89	38.1	28.9	4.8
Finland	30.11	29.2	24.5	1.8
France	27.04	27.5	28.3	8.9
Germany	30.71	27.7	27.2	8.9
Ireland	26.62	23.3	13.6	3.3
Italy	23.23	24.1	24.1	2.4
Netherlands	34.33	32.4	21.8	4.2
New Zealand	22.09	17.1	19.2	19.5
Norway	37.22	38.3	23.0	4.1
Sweden	32.84	39.1	28.6	5.4
Switzerland	22.47	29.8	25.4	19.3
United Kingdom	24.57	23.4	21.7	4.0
United States	18.39	13.8	14.2	11.1

Source: Scruggs 2004; Esping-Andersen 1990 (52).

Note: The Scruggs index measures decommodification in the year 2000, and the Esping-Andersen index measures decommodification in the year 1980. Social expenditures are measured in the year 2000 using data from the OECD Social Expenditure Dataset (2004).

uses Esping-Andersen's threefold typology but employs the new Scruggs decommodification score for the year 2000. Also, as expected, there is an association between the newer Scruggs measure and the original Esping-Andersen measure and total social expenditures although the latter is stronger (.73) than the former (.55).

From a theoretical perspective, the most intriguing question is: why should it make a difference in terms of trust, nativist resentment, or support for the welfare state whether the system of social welfare provision is means tested or universal? Titmuss suggested some hypotheses when he highlighted the stigmatizing effect of means-tested arrangements, which single out particular groups of people, thus making them "different" from others. People who are singled out for means testing in general are already disadvantaged in terms of income and education, and highlighting their status is particularly damaging psychologically, leading to a clear separation between those who need state support and those who do not. Such inequality is detrimental to establishing a sense of a common humanity or a universal sense of belonging, which should manifest itself in mutual distrust. Means-tested programs tend to establish hierarchies, accentuate differences, highlight inequalities, and denigrate the self-esteem of welfare recipients. This leads to a further fraying of already gossamer bonds, weakening them to such a degree that they are unable to sustain a solid sense of a shared destiny. Staffan Kumlin (2002) found that when people experience welfare institutions that are of universal character their support for the welfare state and state intervention in general was stronger than when they experienced institutions that were based on means testing.

This difference should be visible in terms of lack of trust originating both from the side of the receiver of means-tested benefits and from the viewpoint of those who fund such programs, undermining the sense of a collective, organic society. In means-tested systems, it is much easier to identify the "other," while in universal systems in which everybody essentially pays and receives the redistributive effects are much more difficult to ascertain, which may actually generate a sense of equality among members of such a welfare regimes. Thus, "the strategy of universal provision will lead to the strongest support for a welfare regime" (Papadakis and Bean 1993, 234). Examining Sweden, Stefan Svallfors (2002, 199) argues similarly when he claims that "it is the universalism of the Swedish welfare state institutions that tend to create support for welfare policies." "Universal programs do not cast aspersions on the responsibility of benefits," Bo Rothstein and Eric Uslaner (2004, 12) state, "and thus do not destroy trust. When they work well, they can even help to create it."

In order to establish a stable measure of trust, three comparative surveys are examined and the average trust scores calculated. This should reduce any survey-specific bias as a result of sampling, slight differences in wording, or other differences in the administration of the surveys. Table 5.2 shows results of the trust questions across three different surveys. The countries are ordered according to Esping-Andersen's threefold classification of liberal, conservative/corporatist, and social-democratic welfare state clusters. However, the updated results from the Scruggs decommodification score are used to classify various countries into their clusters.

Table 5.2 indicates trust measured in three different surveys using almost the same wording. In terms of time the three surveys were taken within four years of each other. What is remarkable are the sometimes dramatic differences in trust levels between the three surveys, such as in Switzerland, where the WVS indicates 36.9 percent while the ISSP two years earlier found 64.2 percent, or in Austria, where the WVS indicates 33.4 percent and the ISSP 53.0 percent two years earlier. In general, it appears that the ISSP surveys tend to generate higher numbers than the other two. There are many reasons why these differences are observable, some of which have to do with the different time points in which the interviewing took place and the differing answer options across the three surveys. Undoubtedly, different sampling methods and differences in administering the surveys may be responsible for these differences.

However, what is remarkable is the similarity in the *direction* of trust across the three surveys. The correlation coefficient of trust between the ISSP and ESS measure is .84, between the WVS and ISSP measure is .78, and between the WVS and ESS measure is .9. So, while there are some drastic differences in levels of trust across the surveys, in terms of the relative direction there is a very strong correlation between them.

Column 4 in table 5.2 depicts the average of the three surveys for each country and each welfare regime cluster. It represents a poll of polls. Closer inspection of column 4 reveals that there is very little difference in terms of trust between the liberal (43.8 percent) and conservative/corporatist (45.3 percent) cluster. The conservative/corporatist regime cluster indicates less than 2 percent more trust than the liberal one. This is a disappointing performance for the conservative/corporatist welfare states, which are understood to be decommodifying and relatively generous

(Esping-Andersen 1990). It may be possible that this low capacity to generate social trust may be caused by the strongly earnings-driven logic of this type of welfare state, which extends support to recognized groups and people who must demonstrate a prior earnings history before being

TABLE 5.2.   Worlds of Welfare and Worlds of Trust

	Trust (WVS)	Trust (ESS)	Trust (ISSP)	Trust (average)
Liberal Welfare States				
Australia (18.16)	40	n.a.	54.4	47.2
United States (18.39)	36.3	n.a.	49.8	43.1
New Zealand (22.09)	49	n.a.	56.1	52.6
Switzerland (22.47)	36.9	51.5	64.2	50.9
Italy (23.23)	32.6	33.6	19	28.4
United Kingdom (24.57)	28.9	43.1	49.4	40.5
Average	37.3	42.7	48.8	43.8
Conservative/Corporatist Welfare States				
Canada (25.80)	37	n.a.	55.7	46.4
Ireland (26.62)	36	50.9	44.5	43.8
France (27.04)	21.3	28.0	38.5	29.3
Austria (28.65)	33.4	41.9	53.0	42.8
Finland (30.11)	57.5	71.0	n.a.	64.3
Average	37.0	48.0	47.9	45.3
Social-Democratic Welfare States				
Germany (30.71)	37.5	33.0	48.2	39.6
Belgium (30.87)	29.2	40.2	n.a.	34.7
Sweden (32.84)	66.3	61.1	67.4	64.9
Netherlands (34.33)	60.8	58.4	65.2	61.5
Denmark (34.89)	66.5	74.6	66.0	69.0
Norway (37.22)	65.1	72.5	78.7	72.1
Average	54.2	56.6	65.1	57.0

Source: Data from World Values Survey 2000, European Social Survey 2002, and International Social Survey Program 1998.

Note: Numbers in parentheses following country names refer to the Scruggs (2004) decommodification score in year 2000. Worlds of trust are percentage of people indicating trust in 1998 (ISSP), 2000 (WVS), and 2002 (ESS).

n.a. = not available.

"Trust" refers to the standard trust question in the WVS: "Do you think most people can be trusted or you can't be too careful?" (the percentage indicates those who answered that most people can be trusted). This is a dichotomous measure. Universal trust cannot be used since the question on which that index is based was only asked in eleven countries.

"Trust" in ESS uses a slightly different wording: "Using this card, generally speaking, would you say that most people can be trusted, or that you can't be too careful in dealing with people? Please tell me on a score of 0 to 10, where 0 means you can't be too careful and 10 means that most people can be trusted." Following Uslaner (2002), responses from 0 to 5 were coded as 0, and answers from 6 to 10 were coded as 1, meaning trust. "Trust" in the ISSP employs exactly the same wording as in the ESS. However, the answer options are again different. They range from 1 to 4, 1 meaning "People can almost always be trusted," 2 meaning "People can usually be trusted," 3 meaning "You usually can't be too careful in dealing with people," and 4 meaning, "You almost always can't be too careful in dealing with people." The data were recoded with answer options 1 and 2 representing trust (1) and the last two options (3 and 4) indicating distrust (0).

eligible to draw welfare benefits. The prime example is the degree to which the governments of Austria and Germany (which barely made it into the social-democratic cluster) protect their public servants while other sectors are much less protected. This may give rise to a sense of inequality in public protection of more or less important sectors of society that the state deems worthy of support, which may undermine social trust (Uslaner 2002).

However, social-democratic welfare regimes show much higher levels of trust (57 percent) than the other two, demonstrating an association between type of welfare state and interpersonal trust. In fact, that cluster is hampered by the low trust levels of Germany and Belgium. If only the three Scandinavian countries in that cluster are examined, their average trust levels across the three surveys would rise to 68.7 percent!

The relationship between welfare regimes and their effect on trust can be examined more formally by probing the relationship between the decommodification scores and trust rather than relying on the relatively impressionistic threefold categorization. Figure 5.1 displays the relationship between decommodification (Scruggs 2004) and social trust. Social trust is the dependent variable derived from column 4 in table 5.2 and represents the "poll of polls," that is, the averages of the three surveys. This should help reduce any anomalies in the three surveys and produce a more robust measure of social trust.

A positive, statistically significant relationship is visible, indicating that more universal welfare regimes tend to create higher social trust. In addition, when the decommodification index is replaced with simple dummy variables for the Scandinavian countries (Norway, Sweden, Denmark, and Finland) the positive relationship becomes significant at the $p < .000$ level, clearly indicating that the highly decommodifying, universal, Scandinavian welfare states positively and significantly affect levels of social trust. Running the model with robust regression estimates, that is, estimates that reduce the effect of observations that are located farther from the regression line in order to reduce the effects of outliers, thereby establishing a truer relationship between the variables, does not markedly change the results. This means that the relationship is not driven by outliers or points with high leverage (Belseley, Kuh, and Welsch 1980).

It is conceivable that the levels of trust may be affected by the foreign resident population. Table 5.1 shows that the Scandinavian countries do have a lower percentage of foreign residents than the continental European states and certainly less than traditional immigration countries such

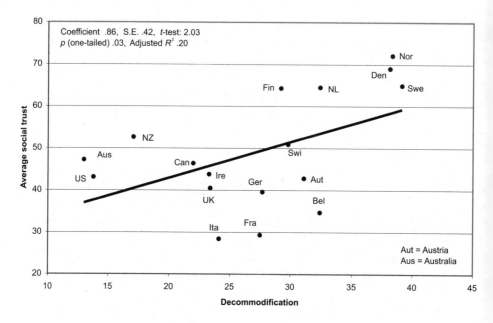

Fig. 5.1. Relationship between levels of decommodification and social trust in
17 modern societies

as Australia, Canada, New Zealand, and the United States. Thus, it is ad-
visable to add the percentage of the foreign-born population to test
whether the initial association is still valid.

Even controlling for the foreign-born population, table 5.3 shows
that the statistical association between decommodification or the
dummy variable for Scandinavia (Norway, Sweden, Denmark, and Fin-

TABLE 5.3. Multiple Regression of Decommodification and Percentage of
Foreign-Born Population on Social Trust

	Coefficient	S.E.	p-Value	Adj. R^2
Model 1				
Decommodification	1.83	.65	.014	
Foreign-born population	.64	.53	.25	
Intercept	−7.3	21.47	.74	.29
Model 2				
Dummy for Scandinavia	27.3	5.5	.000	
Foreign-born population	.46	.35	1.31	
Intercept	38.4	4.5	8.5	.60

Source: Data from OECD 2003, Scruggs 2004, and World Values Survey 2000/01.
Note: S.E. = standard error.

land) and social trust is still valid. Model 1, using decommodification scores, clearly indicates that higher decommodification leads to higher social trust, and model 2 suggests that the Scandinavian countries are particularly apt in establishing social trust.

These findings show that institutional context matters. It appears that social trust is an outcome of universal welfare regimes, which, by avoiding stigmatization and establishing equal access to welfare benefits, have the capacity to attain higher levels of social trust, which in turn, as was demonstrated in chapter 3, can blunt nativist resentment. By reducing publicity about who the receivers of welfare are, universal welfare states make it more difficult to determine who the other is and establish a sense of equality and common humanity above and beyond the security function for which the welfare state was originally devised. Trust, it seems, is an outflow of institutional design.

Worlds of Welfare and Welfare Chauvinism

Just as the universal welfare state can mollify differences between the rich and poor by creating higher social trust, the same logic may also work in blunting welfare chauvinism as natives encounter immigrants receiving welfare support. Can the same logic of the trust-creating welfare state also be applied in societies characterized by increased diversity? Is welfare chauvinism blunted in universal welfare states or does the provision of welfare services to immigrants heighten welfare chauvinism in universal systems? As previously homogeneous societies, such as the Nordic countries, are becoming more diverse and "visible" minorities are emerging in larger numbers, often in concentrated areas, is it possible that the logic of the universal welfare state, which is that it is much more difficult to recognize who the other is, coming apart in the face of clearly visible minorities who are also receivers of welfare benefits? Michael Bommes and Andrew Geddes (2000, 251) argue that "immigrants appear as illegitimate if they are seen as claiming support from the welfare state and thereby claiming access to resources which are viewed as reserved for members of the community of legitimate welfare receivers." Herbert Kitschelt (1995, 252) argues that welfare chauvinism may in fact be a "rational" response by the marginalized insofar as incoming immigrants may threaten their survival by putting enormous pressures on it rather than being driven by cultural differences. "Welfare chauvinism is likely to appeal particularly to less well-off members of the community," he explains, those "who expect to gain from the redistributive welfare state but fear an anti-welfare state backlash if the number of net beneficiaries swells due to the special needs of immigrants."

Welfare chauvinism can be divided into two parts: first, the fear that immigrants will come in and steal the jobs of natives; and, second, that they will "free ride" on the welfare state. As newcomers arrive, they initially place a greater burden on the welfare system in terms of their needs for housing and health care. Still, of the two, the fear that immigrants take jobs away is probably more powerful than the fear that they abuse the system of social benefits. For instance, in the United States there was resentment against immigration long before there was a welfare state of any sort, and this resentment was fueled by fear for jobs. This is still the case today.

The fear of losing one's job and the degree to which a welfare state "decommodifies" one's life chances are related, however. The fear of losing a job to immigrants should be higher in a weak welfare state, where there is no safety net to catch those who fall victim to a major economic crisis. Where there is a very well developed welfare state, the fear of losing a job should be ameliorated by the knowledge that the state will take care of those who are affected by such an economic crisis. In other words, a strong welfare state that guarantees that the loss of a job will not be a catastrophic event ought to ameliorate the fear of immigrants taking over jobs. This is the same logic that makes the welfare state into a trust-generating device. It is easier to go out on a limb and trust knowing that if one's trust is exploited the sucker's payoff will be less painful as a result of the existence of an encompassing welfare state. It is precisely the sense of economic security provided by the welfare state that makes trusting relationships between people more likely.[5]

Two outcomes are possible. It is not inconceivable that in comprehensive welfare systems the challenges of race, ethnicity, and otherness prove to be more benign than in means-tested ones. Just as comprehensive systems of social provision can generate more social trust, so welfare chauvinism may prove to be less of a lightning rod issue than in means-tested welfare states, where the stigmatized welfare receivers are singled out for everyone to see. Particularly if welfare receivers belong to a "visible" minority, the mechanisms of universal welfare delivery make them indistinguishable from natives. On the other hand, if visible difference is reinforced with stigmatization of welfare receivers, public reaction against such groups may be more pronounced and virulent. Thus, there is a greater chance of "ethnicization" of welfare politics in means-tested environments than in universal ones. Redistributive struggles between natives and foreigners may be reduced in institutional contexts of more comprehensive social protection while the opposite may be the case in contexts in which less comprehensive systems put the politics of identity into sharper relief. In addition, the charge of abusing the welfare system is simply less likely to develop in universal than in means-tested arrangements (Rothstein 2002). This is essentially the same argument made by those who have examined the origins popular support for the welfare state in general without focusing on immigrants. Support for the welfare is argued to be greater in universal systems because everybody is benefiting from it. The coalition of receivers of benefits is larger than in means-tested ones, and thus there should be more support for such policies (Papadakis and Bean 1993).

However, the opposite may be true also. It is not counterintuitive to argue that precisely because a welfare regime is universal, and widely known to be universal by members of the host society, welfare chauvinism should be more pronounced than in means-tested ones. Means-tested regimes are more meager to begin with, and natives may feel that means testing will ensure that only those who are "deserving" of welfare are in fact receiving the meager support. This is not the case in universal systems, where everybody, including immigrants, is eligible for rather generous welfare support (Guiraudon 1998; Banting 1999). This has given rise to the suspicion of many natives that immigrants choose their target country on the basis of the generosity of its welfare state. As already mentioned, there is a whole class of immigrants, in Hammar's term "denizens," who are enjoying extensive social protection even though full membership in the host society is denied (Hammar 1990).

The groups that are generally in the most precarious position are asylum seekers. In many countries, such as Germany and the United Kingdom, they are not allowed to work while their cases are being processed, yet they have significant welfare needs. As they are awaiting their fate, sitting in public parks and languishing on street corners while at the same time receiving benefits, they tend to construct many natives' image of the jobless asylum seeker who came to exploit "their" welfare state. Oftentimes such images are overdrawn by the sensationalist media and help establish a potent perception of welfare chauvinism that radical right-wing parties are more than ready to exploit. On the other hand, over the past two decades Western countries received about nine million applications for asylum and only one-third of them were granted, increasing suspicions that many such applications are in fact fraudulent (Spencer 2003). As a result, some call for policy reform allowing asylum seekers to work while their status is examined (Spencer 2003). Thomas Faist reports that during the 1980s in Germany the financial burdens on local communities that were paying for food and housing for asylum seekers became so heavy that the communities began granting work permits to alleviate those burdens. However, the granting of work permits to asylum seekers increased the number of applications, and thus, "the liberal handling of work permits was restricted again until 1991 when asylum seekers were eligible for restricted work permits after a waiting period" (Faist 1994, 442).

For these reasons it is possible that welfare chauvinism is more pronounced in universal (health care, child benefits, pensions) welfare states than in more limited ones precisely because of the high visibility of immigrants combined with the universal provision of welfare and the perhaps "rational" perception that further immigration will put unbearable strains on the welfare state, threatening the security of the local population, which depends on public assistance. In more residual welfare states, means testing may help establish a sense that only the deserving are being supported and help reduce the suspicion that large portions of the population are abusing public assistance.

An additional reason why universal welfare provision may increase welfare chauvinism among natives is that generous welfare support obviates the need for immigrants to integrate into the host society, in terms of establishing contacts at the workplace, or engaging in common activities with members of the host society. Generous welfare provision may facilitate the establishment of "parallel" societies, with little interaction between immigrants and natives. If a public perception develops that links the ability of immigrant subcultures to exist independent of the host society as a result of the welfare state, such sentiments should manifest themselves in an acute form of welfare chauvinism.

In the post–9/11 period, the way in which natives perceive foreigners, particularly Muslims, could have drastic consequences for domestic peace. The specter that is haunting Europe, not only since 9/11 but since the early 1990s, is "Islamophobia." Differences in the institutional setup of the welfare state could either heighten or mollify potential racial, ethnic, or religious conflicts. Depending on how comprehensive forms of social protection are organized, welfare states may play a much more fundamental role than just delivering economic security; they may deliver social harmony in times when racial, ethnic, and religious bonds seem particularly frayed. This is not to say that they are a panacea. After all, the social instability in the wake of the Van Gogh murder in the Netherlands, a rather generous welfare state, proved that even such systems are no guarantee that such horrific acts will not occur. Yet welfare states are about who is "in" and who is "out," at least in the perception of many natives, academic findings of "denizenship" notwithstanding. Already frayed relationships based on primordial differences can become seriously accentuated when they are overlaid with perceptions by natives that foreigners are undeserving receivers of welfare benefits. The crucial question to be answered is: does the type of welfare regime make a difference when it comes to welfare chauvinism?

Fortunately, over the last few years the various large-scale opinion surveys have polled European publics precisely along these lines. Table 5.4 shows the "three worlds" again, as classified along Scruggs's (2004) levels of decommodification, and their attendant levels of welfare chauvinism.

Table 5.4 reveals some unsettling results. If we define *welfare chauvinism* as a widespread perception that foreigners undermine the protective umbrella of the social welfare state, to which the natives' life chances are directly linked, by abusing and misusing social services, claiming benefits for which they are not eligible, and taking jobs away, the results in table 5.4 demonstrate widespread levels of welfare chauvinism. For example, column (a) shows that the most protective responses were elicited by people in the conservative/corporatist clusters who favored giving jobs to locals when jobs are scarce. An average of more than 69 percent agreed with the statement that "when jobs are scarce, employers should give priority to [nationals] over immigrants." This may be caused by the strongly earnings driven logic of this type of welfare state, which extends support to recognized groups and people who must demonstrate a prior earnings history before being eligible to draw welfare benefits. This can clearly be seen in the case of Austria, where over 80 percent of respondents "agreed" with the statement. Austria represents a prime example of a country where public support depends on a prior earnings history. In other words, in such systems having a job means not only "having a job" but also being protected in times when the job is gone.

In striking contrast to Austria stands Sweden, where not even 13 percent of respondents felt the same way. Based on the new welfare state entitlement data set, Austria falls into the conservative/corporatist cluster while Sweden remains in the social-democratic cluster. The difference

TABLE 5.4. Worlds of Welfare and Welfare Chauvinism

	(a)	(b)	(c)	(d)	(e)	(f)
Liberal Welfare States						
Australia	47.9	n.a.	n.a.	n.a.	n.a.	n.a.
United States	55.9	n.a.	n.a.	n.a.	n.a.	n.a.
New Zealand	35.5	n.a.	n.a.	n.a.	n.a.	n.a.
Switzerland	73.5	n.a.	48.3	72.4	28.5	43.7
Italy	75.2	41.5	42.3	47.0	46.0	36.0
United Kingdom	65.0	57.8	50.4	74.6	41.5	37.0
Average	58.8	49.7	47.0	64.7	38.7	38.9
Conservative/Corporatist Welfare States						
Canada	57.2	n.a.	n.a.	n.a.	n.a.	n.a.
Ireland	78.6	56.5	50.6	79.0	46.0	39.2
France	59.7	65.3	55.0	67.3	30.3	47.9
Austria	81.1	46.1	47.5	65.8	35.7	36.9
Finland	69.3	55.0	48.9	70.0	29.1	38.7
Average	69.2	55.7	50.5	70.5	35.3	40,7
Social-Democratic Welfare States						
Germany	73.5	56.9	55.8	80.8	46.4	37.7
Belgium	53.6	65.8	42.5	74.4	42.0	28.9
Sweden	12.6	46.4	24.0	60.0	12.0	15.2
Netherlands	29.2	48.6	39.0	66.6	21.0	21.8
Denmark	39.0	51.9	35.4	72.2	14.0	37.7
Norway	55.4	n.a.	30.0	60.0	18.0	12.0
Average	43.9	53.9	37.8	69.0	25.6	25.6

Source: Column a, World Values Survey 2000; column b, Eurobarometer 53 2000; columns c–f, European Social Survey 2002.

Note: The percentages in column a represent answers to the following question (WVS, 1999/2000): "When jobs are scarce, employers should give priority to [Nation] people over immigrants." Answer options: (1) agree; (2) disagree. The numbers represent the percentages of those respondents who indicated "agree."

Column b represents the precentages of respondents who indicated "tend to agree" (with the other option being "tend to disagree") to the following question: "The people who live in [our country] come from different races, religions, or cultures. They form different groups of varying sizes which are more or less homogenous. For each of the following opinions, please tell me whether you tend to agree or tend to disagree: People from these minority groups abuse the system of social benefits" (Eurobarometer 53 2000).

For column c the item reads as follows: "People who come to live and work here generally harm the economic prospects of the poor more than the rich." The numbers represent the percentages of the sum of those who indicated either "strongly agree" or "agree."

Column d represents percentages of people who fell into the 0–4 range (of a total of 0–10), with 1 meaning "Generally take out more" and 10 meaning "Generally put in more." The question was as follows: "Taxes and Services: Immigrants take out more than they put in."

The e column represents percentages of people who indicated any of the first four answer categories (out of 10) to the following question: "Using this card, would you say that people who come to live and work here generally take jobs away from workers in [your country], or generally help to create jobs?" (0 = take jobs away; 10 = create new jobs).

The last column, f, reflects reactions to the following statement: "Average wages/salaries are generally brought down by immigrants." The numbers represent percentages of the sum of those who indicated either "agreed strongly" or "agreed." Question items c–f are from the European Social Survey 2002.

n.a. = not available.

between the public reactions to this question may be found in the different institutional setups of the two types of welfare states.

Columns (b–f) in table 5.4 are based on the ESS and the EB surveys.
The limitation of both European surveys is of course that they do not
include the United States, Canada, Australia, and New Zealand, limiting
the liberal welfare regime cluster, according to Esping-Andersen, to only
Ireland and Great Britain and reducing the total number of observations
of modern, established welfare states to 11 in the Eurobarometer data series and 14 in the European Social Survey series.

Even in Sweden, which otherwise appears to be the paragon of a
high-trust and egalitarian society, over 46 percent of respondents believe
that minorities abuse the system of social benefits. Column (d) also reveals high levels of welfare chauvinism even in the Nordic, high-trust
countries. For instance, Denmark shows almost three-fourths of the
population believing that "immigrants generally take out more" in taxes
and services than they put in. In both Sweden and Norway that percentage drops to 60, which still indicates that large swaths of Nordic populations believe that immigrants are a drain on public services.

It is surprising that public opinion does not seem to vary much with
the percentage of foreign-born population in those countries, a finding
also noted by Citrin and Sides (2004). For example, the foreign-born
population reached about 1.8 percent in Finland in 2000 and 5.4 percent in Sweden. Even though the foreign-born population in Sweden is
three times higher than in Finland, the latter indicates higher welfare
chauvinism across all six measures in table 5.4. On some issues, Finland
shows much higher welfare chauvinism, as evidenced in its public reaction to item (a), where almost 70 percent of Finns indicated their belief
that "when jobs are scarce, employers should give priority to Finnish
people" while less than 13 percent of the Swedish public felt that way. A
similar picture emerges when Australia, a traditional immigration country, and Germany, which until recently was not considered a traditional
immigration country, are compared. In the year 2000, Australia's foreign-
born population was over 23 percent while in Germany that percentage
stood at just under 9. Yet not quite 48 percent of Australians believed that
jobs in Australia should be given to Australians while 73.5 percent of
Germans thought that when jobs are scarce they should be given to
Germans. It could be that the national percentage of foreign-born population may not be the appropriate measure. It may be that the "visibility" of immigrants is what drives welfare chauvinism. However, when

the percentage of non-EU immigrants is regressed against the six mea-sures of welfare chauvinism in table 5.4, in no instance did that relation-ship reach statistical significance. Another explanation may be found in the residential density of immigrants, that is, even though as a percentage of the national population immigrants may not be high in number, if they live in concentrated areas this may lead to higher welfare chauvin-ism. This question, however, takes us too far afield from institutional is-sues examined in this section.

Nevertheless, some general conclusions from table 5.4 can be drawn. In four of the six measures of welfare chauvinism, the social-democratic cluster indicated the lowest levels of welfare chauvinism. Regressing Scruggs's measure of decommodification and controlling for the per-centage of foreign-born population (not shown), the coefficient of de-commodification is significant at the .05 level for four (items a, c, e, and f) out of the six measures. In two cases, the decommodification mea-sure is not significant, although it is in the predicted direction (items b and d).

These results provide remarkable evidence that the universal welfare state indeed reduces welfare chauvinism rather than heightening it. En-dogeneity (i.e., that chauvinist attitudes lead to the institutional config-uration of welfare states) is illogical, as the welfare state was long estab-lished before any immigrants arrived. Welfare chauvinism is lower the higher the level of decommodification. This suggests that the most effec-tive way to deal with immigrants is to include them in the systems of public welfare provision rather than excluding them. It is not *despite* the universality of these welfare states but *because* of their universality that they have been successful in reducing widespread negative sentiments against immigrants and the welfare state. The salience of the "politics of difference" is likely to increase in the coming years and decades with tremendous potential for civil unrest between immigrants and natives. Inclusion of foreigners in the family of universal welfare supporters and recipients assists them in integrating into their new homelands. But per-haps more importantly from the standpoint of citizens, the welfare state remains not only a viable tool for integrating foreigners but a tool that continues to foster a sense of security and equality, highlighting the con-tinued viability of the modern welfare state.

What precisely is the influence of "context" on such individuals' at-titudes? How much of the variation in such attitudes can be explained by individual-level characteristics and how much can be explained by the welfare regimes themselves? To answer these questions requires a short excursion into multilevel, hierarchical analysis.

A MULTILEVEL ANALYSIS

Hierarchical linear modeling (HLM) has only been possible for about one and a half decades (Raudenbush and Bryk 2002). The use of multilevel analysis originated in the field of education. Students of education have long understood that a pupils' performance is not just a matter of their innate capacity and work ethic. Typically, performance of students is also a matter of, for instance, class size (large or small), the type of school (private or public), the type of county (agricultural or industrial), characteristics of the state (northern or southern), and perhaps even characteristics of the country compared to those of other countries. Obviously, such nested data structures occur not only in the field of education but also in sociology, economics, geography, and social psychology and certainly in political science. Whenever someone attempts to explain individual differences in outcomes on the basis of "institutions," for instance, the researcher assumes a nested data structure, that is, citizens are exposed to structural and organizational features that are the same for all of them but vary across groups. For instance, Erik Bleich (2003) has argued that in managing race relations policy differences between Great Britain and France are driven by differences in "frames," that is, different ideas about how to implement racial policies. These frames, if shared very widely, establish the context in which policy unfolds, and this may differ from country to country. In fact, hierarchical data structures are a very common phenomenon since people tend to exist within larger organizational units such as families, counties, cities, states, provinces, countries, and many other groupings.

Ordering the results of individual attitudes along lines of welfare regime clusters means that such individual attitudes are seen to be driven by the institutional contexts. In other words, such attitudes are "nested" within particular groups, which are believed to be responsible for the individual differences. In other words, individual attitudes are a function of sociodemographic predictors of individual-level variables such as income, gender, and education in addition to high-level variables such as institutions. To model such multilevel effects correctly, HLM is necessary to capture appropriately the high-level effects on individual-level attitudes.[6]

The advantage of multilevel analysis is that it recognizes this nested, hierarchical structure. The two traditional methods of analysis, aggregate-level and individual-level analysis, have serious drawbacks. In aggregate data analysis, individual data are aggregated to the organizational units, leading to the wasting of information and the well-known ecological fallacy. Using individual-level analysis creates different problems. Disaggregating information to the individual level across different contexts violates the crucial assumption of independence of observations. In other words, people who come from a particular county, city, region, or other organizational grouping have more things in common (morals, income, ethnicity, religion, education, etc.) than if they were drawn randomly from the whole population. Thus, because such individuals share certain characteristics, observations based on these individual-level data are not fully independent. Moreover, using large-scale individual-level analyses tends to lead to type I errors (false positives). Analyzing nested and cross-level relationships using the familiar ordinary least squares (OLS) regressions results in biased estimates (inaccurate estimates) and inefficient estimates (wrong significance tests). These problems are aggravated as the level of nonindependence across units increases. Hierarchical linear modeling estimates two different models simultaneously: first, it estimates relationships within each of the lower-level units (level 1); and, second, it models the ways in which level 1 relationships vary between units (level 2 model).[7] National levels of decommodification establish the context (level 2) while individual characteristics such as income, gender, and education are measured at level 1. Figure 5.2 shows how multilevel analysis is used to explain levels of welfare chauvinism.

There is a multitude of items from the ESS (2002) that could be used as dependent variables to tap welfare chauvinism. In order to take maximum advantage of the many items in that survey a principal component factor analysis was conducted. Five items were entered into the principal component factor analysis. All five were found to have one shared commonality, as only one factor emerged after a varimax rotation (not shown). The latent concept that emerges is called "welfare chauvinism." The five items, which all originate from the European Social Survey, are as follows.

1. "Most people who come and live here work and pay taxes. They also use health and welfare services. On balance, do you think people who come here take out more than they put in or put in more than they take out?"

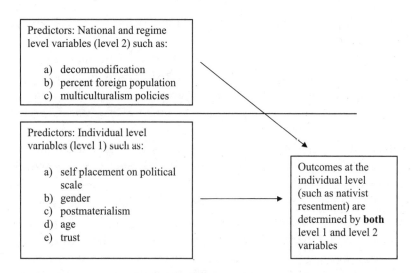

Fig. 5.2.   Contextual and individual predictors of welfare chauvinism

2. "Using this card, would you say that people who come to live and work here generally take jobs away from workers in [your country], or generally help to create jobs?"
3. "Using this card, please say how much you agree or disagree with each of the following statements: "Average wages/salaries are generally brought down by immigrants.""
4. "Using this card, please say how much you agree or disagree with each of the following statements: If people who have come to live here commit any crime they should be made to leave."
5. "Using this card, please say how much you agree or disagree with each of the following statements: If people who have come to live and work here are unemployed they should be made to leave."

The first three items are familiar from table 5.4. Item 4 is also tightly connected to the other economic items. The reason could be that natives may think that rather than letting foreigners who have committed a crime become a public burden it is better to send them back. The fifth item captures a similar economic motive that corresponds well to the concept of welfare chauvinism: rather than having the unemployed become a burden on the public it is better to make them leave the country. Cronbach's alpha, the measure that captures the interitem reliability for the five items is .71, which is considered to be in the "acceptable" range (Nunnaly 1978).

In multilevel models there are no readily available measures that capture the "fit" of an overall model, such as the R^2 in regression analysis. However, it is possible to measure the "proportionate variance," that is, the amount of variance that is explained by the variables at each level of the hierarchy. In table 5.5, 29 percent of the variance of level 2 is explained by the percentage of foreign-born population and decommodification, and 21 percent is explained by the various independent variables at the individual level. The reduction of deviance that the full model accounts for (from a Chi-square statistic of about 8,089 down to 7,274) is statistically significant, indicating that the model contributed significantly to the explanation of the variation in welfare chauvinism.[8]

Even when controlling for the percentage of foreign-born population, the multilevel analysis in table 5.5 demonstrates that welfare chauvinism is significantly lower when decommodification, a contextual effect, and trust, an individual-level variable, are high. Contextualizing individual sentiments by taking regime clusters seriously, this multilevel analysis provides strong evidence that regimes matter. Nativist concerns that immigrants take their jobs away or that they abuse the welfare state

TABLE 5.5.   Multilevel (HLM) Analysis of Welfare Chauvinism

Regime Level Predictors ($N = 13$)	Welfare Chauvinism
Foreign-born population	.002 (.009)
Decommodification	.025 (.008)**
Individual level predictors ($N = 16,729$)	
Self-placement on left/right scale	−.0056 (.008)***
Female	−.09 (.034)**
Education	.15 (.014)***
Age	−.005 (.00016)**
Unemployment	.034 (.035)
Trust	.29 (.036)***
Between country variance explained (level 2)	29%
Within country variance explained (level 1)	21%
Deviance of intercept-only model (not shown)	8,088.73710
Deviance of model shown	7,274.38545
Deviance reduction: Chi-square ($df = 35$)	814.35165
p-value:	.000

Source: European Social Survey 2002.
Note: Two-tailed tests. Population weights are applied but not shown.
**$p < .01$; ***$p < .001$.

are less pronounced in comprehensive regimes than in liberal regimes, controlling for individual levels of trust, education, self-placement on the political scale, gender, and age. Apparently, episodes of unemployment in the past do not affect people's misgivings about foreigners. People who place themselves on the political right show significantly higher levels of welfare chauvinism than people on the left. Also, and this is somewhat surprising, females tend to indicate higher levels of concern that foreigners take away jobs and abuse the welfare state. These sentiments are shared more when people get older. On the other hand, respondents with higher trust and higher education show significantly lower levels of welfare chauvinism.

Social-democratic welfare states do not have to fear a backlash from their native populations in terms of being too generous with foreigners. This finding is not intuitive. Precisely because social-democratic welfare states are more generous, more welfare chauvinism might have been expected, particularly in the relatively homogeneous Nordic societies. All the data were measured at the beginning of the new millennium after many decades of influx of foreigners into these societies. It appears that universal welfare institutions and high levels of trust combine to stave off misgivings about foreigners in these advanced societies. Extensive welfare states can absorb immigrants with much less groaning and moaning from their native populations than residual welfare states can, giving credence to Titmuss and other early welfare state pioneers, such as Tawney, who understood very clearly that in order for welfare states to be effective it is important to treat people equally and with respect.

Comprehensive welfare systems reduce welfare chauvinism and experience fewer conflicts in the area of politics of identity than in liberal regimes. To be sure, this is not to say that redistributive conflicts between natives and immigrants will not occur. However, for policymakers this is a most important finding as demand for foreign workers will increase as a result of the graying across developed nations. Immigration will most likely supply the necessary workforce in the future, and if regimes are structured so as to facilitate integration of foreigners into a system of social provision that does not lead to adverse nativist reactions disputes between natives and newcomers are more likely to be limited. Universal provision of welfare makes it more difficult to recognize who the other is, to avoid stigmatization, and as a result public welfare chauvinism is more muted in such regimes. It is also more difficult for foreigners to establish a reputation as cheaters in a universal welfare regime than in a means-tested one. This may also help explain why welfare chauvinism is more blunted in social-democratic regimes than in liberal ones. Titmuss appears to have been correct when he argued that universal provision of welfare leads to a more collective, organic, and egalitarian society in which racist and welfare chauvinist voices are more muffled and trust thrives. The findings in table 5.5 demonstrate that societies based on universal welfare regimes not only protect their populations more effectively from the vagaries of the market but also help integrate newcomers into society with fewer adverse reactions from the natives.

Against the backdrop of these findings, the claim of the "Americanization of the European welfare state" is too sensationalist. This finding supports the hunch Harold Wilensky (2002, 653, 654) expressed when he said, "I doubt that the European democracies . . . as they experience increased immigration, must necessarily produce an alienated underclass, the target of a middle mass revolt, American style. Only if they abandon the public policies that encourage labor peace and kept their poverty rates low—family policies, an active labor-market policy, an accommodative framework for industrial relations, a universalistic welfare state—will they drift into the Anglo-American pattern."

It is well known that welfare states tend to equalize people's "life chances," and that is certainly one of the central reasons why genuine welfare states nurture trust. The welfare state creates equality also at a deeper level, what might be called "equality of control," meaning a similarity in the capacity to shape one's own life as well as the lives of others. As such the welfare state equalizes not only living conditions but also power. As a result, welfare states reduce the threat potential among citizens, and that may be another reason why trust flourishes with more abandon in such regimes. The social-democratic welfare state reduces the vulnerability of both immigrants and natives and gives both strata a sense of protection from the vagaries of market forces. The universality of the welfare state prevents an exceedingly stark separation between "us" and "them," thereby establishing trust, which results in lower welfare chauvinism and in turn helps build bridges between immigrants and natives.

CHAPTER 6

To Belong or Not to Belong
Incorporation and Integration
Policies in Modern Welfare States

I am a part of all that I have met.
—Alfred Tennyson

FROM THE PERSPECTIVE OF POLICYMAKERS, the findings in chapter 5 are extremely relevant: the more decommodifying national systems of welfare provision are the lower are the levels of welfare chauvinism among natives. This chapter will probe the determinants of nativist resentment and welfare chauvinism further, and it contends that two additional factors may be crucial in understanding prejudice and resentment. First, it is argued that the pattern by which foreigners are turned into citizens, that is, the type of "incorporation regime," is important. A society with liberal immigration regimes that absorb foreigners relatively quickly blurs the distinction between insiders and outsiders. As a result, public sentiments that foreigners are abusing the welfare state should be more muted and "detachment" by natives from the welfare state should be less expected. Conversely, immigration policies that make it very difficult, if not impossible, for foreigners to ever become members of the host society maintain the "us" versus "them" dichotomy and allow the scapegoating of foreigners. Such policies should increase welfare chauvinism and consequently may lead to the waning of public support of the welfare state. "Citizenship is not only a legal status but also an identity," Christian Joppke reminds us. "As an identity, citizenship depends on and reinforces shared values and understandings, that is, a common culture" (Joppke 1999, 7).

Second, once newcomers become citizens the degree to which states attempt to integrate them into society matters. The two contending approaches at the extremes are "multiculturalism" on the one hand and "assimilation" on the other. Depending on which policies are enacted, support for the welfare state may be differentially affected. Multiculturalism policies (MCPs) not only recognize the ethnic, racial, and religious differences of newcomers but actively support them through state-sanctioned efforts designed to protect and further the interests of such groups. Assimilation, or perhaps more properly integration, is an alternative strategy that calls for newcomers to adjust and ultimately blend into the host society. Precisely because multiculturalism strategies highlight the differences in the new resident population, such policies may lead to more adverse reactions by natives than policies of integration. It may very well be that the more intense the attempts of nations to engage in multiculturalism policies are the lower the support for the welfare state will be. As highlighted in chapter 1, many scholars believe that redistribution schemes such as the welfare state are only viable in relatively homogeneous societies. This chapter will examine whether multiculturalism policies erode support for the welfare state.

While much empirical data have been amassed over the years in terms of differing levels of decommodification and social expenditures, allowing for large-N statistical analyses, there are comparatively few empirical data available that measure "degrees of incorporation" of immigrants or "levels of multiculturalism" across countries. Not only are there very few empirical data, but few authors have connected variations in incorporation regimes with other policy fields, leading Adrian Favell to argue that much of the literature highlighting different incorporation regimes fails to make connections with "wider questions of political economy, welfare, inequality, and democracy in Europe" (1998, 13).

Very recently, Keith Banting and Will Kymlicka (2003) presented the first empirical attempt to measure multiculturalism policies across modern industrialized societies. Similarly, Harald Waldrauch has attempted to empirically measure the integration of foreigners in seven EU countries along several dimensions, including residential requirements, civil and political rights, and social rights (Waldrauch 2001). These are commendable attempts since more empirical support is sorely needed in this field of immigration studies, which is replete with much description but little theory and empirical testing.

TYPES OF INCORPORATION REGIMES AND THE
WELFARE STATE

The degree to which natives are willing to share their society with new-comers is partly determined by the way society allows newcomers in. The policies that regulate inclusion, or exclusion, as the case may be, re-flect the self-image of the nation. That is to say, the contours of immi-gration policies may be driven by deeply held conceptions of the mean-ing of *nation* and the degree of a sense of shared fate that developed during the wrenching process of nation building. As such, these "models" of incorporation of foreigners are themselves based on historical con-structions of what it means to be German, Swedish, or American. In other words, policies on immigration reveal the underlying "political philosophies of integration" (Favell 1998) of the respective nations.

Just as the "varieties of capitalism" literature finds systematic differences in the degree to which countries deal with production structures, de-industrialization, or globalization, are there systematic differences observ-able in the "varieties of integration" different countries pursue? The pol-itics of race, and the problems of welfare chauvinism and nativist resent-ment may be directly linked to the policies and models of integration that different states use. More specifically, is there less nativist violence, preju-dice, and welfare chauvinism in some countries than in others as a result of integration policies?

Mapping the topography of current immigration policies and locat-ing the source of their differences in the historical unfolding of nations was the seminal contribution of Rogers Brubaker in his *Citizenship and Nationhood in France and Germany,* which appeared in 1992. It coincided with the end of the cold war and the breakdown of multiethnic states, raising the burning question of identity and belonging. This timing was both felicitous and infelicitous. It was felicitous because the end of the cold war unleashed significant migration movements, making issues of immigration and multiculturalism salient virtually overnight. It was in-felicitous because the same events started the slow but unstoppable ero-sion of the autonomy of the state, ironing out those very differences and converging toward more uniform immigration policies.

Brubaker's central claim was a path-dependent argument, which es-sentially states that the policies that structure the pathways to citizenship are part and parcel of the processes of nation building and reflect the very self-image of the state. This state-centered approach has been questioned by Yasemin Soysal's concept of "postnationality," which is fed by growing "globalization," raising the paradox between the "universal status of individuals and their rights" detached from the nation-state and the "principle of sovereignty that reinforces national boundaries and invents new ones" (Soysal 1994, 156). In a sense the Brubaker-Soysal debate replicates the "globalists" versus "statists" debate in comparative politics. Any argument claiming that international forces are hollowing out the sovereignty of the state does not sit well with statecentric arguments that insist on the sovereign decision-making capacity of states.

Creating conceptual order is often aided by establishing distinct categories. Since Brubaker's study, there has been a flurry of such attempts to connect policies to predominant ideas. Adrian Favell (1998, 2) speaks of "philosophies of integration" that distinguish British and French approaches to immigration policies, with France relying on republican ideas of *citoyenneté* and *intégration* and Britain attempting to deal with its ethnic dilemma using concepts such as *race relations* and *multiculturalism*. Erik Bleich (2003, 14) identifies different "race frames" that inform British and French policymakers, with the British largely accepting the categories of race and ethnicity while the French "have downplayed or denied the categories of race and ethnicity." Race frames find their origins in the "lived experiences and discourses" of British policy experts and the "coterie of policy experts engaged with the issue of racism" in France (191). The comparative political economy literature does not escape such categorizations either. The "varieties of capitalism" debate has been smoldering, and sometimes burning, at least since Andrew Schonfields' *Modern Capitalism* (1965).

Most recently, with Germany abandoning jus sanguinis, the principle that locates citizenship on the basis of descent, and moving toward jus soli, the principle that recognizes citizenship on the basis of territory, the debate about "historical legacies" in explaining immigration practices has lost some of its edge. In other words, the "differential" policies of including newcomers in Germany compared to France have begun to converge rather than diverge. Even Brubaker admits that "while the 1980s and 1990s witnessed an unprecedented efflorescence of differentialist discourse—and differentialist policies . . . in the domain of immigration, there are signs that the differentialist tide may have begun to ebb" (Brubaker 2001, 532–33). There are others, more skeptical about Brubaker's elegant dichotomy, who have argued that there is more contestation and contingency in immigration policies than Brubaker allows and that liberalism tends to undermine differentialist approaches to immigration policies (Joppke 1999, 1998; Joppke and Morawska 2003).

One such contingency for successful integration is economic opportunity for minorities. The French riots in November 2005 revealed the inadequacy of the Republican model of integration. This model essentially holds that all French citizens have the same cultural identity, that is, French. In fact, being French is the only acceptable identity. No hyphenated names, no special recognition of minorities—everybody is supposed to be equal in this model insofar as all French citizens are the same "children of the Republic," as Jacques Chirac declared at the height of the riots. The French model of integration is an assimilationist model, which requires that everybody speak the same official language and go through a common curriculum in school. Another element of the French Republican model is that the government does not keep official statistics on ethnicity, religion, or social class since this would "violate the Republican tenet that France is 'one and indivisible'" (Stepan and Suleiman 2005).

It is a bitter irony that this model, which was supposed to create a sense of French identity based on common Republican principles, did exactly the opposite, revealing dramatic differences in life chances between two classes of citizens: the "native" French, with French-sounding names, city-center addresses, and white skin color; and second- or third-generation French citizens with dark skin, Muslim-sounding names, and addresses in the dilapidated suburbs. French identity was not enough of a glue to bridge the chasm between those of privilege and poverty in addition to the racial frictions. In the wake of the riots, French prime minister Dominique de Villepin suggested more government involvement in integrating minorities, renovation of some run-down apartment buildings and the destruction of others, and increasing the government's support for those living in deprived neighborhoods by tripling the number of boarding school scholarships given to children from these areas. It appears that the paths these historical legacies have taken are not as constraining as originally thought.

Yet there is no denying that national self-images shape policies. Without intending to reify concepts such as the "nation" it is irrefutable that particular "images of nations," with their own material force, are revealed in comparison with others. A fundamental part of how a nation conceives of "itself" is found also in its political economy and the willingness of the population to support redistributive regimes.

Debates about whether corporatist models, a specific form of cooperation among the state, labor, and employers' organizations, have been
undermined by "globalization" have been going on for the last two
decades, and some scholars have made careers out of endlessly debating
whether country-specific institutions are under attack by "global forces,"
whether there will be a convergence of nation-specific industrial policies, and whether globalization will sound the death knell of corporatism (Katzenstein 1985; Swank 2002; Gourevitch 1978; Strange 1995;
Crepaz 2002; Boyer and Drache 1996; Keohane and Milner 1996; Hirst
and Thompson 1996; Rodrik 1997). The similarities between this debate
and the one between Brubaker and Soysal are uncanny.

The problem of establishing models of such complex arrangements as
political economies, incorporation, and integration policies is that reality
is never as tidy as these carefully drawn typologies suggest. Germany's
turn toward jus soli has put a serious dent in Brubaker's theory that state-
centered traditions have "locked in" policies of incorporation. "With regard to Germany, what Brubaker deemed 'unthinkable' in 1992 ... has in
large measure come to pass," reports Triadafilos Triadafilopoulos (2004, 5),
who argues for an approach that bridges the "internal–external divide,
recognizing the importance of global culture, national traditions, and liberal democratic norms."

Still, the French anthropologist Emmanuel Todd (2002) argues that
intermarriage rates (exogamy or marriages across ethnic and racial
boundaries) are important indicators of tolerance. He finds that relatively few Turkish women marry German men while in France young
maghrebin women marry French men, leading to higher exogamy rates
in France than in Germany. Todd explains this, as Brubaker does, on
the basis of the French Republican tradition, which has managed to go
beyond markers of race and ethnicity and anchor identity in civic
ideals, reducing the effect of ethnicity and race. Germany, which defined itself for long periods of time on the basis of blood relationships,
finds it much harder to engage in exogamous relationships, leading to
lower intermarriage rates. Todd speaks of the "omnipotence of the host
country" in defining the terms of inclusion and classifies Germany as
still a relatively closed society. However, he believes that such differences are radically disappearing, increasing the chances for successfully
dealing with the challenges of integration (taz, die tageszeitung, 19 August 2002).

In stark contrast to the German incorporation regime stands the American regime. The United States is, of course, the worlds' classic settler nation, where "immigration has been a nation founding myth" (Joppke 1999, 8). Although America has not always welcomed immigrants (see chap. 2), the 1965 Hart-Celler Immigration Reform Act, which replaced the National Origins Act of 1924, which allowed immigration from only a few selected Northern European countries, opened U.S. borders to immigrants. In the appendix of his *A Nation of Immigrants,* published posthumously in 1964, President John F. Kennedy affectionately speaks about the various nationalities that came to the United States during the nineteenth and twentieth centuries. Among other immigrants, he speaks of the "bold, imaginative Irish," "from Germany came the liberals and those who fled persecution," "the Japanese and the Chinese brought their gentle dreams," and "the Scandinavians brought their knowledge of agriculture." He concludes his appendix with the statement: "These are some of yesterday's immigrants who have supplied a continuous flow of creative abilities and ideals that have enriched our nation. The immigrants we welcome today and tomorrow will carry on this tradition and help us to retain, reinvigorate and strengthen the American spirit" (Kennedy 1964, 85).[1] Once admitted, the children of immigrants born on American soil automatically receive American citizenship, making the United States a case of jus soli.

It is beyond the scope of this book to describe the incorporation regimes of over a dozen countries in detail. The German, French, and American examples, however, highlight rather significant differences in the ways foreigners are turned into citizens. Table 6.1 lists the incorporation regimes and multiculturalism policies in 17 modern, capitalist societies.

It is tempting to theorize whether different incorporation regimes have a measurable effect on levels of prejudice and resentment in Western societies. When foreigners, no matter how long they have lived in the host country, have no chance of ever becoming citizens of their place of residence, they have no incentive to make any effort to "integrate" with the native population. There will always be a hard, legal wall between them and the majority population. The existence of that legal difference establishes inequality where it matters most: in the political arena. Although some countries allow foreigners to vote in local and even regional elections (Waldrauch 2003), not being able to take part in national elections enshrines the deepest separation between foreigners and natives, namely, that their fates are nor linked. Being excluded from the community of citizens, why should natives care about foreigners and vice versa? This is not to say that human relationships can flourish only on the basis of legal membership in a community, but it certainly does not help if a group is stigmatized as an outsider as a result of legal separation. Harold Wilensky (2002, 652) speaking specifically about the German incorporation regime, states, "The German policy of ethnic exclusion based on descent and combined with wide open access to refugees up to 1993 (perhaps driven by historical guilt) makes the cultural and social integration of minorities difficult, no matter how long they stay." This raises a related issue, which played a crucial part in the myth of American nation building: the concept of taxation without representation. Clearly, an overwhelming number of foreigners pay taxes, but how compatible is that with them being excluded from the national political process?

Viewed from the perspective of members of the native population, knowing that foreigners are not citizens, they tend to treat them as others, as members of an out-group. Clearly, demarcated membership tends

TABLE 6.1. Types of Incorporation Regime and Levels of Multiculturalism Policies (late 1990s)

	Incorporation Regime	Multiculturalism Policies
Australia	0	1
Austria	1	0
Belgium	1	.5
Canada	0	1
Denmark	1	0
Finland	1	0
France	0	0
Germany[a]	1	0
Ireland	1	0
Italy	.5	0
Netherlands	0	.5
New Zealand	0	.5
Norway	1	0
Sweden	0	.5
Switzerland	1	0
United Kingdom	0	.5
United States	0	.5

Source: Incorporation regimes (Lahav 2004, 256); multiculturalism policies (Banting and Kymlicka 2003, revised version, 25–26).
Note: 1 = jus sanguinis; 0 = jus soli.
[a]Germany changed from jus sanguinis to jus soli on January 1, 2000.

to lead to constructed conflicts, as shown in the famous Robbers Cave experiment, elaborated in chapter 2. Many foreigners find that on a daily basis natives do not think of them as having "equal social worth" (Marshall 1950). They are perceived by the majority as "exiles from society" (Moon 1988, 43), very much like the poor, who, as a result of capitalist market forces, have become outsiders, lacking the "means for self respect and the means to be recognized by fellow citizens as of equal worth to themselves, a recognition basic to democracy" (Pateman 1988, 235). Henri Tajfel, the founder of social identity theory, realized that merely placing someone in a group is enough to trigger out-group discrimination. Not only does group membership convey positive emotions of belonging to the in-group, but it also leads to sentiments of superiority over those who are not in the group (Tajfel 1982). With in-group favoritism comes out-group hostility. This is why the label *Ausländer* connotes not only outside status but inadvertently lower status. The ultimate outsiders are foreigners without political rights. In that sense, incorporation regimes based on jus sanguinis, where citizenship is conferred on the basis of descent, should demonstrate more prejudice and resentment than regimes that are more liberal. Harald Waldrauch and Christoph Hofinger (1997, 271), who have been engaged in a most laudable effort to develop "an index to measure the legal obstacles to the integration of migrants," argue similarly: "We believe that the systematic prolongation of legal differences between citizens of a state and immigrants reinforces social and cultural discrimination against the latter."

This is not to say that once citizenship is attained discrimination will stop. Blacks in America have been full citizens at least since the passing of the Civil Rights Act, yet there is no question that discrimination, in perhaps subtler forms, still exists. But when existing prejudice is reinforced with legal separation discrimination is likely to be higher than when there is no legal separation between immigrants and natives.

To test this hypothesis, multilevel modeling is used again in order to examine the effect of the incorporation regime on individual attitudes. To measure the degree of prejudice, I use the familiar question, "On this list are various groups of people: could you please sort out any that you would not like to have as neighbors?" The dependent variable reflects the percentage of those who have mentioned "immigrants" as undesirable neighbors. The central predictor variable for incorporation regimes is the designation of either jus soli or jus sanguinis in table 6.1.

Since in this multilevel model the dependent variable is dichoto-mous (not wanting immigrants as neighbors was either mentioned or not), a nonlinear logit model is the appropriate functional form.[2] Rather than showing the nonintuitive logit coefficients, table 6.2 indi-cates the odds ratios and their significance. Odds ratios above 1 indicate a positive probability (positive impact of variable) and odds ratios below 1 indicate a negative probability (negative impact of variable). For ex-ample, the odds ratio of 1.19 for the variable "interest in politics" (ques-tion item: "How interested would you say you are in politics? 1 = very interested, 2 = somewhat interested, 3 = not very interested, 4 = not at all interested") in the table indicates that people who are less inter-ested in politics are 19 percent more likely to indicate that they do not want immigrants as neighbors than people who are more interested in politics. The more ignorant people are of politics, the more prejudiced they are. Odds ratios below 1, such as the one for "female" at .78, indi-

TABLE 6.2.   **Multilevel Logit Analysis (HLM): Dependent Variable, Immigrants Not Liked as Neighbors (0 = not mentioned; 1 = mentioned)**

Regime Level Predictors (N = 17)	Odds Ratios
Incorporation regime (jus sanguinis = 1; jus soli = 0)	1.65**
Individual level predictors (N = 12,820)	
Life satisfaction	.91***
Interest in politics	1.19***
Self-placement on political scale (1 = left; 10 = right)	1.14***
Age	1.01***
Education	.89***
Income	.94*
Trust	.57***
Female	.78***
Intraclass correlation	20.2%
Deviance of intercept only model (not shown)	31,846.62
Deviance of model shown	31,415.61
Deviance reduction: Chi-square (df = 9)	431.01
p-value	0.000

Source: World Values Survey 2000.

Note: Two-tailed tests. Population weights are applied but not shown.

*$p < .1$; **$p < .05$; ***$p < .01$.

Question items

The precise wording for "life satisfaction" is as follows: "All things considered, how satisfied are you with your life as a whole these days? 1 = dissatisfied; 10 = satisfied."

"How interested would you say you are in politics? 1 = very interested; 2 = somewhat interested; 3 = not very interested; 4 = not at all interested."

cate that females are 22 percent (100–78) less likely than males to indicate that they do not want immigrants as neighbors.

Respondents who are happy with their lives, have higher incomes, are educated, and are female all show significantly less nativist resentment than unhappy people who are less well off, less educated, and male. The strongest of all predictors is trust: the more people trust the less prejudiced they are. However, the more people place themselves ideologically on the right the more likely they are to be prejudiced against immigrants. Similarly, age is also positively related to resentment.

These results are beginning to sound very familiar as they confirm yet one more time the impact of sociodemographics, ideology, and trust on nativist resentment. The emphasis in this chapter is of course on incorporation regimes. Table 6.2 shows that indeed the fashion in which foreigners are turned into citizens matters. Incorporation regimes based on jus sanguinis are 65 percent more likely to create prejudice than regimes based on jus soli. That relationship is significant at the .05 level.

The intraclass correlation of 20.2 indicates that slightly over 20 percent of the overall variance in the model is explained by level 2 variables while around 80 percent is explained by individual-level variables. The reduction of deviance that the full model accounts for (from a Chi-square statistic of about 31,846 down to 31,415) is statistically significant, indicating that the model contributed significantly to the explanation of the variation in whether or not respondents wanted immigrants as neighbors.[3] Similar results were obtained when "people of another race" as a neighbor category was used as a dependent variable. However, for the sake of economy of presentation, they are not shown.

These findings suggest that incorporation regimes matter in reducing prejudice and resentment. Societies that allow a relatively "easy" and quick transition from foreigner to "one of us," at least in legal terms, display less xenophobia than societies in which it is practically impossible to achieve that inclusive status, where otherness not only is maintained in terms of culture and lifestyles but is enshrined in the starkest form possible: legal exclusion from membership in the host society. When existing differences on the basis of culture and lifestyles are reinforced with legal exclusion, it is no small wonder that both natives and foreigners have no incentives to make an effort to integrate. Legal exclusion from membership means that it is officially sanctioned that fates are not interlinked. Is it really surprising that in such societies there is more xenophobia, hate, and racism than in societies where the paths toward membership are less restrictive?

The Impact of Multiculturalism Policies
on the Welfare State

It is important to draw clear distinctions between incorporation regimes (how foreigners are turned into citizens) and multiculturalism policies (what is done in terms of integrating newcomers once they have become residents) for they are substantively different concepts. However, empirically they may not be as distinct as they appear. Just as the degree of liberalism in incorporating citizens can be thought of as a measure of tolerance of the receiving society, so can the level of integration policies (ranging between the extremes of "radical" multiculturalism and assimilation) be thought of as a measure of tolerance. There is also good empirical evidence that these two measures are related. The Pearson's r correlation coefficient between incorporation regime and multiculturalism policies is .64 based on the data in table 6.1. Those who favor "easy" incorporation of foreigners should also support multiculturalism policies. Surprisingly, this is not the case. Banting and Kymlicka argue that "many critics of multiculturalism policies are in fact defenders of more open borders: they are happy with the idea of greater ethnic and racial diversity in the population, but simply oppose any government recognition or accommodation of this diversity through multiculturalism policies" (Banting and Kymlicka 2003, 15). They understand British immigration policies to follow that pattern where the government is hoping that British citizens will accept multiculturalism policies for those immigrants who are already in Britain while in turn the government will allow fewer new immigrants in.

Canada was the first country to establish official multiculturalism policies in 1971. These were designed to, among other things, "assist cultural groups to retain and foster their identity; to promote creative exchanges among all Canadian cultural groups; and to assist immigrants in acquiring at least one of the official languages."[4] In 1988, the Canadian Multiculturalism Act was passed by Parliament to give a clearer architecture and more purpose to the earlier expressions of multiculturalism. These policies were intended, among other things, to "recognize and promote the understanding that multiculturalism reflects the cultural and racial diversity of Canadian society," to "foster the recognition and appreciation of the diverse cultures" and "promote policies, programs and practices that enhance the understanding of and respect for the diversity of the members of Canadian society" (Canadian Multiculturalism Act).[5]

However, these policies were contested almost from their inception (Bissoondath 1994; Gwyn 1995; Granatstein 1998). While these critics were specifically writing about the Canadian case, the critiques are so general that they can be applied to any other country. The critiques against multiculturalism generally center around the perceived loss of the majority identity, what Brian Barry called, "losing our way" (2001, 1). In addition, critics of multiculturalism policies argue that by highlighting differences between different groups the sense of a common identity, which is necessary for the welfare state to command support, is undermined. Finally, focusing on identity politics, so the critics argue, directs attention away from truly important issues such as growing inequality and issues of economic redistribution (Wolfe and Klausen 1997), as is so powerfully stated in one of Todd Gitlin's (1995, 126) chapter titles, "Marching on the English Department While the Right Took the White House."

This is not to suggest that multiculturalism policies, once created, are set in stone. The Netherlands for example, experienced a move from an expressly multicultural approach in the 1980s to an integrationist approach in the late 1990s. In the early 1980s, when there still was a belief that the temporary "guests" would eventually leave, the Dutch government established policies to ensure their cultural identity. Employers were required to provide acceptable accommodation for immigrants, and most welfare provisions, such as unemployment benefits, housing allowances, public assistance and health care, were extended to the Dutch "guest workers." Native-language instruction for the children of migrants was provided in order to assist them when they returned to their homelands.[6] Han Entzinger describes this policy as "integration with retention of identity."

By the 1990s, however, ethnic minorities had almost doubled in size as a result of both continuing immigration and high fertility rates among resident immigrants combined with the proliferation of different immigrant groups and more diversity within each group. This began to challenge the earlier multiculturalist orientation (Entzinger 2003). The multiculturalist policies failed to improve the migrants' socially impoverished position, ethnic segregation was increasing, and unemployment among immigrants was significantly higher. In 1994, the earlier multicultural policy was replaced with an integration policy. *Integration,* according to Entzinger (2003, 72), was "a term almost taboo in political circles until then."

Since the killing of Pim Fortuyn, and even more so after the assassination of Theo van Gogh in 2004, the terms of discourse have dramatically changed. A colder wind is blowing in the Netherlands. On November 19, 2004, at a European Union justice and interior ministers meeting, the Dutch immigration minister, Rita Verdonk, said: "It's not that we are against immigration. If you want to live in the Netherlands, you have to adhere to our rules . . . and learn our language." With this statement Verdonk seems to have abandoned even the rhetoric of multiculturalism let alone the policies. But even before Van Gogh's murder it was noted that "integration policies in the Netherlands no longer are as outspokenly multiculturalist as they have been in the past. The initial multiculturalist approach was ill-conceived" (Entzinger 2003, 84).

The United Kingdom also appears to be moving away from multiculturalism policies. Ever since the summer riots of 2001 in Burnley, Oldham, and Bradford, the concept of multiculturalism has come under scrutiny as it became clear that the roots of the riots were found in the segregated neighborhoods, segregated schools, segregated workplaces, and lack of economic opportunities for Asians. A British government report found "shockingly divided" communities with very little interaction between whites and Asians, who were mostly of Pakistani descent (Kelly 2001). In 2004, Trevor Phillips, chairman of the Commission for Racial Equality, denounced multiculturalism and declared, "We need to assert there is a core of Britishness" (Portillo 2005). And in the wake of the deadly July 7, 2005, bombings in London, which killed 56 people and injured 700 others, Prime Minister Tony Blair proposed strict anti-terror measures, including surveillance of mosques, extremist Web sites, and bookstores and deportation of radical Islamic leaders who were inciting anti-Western feelings among impressionable Muslim youths. Blair used strong language to defend his controversial deportation policy: "The rules of the game are changing. . . . We are angry. We are angry about extremism and about what they are doing to our country, angry about their abuse of our good nature. . . . We welcome people here *who share our values and our way of life*. But don't meddle in extremism because if you meddle in it . . . you are going back out again" (emphasis added) (Bellaby 2005).

Critics have been unsparing in the demolition of multiculturalism, particularly the essential claim of multiculturalists that different groups must not only be recognized but their interests must be specifically supported by the state. One defender of nationality, David Miller, has argued that such singling out of groups "is liable to backfire, by exposing groups to outright rejections and rebuffs which they would not experience under a less politically charged regime of toleration" (Miller 2000, 75). Brian Barry (2001, 21) echoes that view, scolding that "the politics of difference is a formula for manufacturing conflict, because it rewards those groups that can most effectively mobilize to make claims on the polity."

Multiculturalists such as Will Kymlicka, of course, take a very different view, claiming that at least as far as Canada and Australia are concerned evidence indicates that multiculturalism policies have not eroded social unity. If anything, Kymlicka argues, such policies have enhanced social unity, as evidenced by "increases in the levels of interethnic friendships and intermarriage." He claims that Canada and Australia "do a better job integrating immigrants into common civic and political institutions than any other country in the world" (2001, 37).

Rather than detailing the vast and sometimes vitriolic debate about multiculturalism, the focus here will be on what Banting and Kymlicka call the "corroding effect," which argues that "multiculturalism policies erode solidarity because they emphasize differences between citizens, rather than commonalities. Citizens have historically supported the welfare state, and been willing to make sacrifices to support their disadvantaged co-citizens, because they viewed these co-citizens as 'one of us,' bound together by a common identity and common sense of belonging. However, multiculturalism policies are said to corrode this overarching common identity" (Banting and Kymlicka 2003, 4).

For the case of immigrant groups, Banting and Kymlicka (2003, 25) define multiculturalism policies as: (1) parliamentary affirmation of multiculturalism; (2) the adoption of multiculturalism in school curricula; (3) the inclusion of ethnic representation/sensitivity in the mandate of public media or media licensing; (4) exemptions from dress codes, Sunday closing legislation, and so on; (5) allowing dual citizenship; (6) the funding of ethnic group organizations or activities; (7) the funding of bilingual education or mother-tongue instruction; and (8) affirmative action. The time period for which they examine these policies ranges from 1980 to the late 1990s. Depending on whether a country adopts most or all of these policies, the country gets either a "weak," "modest," or "strong" rating (26). The countries with strong multiculturalism policies receive a value of 1, those with modest policies a .5, and those with weak policies a 0. The countries and their scores are depicted in table 6.1.

With this categorization of multiculturalism policies in place, it is tempting to examine whether there are associations between such policies and the welfare state. Such associations can be measured at different levels. The multiculturalism policies are aggregate-level data, and they can be correlated with aggregate-level data on the extent of decommodification and on various welfare measures, total social expenditures, or disaggregated measures of social expenditures. It is important in this context to realize that "change in rate" of welfare measures is the appropriate measure rather than the actual "level" of welfare expenditures. The reason for this is that variations in different levels occurred long before multiculturalism policies came into being and are driven by political parties, the degree of pluralism and corporatism, types of political institutions, and a whole host of other factors.

The question to tackle is this: have welfare states become diminished between 1980 and the late 1990s, for which the Banting and Kymlicka data set is applicable, as a result of multiculturalism policies? This requires comparing the change in the generosity of welfare states between 1980 and 1999 with multiculturalism policies. Fortunately, the social expenditures database of the OECD has very detailed accounts of measures such as expenditures for old age, unemployment compensation, health care, survivors' benefits, and incapacity-related programs.

There is particular pressure on two types of expenditures as far as immigrants are concerned: health care and unemployment compensation. In almost every country in Europe, the percentage of unemployed immigrants is on average twice as high as the percentage of unemployed natives (OECD 2003). Similarly, immigrants have greater health care needs than the average population. Any manifestation of adverse native reaction against redistributive mechanisms should be visible in these two measures. According to the "corroding effect" hypothesis, public support for such expenditures should wane among natives since the receivers of such support are perceived to be "not one of us." The overarching identity that enabled the establishment of such redistributive schemas in the first place, so the critics say, is diminishing as a result of multiculturalism policies. This should ultimately be reflected in reduced rates of growth or even absolute reductions in unemployment compensation and health expenditures.

The third aggregate measure used is Scruggs's decommodification measure. This taps a separate dimension of public insurance insofar as it does not reflect "expenditures" but programmatic elements of redistribution, capturing factors such as replacement rates, duration of benefits, and generosity of benefits in the areas of unemployment, pension, and health

benefits. The time period over which change in these measures is calculated is the same as in Banting and Kymlicka 2003 (from 1980 to 1999).

A cursory look at table 6.3 reveals that in terms of health and unemployment benefits, as well as their programmatic features, welfare states
expanded between 1980 and 1999. Cutbacks occurred in Sweden, Denmark, and Ireland in the area of health benefits, while unemployment
benefits were reduced, among other countries, in Canada, Denmark, the
United Kingdom, and the United States. The widest measure of the
three, the decommodification score, indicates reductions in the ability to
make one's life chances independent of market forces in Australia,
Canada, France, Germany, New Zealand, Sweden, Switzerland, and the
United States.

Table 6.4 shows the effect of multiculturalism policies on the three
measures of change in health and unemployment benefits and in
the change of the decommodification index. All three change models
were estimated using robust regression estimates. This regression technique reduces the impact of outliers and/or leverage points the farther
away they are from the regression line. Such outlying points can have
"undue" effects on the regression slope, particularly when the number of
observations is low, as is the case in table 6.4. Robust regression estimates

TABLE 6.3. Percentage Change in Health Benefits, Unemployment Benefits (both measured as percentage of GDP), and Decommodification from 1980 to 1999

	Health Benefits	Unemployment Benefits	Decommodification
Australia	36.4	42.8	−9.0
Austria	3.8	0	2.7
Belgium	14.8	−8.0	.3
Canada	21.2	−33.3	−1.2
Denmark	−13.8	−36.7	4.3
Finland	4.0	228.6	7.9
France	22.4	−25.0	−3.2
Germany	17.6	160.0	−.4
Ireland	−30.9	−67.6	21.5
Italy	0	16.7	24.7
Netherlands	5.8	−5.9	8.5
New Zealand	17.3	220.0	−7.6
Norway	23.7	25.0	5.0
Sweden	−14.3	300.0	−9.2
Switzerland	63.9	700.0	−29.2
United Kingdom	16.3	−63.6	6.3
United States	56.8	−57.1	−1.5

Source: OECD Social Expenditure Dataset 2004; Scruggs 2004.

are obtained by using the reweighted least squares method, which assigns less weight to points farther from the regression line. As a result, if there are outlying data points, their effect is reduced, thereby increasing the robustness of the findings (Belseley, Kuh, and Welsch 1980). In other words, robust regression estimates ensure that the relationships are not driven by either outliers or points with high leverage on the regression slope.

None of the three models is statistically significant, and their explanatory power is very low. This aggregate data analysis does not support the claim that multiculturalism policies adversely affect such critical components of the welfare state as health and unemployment benefits and the overall decommodification index.

What about attitudinal changes over time? Is support for the welfare state changing over time as a result of MCPs? In terms of attitudes toward redistribution, there are few items in the WVS survey that have been asked consistently over time and in enough countries to allow a fruitful comparison. One item that will be used throughout this chapter, however, aptly captures the essence of the philosophy of the welfare state and has been asked over time in most countries. The exact wording of the item is: "Now I'd like you to tell me your views on various issues. How would you place your views on this scale? 1 means you agree completely with the statement on the left, 10 means you agree completely with the statement on the right; and if your views fall somewhere in between, you can choose any number in between. 1: people should take more responsibility to provide for themselves. 10: The government should take more responsibility to ensure that everybody is provided for" (this is variable v127 in WVS 1–3 and e037 in WVS 4). Thus, this variable has a 10-point scale. Entries in table 6.5 represent the sum of those who have indicated options 6–10 of that variable. The validity of this item derives from the explicit mention of who should do the providing

TABLE 6.4. Robust Regression Estimates of Changes in Health Benefits (1980–99), Unemployment Benefits, Decommodification, and Trust: Independent Variable, Multiculturalism Policies

Model	Coefficient	S.E.	p-Value	Constant	R^2
Δ Health benefits	20.15	16.1	.29	6.1	.01
Δ Unemployment benefits	−20.32	16.3	.8	16.3	.02
Δ Decommodification	−11.9	6.9	.11	6.0	.01

Source: OECD 2004, Banting and Kymlicka 2003.

Note: S.E. = standard error; Δ = "change in."

("people" or "the government"). Any misgivings by the public about government-supported MCPs should manifest themselves in an increase in support for the "people" rather than the "government" option.

These attitudes should also be affected by the percentage of foreign population in the respective countries.[7] It is intuitive to believe that the higher the percentage of the foreign population the more the effects of MCPs are brought into sharp relief and any "withdrawal" from public redistribution schemas should be more visible when the percentage of foreigners is higher.

A total of four waves of the WVS have been administered: in 1981, 1990–91, 1995–97, and 1999–2001. Unfortunately, the "government should provide" question was not asked in 1981. It was asked in the 1990–91 and 1999–2001 surveys but was posed in only a few countries in 1995–97. This means that there are basically only two complete time periods in which this question was posed: 1990–91 and 1999–2001. This is the reason why the percentage of foreign population was collected for the years 1988 and 1998. In order to predict attitudes in 1990–91 and 1999–2001, the percentage of foreign population in 1988 and 1998, respectively, are used.[8] In order to capture the extent of change of both distributional attitudes, as well as percentage of foreign population, table 6.5 also lists the Δ (change) measures for attitudes (measured between the two longest possible time frames in the cases in which three observations were given—1990 to 1999–2001—as opposed to the cases in which data for only two time points were available).

A glance at the percent change in attitudes (Δ percent Att.) in table 6.5 indicates that, on average, redistributive attitudes increased by almost 22 percent between 1990 and 2000. Although there are countries in which support for state-led redistribution has decreased, including Denmark (−2.2), France (−5), Ireland (−16), and the United Kingdom (−37), the overall direction is a positive one. Over the period 1988–98, on average, the percentage of foreign population grew by about 18 percent from 7.0 percent in 1988 to 8.25 percent in 1998.

Are these changes in attitudes correlated with the strength of MCPs? Only two countries are indicated to have "strong" MCPs (Australia and Canada), five countries are indicated to have "modest" MCPs, and nine are indicated to have "weak" MCPs. The average percent change in attitudes for the strong group of MCPs is 22, for the modest group 40.6, and for the weak group 20.6. This means that the strongest growth of support for redistributive policies has occurred in countries with modest MCPs, the next strongest in countries with strong MCPs, and the smallest in countries with weak MCPs. These initial descriptive findings are at odds with those who claim that MCPs corrode the welfare state. In terms of public opinion, at this stage there is no systematic negative association between MCPs and redistributive attitudes. If anything, a slight positive connection is observable.

To analyze this relationship more formally, two methods are applied. First, MCPs are regressed on changes in attitudes (Δ percent Att.) as the dependent variable with changes in the percentage of foreign population as an additional predictor. It is possible that societies that experience dramatic increases in foreign population feel especially threatened. If that is the case, according to the critics of MCPs this should undermine the willingness of the public to continue supporting the welfare state.

TABLE 6.5.   Public Perceptions on "Government Should Take More Responsibility" (1990, 1995, and 2000), Multiculturalism Policies, and Percentage Foreign Population

| | 1990 | 1995 | 2000 | Δ% Att. | MCP | Foreign Population | | Δ% FP |
						1988	1998	
Australia	n.a.	43.0	43.0	0	1	22.1	23.2	5
Austria	17.8	n.a.	23.1	30	0	3.9	9.1	33.3
Belgium	35.2	n.a.	39.9	13	.5	8.8	8.7	−1.2
Canada	26.5	n.a.	38.3	44	1	17.1	17.9	5
Denmark	24.0	n.a.	23.5	−2.2	0	2.8	4.8	71
Finland	24.8	47.2	34.8	40	0	.4	1.6	400
France	23.7	n.a.	22.6	−5	0	6.5	5.5	−16
Germany	28.3	46.7	37.1	31	0	7.3	8.9	22
Ireland	37.1	n.a.	31.1	−16	0	1.9	3.0	58
Italy	48.5	n.a.	50.3	4	0	1.1	2.1	91
Netherlands	32.5	n.a.	33.7	4	.5	4.1	4.2	2.5
Norway	28.9	50.3	50.4	74	0	3.2	3.7	16
Sweden	14.6	18.9	25.5	75	.5	5	5.6	12
Switzerland	n.a.	20.8	20.8	0	0	15.2	19.0	25
United Kingdom	45.1	n.a.	28.4	−37	.5	3.2	3.8	19
United States	17.7	27.5	30.6	74	.5	9.5	10.9	15
Average	28.9	36.3	33.3	21.9		7.0	8.25	18[a]

Source: Attitudes, World Values Survey 1990, 1995/97, 1999/2001. Percentages represent the sum of answer options 6–10. Multiculturalism policies (0 = weak; .5 = modest; 1 = strong), Banting and Kymlicka (2003, revised version, 25–26). Stocks of foreign population, OECD (1993, 2003).

Note: n.a. = not available; Δ% Att. = percentage change in attitudes; MCP = multiculturalism policy; Δ% FP = percentage change in foreign population.

[a]This is not the average percentage change in each country, as the case of Finland, which experienced a 400 percent increase in foreign population, would dramatically distort that mean. Rather it is the calculated average increase from 7 to 8.25 percent foreign population, which equals around an 18 percent average increase between 1988 and 1998.

The second method uses absolute levels of attitudes in 1990 and 2000 as dependent variables and MCPs and absolute levels of foreign population in 1988 and 1998 as independent variables. This doubles the number of observations from 16 to 32 and introduces a short time element in this cross-sectional/time series panel analysis ($N = 16$, $t = 2$).[9] The level of foreign population in 1988 is used to explain attitudes in 1990 in country A followed by the same variables but shifted one time frame to 1998 and 2000, respectively, in the same country.

Both models in table 6.6 were estimated using robust regression estimates. Neither of the two models in table 6.6 is statistically significant, and their explanatory power is very low. In other words, MCPs do not affect redistributive attitudes either negatively or positively in a significant fashion. That is to say, there is no connection between MCPs and support for redistributive policies. These aggregate data analyses do not support the claim that multiculturalism policies adversely affect public support for redistribution even when controlling for the effect of foreign population.

Despite these findings, there are limitations to examining aggregate data. The most serious limitation is that the theoretical claims skip an important link in the causal chain. Proponents of the "corroding effect" hypothesis claim that multiculturalism policies lead to a fragmenting of community, which will ultimately be visible in reduced aggregate welfare measures. Welfare measures such as health policies and unemployment compensation are very complex policy outputs that reflect the vector sum of many different, often crosscutting interests.

TABLE 6.6.   Effects of Multiculturalism Policies and Foreign Population on Redistributive Attitudes

	Coefficient	S.E.	*t*-Test	*p*-Value
(a) Change model ($N = 16$): Δ% Att. is the dependent variable.				
MCPs	3.4	34.9	.1	.92
Δ% FP	−.22	.44	−.52	.61
Constant	22.5	21.2	1.06	.31
$R^2 = .02$				
(b) Cross-sectional/time series "panel" model ($N = 32$): Δ% Att. is the dependent variable.				
MCPs	11.5	7.3	1.6	.12
Δ% FP	−.18	3.17	−.45	.66
Constant	27.6	3.2	8.7	.00
$R^2 = .03$				

Source: Banting and Kymlicka 2003; OECD, *Trends in International Migration* (various years); WVS (various waves).

Note: Δ% Att. = percentage change in attitudes; Δ% FP = percentage change in foreign population.

However, before multiculturalism policies manifest themselves in concrete policy outputs they affect public opinion. Public opinion can be thought of as an early warning indicator of the acceptance or rejection of such policies and thus theoretically prior to policy outputs such as health care policies or policy outcomes such as the health of society.

Hence, the most persuasive empirical evidence about the effect of multicultural policies in the welfare state would come from multilevel models, that is, models that specifically take into account the effect of national policies such as MCPs on individual attitudes. If there is any truth to the corroding effect of multiculturalism policies (i.e., that such policies corrode the "fellow feeling" among natives, an undermining of the sense of "that could be me in need of help"), such changes should become visible in public opinion surveys long before they manifest themselves in aggregate statistics. Therefore, the next section maps the extent of multiculturalist attitudes across modern societies.

FOR ELITES ONLY?
THE EXPANSE OF MULTICULTURALISM ATTITUDES ACROSS MODERN SOCIETIES

This section explores the public support and distribution of multiculturalism attitudes across modern societies. Many critics of multiculturalism claim that these policies are "out of touch" with "the people" and are driven by elites such as "advocacy groups, judges and educational bureaucrats" (Barry 2001, 228), who impose these policies on the common man. According to Barry, these "behind the scenes manipulations" have "strong[ly] anti-majoritarian implications" and thus are inconsistent with democratic principles. Barry (2001, 299) goes on to explain: "That multiculturalist policies continue to be pursued in the face of a high degree of public hostility is a remarkable tribute to the effectiveness of the elites who are committed to them."

How widespread are multiculturalism attitudes? There are very few comparative surveys that have specifically tapped such attitudes. Among the "big four" surveys, the ISSP (International Social Survey Program), the WVS (World Values Survey), the ESS (European Social Survey), and the EB (Eurobarometer), only the latter has specifically asked European publics about MCPs. Most surveys ask more general questions (e.g., whether ethnic and racial minorities should keep their customs or whether they should adapt to the larger society). For example, the WVS in 2000 asked the question: "Which statement is nearest to your opinion? Immigrants should 1) maintain distinct customs and traditions; 2) take over the customs of the country." Most proponents of multiculturalism would take the answer option "maintain customs and traditions" as the central goal of multiculturalism. On average, across 11 countries (Austria, Belgium, Denmark, Finland, France, Germany, Ireland, Italy, the Netherlands, Sweden, and the United Kingdom), 33.7 percent of the respondents indicated that immigrants should maintain their customs and traditions and two-thirds thought that immigrants should adopt the customs of the country. However, in Ireland and Italy there was a majority of 56.8 and 59.7 percent, respectively, favoring multiculturalism.

In 2002 the ESS asked a similarly worded question: "Tell me how much you agree or disagree with each of these statements. It is better for a country if almost everyone shares the same customs and traditions." On average across 13 European countries (Austria, Belgium, Switzerland, Denmark, Finland, France, United Kingdom, Germany, Ireland, Italy, the Netherlands, Norway, and Sweden) around 58 percent either agreed strongly or agreed with this statement while 42 percent disagreed or disagreed strongly—with the latter 42 percent, of course, representing the multiculturalist option. Interestingly, across this sample there was one only country in which there was a majority that disagreed with that statement: Switzerland. Its reaction is not surprising since Switzerland has a long tradition of giving political, linguistic, and ethnic autonomy to the people in its cantons.

With the recent publication of ISSP's National Identity II module, it is possible to gauge change in multiculturalist attitudes over time. The 1995 data can now be complemented with data collected in 2003. When respondents were given the choice to indicate whether they believe it is "better for a country if different racial and ethnic groups maintain their distinct customs and traditions" or whether "it is better if these groups adapt and blend into the larger society," the tendency appears to be toward people believing that ethnic groups should adapt and blend into the larger society.

Large segments of the eleven countries already believed in 1995 that immigrants should adapt to the host society even in those societies which are characterized specifically as multicultural, such as Australia and Canada. In Australia, 83 percent of the population in 1995 believed that immigrants should adapt to the host society; in Canada, this was true for 64 percent of the population. The 2003 data points show that respondents feel even stronger that immigrants should adapt to their host society and not maintain their distinct customs and traditions. The largest increases in "assimilationist" tendencies are observable in both East and West Germany, Austria, and Canada. Only three countries revealed a trend toward more multiculturalism: Australia (although a 1 percent reduction is not significant), United Kingdom, and the United States.

The Australian case is noteworthy because it indicates little impact of the nationalist and anti-immigrant "One Nation" party created by Pauline Hanson, David Oldfield, and David Ettridge. Even though the party won an astonishing 22.7 percent of the vote in Queensland, the party has fizzled out recently. The *Economist* (May 7, 2005, 13) described Pauline Hanson and her party as "merely a footnote in history."

Table 6.7 shows results of a most poignant question, that is, whether the state should give ethnic minorities financial assistance, a cornerstone of multicultural policies. Inspection of people's attitudes reveals that from 1995 to 2003 there are mostly decreases observable in the public's belief that the state should give ethnic minorities financial assistance. In 6 of the 11 countries, support for such policies has declined, while it stayed the same in New Zealand, increased very slightly in Australia and the United Kingdom, and a little more robustly in Sweden and the United States. The most massive collapses of such support occurred in East and West Germany and in Ireland. With the exception of East Germany, which stands at only 50 percent, in none of the 11 countries is there a majority of respondents who believe that the state should give ethnic minorities financial assistance.

Examining multiculturalism attitudes in Eastern Europe reveals an intriguing picture. When asked the same question as mentioned earlier—whether respondents believe it is "better for a country if different racial and ethnic groups maintain their distinct customs and traditions" or whether "it is better if these groups adapt and blend into the larger society"—figure 6.1 shows that there tend to be large majorities who favor that ethnic groups maintain their customs and traditions.

Does that mean that Eastern Europeans are more multiculturalist than West Europeans? What could explain these differences between Eastern and Western Europe? The difference between Eastern and Western Europe (in political terms) is most likely explained by the different types of minorities that reside in the two parts of Europe. The lower support in Western Europe may be driven by the fact that these minorities are relatively new (i.e., immigrant minorities) while the Eastern European minorities are "historic" minorities. When publics in Eastern Europe are asked whether "groups" should maintain their customs and traditions, they think first and foremost of long-standing, historic minorities, not recent immigrants groups, of which there are few if any in these societies. For instance, people in Bulgaria would be thinking about their historic Turkish minority, and people in Slovakia would be thinking about their historic Hungarian minority. While oftentimes relationships with these minorities are tense, the basic legitimacy of their existence as culturally distinct groups is largely unquestioned since they have been living side by side with the majority group for centuries and can plausibly claim that this is their homeland too.[10]

In Western Europe, on the other hand, the minorities are "new" (immigrant minorities) as opposed to the historic minorities in Eastern Europe. Thus, most West Europeans will interpret the survey question as referring to the rights of newcomers who have no historic claim to practice their traditional culture in their new country of residence. After

TABLE 6.7. Multicultural Attitudes and Their Change from 1995 to 2003
(percent responding)

Country	Immigrants Should Adapt and Blend into Larger Society			State Should Give Ethnic Minorities Financial Assistance		
	1995	2003	Δ	1995	2003	Δ
Austria	57	68	10	40	37	−3
Australia	83	82	−1	16	17	1
Canada	64	71	7	19	17	−2
West Germany	38	64	26	41	30	−11
East Germany	48	62	15	70	50	−20
Great Britain	81	75	−5	16	18	2
Ireland	60	66	6	52	40	−12
New Zealand	65	69	4	18	18	0
Norway	75	80	5	20	17	−3
Sweden	81	85	4	20	24	4
United States	58	53	−6	17	23	6

Source: International Social Survey Program (ISSP). National Identity (Module I and II). *Zentralarchiv für Europäische Sozialforschung,* Köln, Germany.
Question wording:
For "immigrants should adapt": Some people say that it is better for a country if different racial and ethnic groups maintain their distinct customs and traditions. Others say that it is better if these groups adapt and blend into the larger society. Which of these views comes closer to your own? (1) It is better for society if groups maintain their distinct customs and traditions; (2) It is better if groups adapt and blend into the larger society.
For the "financial assistance" question: how much do you agree or disagree with the following statements? Ethnic minorities should be given government assistance to preserve their customs and traditions. (Entries reflect the sum of those who "strongly agreed" and "agreed" with that statement).

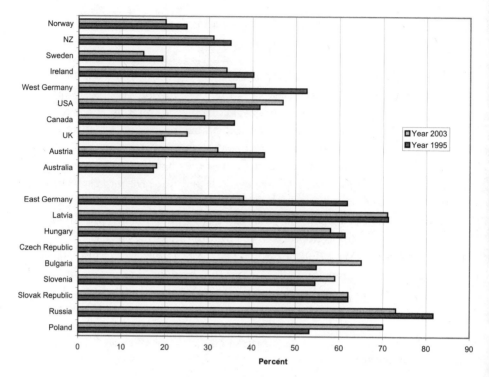

Fig. 6.1.   Multiculturalist attitudes in Eastern and Western Europe over time
(1995–2003). (Data from ISSP National Identity Module I [1995] and II [2003].
Entries represent the percentage of those who believe that it is "better for society
if groups maintain their distinct customs and traditions" as opposed to that
"groups adapt and blend into larger society.")

all, they have voluntarily left their homelands and as a result may be
thought of as having waived their right to practice their traditional culture (Kymlicka 1996). As a result, West European publics are more hesitant to allow immigrant minorities to practice their culture and customs,
which manifests itself in lower scores on that particular survey question
compared to the scores of Eastern European countries.

Asking more specifically about public support for MCPs, the Eurobarometer series in the year 2000 asked publics across Europe how much
support there is for such policies (EB 53, fieldwork: April–May 2000).
The precise question was: "What do you think ought to be done to improve the relationship between people of different races, religions or cultures in [your country]?" Respondents could either "mention" or "not
mention" the respective policies. The bars in figure 6.2 represent percentages of people who mentioned the following policies.

1. Do nothing
2. Promote understanding of different cultures and lifestyles in [your country]
3. Promote equality of opportunity in all areas of social life
4. Encourage the creation of organizations that bring people of different races, religions, or cultures together
5. Promote the teaching of mutual acceptance and respect in schools

Figure 6.2 reveals a rather intriguing picture. There is strong support across European publics for the teaching of "mutual acceptance and respect" in schools (on average over 55 percent) and also for promoting policies that assist in understanding different cultures and lifestyles (on average 42 percent). When it comes to promoting equality of opportunity, European publics are becoming a bit more hesitant, with only 38 percent mentioning this option. Less than a third (31.5 percent) encourage the creation of organizations to bring together people of different races, religions, and cultures. When asked whether nothing should be done to "improve the relationship between people of different races, religions, and cultures" only around 6 percent of respondents mentioned this option.

Finally, using the same Eurobarometer survey the public's attitudes toward minorities and diversity in general are examined. Four items in particular are relevant in gauging support for multiculturalism across European publics. The lead statement is: "Now can we talk about the place of people belonging to minority groups in terms of race, religion or culture within [nationality] society. For each of the following opinions, could you please tell me whether you tend to agree or tend to disagree?"

1. In two or three generations' time, people belonging to these minority groups will be like all other members of society.
2. In order to be fully accepted members of [nationality] society, people belonging to these minority groups must give up their own culture.
3. [Country's] diversity in terms of race, religion or culture adds to its strength.
4. It is a good thing for any society to be made up of people from different races, religions or cultures.

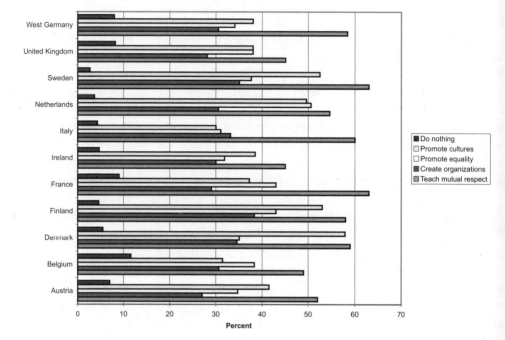

Fig. 6.2. Support for policies affecting people of different races, religions, and cultures. (Data from Eurobarometer 53 [2000].)

Figure 6.3 shows rather strong support for what might be called "multiculturalist attitudes," such as the belief that diversity adds strength to the nation (on average 57 percent tend to agree with that statement across Europe) and the belief that it is good if society is made up of minorities (73 percent on average), and low percentages for those who believe that in order to become fully accepted members of the dominant society minorities must give up their culture (around 26 percent). Respondents also tend to believe that minorities will eventually melt into the larger society. On average, over 63 percent indicated that in time members of minority groups will become just "like other members of society." This stands in stark contrast to the recent talk about "parallel societies," "ethnic enclaves" that are said to have developed in many big European cities, and the struggle over the term *Leitkultur* (guiding culture) in Germany.

These numbers reveal more support and tolerance for minorities and diversity in Europe than what one may glean from reading the headlines of major American and European newspapers. Still, figure 6.1 reveals that there is not much support among Western European publics for the

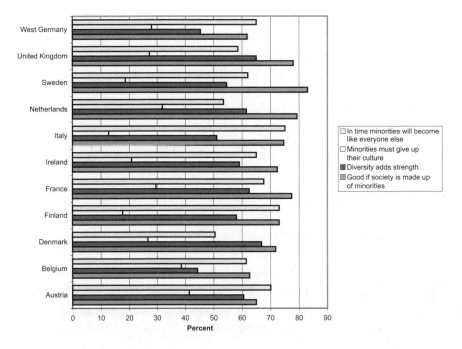

Fig. 6.3. Support for diversity and minorities across European countries. (Data from Eurobarometer 53 [2000].)

view that ethnic and racial groups should maintain their distinct customs and traditions. It is likely the case that attitudes have hardened against minorities in the wake of 9/11, the gruesome assassination of Theo van Gogh in the Netherlands, and the terrorist attacks in London in the summer of 2005. On the other hand, to describe multiculturalism policies as encountering a "high degree of public hostility," as Barry does, seems unwarranted given solid majorities in favor of at least part of such policies. Particularly figure 6.2 shows a much more widespread prevalence of what might be called "multiculturalist attitudes" than what Barry's comment suggests. These results are especially relevant as they are specifically tapping attitudes about MCPs—and these attitudes are relatively friendly toward MCPs.

ESTIMATING THE EFFECTS OF MCPs ON INDIVIDUAL ATTITUDES: MULTILEVEL ANALYSIS

Multilevel analysis again is highly appropriate as it allows for the exploration of the effects of state-level differences on individual attitudes.

More specifically such models capture the institutional effects on individual-level attitudes. In order to test the claim that multiculturalism policies lead to the erosion of the welfare state, individual attitudes on the redistributive role of the state are used as dependent variables. Table 6.8 shows multilevel analysis based on the following question item used as a dependent variable: "How would you place your views on this scale? 1 means you agree completely with the statement on the left. 10 means you agree completely with the statement on the right; and if your views fall somewhere in between, you can choose any number in between. 1 = people should take more responsibility to provide for themselves. 10 = the government should take more responsibility to ensure that everybody is provided for." This question is particularly appropriate to capture attitudes about the welfare state as it starkly contrasts the concept of private provision of social insurance with public provision. "The government should take more responsibility to ensure that everybody is provided for" concisely sums up the very idea of the welfare state. Since responses to that question represent individual-level attitudes, any doubts about growing societal heterogeneity should be reflected in the answers to this question.

TABLE 6.8.   Multilevel Analysis (HLM) of Regime-Level and Individual-Level Variables on Attitudes about the Welfare State

Regime-level variables ($N = 17$)	
Multiculturalism policies	1.33 (.14)★★★
Degree of decommodification	−.01 (.22)
Individual level variables ($N = 13,646$)	
Satisfaction with life	−.08 (.016)★★★
Self-placement on political scale	−.20 (.03)★★★
Age	−.0086 (.0019)★★★
Education	−.053 (.021)★★★
Income	−.25 (.042)★★★
Trust	−.027 (.046)
Female	.17 (.06)★★
Proportionate variance explained at level 1	6%
Proportionate variance explained at level 2	12.5%
Deviance of intercept only model (not shown)	64,042.29
Deviance of full model (shown)	63,273.94
Deviance reduction: Chi-square	768.35
p-value	.000

Source: World Values Survey 2000; Banting and Kymlicka 2003; Scruggs 2004.
Note: "People (1)/state (10) should take more responsibility to provide for themselves" is the dependent variable. Entries indicate odds ratios.

Table 6.8 provides evidence that multiculturalism policies have a positive impact on attitudes as far as the welfare state is concerned—exactly the opposite of what the corroding effect hypothesis claims. If the public's support of the welfare state became fragmented as a result of multiculturalism policies that heighten differences between "them" and "us," such effects should be visible first in public opinion surveys. However, this multilevel analysis shows that this is not the case. In fact, the opposite is the case. Countries with strong multiculturalism policies show statistically significant public support for the welfare state compared to those with weaker multiculturalism policies. More specifically, the odds ratio of 1.33 indicates that a one-unit increase in multiculturalism policies (in effect, from "weak" to "strong" multiculturalism policies) increases the likelihood by 33 percent that on average a respondent in the sample tends to support the view that it is the state that should ensure that everybody is provided for.

What is interesting is that the degree of decommodification does not show a significant impact on welfare state support. This can be explained as a result of the declining marginal utility of the welfare state. In those countries that enjoy more generous public protection, such as the Nordic countries, relative public support for the welfare state is not as strong as in societies with less public protection. A similar finding was reported by Gelissen (2002).

Among the individual-level predictors, most are negative, that is, the older people are the more they place themselves politically on the right, the more satisfied they are with their lives and the more educated they are and the more income they have the more they prefer that people should take responsibility to provide for themselves rather than the state. The only two exceptions to that pattern are females, who think that the state should be more involved, and people with higher trust. However, while gender is statistically significant, trust is not. This stands in apparent contrast to the findings in chapter 3, which showed that universal trusters favor government redistribution. The difference is that in all the models in chapters 5 and 6 the general trust question was used ("Do you think most people can be trusted or that you can't be too careful?") to gauge its effect on various outcomes. The reason why the universal trust concept cannot be used is that the question items used for refining the concept of trust into primordial and universal was asked in only 11 countries. Using the universal trust measures would have reduced the number of observations too much to run legitimate HLM analyses.

How do multiculturalism policies affect nativist resentment and welfare chauvinism? There are good reasons to believe that multiculturalism policies may engender both adverse and positive public reactions. One of the main findings throughout this book has been that people with higher education, as well as people who actually have had contact with immigrants, have a much more positive view of them than do those who are less educated and have very little or no contact with foreigners. Multiculturalism policies that convey information about the culture and history of the newcomers, as well as newcomers learning about the culture, language, and history of the receiving society, should create more tolerance and understanding. This works, of course, only if newcomers and natives engage with *the other's* traditions, history, and culture. As Banting and Kymlicka (2003, 8) put it, "By adopting multiculturalism policies, the state can be seen as trying both to encourage dominant groups not to fear or despise minorities, and also to encourage minorities to trust the larger society." Iris Young (1990, 174), a proponent of group rights, argues similarly: "Groups cannot be socially equal, unless their specific experience, culture, and social contributions are publicly affirmed and recognized."

On the other hand, it is just as plausible that policies that highlight the differences between newcomers and natives, for example, bilingual education; school curricula specializing in the history, culture, and traditions of the newcomers; dual citizenship; and exemptions from dress codes. The best-known example of how dress codes challenge the identity of nation-states is the *l'affaire du foulard,* the head scarf debate that has plagued France since 1989, when two schoolgirls wearing the traditional Muslim head scarf (*hijab*) were expelled from a public school. On March 15, 2004, French president Jacques Chirac signed a law banning the wearing of conspicuous religious symbols in schools in the belief that such symbols undermine the separation of church and state (*laïcité*) and national cohesion. The law went into effect on September 2, 2004, at the beginning of the new school year.[11]

Such debates are often very bitter as they reveal, more than many other issues, the self-image of a society. The head scarf debate proves very illuminating because it brings choices between identity and liberalism into sharp relief. Both values, identity as well as liberalism, are important for the self-image of a democratic society. Alas, maximizing one of the two values comes at the cost of reducing the other. Alan Riley's (2005) interpretation is that "the French government has argued that it is seeking to maintain the sacred Republican principle of secularism." France, by banning head scarves and other religious symbols, has chosen to protect its sense of identity, which is the principle of *laïcité,* to the detriment, as some might argue, of freedom of expression or with the European convention on fundamental human rights.[12] Similar debates over the wearing of religious symbols in public schools have occurred in Germany, Switzerland, and Italy.

Critics of multiculturalism tend to favor *integration* or, to use a term that has been pushed to the margins of academic discourse, *assimilation.* This is not to suggest that integration and assimilation are the same. What separates them are matters of degree. It seems that assimilation would require a much more thorough process of becoming like the majority native population than integration would. The Procrustean bed of assimilation was particularly painful for German settlers in the American Midwest, especially after World Wars I and II. Before World War I, German was taught in public schools in states with significant German populations. Germans demonstrated great pride in their heritage and maintained their social, cultural, and athletic institutions. In the wake of the world wars, however, these German institutions were dismantled as a result of "American chauvinism—or, if you will, patriotism," with the effect that many immigrants' loyalty to their former people or country disappeared. "This was the melting pot in operation, with a vengeance" (Glazer 2004, 62). Wars had the unintended consequence of imposing assimilation based on the strongest of all possible justifications: national security. Wars fired the pot that allowed melting to take place. Germany engaged in its own version of assimilation, of course, as when "ethnically despised Polish labor migrants in the German Ruhr Valley had to trade in their language and 'Germanize' their names as the price of their acceptance" (Joppke and Morawska 2003, 4).

It is not obvious why people who voluntarily left their homelands to pursue their dreams in another country should be able to make any claims on their newly chosen country to support their pursuit of maintaining their languages, customs, and traditions. This is of course different for asylum seekers and members of ethnonational groups such as the Maori in New Zealand, the Catalans in Spain, or the Sicilians in Italy. After all, they did not leave to join empires or nations. Rather, empires or nations came to them. Will Kymlicka (1996, 96) makes that point

quite explicitly: "In deciding to uproot themselves, immigrants voluntarily relinquish some of the rights that go along with their original national membership." However, what they are entitled to, according to
Kymlicka, are so-called polyethnic rights, meaning rights that allow
them to express themselves as a group without being disadvantaged by
the dominant society for doing so.

It may be argued that the less stringent such integration procedures
are, combined with more extensive multiculturalism policies, the more
the differences between natives and others are highlighted. This may precisely lead to more prejudice and nativist resentment than policies that
aim toward deeper integration of newcomers. Harold Wilensky (2002,
653) bluntly makes this point when he says, "A country that makes a serious effort to . . . assimilate immigrants via inclusionary naturalization
policies; job creation, training, and placement; and language training and
citizenship education will minimize nativist violence."

This discussion has examined theoretical reasons why multiculturalism policies could lead to either more or less nativist resentment and
welfare chauvinism. Table 6.9 shows the results of two more multilevel
analyses that use the familiar "no immigrants as neighbors" and "if jobs
are scarce, employers should give preference to [nation] people over
immigrants" questions. Again, success or failure of multiculturalism
policies should become visible first in public opinion surveys. Since the
dependent variable in both models is dichotomous, nonlinear logit
models are the appropriate functional form. Instead of showing the
hard to interpret logit coefficients in the table, the odds ratios are
shown.

The precise wording of the two dependent variables is: "If jobs are
scarce, employers should give priority to [nation] people over immigrants. 0 = agree, 1 = disagree." For the "no immigrants as neighbors"
model: "On this list are various groups of people. Could you please sort
out any that you would not like to have as neighbors: immigrants: 0 =
not mentioned, 1 = mentioned."

The "jobs to nationals" model in table 6.9 is a measure of "welfare
chauvinism" while "no immigrants as neighbors" may be thought of as
tapping prejudicial attitudes or what was referred to earlier as nativist
resentment. Both models essentially show very similar results. In both,
multicultural policies helped reduce welfare chauvinism and nativist resentment. A one-unit increase in multiculturalism policies (essentially
moving from "weak" to "strong" multiculturalism policies) increases the

chance by almost three times that respondents will disagree with the statement that jobs should go to nationals if jobs are scarce and are 53 percent less likely to mention that they do not want immigrants as neighbors. Political institutions with higher degrees of decommodification also reduce welfare chauvinism, which is consistent with the findings in chapter 5. Although the sign (smaller than 1 in odds ratios) is correct for the "no immigrants as neighbors" model, the variable decommodification fails to reach statistical significance. Respondents who are satisfied with their lives show less welfare chauvinism and prejudice. Rather unsettling is the consistent finding throughout this book that people who are not interested in politics are significantly more prejudiced. For example, a one-unit increase in "interest in politics," say, from "somewhat interested" (2) to "not very interested" (3), leads to a 22 percent higher chance that such respondents will agree that jobs should go to nationals. Conversely, the same step in "interest in politics" leads to a

TABLE 6.9.   Multilevel Logit Analysis (HLM) of Regime Variables (Multiculturalism Policies and Levels of Decommodification) and Individual-Level Attitudes about Nativist Resentment

	Jobs to Nationals (0 = agree; 1 = disagree)	No Immigrants as Neighbors (0 = mentioned; 1 = not mentioned)
Regime-level variables (*N* = 17)		
Multiculturalism policies	2.9★★★	.47★★
Degree of decommodification	1.08★★	.99
Individual-level variables (*N* = 12,928)		
Life satisfaction (1 = dissatisfied; 10 = satisfied)	1.03★	.92★★★
Interest in politics (1 = very; 4 = not at all)	.78★★★	1.19★★★
Self-placement on political scale (1 = left; 10 = right)	.87★★★	1.13★★★
Age	.99★★★	1.01★★★
Education	1.18★★★	.89★★★
Income	1.07★★★	.97
Trust	1.7★★★	.61★★★
Female	1.02	.78★★★
Deviance of intercept-only model (not shown)	39,888.58	32,086.68
Deviance of model shown	38,703.92	31,678.31
Deviance reduction (Chi-square: *df* = 10)	1,184.66	408.31
p-value	.000	.000

Source: World Values Survey 2000.

Note: Two-tailed tests. Population weights are applied but not shown. Decommodification refers to the Scruggs 2004 measures; multiculturalism policies are from Banting and Kymlicka 2003, revised version. Entries indicate odds ratios.

★*p* < .1; ★★*p* < .05; ★★★*p* < .01.

19 percent increase in the probability that respondents will mention
that they do not want immigrants as neighbors. As far as self-placement
on the political scale and age are concerned, people who rate themselves on the right and are older show more welfare chauvinism, as well
as higher levels of prejudice. However, respondents who are more educated, have higher incomes, and are female all indicate lower prejudice
and less welfare chauvinism than do less educated people, people with
lower incomes, and males. Predictably, respondents with higher trust
show significantly lower levels of prejudice and welfare chauvinism.

These are tantalizing results. Multiculturalism policies appear to reduce prejudice and welfare chauvinism, in addition to establishing support for the welfare state. The widespread notion that multiculturalism
policies heighten the difference between natives and newcomers, and
thereby create tensions between the in- and out-groups, does not appear
to be true. If anything, the opposite is the case! The stronger the multiculturalism policies are the more they tend to blunt prejudice and welfare chauvinism. These findings provide strong evidence against the view
that multiculturalism corrodes the fabric of society or that the dominant
society is "losing its way." What they show is that they lower the cultural
distance between members of the dominant society and minorities and
as a result lead to a better understanding between these two groups.
From a policymaker's point of view, multicultural policies yield more benign interactions between the in- and out-groups of society. Immigration appears to be tolerated more in societies with such policies, and the
"nativist impulse" to exclude foreigners from the job market is reduced.
All of this can only bode well for public support of the welfare state. It
bodes well because multiculturalism policies do not lead to a fragmentation of society to such a degree that the "fellow feeling" necessary to
maintain the welfare state is undermined.

These are findings are based on large-N analyses. However, the conclusions drawn from these cross-sectional analyses do not necessarily
apply with equal force to each country. To add historical and case-specific
context, the next chapter will examine the incorporation and multiculturalism policies of Germany, Sweden, and the United States. These three
countries are paragons of different welfare regimes. The task in the next
chapter will be to examine whether as a result of immigration-driven diversity these three countries experience similar or different pressures on
their welfare states. This "thick description" should bring similarities and

differences into sharper relief. Will Sweden be able to retain its generous protection levels in the face of immigration? What is the politics of moving from jus sanguinis to jus soli in Germany? How does the United States balance restriction of immigration and freedom of movement? Above all, is there evidence that immigration is undermining public support for funding the welfare state in these three countries?

CHAPTER 7

The Politics of Immigration and the Welfare State in Germany, Sweden, and the United States

*Politics is not the art of the possible. It consists in choosing
between the disastrous and the unpalatable.*
—John Kenneth Galbraith

THIS CHAPTER WILL EMPLOY A "most similar systems design" by
examining Sweden, Germany, and the United States. They are most similar
in that they all are developed, affluent, democratic, and "modern" societies.
They differ on one institutional feature: each of these countries represents
the prototypical case of a member of a distinctive welfare state "regime"
(Esping-Andersen 1990). Sweden is the most "welfarist" of the three systems based on universal coverage. This means that benefits and services are
intended to cover the whole population without incurring the stigmatization associated with poor relief. The benefits are generous, and so is the
tax burden. Germany, on the other hand, is the archetypal example of a
"corporatist" welfare regime that consists of a contributory scheme and
sees the welfare state as primarily a facilitator of group-based mutual aid
and risk pooling. It is based on collective bargaining with benefits going
to recognized groups. Both the tax burden and benefit levels are generally
lower than in Sweden. Finally, the United States is the prototypical example of a liberal, residualist welfare state in which the market is seen as
the primary allocative device for the distribution of "life chances." The

United States uses means testing to identify the "deserving poor" and is very limited in the benefits it provides. As a result, the tax burden is lower than in Germany or Sweden. With Germany having adopted jus soli in the year 2000 as its incorporation regime, all three countries now adhere to this territorially based form of immigration policy.

Immigration and domestic welfare have been at cross-purposes since the very founding of states. In fact, keeping the poor outside of state boundaries was one of the central purposes of establishing the Prussian state in 1842. Faced with migrant poor, the challenge of the founders of the Prussian state was how to establish a state in such a way as to exclude the poor. The answer was to make it a membership institution, independent of residence, allowing the state to decide who is a member and who is not. The increased mobility of the itinerant poor, who moved from town to province or principality during the first half of the nineteenth century in Germany, "had given the state the incentive it formerly lacked to defined membership systematically and precisely as a legal quality independent of residence" (Brubaker 1992, 71). In order to exclude the poor, the state needed to invent new categories of belonging that did not depend on claims of territory but on the capacity of the state to discriminate between those who are in and those who are out. In that sense, the state literally became a "gatekeeper" with full discretionary power over membership claims. As a result, "state membership could now serve as an instrument of closure against the migrant poor" (71).

Similarly, American immigration policies have long used poverty as a reason for exclusion. Those immigrants who were likely to become "public charges" were not admitted. During 1893 and 1916, claims that immigrants from Southern Europe would become public charges were often heard as a reason for exclusion. Exclusion policies on the basis of the likelihood of becoming a public charge are also driven by the economic situation of the receiving country. In 1930, President Herbert Hoover told Congress: "Under conditions of current unemployment, it is obvious that persons coming to the United States seeking work would likely become either direct or indirect public charges. As a temporary measure the officers issuing visas to immigrants have been instructed to refuse visas to applicants likely to fall into this class" (President Hoover. Quoted in Meyers 2004, 37). Within five months, this policy succeeded in cutting European immigration by 90 percent.

The discriminatory power to decide who belongs and who does not lies within the purview of the state. Yet not all states follow a simple utility-maximizing principle. As was examined earlier, there are different models of incorporation, as well as integration, of foreigners that reflect different national models. Similarly, there are different welfare state models. Immigrants themselves are aware that some states offer more generous benefits than others. In fact, the more generous a welfare state is believed to be among immigrants the more attractive it becomes as a possible destination. This imposes on receiving states a particular need to scrutinize the motives of the immigrants, particularly those of asylum seekers. Some scholars have found that countries with greater welfare benefits do attract more migrants and thus function as "welfare magnets" (Bruecker et al. 2002) while others did not (Neumayer 2004). More relevant for this project is the following question: do these national models still make a difference in terms of how immigration-induced pressures on the welfare state are refracted? In other words, do more generous welfare states do a better job of integrating migrants than less generous ones?

Or have welfare states themselves lost the capacity to establish idiosyncratic models of protection for the most vulnerable members of society? Alan Wolfe and Jytte Klausen (1997) have argued that the welfare state is undermined both from "below," as a result of rising demands by identity groups, and from "above" as a result of globalization undermining the very essence and effectiveness of the nation-state. Since the mid-1990s the field of comparative political economy has seen an upsurge in studies on the decline of the nation-state as a result of mobile capital that is "footloose." Buttressed by advances in communications and transportation technologies, so the argument goes, mobile asset holders now have an "exit option" to move their capital to areas with less regulation, lower taxes, and lower wages. This forces national governments to engage in a bidding war to induce such asset holders to stay put or to attract foreign direct investment by lowering taxes, wages, social welfare transfers, and public services in general, leading to a "race to the bottom" and culminating in a "diminished democracy" (Swank 2001, 136). In a similar vein, Rogers Brubaker (1992, 187) opined in the last pages of his influential book that the "post-national vision may come to fruition." In stark contrast to these visions of a "defective state" (Strange 1995), Michael Bommes and Andrew Geddes (2000, 251) warn researchers that "we need to focus on national settings, on national political institutional repertoires that structure migration regimes and on the immigration and immigrant policies that all pave the path to social participation."

In this spirit, this chapter examines "social participation" in these three "classic" cases of welfare states. It attempts to put an "empirical baseline" under some of the public opinion data in Germany, Sweden, and the United States that have been used for empirical analyses in the preceding chapters. Chapter 5 demonstrated that more decommodifying welfare states showed less nativist resentment and welfare chauvinism than more market-conforming ones. This chapter concentrates on a crucial origin of prejudice against foreigners: the degree of unemployment of immigrants and their attendant welfare "uptake." These are important measures for they are the root causes of much of the dominant society's impression that foreigners are living on the dole while natives, via their tax contributions, support their idleness. The bigger the chasm between the life worlds of immigrants and natives the more likely it is that natives will harbor prejudices and resentment against newcomers.

This is why functioning integration policies are essential in order to minimize violence. From a policymaker's perspective, it is crucial to integrate newcomers as successfully as possible. If they are not integrated well, that is, if they stay unemployed, do not intermarry, engage disproportionately in crime, and live in "parallel" societies, public opinion tends to become excessively hostile, limiting the range of possible immigration policies available to basically only restrictionist ones. This was demonstrated in Otto Schily's exasperated attempt to put a stop to immigration in Germany in December 1998. The Social Democratic interior minister claimed that Germany had "reached the limits, the point where we have to say we cannot bear any more. The majority of Germans agree with me: Zero immigration for now. The burden has become too great. I would not even dare to publish the costs that stem from immigration. The Greens say we should take 200,000 more immigrants a year. But I say to them, show me the village, the town, the region that would take them. There are no such places" (Otto Schily. Quoted in Martin 1999, 5).

It is important to state up front that statistics on immigrant unemployment and crime, or welfare uptake, do not show that the welfare state in general is declining. Such numbers cannot show that. It is equally true that legal immigrants support the economy, pay taxes, and are productive members of the community. Whole service industries, such as nursing in Great Britain, depend on immigrants. In a survey of the city of New York, the *Economist* recently reported that in the 1990s immigrants flooded into the city in greater numbers and from more countries than ever before and currently, of the 8.1 million residents of the city, 36 percent are immigrants. "The impact of these multifarious new New Yorkers is easily summed up. They saved the city, and they are helping to rebuild its neglected neighborhoods. In the disastrous 1970s, New York lost 10 percent of its population and more or less went bankrupt. Without the influx of some 780,000 foreigners in that decade, things would have been much worse. And ever since then, immigration has helped New York to avoid the decline that beset most of America's other big, old cities" (*Economist*, "The town of the talk," 2005, 3).

Few studies have engaged in authoritative examinations of the macroeconomic impact of immigration. Concentrating on immigrant unemployment, immigrant crime, and welfare uptake does not show that immigrants are a drain on public services. It is equally important to examine their contributions, such as paying taxes, opening businesses, buying products, and making investments. Establishing a clear-cut relationship between rising diversity and erosion of the welfare state is not straightforward. If as a result of immigration-driven diversity social expenditures rise as immigrants make use of unemployment benefits, health care, subsidized housing, and so on, one cannot speak of a "decline" of the welfare state. After all, expenditures are rising. Critics maintain that the welfare state can only expand so far before it collapses. Thus, only if expenditures or programmatic requirements are curtailed, that is, only if a *reduction* in welfare programs are visible, is it possible that increasing immigration may be the reason, though this may still only be an association rather than a causal connection.

In the sections that follow, more attention is paid to Germany than to Sweden and the United States. The reason for this is that, as opposed to Sweden and the United States, Germany underwent a historic change in its immigration policy, from jus sanguinis to jus soli, in the year 2000 and again with a new law starting in 2005, reflecting a significant change in the country's self-image. Consequently, more space is devoted to tracing the roots of these changes so as to provide brief analyses of what drove those changes and an interpretation of what the new immigration law means for Germany.

GERMANY: FROM JUS SANGUINIS TO "JUS UTILITARIS"?

> 1933 wollten viele aus Deutschland raus. Heute wollen viele
> rein. Das muss doch was bedeuten?
> —Sir Peter Ustinov

"The soul lives in the blood" said Intschu-tschuna, the chief of the Apache Indians, as he prepared to bond Winnetou, his son, with Old Shatterhand through a ritual called *Blutsbrüderschaft* (brothers in blood). The two heroes cut the palms of their hands, and as the passionate embrace of their interlaced fingers culminated in the intermingling of their blood, "they became one soul with two bodies."[1] It is an unlikely union between the agile Winnetou and the "greenhorn" with German roots from the eastern United States, yet the mixing of their blood enabled them to "understand each other without having to communicate our emotions, thoughts and decisions" (Karl May, Winnetou I, 416–17).

This is the fanciful story of the adventures of Winnetou, and Old Shatterhand in the Wild West as told by one of the most influential and widely read German authors, Karl May. His books are read by almost every German, Swiss, and Austrian youth and were read at the time by the likes of Hermann Hesse, Albert Schweitzer, and Albert Einstein. When Karl May began to write these imaginative, colorful, and arresting stories in 1896, Germany was a very young country barely 25 years old. It is not accidental that May emphasized the importance of blood relationships and the notion that true friendship is only possible as a result of consanguinity.

The peculiar German emphasis on blood as an identity-creating force has become the master narrative of German history. Walker Connor describes the saying "*Blut* will zu *Blut*" (roughly translated as "people of the same blood attract") as a "German maxim" (Connor 1994, 203). Johann Gottfried Herder "envisioned the German nation as an organic entity based on essential affinities of blood, language and culture" (Doyle 2002, 15),[2] even though "Germany," at that time was a multinational mélange. The *Turnvater* Friedrich Ludwig Jahn (founder of the German calisthenics movement), railed against the *Kleinstaaterei* (independence of every principality, town, or province) and French occupation and in the early nineteenth century agitated for a unified, healthy Germany based on a form of organic solidarity. Appeals to blood in the early phases of the

German nation-building process, such as Bismarck's exhortation, "Germans, think with your blood" (quoted in Connor 1993, 377) or the spiritual connection between ethnicity and territory as contained in the couplet "*Blut und Boden*" (blood and soil), prepared Germans for many of Hitler's (who was not German) ravings about the superiority of the German race.

However, this purported *völkisch* (ethnic) character of German identity, this notion of *Kulturnation*, is only part the story. After all, it developed from the romantic roots of German nationalism in the late eighteenth century, almost a hundred years *before* the German state was created. Nevertheless, references to such romantic concepts as *Blutsbrüderschaft* still resonated with Germans in the late nineteenth and early twentieth centuries when Karl May wrote his novels.

The other part of the story is contained in the deep-seated respect of Germans for the "state." Prussia, the most influential of German states, was itself highly heterogeneous in addition to the multitudes of towns, principalities, and provinces that were to become part of "Germany" in 1871. It was precisely this heterogeneity that made appeals to some mythical ethnonational origins necessary to establish Germany's identity as a state. In addition to attempting to establish identity on the basis of *Volk* (people), Prussia attempted to integrate its subjects on the basis of a state, with a capital *S*, "the state as an end in itself rather than as a means to a particular social or political end" (Schirmer 2004, 44). The centrality of the state in Prussia could be seen in the extensive authority state agencies had. In addition, Prussia nurtured a very strong civic sense, which manifested itself in the well-known *Beamtentum* (officialdom), which sheltered and insulated officials like no other professional group. This continuity of the importance of the state survived the Third Reich and can be found in contemporary terms such as *Verfassungspatriotismus* (constitutional patriotism) and *Verfassungsschutz* (protection of the Constitution), which clearly refer not to national but to state and civic concepts.

Germany became a "nation-state" in 1871, and "on the ethnocultural understanding of nationhood, the Bismarckian state and its citizenship were only imperfectly national" (Brubaker 1992, 52). The overlap between "nation" and "state" was *unvollendet* (incomplete). Precisely because of the social, religious, and cultural heterogeneity of the various German jurisdictions, the myth of the state had to be invented. Finally, the creation of the German Reich "forced the principles of nationalism and statism into congruency," leading to a "dramatic closing of the lens on matters of membership rights" (Schirmer 2004, 37). Appeals to state as well as the nation culminated in the German Imperial and State Citizenship Law of 1913, which codified that German identity as based on jus sanguinis—until January 1, 2000, when a new law came into effect.

In the early morning of January 1, 2000, a baby girl named Seyma Nur Kurt was born to Turkish parents in the Kreuzberg district of Berlin. This birth was celebrated across Germany as a new symbol of openness and inclusion because by being born on German soil she automatically became a German citizen, even though not a drop of German blood flows in her veins.[3] The first visitors to the proud mother and daughter were the federal commissioner for foreigners (*Bundesausländerbeauftragte*), Marie-Luise Beck, and Berlin's commissioner for foreigners (*Ausländerbeauftragte*), Barbara John (*Berliner Zeitung,* January 4, 2000, 20).

This new law introduced the principle of jus soli, which states that anybody born on German soil is automatically a German citizen. When Seyma reaches maturity she will have to decide whether the keep her German citizenship or choose Turkish citizenship, but she cannot keep both. This birth was hailed across Germany as a symbol of historic change. This law, called *Ausländergesetz* (law for foreigners) was revised again, and, starting on January 1, 2005, there is a still more comprehensive law on the books, the so-called *Zuwanderungsgesetz* (immigration law), which renders the 1999 *Ausländergesetz* obsolete. It is more comprehensive insofar as it not only spells out immigration but also integration policies. The new law "finally does away with the decades-long life-lie (*Lebenslüge*) that Germany was not a country of immigration,"[4] commented Steffen Angenendt (2005), who was a member of the Süssmuth Kommission, which was charged with hammering out the new immigration law.

How did this fundamental change happen? Five brief explanations are offered. First, the fall of the Berlin Wall on November 9, 1989, brought the contradictions of the German immigration law into sharp relief. With the opening of the iron curtain, all those ethnic Germans who lived on the eastern side of it began to migrate into Germany first mostly from Poland and after 1991 from the former Soviet Union. Between 1990 and 2003 almost 2.4 million so-called *Aussiedler* or *Volksdeutsche* (ethnic Germans) migrated to Germany (Beauftragte der Bundesregierung fuer Migration 2004, 15). The ethnic Germans who returned after 1996 are referred to as *Spätaussiedler.* This migration was possible on the basis of paragraph 116 of Germany's *Grundgesetz* (Basic Law), which states that the "offspring" (*Abkömmlinge*) of refugees and exiles of German descent (*Volkszugehörigkeit*) are Germans if their ancestors lived in the territory of the German empire after December 31, 1937. Germany is only one of two countries, the other being Israel, that "allow their scattered tribes a right of return" (Ignatieff 1993, 99). Russians and members of other nationalities are returning to Germany on the basis of being ethnic Germans, although they have lived for generations in far-flung corners of Russia, have no language competency or immediate history of residence in Germany, and are admitted as Germans even though "intermarriage has thinned the tie that binds to vanishing point" (Ignatieff 1993, 100).

On the other hand, no matter how long foreigners had lived in Germany and no matter how "German" they were in language and culture, they could never become full members of society.[5] This clash of "foreigners with a German passport" (that is, the ethnic Germans) with "Germans without a passport" (that is, acculturated Turkish citizens) highlights the absurdity (Ignatieff 1993, 101) of the German immigration law. The fall of the Berlin Wall, that "violent incursion into the fantasy of Germany identity" (Ignatieff 1993, 101), forced German elites, as well as the public, to rethink what it means to be German. The abolition of jus sanguinis in 1999 may represent a transition from ethnic nationalism to civic nationalism and, as a result, "may bury the idea of a German *Volk* altogether" (Ignatieff 1993, 102). The pendulum that swung so often between state and nation in Germany may finally come to rest closer to the side of the state than the nation.

In light of the emphasis on "blood" as the reason for their immediate citizenship, it is ironic that the *Aussiedler* have proven to be particularly difficult to integrate. While immediately German, their lack of language and other skills has created a new *Armutsproletariat* (impoverished class), as dubbed by the German newsmagazine *Der Spiegel*. They are disproportionately involved in crimes such as drug dealing and theft (*Der Spiegel,* February 24, 2003). It is clear according to the Bavarian social minister, Christa Stewens (CSU party), that "the *Spätaussiedler* have become a particularly problematic group as far as integration is concerned" (*Der Spiegel,* February 24, 2004).[6]

A second factor in changing the German immigration policy is the increasing assertion of the European Union. The signing of the Maastricht Treaty in 1992 not only established the European Union but also EU citizenship. This means that anyone who is considered a national of

a member state is also a citizen of the EU. The Maastricht Treaty relent-
lessly gnaws away at the foundations of national membership and identity. Klaus von Beyme makes a strong case in this regard, and it is worth
quoting him at length.

> German elites may dislike it, but Maastricht clearly decouples cit-
> izenship from *ethnos* or *Volk*. ... Citizenship in Europe is set on the
> road of constitutional patriotism. The European Community re-
> quires a decoupling of the "European peoplehood" from natural,
> organic, ontological categories such as *Volk,* nation, and even the
> state—so dear to many German lawyers. (2001, 74)

In 1995, the EU expanded to 15 countries, and on May 1, 2004, it
added another 10, mostly Eastern European countries. Accession of these
10 countries meant 75 million new EU citizens. While there are transition periods of migration in place for some of the newly joined Eastern
European countries, it is just a matter of time until Poles, Hungarians,
Czechs, and others will become EU citizens with full rights to travel,
settle, work, or study across all 25 EU countries. And as of this writing
plans are under way to start negotiations over Turkey's accession to the
EU. Citizenship in the EU is of course in addition to national citizenship, which still regulates specific national areas such as eligibility for
welfare, but, as Tomas Hammar (1990) demonstrated, access to welfare
support was possible even without being a citizen of the benefit-grant-
ing state. Such developments are simply incompatible with an attempt to
regulate immigration on the basis of descent.

The EU represents the most massive incursion into the sovereignty of
nation-states in the history of nation-states. Arguably this process of erosion of sovereignty began with the very formation of the European Economic Community (EEC) in 1958. In the mid 1970s Germany opposed
the widening of the European Community (EC) to include Greece,
Portugal, and Spain on the basis that it would "adversely affect migration
into Germany" (Marshall 2000, 118). While conservatives in Germany,
such as the Christian Democratic Union party leader Friedrich Merz,
argued in October 2000 that immigrants should conform to a German
Leitkultur, or "dominant culture," to others such as the Foreign Minister
Joschka Fischer, it is clear that such talk about *Leitkultur* is out of touch
with the integration that is happening across the EU. Fischer countered
that "Merz is still living in the 19th century, still believing in a German

nationhood defined by blood, still resisting an immigrant culture when the fact is we have to open up for economic reasons. This idea of *Leitkultur* today, in a post-national Europe, is completely crazy" (Cohen 2000). But national sovereignty is not only affected from without by the EU or international refugee and human rights organizations; it is also undermined from within. Groups such as "the legal establishment—trial lawyers, civil libertarians, and the courts . . . , intellectuals, broadly construed . . . , [and] anti-racist movements . . . , are only a few of the possible protagonists in a political struggle over control of immigration policy" (Freeman 1998, 103).

The third reason why Germany changed its immigration law is what is termed "globalization." Jürgen Habermas speaks of the "post-national constellation," by which he means the process of globalization such as telecommunications, mass tourism, and arms and human trafficking. However, "the most significant dimension is economic globalization, whose new quality can hardly be doubted" (Habermas 2001, 66). While some proponents of globalization have exaggerated the paralysis of nations, it is also clear that as a result of modern technologies and international regimes such as the World Trade Organization the capacity to steer nation-specific, idiosyncratic policies is rapidly declining. The increasing importance of global human rights norms put additional pressures on states that want to maintain rigorous control over their borders.

Yasemin Soysal made that point earlier, arguing that the proliferation of global human rights instruments in the postwar period has created a "new and more universal concept of citizenship . . . whose legitimizing principles are based on universal personhood rather than national belonging" (Soysal 1994, 1). Other observers, such as Saskia Sassen, have found that "where the efforts towards the formation of transnational spaces have gone the furthest and been most formalized, it has become very clear that existing frameworks of immigration policy are problematic" (Sassen 1998, 72).

The fourth reason why Germany changed its immigration laws was the tragic events of 1992 and 1993, which involved the firebombing of Turkish families, Vietnamese foreign laborers, or asylum seekers from Kosovo, in Mölln, Hoyerswerda, Solingen, and Rostock. In addition, Jewish cemeteries were victimized and places such as the Nazi Death March Museum in the Belower Woods, 65 miles northwest of Berlin, were firebombed in September of 1992. Pictures of charred buildings and skinheads with swastikas tattooed on their forearms went around the world. The official tally of "racially motivated attacks jumped from a dismal 2,426 in 1991 to an astonishing 6,336 in 1992" (Triadafilopoulos 2004, 30).

The attacks in Mölln sent shock waves across Germany and Europe. At the same time it provoked sympathy for the victims and their families. For weeks after these horrible events, hundreds of thousands of people took to the streets in demonstrations, protest marches, and so-called *Lichterketten* (candlclight vigils) to protest xenophobia. These events "served as a turning point in policy terms; grief and indignation were quickly channeled into demands for change, with the abolition of the 1913 RuStAG (*Reichs- und Staatsangehörigkeitsgesetz*) emerging as a unifying theme" (Triadafilopoulos 2004, 31).

However, as long as the CDU/CSU coalition was in power, serious attempts to abolish that law were not undertaken. This changed with the victory of the Social Democrats in 1998, who, together with the Greens, formed a coalition government. This political change marks the fifth explanation of why Germany changed its immigration law. The new government controlled both the Bundesrat (Upper House) and the Bundestag (Lower House) and made reform of Germany's citizenship law a legislative priority. The original plan of the government was to grant German citizenship to children born in Germany through the principle of jus soli. In addition, the children could maintain their parents' nationality, thereby becoming dual citizens. However, in 1999 *Landtagswahlen* (regional elections) occurred in the *Bundesland* (state) of Hesse, and the ruling SPD/Green coalition was defeated, thereby losing its majority in the Bundesrat. As a result, the CDU/CSU could now block the government's reform proposals. The reforms that were eventually enacted in 1999 represented a compromise: they retained jus soli but not the idea of dual citizenship. In addition, children must decide when they reach the age of majority whether they will accept German citizenship or take on their parents' citizenship.

Thus, the factors that shaped Germany's abolition of its 1913 immigration law were not only "internal" or "external." Rather, they combined the growing importance of transnationalism through the EU and globalization, a newfound sensitivity to international norms, epochal historical conjunctures, a more active civil society, and old-fashioned politics. In 2002 the SPD/Green coalition won another election victory and introduced a new law, the so-called Zuwanderungsgesetz, or more precisely the "Act to Control and Restrict Immigration and to Regulate the Residence and Integration of EU Citizens and Foreigners (Immigration Act) of 30. July 2004," which went into effect on January 1, 2005. *Nomen est omen*—and in this case the title of the new law appropriately captures its intent.

This new law is intended to "bring the legal framework into congruence with societal realities," according to Interior Minister Otto Schily (2005, 1). This new law was designed, among other elements, to attract highly qualified immigrants. Employers are allowed to do business in Germany if they invest at least one million euros and create at least 10 jobs, and foreign students are able to stay one more year after finishing their degrees to find a job in Germany. People who are not highly qualified will not be allowed to work in Germany.

In addition, the new law codifies for the first time integration policies affecting those who are already here. Newly arrived immigrants must participate in an "integration course" in which they must learn the German language and German laws, history, and culture. Participation in such a course is mandatory. Without completion of this course, permission of stay (*Aufenthaltserlaubnis*) will not be renewed. For those who have lived in Germany for a longer period of time, who receive unemployment support (*Arbeitslosengeld II*), or who are in special need of integration (*besonders integrationsbedürftig*) can be obligated to participate in such courses. If they refuse, their social benefits will be reduced by 10 percent. German authorities estimate that the cost of these integration programs, which will affect between 280,000 to 336,000 immigrants, will run from 380 to 456 million euros. Immigrants will have to pay part of the costs of the integration course, an amount between 30 and 50 euros (38 to 65 U.S. dollars). Family members of *Spätaussiedler* or *Aussiedler* who are not of German descent (i.e., who are the spouses of ethnic Germans and have arrived after 1994) must also participate in language courses. Moreover, particular emphasis in this law is placed on security, influenced by the terrorist attacks of September 11, 2001. If there is proof that people have been engaged in terrorist activities or belong to terrorist organizations, they will be expelled. Similarly, human traffickers who bring refugees into the country will be deported, as well as the so-called *geistige Brandstifter* (demagogues intending to incite violence).

The preamble of this law states that its purpose is to "guide and limit the migration of foreigners" into Germany. It "enables and organizes immigration with due regard for the capacities for admission and integration and the interests of the Federal Republic of Germany in terms of its economy and labor market." The Web site of the Interior Ministry touts the new law as making it "easier for highly qualified workers to move to Germany, making the country more competitive in the global market for the brightest minds." The two principles on which the 2005 law is built are security and utility. It brought restrictions to migrants who depended on the welfare state, and it also highlighted the need for security. The creators of this law were clearly interested in establishing a law that reflects the realities of globalization and the need for highly qualified workers in Germany while at the same time increasing control over asylum seekers in conjunction with making it easier to deport or arrest suspected terrorists and human traffickers. Aristide Zolberg (1987) described alien labor in Germany as "wanted, but not welcome." Based on the new immigration law, the situation of foreign labor may now be described as "only those that are needed are welcome."

Starting with the 2000 shift from descent-based to territorially based citizenship, a historic change has been put into motion. The term *Ausländerpolitik* will soon take on a different meaning: from January 1, 2000, through December 2003, over 660,000 naturalizations took place in Germany, significantly more than occurred between 1996 to 1999 when just over 400,000 took place (Beauftragte der Bundesregierung 2004). While certainly a significant increase, it does not represent an "explosive" rise in naturalizations. The explanation lies in the fact that German "social citizenship" always meant that most social provisions are accessible to foreigners anyway and they do not see a marked improvement in their situation by actually becoming German. More important, however, is the fact that by becoming German foreigners gain the right to vote in national elections and as such are suddenly appearing on the radar screens of political parties.

In the United States, electoral strategies regularly include how best to win over the "Latino" or "black" vote. Currently, immigration reform is dividing the American Republican Party more than any other issue. Germany has been immune to this calculus as very few foreigners became immigrants. However, appealing to the "Turkish vote" in Germany, while it still sounds somewhat strange, will soon become as familiar as the well-worn statements of American political hopefuls addressed to Latinos, blacks, and other minorities. Before the 2002 election the Turkish community in Germany endorsed the Red/Green coalition and asked its members to vote for it. Election analyses have shown that 80 percent of all Turks voted for the Red/Green coalition while the ethnic Germans, mostly from Russia, supported the conservative coalition. In fact, just as Karl Rove uses immigration reform in an attempt to solidify a perpetual Republican majority in the United States, so do conservative German politicians. Axel Fischer asserts that the reason why the Red/Green coalition pushed so hard for a new immigration law in 2002 was to win the elections with the help of immigrants. According to him, both ruling coalition parties are using the immigrant vote as a strategy to "cement their political power forever" (*Der Selbständige,* summer 2003, 3).

The pressures of globalization have led to the establishment of laws that increase the sovereignty of the state while at the same time opening Germany's borders to individuals who further the national interest. This can clearly be seen in the 1993 modification of Germany's asylum law,[7] the categories of migrants Germany accepts, and the state's capacity to arrest or deport suspects. Germany is in dire need of people in areas such as nursing, high technology, and education (Zimmerman et al. 2001) while at the same time suffering from record unemployment. Germany's move to a utility-based immigration policy (i.e., allowing access to those who are needed and keeping others out) is compatible with its labor market needs. Germany clearly has been very successful in curbing immigration, particularly by asylum seekers, whose numbers today are at a historical low, and it has become very choosy as to for whom it will open its doors. This is the dawn of a new phase in Germany's immigration policy, which might most appropriately be called jus utilitaris.[8]

Economic Integration of Foreigners in Germany

Many Germans take great pride in the principle of the *soziale Marktwirtschaft* (social market economy), in which organized unions and employers' organizations engage each other on the basis of social responsibility to avoid the egregious failings of a pure market economy such as widespread poverty and drastic income inequality. Democracy in Germany extends all the way from the shop floor to the highest levels of decision making in large private corporations, where workers together with owners and managers make collective decisions with respect to industrial policy. This form of *Mitbestimmung,* or codetermination, has been a central marker of the German variety of capitalism.

However, at the beginning of the 1990s, and particularly in the wake of unification, doubts about the viability of *Modell Deutschland* have increased. Christopher Allen has argued that as a result of high unemployment, unexpectedly soaring costs of unification, and racial tensions, particularly in the new *Bundesländer,* policymakers, including the former conservative chancellor Helmut Kohl and the Social Democratic/Green coalition government under Chancellor Gerhard Schröder, are increasingly drawn to more American-style, "laissez-faire" policies. He argues that policy-making elites are suffering from a sort of "amnesia" in which "German policymakers lost their 'institutional memory' regarding their past successes during the *Wirtschaftswunder"* (Allen 2004, 1134).

In February of 2005, Germany's unemployment rate reached an all-time high of 12.6 percent, the highest rate since World War II, affecting 5.2 million people. This represented a dramatic jump from December 2004, when the unemployment rate was around 10.8 percent. This sudden increase is the result of the introduction of HARTZ IV, a new law that went into effect on January 1, 2005. According to the new law, recipients of social benefits (*Sozialhilfeempfänger*) are now counted as unemployed and will receive the so-called *Arbeitslosengeld II* (unemployment benefits II), which is 345 euros a month. The new law is named after Peter Hartz, who is head of personnel at Volkswagen, the German car giant. Beneficiaries, however, must be ready to accept a wide range of jobs, such as the so-called 1-euro jobs, that pay less than the collectively agreed upon wage agreements (*Tariflohn*) and "minijobs," which do not provide encompassing insurance (*Frankfurter Rundschau,* March 28, 2005).

The German union IG-Metall believes that 27 percent of the long-term unemployed will lose all of their benefits and 48 percent will see drastic reductions. The government claims that these are exaggerated numbers and "only" 10 percent will lose all their long-term unemployment benefits (*Deutsche Welle,* January 3, 2005). HARTZ IV will involve stringent means testing, including the size of an apartment and people's savings. People who have not worked for at least 12 months in a two-year period will not get any support (*Frankfurter Rundschau,* March 28, 2005).

These drastic cuts led to massive demonstrations, particularly in the former East German *Länder,* in an attempt to persuade Schröder to abandon the law. Thousands of protesters gathered in the eastern cities of Leipzig and Halle on Mondays. These "Monday demonstrations" were reminiscent of the Monday demonstrations in the fall of 1989, which eventually brought down the East German government. But Schröder incited even more vitriol by stating, "In both the east and the west, there's a mentality which extends well into the middle class that you should claim state allowances wherever you can get them, even when there's an adequate income in the family. No welfare state can reasonably expect to manage such a burden" (*Deutsche Welle,* September 18, 2004). The word *HARTZ IV* has even entered the national lexicon, having been designated the "word of the year" by the Gesellschaft für die Deutsche Sprache, the German Language Society (*Deutsche Welle,* December 30, 2004).

Thus, HARTZ IV represents drastic liberalization measures that may spell the end of *Modell Deutschland.* Even so, Rainer Apel (2004) describes in rather shrill tones the law as representing "the deepest cut— the worst threat to existing living standards to millions of Germans— since the founding of this republic in 1949" and compares HARTZ IV with the austere economic policies of Hjalmar Schacht who was the governor of the German Reichsbank and Hitler's economics minister from 1934 to 1937. Such comparisons are much exaggerated. However, this law does reduce access to social benefits, creates "junk jobs," and exposes many more people to the vagaries of the market. With HARTZ IV, Germany has moved from a concept of "organized capitalism" to "capitalism" under the motto "Jeder job muss angenommen werden" (any job offered must be taken); otherwise *Arbeitslosengeld II* will be cut. In fact, the only jobs the unemployed can legitimately reject are those that are *sittenwidrig* (perverse or immoral).

It is against this background of rising unemployment and radical measures intended to rein in the welfare state that immigrants appear particularly vulnerable. In hard times, immigrants are easily made into scapegoats. Hard economic times sharpen the differences between immigrants and natives, increasing the potential for conflicts. This can most clearly be seen in the unsettling successes of two radical right-wing parties in Germany in the September 2004 *Land* elections in Saxony and Brandenburg, both of which are located in the former East Germany. In Saxony, the Nationaldemokratische Partei Deutschlands (NPD), the National Democratic Party of Germany, gained 9.2 percent of the popular vote and elected 12 members to Saxony's Parliament. In Brandenburg, another radical right-wing party, the Deutsche Volksunion (DVU), the German People's Union, gained 6.1 percent of the popular vote, which translated into six seats.

The political success of these parties is directly related to the government's attempts to cut back the welfare state (Wallace 2004; Traynor 2004). One of the central planks on which both parties campaigned was *against* cutbacks in the welfare state. In some areas of Saxony, unemployment has reached 25 percent and more. Much of the support for the radical right-wing parties came from workers who did not want to see their social benefits reduced. "For us the social question is closely connected to the national question," says Holger Apfel, the leader of the NPD, and "the solution for Germany's unemployment problem is to first create jobs for Germans, and later create a foreigner re-patriation policy, so we can free up jobs for Germans, and especially sending home foreigners who are on the dole and who are criminals" (National Public Radio [NPR], November 23, 2004). Paradoxically, ethnic Germans will be just as affected as foreigners by HARTZ IV. Many have few language and job skills, and even though they are German they may find themselves in direr straits than they expected before they started their migration west. With the drastic reduction in the generosity of the German welfare state, many may ask themselves why they went there in the first place.

The more the most vulnerable members of society see their life chances reduced by official government policy the more they become attuned to the demagoguery of the radical right. The trust-generating logic of the welfare state is undermined by such cutbacks. If people's lives are made more precarious, their readiness to trust foreigners will diminish, making them easier targets for radical right-wing parties. As not only foreigners but also natives become increasingly unemployed, nativist resentment and welfare chauvinism are bound to increase. The picture of the idle foreigner, the ones who came to exploit the welfare state, unflatteringly called *Sozialschmarotzer* (social parasites), represents a powerful potion of prejudice. Are foreigners more unemployed than natives?

Figure 7.1 indeed indicates that unemployment of foreigners is significantly higher in Germany than across the total German population. The chasm between foreign unemployment and German unemployment has been widening since 1990, and in 2003 unemployment of foreigners was more than twice (21.5 percent) as high as that of Germans (10.1 percent). With higher unemployment also comes the need for higher welfare dependency. The reason why unemployment is higher among migrants is directly connected to their human capital: they tend to have less education, a smaller skill set, more children, and greater health care needs than natives. However, once education, age, and family size are controlled for, "foreigners are equally or even less likely to

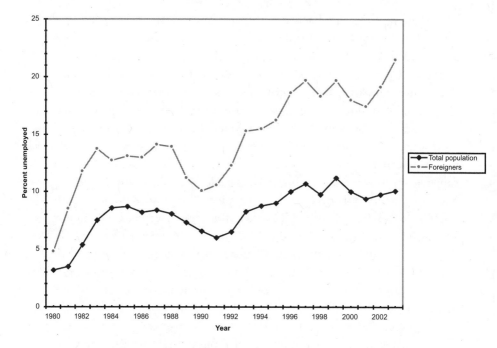

Fig. 7.1.   Unemployment rates of foreigners and Germans as a percentage of total population (1980–2003)

depend on welfare than natives" (Bruecker et al. 2002, 67).[9] In other words, immigrants suffer from an "opportunity gap" as a result of their below-average level of human capital, very much like native Germans who are just as likely to be unemployed as the Turks if not more so. Given Germany's laws ethnic Germans cannot be kept out of the country, even though their human capital profile is in many cases lower than that of second-generation Turks. Particularly ethnic Germans from the former Soviet Union perform worse in the German labor market than ethnic German immigrants from Poland or Romania (Bauer and Zimmermann 1997). With many migrants and ethnic Germans already on home territory, the new Zuwanderungsgesetz is precisely an attempt to deal with the opportunity gap: integrate those who are already here by offering language, history, and civics courses; let only qualified workers in; and keep unskilled and dangerous workers out. This is the gist of the new German immigration law.

As a result of higher unemployment, the welfare uptake of immigrants is also higher. Between 1984 and 1991, foreigners receiving welfare payments increased from around 5 to 17 percent while for natives the rate remained stable at around 4 percent during the same time period (Chapin 1997, 60). In 1996 foreigners made up 9.8 percent of the labor force but accounted for 23.5 percent of social assistance recipients (Marshall 2000, 52). Ethnic Germans and asylum seekers tend to put particular pressure on the welfare state. The lack of human capital in both groups, particularly the inability to speak German well enough to find employment, is a major reason for "the disproportionate rise in the levels of unemployment among ethnic Germans and their increasing demands on the welfare state in the form of unemployment benefits and social assistance" (54).

However, none of these data show that the welfare state is declining as a result of immigration. If anything, strict examination of the numbers would of course show the opposite: welfare expenditures are increasing as a result of the higher welfare uptake of immigrants. The more relevant issue is: did the arrival of immigrants create "net benefits" to or a "net drain" on the overall macroeconomy of Germany? This is a technically complex question, let alone a politically explosive one, and there are very few authoritative studies. There are good reasons to believe that the early migrants, healthy young men with relatively few health needs and jobs aplenty,[10] had a positive effect on the overall economy. After all, they were paying taxes, bought goods, and as a result put little strain on the welfare state. It is likely that in those years they produced a net benefit to the German welfare state. As a result of family unification, which began after 1973 and increased the number of immigrants, particularly ethnic Germans who arrived with their extended families, there is evidence that that trend has reversed.

Hans Werner Sinn, head of the Institute of Economics at the University of Munich, has calculated that if migration to Germany occurred less than 10 years ago the net cost to the German welfare system per immigrant is 2,400 euros (around 3,000 U.S. dollars). Continued competition between states to reduce the generosity of their welfare systems in order to deter immigrants will lead to erosion of the German welfare state, so that "in 50 years we'll have a situation like that in America" (Hans-Werner Sinn, quoted in Gatzke 2004). In a popular book with the alarming title *Ist Deutschland noch zu retten* (Can Germany Yet Be Saved? 2004), Sinn argues that salaries in Germany are kept artificially high as a result of generous welfare benefits. He argues that a family in eastern Germany can collect four times the average income of a family in

Poland and six times the income of a family in Hungary. As a result, he suggests that social benefits should be reduced in order to give incentives to natives to take up work and at the same time give disincentives to migrants to come to Germany (Sinn 2004). Moreover, he suggests that with the accession of 10 Eastern European countries to the EU the most generous welfare states will become magnets for many immigrants from the east. According to Sinn, countries will be forced into a "race to the bottom" in terms of which country offers lower welfare support in order to deter immigrants, thereby hollowing out the welfare state (Sinn, quoted in Gatzke 2004). These suggestions have been strongly criticized by other economists, who are appalled at the suggestion that German social benefits should be adjusted to match the low wages in Eastern European countries (Hickel, Focus Money, February 2004).

However, focusing solely on the "welfare drain" of immigrants distorts the picture. Turks in Germany have been exceptionally successful in becoming self-employed, like many other immigrant groups such as the Koreans in the United States. Between 1985 and 2000, the number of self-employed Turkish immigrants in Germany almost tripled from around 22,000 to nearly 60,000. These businesses employ almost 300,000 workers and ring up billions in sales every year. In conjunction with the consultancy group KPMG, the Association of Turkish Businessmen and Industrialists in Europe estimates that by 2010 the number of entrepreneurs of Turkish descent will reach 106,000, creating a "Turkish middle class in Germany" (German Embassy 2004).

In addition, there is, despite all the talk about parallel societies and *Kulturkampf,* evidence that Germany is becoming a melting pot of sorts. In the year 2003, 18.5 percent of all marriages involved at least one "foreign" partner. Exogamy (marriages across ethnic lines) increased from 4 percent in 1960 to 18.8 percent in 2000 (Beauftragte der Bundesregierung, 2004, 8). In fact, one of the sons of former conservative chancellor Helmut Kohl is married to an ethnic Turk (*Economist* 2005, 4).

In an era of tight budgets, globalization, and international terrorism, it is easy to blame problems on those who are different, even if they were central in the reconstruction of Germany. Sentiments against foreigners have changed since the 1960s, when one day a slightly bewildered Turk was presented with a scooter as he was the one-millionth *Gastarbeiter* (guest workers) crossing into Germany. Sentiments have changed mostly because external conditions have changed. In the German case, unification meant the absorption of an impoverished East, which meant massive

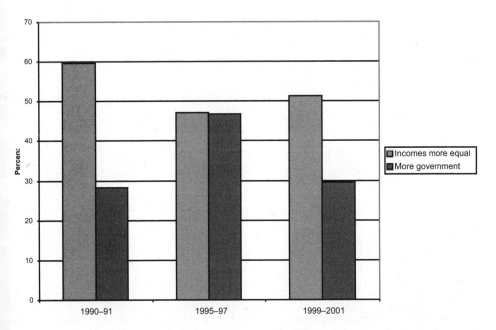

Fig. 7.2. Welfare state attitudes in Germany over three waves of the World Values Survey

financial transfers to reconstruct this area. At the same time, massive streams of refugees have moved into Germany while concurrently the strengthening of the EU has undermined the sovereignty of the state. In addition, globalization has increased the mobility of capital, reducing further the wiggle room of government. Finally, since the terrorist attacks of 9/11 in the United States, the attacks in Madrid in March of 2004, and the assassination of Theo van Gogh in the Netherlands, "Islamophobia" has raised its ugly head and brought the tensions between Muslims and natives in Germany and across Europe into even sharper relief.

These events have shaped public opinion, and if there is any connection between immigrant-driven diversity and willingness to support the welfare state it should be visible in such public opinion measures over time. Two such measures that capture welfare state attitudes over time are shown in figure 7.2.

Unfortunately there are only three time points with which to capture the support or lack thereof of the welfare state in Germany. Nevertheless, as can be seen from figure 7.2, there is no clear trend visible with regard to the sentiment that "incomes should be made more

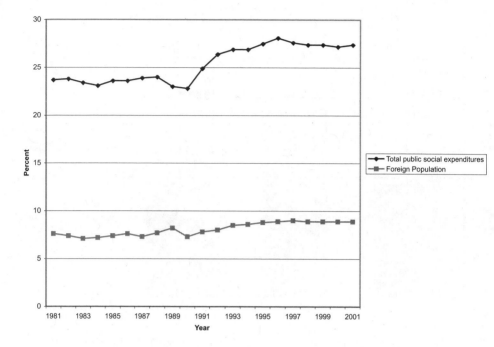

Fig. 7.3.   Total public social expenditures and stock of foreign population in Germany from 1981 to 2001. (Data from OECD Social Expenditures Database [various years]; OECD, *Trends in International Migration*.)

equal" or that the government should ensure that "everyone is provided for." Of course, the last opinion poll was taken before the momentous changes of HARTZ IV. Still, the contours of the immigration debate were well established by the time the fourth wave of the World Values Survey (1999–2001) was conducted. According to figure 7.2, the attitudes of the German public have not, perhaps yet, turned against the welfare state.

This can also be seen by examining the relationship between total public social expenditures and the percentage of stocks of foreign population over time. Since 1997 Germany has hosted about 7.3 million foreigners, which translates to about 8.9 percent of the German population. The claim that immigration-driven diversity leads to cutbacks in the welfare state is clearly not the case, as is shown in figure 7.3.

In fact, figure. 7.3 indicates a positive relationship between the percentage of foreigners and total public social expenditures. The association of the two measures is very strong. The Pearson correlation coefficient is .92. This is not to say that immigrants drive public expenditures in Germany. There is a multitude of other reasons why public expenditures have been rising in Germany. The "bump" in total public expenditures starting in 1990, which is clearly visible in figure 7.3, is directly connected to German unification, when Germany, overnight, inherited the rusty East German economy. Many factories and plants were closed, as they proved to be outdated and noncompetitive, and their workers laid off, increasing dramatically the burden on the German welfare system. Figure 7.3, however, clearly shows that there is no "retreat" from the welfare state taking place as a result of immigration-driven diversity, at least as far as the time period from 1981 to 2001 is concerned.

However, with HARTZ IV there are strong reasons to believe that Germany's welfare state is being undermined. The total impact of the new law is not known yet since it went into effect only on January 1, 2005. However, there is no evidence that these cuts are the result of immigration-driven diversity. HARTZ IV was not passed in order to save the welfare state from abuses by immigrants. It was passed in order to make labor markets more "flexible" by reducing social benefits. This, it is believed, will get Germany out of its sluggishness and give "its young people" a chance to "learn economic dynamism," as the Yale economist Robert J. Shiller (2003, 2) put it. Ultimately, the pressures on the German welfare state originated in the conjuncture of events whose making were mostly determined externally. Unification, the consequent migration flows, and globalization exerted enormous pressure on an already burdened *öffentliche Hand* (public sector), highlighting the role of immigrants as they began to partake of German public expenditures. This raised the profile of immigrants dramatically in the public eye, contributing to rather shrill claims about the decline of the welfare state as a result of rising diversity. In reality, the main reasons for the cutbacks in the German welfare state can be found in attempts to make labor markets more flexible even before unification, the incredible burdens of reconstruction of the former DDR (German Democratic Republic), and the newfound mobility of capital, which constrained the capacity of the state to increase taxes, leaving retrenchment of the welfare state as the only alternative.

SWEDEN: IMMIGRATION, MULTICULTURALISM,
AND THE WELFARE STATE

A lean settlement is preferable to a fat litigation.
—Swedish proverb

Sweden, like its other Nordic brethren, has traditionally been a very homogeneous country, which is partly a result of its geographic location.
In a 1910 census, Sweden was described as being among those countries
in Europe "where the number of foreigners is the smallest, which can
probably be explained by Sweden's remote location" (Jederlund 1998, 1).
The Swedish census of 1930 noted that less than 1 percent of the population was of "foreign stock," including Lapps and Finns (Runblom
1994). It is remarkable that the Swedish census still made that distinction
of Lapps and Finns even though these groups had been living for half a
millennium in the Swedish realm. While during the interwar years the
slogan "Sweden for the Swedes" was rather popular, after World War II
that attitude radically changed. The sources of the change in attitude
originated in the clandestine harboring of Norwegian Jews in 1942 and
"the rescue actions of October 1943 by Danes and Swedes to save the
lives of approximately 6,000 Danish Jews in Nazi-occupied Denmark"
(Runblom 1994, 628).

The close connection between the universal character of Swedish
citizenship and immigrant entitlement was visible during the 1960s
when large-scale labor immigration took place with an influx of between 30,000 and 60,000 people per year from Yugoslavia, Greece, and
Turkey. During this time period, Sweden eschewed a "guest worker"
program. After one or two years in Sweden, migrants could establish
permanent resident status and after five years could become Swedish
citizens. This stood in stark contrast to the German situation, where it
was nearly impossible for migrants to assume citizenship. This liberal
Swedish nationality law was complemented with full "social citizenship" rights. All the social benefits available to Swedes were extended to
migrants, including unemployment benefits. The social-democratic
roots of the Swedish welfare state, "founded on strongly egalitarian principles meant that immigrants were swiftly included as welfare state
members" (Geddes 2003, 119).

This encompassing inclusion of migrants into the Swedish polity is
consistent with Per Albin Hansson's vision of *folkhem,* a "people's home"
in which the welfare of its inhabitants becomes the responsibility of the

state. Hansson was the architect of the Swedish welfare state in the early 1920s. While *folkhem* captures the Swedish bent for social engineering, the word *lagom,* which may be translated as "just right," "suitable," "appropriate," or perhaps more precisely "just share," captures the moral dimension. The term originated from the drinking habits in ancient Sweden, where a jug of beer was passed around among a group of men, with each one taking "his share" by drinking just the right amount—not too much—so as to leave enough for the others but not too little to be unsociable. This sense of mediation, moderation, and fairness is a "peculiarly Swedish concept" and the "secret of Swedish social ethics" (Ruth 1986, 52, 53).

After the first oil crises in 1973, which dramatically slowed economic growth, the Landsorganisationen (Swedish Trade Union Confederation, LO) decided to stop expansive immigration. In rather typical corporatist fashion this decision involved neither the political parties nor the public. While this policy stopped new workers coming to Sweden, it did not stop family unification. On the basis of humanitarian grounds Swedish authorities could not deny the unification of families, leading to a continuous influx of migrants.

Swedish immigration policies reflected an early realization that migrant workers were here to stay and that swift incorporation is preferable to leaving them waiting in the antechamber of citizenship. Moreover, Sweden, as opposed to Germany, realized very early that once migrants had arrived on Swedish territory the most effective way to reduce potential frictions with the dominant society would be to integrate them as fully and quickly as possible. As a result, Sweden embarked on a very ambitious multiculturalism program in 1975, which rested on three cornerstones: "equality," "freedom of choice," and "partnership." The principles of equality and freedom of choice capture the dimensions of the welfare state and multiculturalism. *Equality* meant that the living conditions of migrants or new citizens should be equal to those of Swedes. *Freedom of choice* referred to the cultural autonomy of immigrants, and *partnership* suggested cooperation and solidarity with Swedes. These policies demarcate Sweden as one of the pioneers of multiculturalism among modern nation-states.[11] Not only were social rights extended to immigrants but also political rights. Starting in 1975 local voting rights were extended to migrants after 36 months in legal residence.

Christian Joppke and Ewa Morawska (2003) make the connection between integration and welfare policy explicit by arguing that the

Swedish policy on integration centered specifically on cultural affairs "because with respect to welfare and social services immigrants were included as individuals, not as groups, reflecting the universalism of the Swedish welfare state" (13). There is a spillover from the way states organize their political economies into the area of immigration and integration policies. Certain affinities between the logic of welfare and immigration and integration policies are to be expected. The universal Swedish welfare state is "universal" in ideal terms, which means that such a model "shuns discrimination on the basis of social background or residence in the country" (Brochmann 2003, 5).

And yet Swedish policymakers soon realized that there is a tension between a universal welfare state and extensive multiculturalism. Evidence began to appear that migrants were disproportionately unemployed and their wages were trailing those of Swedes. At the same time, there was a move away from multiculturalism policies "towards an approach that placed more emphasis on Swedish language and culture and adaptation by immigrants" (Geddes 2003, 122). The 1980s was also a decade that witnessed a different kind of migrant: asylum seekers. While the early 1980s were characterized by a relatively small influx of asylum seekers, around 5,000 each year, by the mid-1980s this number had increased to between 15,000 and 30,000 a year and reached its peak in 1992 when 84,000 asylum seekers entered Sweden, mostly from the former Yugoslavia (Geddes 2003). Between 1991 and 1995, 61.5 percent of all immigrants in Sweden were asylum seekers, by far the highest percentage in modern societies, followed by the Netherlands with 29.3 percent. Studies indicate that countries with the greatest share of asylum seekers are also the ones where the largest amount of immigrant unemployment is to be found. This is because asylum seekers represent a lower "quality of immigrants" as measured by the upon-arrival immigrant-native wage gap (Bauer, Lofstrom, and Zimmermann 2001). Mats Hammarstedt (2001) finds that more recent cohorts of immigrants (i.e., asylum seekers) have less disposable income than earlier cohorts do.

By 1998, 5.5 percent of Swedes were unemployed compared to 23 percent of immigrants. The story is similar to that of Germany: immigrants are at significantly higher risk of unemployment compared to natives. Much of this is related to their lack of human capital. However, a number of studies in Sweden indicate that the cause is not only the lack of human capital, including language difficulties, but simply discrimination (Arai and Vilhelmsson 2001).

The official Swedish Social Report 2001 (Socialstyrelsen) speaks of "ethnic segregation" and finds "much higher unemployment among immigrants."[12] The report continues: "Within the Stockholm region in 1998, roughly forty percent of those born in seven countries—Ethiopia, Somalia, Lebanon, Syria, Turkey, Iraq, and Iran—resided in low- and very low-income areas. Previous research shows that residential segregation in itself has social consequences, sometimes referred to as 'area effects.' Such effects tend to accentuate social problems, contribute to the emergence of new problems, and further distort the distribution of welfare."

Immigration has turned Sweden into a multicultural society, and it has not escaped its share of attendant social frictions. In order to facilitate finding housing for immigrants, Sweden engaged in a dispersal policy for the reception of immigrants. Immigrants were to be dispersed across various communities deemed to have suitable characteristics for reception.

The first widespread reaction against refugees came in 1988 when the small, mostly agricultural, southern town of Sjöbo in southern Sweden objected to the dispersal program. Sixty-five percent of the people Sjöbo decided in a referendum not to participate in this program. This is particularly remarkable as the town of Sjöbo had about 15,000 inhabitants and only 15 to 25 refugees per year (later reduced to 15 per year) were scheduled to be settled there (Uddmann 1992). The success of that referendum tapped a deeply felt Swedish uneasiness about strangers, and combined with a charismatic leader (Sven Olle Olson) it put xenophobia on the map in Sweden (Fryklund and Peterson 1992).

By 1991 enough anti-immigrant sentiment had accumulated in Sweden for the nativist New Democracy Party to win 8 percent of the vote in national elections. In 1993, a mosque was burned down and two Somalis were badly beaten in the Swedish town of Tröllhattan (Geddes 2003). And in the fall of 2004 an arson attack destroyed the mosque in the city of Malmö, which has seen a "sudden influx of Muslim immigrants—90 percent of whom are unemployed" (Harrigan 2004). One-quarter of Malmö's population is Muslim. Students aged 10 or 12 who have arrived from countries such as Iraq, Iran, or Lebanon have such poor language skills that classes require interpreters. Immigration and *lagom* do not seem to go hand in hand.

Joppke and Morawska (2003, 14) come to a strongly worded conclusion: "The message is clear: the earlier stress on cultural pluralism had blatantly ignored the socio-economic rift opening up between immigrants and the domestic population, and tackling this rift meant making

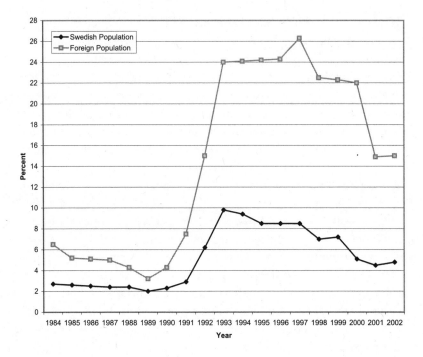

Fig. 7.4.   Unemployment rates of Swedish and foreign population from 1984 to
2002. (Data from OECD Social Expenditure Database 2004.)

immigrants indistinguishable from the domestic population (in this sense,
to 'assimilate' them)—witness the very notion of 'immigrant' has practically disappeared in the new Swedish 'integration' discourse." The rift between immigrants and the domestic population can clearly be seen in the
unemployment rates of the two groups.

Figure 7.4 shows that in 1998 immigrant unemployment was four
times higher among the immigrant population compared to native
Swedes. As might be expected, such a drastic chasm puts tremendous
pressures on the system of social benefits. In fact, by the mid-1990s immigrants in Sweden "accounted for nearly half of the country's expenditures on social assistance" (Hansen and Lofstrom 2001, 1). This is even
more remarkable because foreigners in Sweden account for only about
5.4 percent of the population. As a result of this high unemployment,
immigrants participated to a much larger extent in both the social assistance and unemployment compensation programs than natives did. The
average welfare participation rate for refugee immigrants during the
1990–96 period was roughly six times higher than the average utilization

rate for natives (Hansen and Lofstrom 2001). Very few scholars in the "traditional" welfare state literature have made these connections between immigration and welfare uptake. In the Swedish case, it appears at first glance that immigration is significantly driving the costs of the welfare state. Indeed, if the unemployment benefits expenditures are examined using the OECD Social Expenditure Database, there is a marked increase starting in 1989 of .6 percent of GDP to a peak of 2.7 percent of GDP in 1993 followed by a stabilization at a somewhat lower level of around 2.0 percent through 1998 and a drop to 1.0 percent of GDP in 2001 (OECD, Social Expenditure Database, 2004).

However, overall, Sweden appeared to be able to rein in the costs, partly by cutting the eligibility for unemployment insurance of recent asylum seekers. A look at the overall total social expenditures in Sweden over the last 21 years indicates that Sweden has been able to take control of its expenditures. Figure 7.5 shows a marked "hump" of total social expenditures visible in the first half of the 1990s, culminating in 1993, when Sweden saw its highest level of total social expenditures in the twentieth century. This coincided with low economic growth and attendant high unemployment. It is safe to assume that in this difficult period the extremely high unemployment of immigrants combined with the generous extension of social protection to newcomers have exacerbated the increase in social expenditures. By 2001 Sweden was able to bring down its total social expenditures to lower levels than in 1981 after spiking at around 37 percent in 1993.

The decommodification index also shows a continuous decline after 1988. Decommodification is an index designed to capture the degree to which the life chances of an individual are independent of market forces. The index, rather than capturing expenditures, encompasses programmatic aspects of three elements of the welfare state: pensions, sickness, and unemployment benefits. *Programmatic aspects* refers to things such as replacement rates of pensions or unemployment benefits, the number of waiting days before benefits are paid, the universality of benefits, contribution periods (i.e., for how long are benefits paid), the number of weeks of employment required prior to qualification, and similar features.

Robert Cox (2004) argues that since the early 1990s Sweden has engaged in welfare state reform by making pensions more contributory and less universal, increasing means testing, deregulating the labor market by allowing for more flexible contracts, and decentralizing wage bargaining and government administration (Cox 2004). The effect of part of these

Fig. 7.5.   Decommodification index and percentage of total social expenditures in Sweden from 1981 to 2001

reforms, particularly the pension reform, is reflected in the continuous decline of decommodification in Sweden. Displaying the declines of decommodification in other Scandinavian countries would go too far in this section; however, no other country has seen as tenacious a decline of decommodification as Sweden. Both Denmark and Norway in 2002 show higher decommodification indices than Sweden, with 34.87 and 37.25, respectively, compared to Sweden with 32.53 (Scruggs 2004).

How do these aggregate dynamic data manifest themselves in public support for the welfare state in Sweden? The question that is used to tap welfare support is familiar by now and asks "whether the government should take more responsibility to ensure that everyone is provided for or whether people should take more responsibility to provide for themselves." It is instructive to compare the Swedish results with results obtained from the United States, its diametrically opposed model.

A glance at figure 7.6 reveals a rather surprising picture: for any time period in which the WVS was administered, *more* Americans than Swedes thought that the government, as opposed to "people," should take more

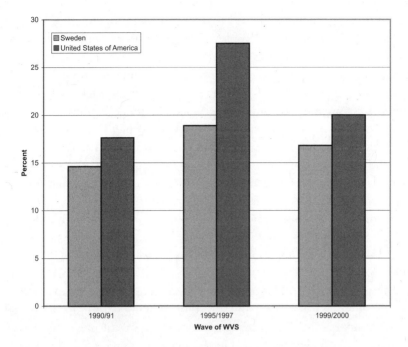

Fig. 7.6.   Swedish and American attitudes about welfare state support. (Data from World Values Survey, various waves.)

responsibility to ensure that everyone is provided for. Certainly the absolute percentages are relatively low, between 17 and 27 percent. However, Swedish public opinion is even less in favor of government provision. In the second wave of the WVS in 1990, 14.6 percent of Swedes thought the government should take care of them. In 1995 that number increased to 18.9 percent, and in 2000 it dropped to 16.8 percent. This is less than what would be expected a priori in such a highly developed welfare state. However, precisely because in Sweden there is already a very high level of public provision and "guided capitalism," Swedish public opinion has reached a saturation point where further increases in state-led public provision is experiencing a declining marginal utility as perceived by public opinion. After all, financing the Swedish welfare state in 1998 took about 59 percent of the pay of people making as little as 30,000 dollars a year (Hoge 1998). It is no small wonder that Swedes do not want more state than they already have.

Nevertheless, as in Germany, there is no indication that in terms of mass public opinion Swedes are retreating from the welfare state. In fact, in 1996, when the fieldwork for Sweden was done, the country had just experienced the highest unemployment rate in its recent history a couple of years before and was still suffering from comparatively high unemployment rates. Yet public support for government-supported provision in such a challenging economic environment was higher than in the other two time periods, which experienced better economic conditions. This confirms much of what was found in chapter 3: hard economic times do not lead to the abandonment of welfare state principles. Rather, just the opposite is the case. It is precisely in challenging economic times that the welfare state is needed the most, and naturally people will be more than willing to pledge their support for it.

In order to examine how the economic crises in the mid-1990s affected Swedish public opinion, the most recent (fourth) wave of the WVS is used in conjunction with the two National Identity I (1995) and National Identity II (2003) panels of the ISSP. The fieldwork for the polls was conducted in 1995, just after Sweden experienced a major economic slowdown and Germany was still struggling with unification, and in 2003 after 9/11. For comparison and economy of presentation, the results for Germany and the United States are presented along with those for Sweden in table 7.1. The picture that emerges from the 10 items in the table is quite consistent with the results shown in table 5.4. In general, nativist resentment and welfare chauvinism are lower in Sweden than in the other two countries.

In the first four WVS items, Sweden shows clearly lower levels of prejudice and welfare chauvinism. The question about not wanting immigrants as neighbors, for example, revealed that in the United States and Germany this percentage is significantly higher by a factor of two to three. Other items within that first group of five show equally strong differences, with the United States and Germany scoring much higher on prejudice and welfare chauvinism, even though item 5 is based on the ISSP survey conducted in 1995 during the height of Sweden's economic crisis. Indeed, the second time point in 2003 for Sweden reveals that the percentage of respondents who believe that immigrants take jobs away from natives is halved from 16 percent to 8 percent, while Germany saw an increase from the 1995 to the 2003 data point from over 26 percent to 39 percent. In the United States, that sentiment slightly decreased from 48 percent to 43 percent.

Natives in all three countries are also becoming less convinced that immigrants improve the host societies by bringing new cultures and

TABLE 7.1. Percentages of Nativist Resentment, Welfare Chauvinism, and Multiculturalism in Germany, Sweden, and the United States

	Germany	Sweden	United States
WVS Items (1999)			
1. Not wanted as neighbors: different race (mentioned)	5.9	2.6	8.1
2. Not wanted as neighbors: immigrants (mentioned)	11.0	2.9	10.2
3. Immigration: strict limits or prohibit immigration? (yes)	63.0	30.0	43.0
4. In case of unemployment, jobs should be given to natives. (agree)	73.5	12.6	55.9

	Germany		Sweden		United States	
	1995	2003	1995	2003	1995	2003
ISSP Items						
5. Immigrants take jobs away from people. (agree)	26.3	39.0	16.1	8.0	48.1	43.0
6. Immigrants open country to new cultures and ideas. (yes)	69.0	56.5	69.8	58.6	62.1	57.2
7. Should number of immigrants be increased? (yes)	3.4	5.4	7.3	12.0	8.6	11.3
8. Ethnic minorities should be given assistance. (yes)	41.4	30.2	20.2	24.2	17.1	23.0
9. Maintain traditions (1) or adapt to society? (2)	47.5	64.2	80.7	66.0	58.3	52.6
10. To become full member sharing traditions is important. (yes)	43.4	55.0	60.7	51.0	35.4	33.0

Source: OECD Social Expenditure Dataset 2004; Banting and Kymlicka 2004.
Question items:
1. On this list are various groups of people. Could you please sort out any that you would not like to have as neighbors? People of a different race (percentage mentioned).
2. On this list are various groups of people. Could you please sort out any that you would not like to have as neighbors? Immigrants (percentage mentioned).
3. How about people from other countries coming here to work? Which one of the following do you think the government should do? (1) Let anyone come who wants to. (2) Let people come as long as there are jobs available. (3) Place strict limits on the number of foreigners who can come here. (4) Prohibit people coming here from other countries. (percentage of sum of 3 and 4)
4. When jobs are scarce, employers should give priority to [Nation] people over immigrants. (1) Agree, (2) disagree, (3) neither. (percentage of 1)
5. How much do you agree or disagree with the following statement? Immigrants take jobs away from people who were born in [Respondent's country]. (1) agree strongly, (2) agree, (3) neither agree nor disagree, (4) disagree, (5) disagree strongly. (percentage of sum of 1 and 2)
6. How much do you agree or disagree with each of the following statements: Immigrants make [Respondent's country] more open to new ideas and cultures. (1) agree strongly, (2) agree, (3) neither agree nor disagree, (4) disagree, (5) disagree strongly. (percentage of 1 and 2)
7. Do you think the number of immigrants to [Respondent's country] should be (1) increased a lot, (2) increased a little, (3) remain the same as it is, (4) reduced a little, (5) reduced a lot. (percentage of 1 and 2)
8. How much do you agree or disagree with the following statements? Ethnic minorities should be given government assistance to preserve their customs and traditions. (1) agree strongly, (2) agree, (3) neither agree nor disagree, (4) disagree, (5) disagree strongly. (percentage of 1 and 2)
9. Some people say that it is better for a country if different ethnic and racial groups maintain their distinct customs and traditions. Others say that it is better if these groups adapt and blend into the larger society. Which of these views comes closer to your own? (1) It is better for society if groups maintain their distinct customs and traditions. (2) It is better if groups adapt and blend into the larger society. (percentage who say: adapt)
10. Now we would like to ask you a few questions about minorities in [Respondent's country]. How much do you agree or disagree with the following statements. It is impossible for people who do not share [Respondent's country's] customs and tradition to become fully (e.g., British). (1) agree strongly, (2) agree, (3) neither agree nor disagree, (4) disagree, (5) disagree strongly. (percentage of sum of 1 and 2)

234 Trust beyond Borders

ideas to it. While majorities in all three countries felt this to be the case, their support has dwindled in all three countries: in 1995, 69 percent of respondents felt that immigrants open the host country to new ideas and cultures, but by 2003 that view has dropped to over 56 percent. Similar decreases are observable in Sweden and the United States.

Very small percentages of respondents believe that the number of immigrants should be increased: in 1995 only over 3 percent of Germans, slightly over 7 percent of Swedes, and not even 9 percent of Americans shared that sentiment. By 2003, however, more people—though still a significant minority—believed that the number of immigrants should be increased as compared to 1995.

There is also little public support for the state giving assistance to ethnic minorities. Across all three countries there is only minority support observable, although in Sweden the percentage of people who believe that the state should support ethnic minorities has increased from 20 percent to over 24 percent, and even in the United States that sentiment has increased from 17 percent to 23 percent. In Germany, on the other hand, there is a drastic drop observable from 41 percent in 1995 to 30 percent in 2003.

Rather intriguing are the responses that are captured under the rubric of "multiculturalism." If multiculturalism is understood to mean the recognition, protection, and active support of minorities' traditions and customs by the host state, Sweden certainly does not appear to be on the leading edge of multiculturalism, at least not in 1995 when the first survey was taken. Over 80 percent of the Swedes thought that immigrants should adapt to Swedish society rather than maintain their traditions. However, by 2003 that sentiment decreased to 66 percent indicating that Swedes may becoming more tolerant of immigrant cultures. The United States also recorded a decrease in its nativist tone, while Germany noted a significant increase in the belief that immigrants should adapt to the host country's culture, from 48 percent to 64 percent.

Finally, the last question also in the multiculturalist mode shows that Americans prove to be the most tolerant. In 1995, slightly over 35 percent believe that in order to become fully American one must participate completely in the customs and traditions of the United States. This was the lowest percentage of all three countries, and by 2003 even fewer Americans, 33 percent, believed that to be the case. The favorable responses for items 9 and 10 can most likely be explained with the argument that immigration is a crucial part of Americans' identity. More

German respondents in 2003 believed that in order to become fully German, immigrants must completely participate in the customs and traditions of Germany. While that percentage stood at over 43 percent in 1995, by 2003 it increased to 55 percent.

Sweden, like the United States, also experienced a reduction in this item, although the 1995 data point indicated that over 60 percent of respondents believed that to become fully Swedish, immigrants must fully absorb the Swedish customs and traditions. It is puzzling that in terms of nativist prejudice or welfare chauvinism Sweden shows a low incidence, but in terms of its level of multiculturalism, at least as the population is concerned, the Swedes are not that much in favor of it despite the early development of multiculturalism policies. It is quite plausible that the rejection of multiculturalism is a function of this particular time frame in which the opinion poll was administered. The mid-1990s was a time when Sweden was still reeling from the economic crises of just a couple of years before. Indeed, by 2003 Swedes seem to have become more tolerant as fewer of them (51 percent in 2003 as opposed to 61 percent in 1995) shared the belief that to fully become Swedish, one must share the customs and traditions of Sweden.

Despite this "native impulse," Swedes seem to be quite willing to mix with other cultures and ethnic groups. Blanck and Tydén (1995, 67) report that "among first generation immigrant couples, approximately half are cohabiting with a Swedish citizen . . . and it is estimated that every third adult Swede has an immigrant relative." The authors take that to mean that there is no "ethnic mosaic" developing in Sweden, that is, exogamy staves off the development of "ethnic enclaves."

Examining the last six items of table 7.1 reveals an intriguing picture. In terms of the direction of change, Germany is clearly becoming less supportive of foreigners, embracing multiculturalism less, showing increases in prejudice and welfare chauvinism compared to the earlier time period. Given its sense of *soziale Marktwirtschaft* and the relatively generous welfare state in the late 1990s, it would have been expected that Germany should come out second after Sweden. However, this is not the case.

More surprising still is the similarity in change in attitudes from 1995 to 2003 between Sweden and the United States. Both countries tend to become more supportive of foreigners, favor multiculturalism more, show less prejudice and less welfare chauvinism than in the earlier time period. In five out of six items, Sweden and the United States change toward more tolerance and acceptance of foreigners, the exact opposite of Germany. The one item where there is an adverse tendency observable is the same for the United States as well as Sweden: in both countries fewer people thought that immigrants open their countries to new cultures and ideas.

While only tentative conclusions can be drawn from these results it appears that among the three models, two of them, Sweden and the United States, seem to be more successful in instilling a more positive perception of foreigners than Germany can. This may have to do with the multitude of economic opportunities in the United States, and the possibility for immigrants to actually become Americans. Until recently, for the majority of immigrants this was not possible in Germany. Also, the recent harsh cutbacks in the German welfare state combined with very high unemployment rates may have heightened differences between natives and immigrants. The German model, forced to reduce public support in the wake of post-unification development needs, may have produced a situation that is worse than either in Sweden or in the United States. Germany has produced a truncated welfare state that only incompletely protects immigrants without having a dynamic, competitive, less-regulated economy that provides economic opportunities for immigrants. In that sense, half a loaf of bread may be worse than no loaf at all.

The Swedish model may also be under some strain, but it is not being abandoned. Carl Bildt, a conservative challenger to the Social Democrats, campaigned for tax cuts in the 1998 general election campaign. He lost to the Social Democrats, who were running on the basis of tax *increases*. Referring to the 1998 general election campaign, "talking about tax cuts in this campaign is like swearing in church," said Toivo Sjoren, the research director of the Sifo opinion survey firm (Hoge 1998). A similar scenario was present during the 2002 campaign. The Swedish prime minister, Göran Persson, leading up to the 2002 election, declared that "Welfare is not free. You have to pay for it, and that is why we say no to the tax cuts." In fact, the incumbent Swedish Social Democratic government has set itself up as the defender of the Swedish model. On the campaign trail in 2002, Prime Minister Persson declared that "Welfare is not about how much money you have in your savings account, but about someone taking care of you when you are weak" (British Broadcasting Corporation, September 14, 2002). The Social Democrats won the election, increasing their vote share from 36.4 percent in 1998 to 39.9 percent in 2002.

In fact, by 2002 the Swedish unemployment rate had dropped to 4 percent, significantly lower than the OECD average, and the economy grew by 2 percent. The government established recruitment subsidies to companies to hire qualified immigrants and established a national fund of 16.5 million euros (20 million U.S. dollars) to improve the employment rate among immigrants. An additional 10 million euros has been allocated to finance language courses for immigrants with a foreign university diploma and programs to promote ethnic diversity. In addition, in 2001 the government presented a national action plan against racism, xenophobia, homophobia, and discrimination (OECD 2003).

The big winner of the last general election in Sweden was the Liberal Party (Folkpartiet liberalerna), which had immigration at the heart of its manifesto. Under the leadership of Lars Leijonborg, the party almost tripled its vote from 4.7 percent in 1998 to 13.4 percent in 2002, which translated into 48 seats out of 349 in the Swedish Riksdag. Leijonborg's main plank was to make a language test a requirement for citizenship and allow further immigration only to qualified workers. In the past, it was not "politically correct" to debate immigration in Sweden. Even so, the Liberal Party actually lost votes and seats in the 2006 election when an alliance consisting of center-right parties won the elections and the Social Democrats, who have ruled for the last 12 years, suffered their biggest defeat since 1914.

Still, embracing immigrants by including them in welfare programs has doused the fires of racism and blunted the effects of xenophobia, at least compared to Germany and the United States. The comparatively friendly public perception of immigrants gives policymakers more room to creatively deal with a potentially explosive issue compared to countries where public sentiments against immigrants have hardened to such a degree that policy is more reactive than proactive.

THE COSTS OF IMMIGRATION AND INTEGRATION: THE UNITED STATES OF AMERICA

Family values don't stop at the Rio Grande River.
—George W. Bush during the 2000 election campaign

It is customary in the United States that newly naturalized citizens receive a "personal" welcome message from the president. The message for those who become naturalized during George W. Bush's administration is addressed "Dear Fellow American" and states, among other things: "Our country has never been united by blood, birth or soil. We are bound by principles that move us beyond our backgrounds, lift us above our interests and teach us what it means to be citizens. . . . Americans are generous and strong and decent not because we believe in ourselves, but because we hold beliefs beyond ourselves."

It is the historical experience as a settler nation that gives such statements plausibility. Only when there is an absence of a long-established history of ethnic, racial, religious, and cultural homogeneity is it possible, and perhaps even prudent, for nation builders to appeal to civic ideals and mold a nation out of creedal principles in order to unite disparate groups. It is precisely this shared principle of political ideals that makes terms such as *un-American* sensible. There is no equivalent of such concepts in Europe. No one has ever heard of "un-Norwegian" or "un-German" behavior. Thus, the central difference between the United States and the previous two cases is that the United States is a classic immigration country, defined as "founded, populated, and built by immigrants in modern times" (Cornelius and Tsuda 2004, 20).

It also has the least-developed welfare state among the three cases examined in this chapter. The United States is the poster child of a "liberal" or "laissez-faire" society with comparatively minimal state intervention in which "society" is strong and the "state" is weak. This is a crucial difference from Germany and Sweden, which requires some explanation, as this structural feature is ultimately the reason why immigration control in the United States takes the form it does and why the welfare state is relatively weak.

From a comparative political economy perspective, the United States can be described as pluralist in nature. If the United States had to be placed on a scale from "corporatism" to "pluralism," most observers would place it on the pluralist end of such a scale (Lijphart and Crepaz 1991; Schmidt 1986; Cameron 1984). Pluralism means that policy in the United States is the vector sum of a multitude of political forces impinging on the state. Political outcomes are the result of a pluralist process of "wheeling and dealing" among multiple actors that are in competition with each other. By contrast, in corporatist societies policy outcomes are goal oriented and based on a small number of actors who are engaged with each other on the basis of accommodation rather than competition. In a pluralist society, the state is rather weak vis-à-vis a strong civil society characterized by highly organized interest groups. In a pluralist political economy, the state is amorphous, with many entry points for private interests shaping public policy. The capacity of governments to keep private interests at "arm's length" is much reduced under pluralism, and as a result so is autonomous policy-making ability (Crepaz 1992).

This is not to say that corporatist countries have been very successful in reconciling policy outputs with policy outcomes. In fact, many of the postwar immigration policies in European countries have been characterized by a slew of unintended consequences, the biggest of which was the belief that guest workers would simply leave when they were not needed anymore. In the oft-repeated phrase by Max Frisch, the labor migrants were like "guests who came for dinner but never left." In the German case, employers insisted on ever longer permits for foreign labor since they did not want to deal with new labor, which needed to be trained again. Also, allowing family visits to labor migrants facilitated their entry into Germany. Finally, granting migrants social rights led to policy *outcomes* that were inconsistent with the intended policy *outputs*.

Wayne Cornelius and Takeyuki Tsuda, who subtitled a chapter in their book "The Limits of Government Intervention," refer to this difference between policy outputs and policy outcomes as the "policy gap" and declare that the "United States has by far the largest gap between the stated goal of controlling immigration and the actual results of policy" (Cornelius and Tsuda 2004, 20). The relative paralysis of American immigration control also motivates Jeffrey Togman's contribution (2002), which finds that compared to France, where immigration was reduced as a solution to rising unemployment between 1962 and 1982, the United States, which was in a similar economic situation with rising unemployment, did not reduce immigration. According to Togman, the French statist tradition allowed France to "act singularly and autonomously on issues of immigration" while in the United States the factors that make immigration policy intractable are "so many actors and so many possible coalitions among these actors. . . . and the fractured nature of the state" (2002, 19).

Gary Freeman made a similar argument in the mid-1990s, building on the work of James Q. Wilson, who examined policies in terms of benefits and costs and whether these elements are either concentrated or diffuse. Freeman applies this framework and concludes that the existence of a gap between restrictionist intentions and expansionist reality is driven by a particular combination of costs and benefits. He concludes that immigration represents a case of concentrated benefits and diffuse costs (Freeman 2001; Freeman 1995). His "client politics" model argues that the United States has lost the capacity to generate an overarching immigration policy as a result of a multitude of private interests that are politically organized and pressure lawmakers to devise policies favoring their interests. As a result of an imbalance in expertise, the political representatives are captured by economic pressure groups. In addition, as the number of naturalized immigrants grows in the United States, they are increasingly becoming an electoral force to be reckoned with. In Freeman's words, "Polls continue to indicate that majorities are opposed to more generous immigration quotas and support stringent measures at the borders. Most voters, however, don't cast ballots on the basis of their immigration views whereas many Latinos do" (2001, 84).

Statistics examining the percentage of foreign-born population indeed indicate a steady increase from 8.7 percent in 1994 to 11.5 percent in 2002 (OECD 2003). A drastic increase occurred between 1999 and 2001, when the number of legal immigrants increased from 646,568 to 1,064,318 as a result of the immigration authorities' successful reduction of the application backlog, which had been accumulating since 1994. In 2001 permanent immigrant status was granted mostly on the basis of family unification (63 percent). In terms of illegal immigration, the U.S. Census Bureau estimates that the number of illegal immigrants in the country doubled between 1990 and 2000 to around 8.5 million (OECD, Sopemi Report, 2003). Other estimates produce numbers up to 15 million.

What are the costs of the immigrants to the American welfare system? Examining national statistics of total social expenditures or decommodification is not that insightful in the American case as much of the funds dealing with welfare are within the purview of the states. There are dramatic differences among states in terms of the social benefits a given family receives. For example, in 1990 a family of three received almost twice as much in social benefits in California compared to the median benefit of all states (Borjas 1999, 116). In New York, such benefits are around 1.6 times higher than the median benefit, and in Texas they are only about half compared to the median benefit of all states. As in Europe, where some observers speculate that immigrants tend to settle in more generous welfare states, George Borjas (1999, 118) concludes that "there might be something to the idea of 'welfare magnets.'"

It is the very federalist structure of the United States that makes a uniform immigration policy, as well as a welfare policy, difficult. This could clearly be seen in the 1996 welfare reform bill. Originally, it postulated that immigrants arriving after August 22, 1996, would be ineligible for food stamps and Supplemental Security Income (SSI) cash assistance for five years, after which time they could apply for naturalization. In the event that the application was successful and they became citizens, they then could partake in the same welfare benefits that were available to American citizens. According to Borjas (1999), almost half of the $54 billion in savings attributed to welfare reform were directly connected to cuts in immigrants' use of welfare. Very quickly a number of powerful proimmigrant interest groups, business lobbies, state governors, and mayors descended on Washington to repeal this law. Senators and state governors, as well as mayors, realized that if these provisions went into effect their states and cities would become responsible for hundreds of thousands of immigrants who previously depended on federal support, including disabled immigrants, who could draw SSI benefits. They lobbied strenuously, and as a result the most stringent features of the immigrant-related provisions were never enforced. The Balanced Budget Act of 1997 restored SSI and Medicaid eligibility for legal residents who were receiving these benefits on August 22, 1996. By 2002, at the urging of President Bush, immigrants became eligible for food stamps after residing in the United States for at least three years.

As in Germany and Sweden, immigrants in the United States partake of welfare benefits disproportionately, although the relative differences are smaller in the United States. While in 2000 around 7 percent of natives received cash benefits, 10.5 percent of immigrants received cash benefits. In terms of all types of assistance, in 1998 around a quarter of immigrant households received some type of assistance while for natives that figure was about 15 percent. As a result, "immigrant households accounted for 14 percent of the cost of means-tested programs, even though they only made up 9 percent of the households in the United States" (Borjas 1999, 108). While clearly disproportionate, this pales in comparison with Sweden, where in the 1990s 5.4 percent of immigrants partook of almost half of the country's social expenditures and the welfare participation rate of immigrants was six times higher than that of natives between 1990 and 1996 (Hansen and Lofstrom 2001). And yet nativist resentment and welfare chauvinism are the lowest in Sweden among all three countries.

The impact of immigrants on the national economy is studied nowhere in more detail than in the United States. However, many of these studies are conducted and financed by special interests in order to support a particular political agenda. One such study that gained a certain notoriety was Donald Huddle's (1993) investigation of welfare uptake by immigrants for the Carrying Capacity Network, an anti-population-growth group. Huddle claimed that the net costs of immigration exceeded $40 billion. His conclusions were quickly questioned by others, including Jeffrey S. Passel and Rebecca L. Clark (Passel and Clark 1994). Harold Wilensky (2002, 649) calls Huddle's investigation "flawed research" and claims that immigrants are probably "ripped off by American taxpayers." He argues that immigrants who pay Social Security and Medicare taxes are overwhelmingly young and as a result place no burden on disability and health care services; help pay for the baby boomers' retirement and medical care; and pay state sales taxes, local property taxes, and gasoline taxes. Their employers pay unemployment insurance and workers' compensation taxes (Wilensky 2002).

What is probably the most authoritative study, *The New Americans* (Smith and Edmonston 1997), conducted by the National Academy of Sciences, examines the economic impact of immigrants on the American economy. Overall, the study concluded that immigrants add between 1 and 10 billion U.S. dollars to the country's gross GDP, largely as a result of increasing the supply of labor and helping produce new goods and services. The gains for the overall American economy are contained precisely in the fact that immigrants work for less, reducing the prices natives pay for many goods. This allows for greater specialization in the more educated, native workforce and thus increases its efficiency. It is not, macroeconomically speaking, efficient to have a university graduate mow the lawns of suburbia. The study concludes that immigration breaks the link between domestic consumption and domestic production, and from this perspective "the effects of immigration are comparable to those of international trade" (Smith and Edmonston 1997, 5).

However, while overall it is positive for the American economy, immigration places heavy a burden on some states and a lighter burden, or even a gain, on others. The National Academy concluded that for two typical immigrant-receiving states, California and New Jersey, the cost of immigration for the typical native household is $1,174 in California and $229 in New Jersey. In other words, without immigration the tax bill for the typical California household would be around $1,200 lower and for the typical New Jersey household around $229 lower (Smith and Edmonston 1997). Interestingly, the study also found that Latin American immigrants tend to put a fiscal burden on some states while Canadian and European immigrants produce a net fiscal contribution.

While it appears that, overall, American taxpayers benefit from immigration, local and state governments are more directly affected. In 1993 in California alone, 1.7 billion dollars were spent educating the children of illegal aliens (Borjas 1999). In 1996, households headed by Latin American immigrants in California "consumed $5,000 more in state and local services, on average, than they paid in state and local taxes" (Martin 2004, 72). Is this is a lot of money? To put this into perspective, the Public Broadcasting Service reported that the complexity of the American tax code costs taxpayers every year around 135 billion dollars. The Internal Revenue Service estimates that the "tax gap" (the difference between the taxes American should pay and the taxes they actually pay) is over a quarter of a trillion dollars, that is, more than 250 billion dollars (National Public Radio, April 15, 2005). Moreover, although educating the children of immigrants, legal or illegal, may be costly in the short run, such expenses are investments in the future of these persons. By increasing human capital through education, such persons are less likely to be unemployed, are likely to be healthier, will obtain higher-paying positions, and in turn will pay more in taxes. There is no doubt that immigrants who are educated pay, over the long term, much more in taxes than they receive in services. Education of immigrants, or for that matter education in general, is never a losing proposition. The unemployment rate for Americans with a four-year college degree is around 3 percent, for high school graduates it is 5.5 percent, and for those who never completed high school it is 8.5 percent (National Public Radio, March 19, 2005).

The bottom line of all of this is that the effect of immigration "is neither overwhelmingly positive nor overwhelmingly negative—and a prudent person would probably conclude that it is pretty close to zero" (Borjas 1999, 126). In fact, evidence indicates that since 1999 the effects of immigration on the American economy have been slightly positive. In 2002, the President's Council of Economic Advisers put the gain of immigration for American taxpayers at close to 14 billion dollars (*Economist,* March 12, 2005), dispelling the myth that immigrants do not pull their own weight. Most recently, in 2005 *Time* magazine reported that illegal immigrants had paid 7 billion dollars in Social Security taxes, even though they would not receive the benefits, and that 10 percent of the previous year's Social Security surplus was made up of contributions by illegal immigrants. Illegal immigrants are also estimated to have paid 1.5 billion in Medicare taxes, another benefit for which they are ineligible (*Time,* April 18, 2005).

In September of 2004, National Public Radio, together with the Henry J. Kaiser Family Foundation and Harvard University's School of Government, published a public opinion survey called "Immigration in America." It was based on phone interviews and included 1,104 interviews with nonimmigrants and 784 interviews with immigrants. When the question was asked: "Do you think recent immigrants take away jobs from Americans who want them, or not?" 51 percent of natives thought immigrants do take jobs away while 48 percent thought this was not the case. Among immigrants, 17 percent thought they take jobs away while 81 percent thought this was not the case.

Asked whether most recent immigrants pay their fair share of taxes, 64 percent of immigrants thought that they do, while only 28 percent of natives thought so. While 62 percent of natives thought that recent immigrants do not pay their fair share of taxes, 28 percent of immigrants agreed with them. Forty-three percent of immigrants said they send most of their money back to the country they came from while 60 percent of natives thought that this was the case. Amazingly, when asked whether they believe that most recent immigrants to the United States are legal or illegal, 50 percent of the *immigrants* thought that most immigrants are illegal and 54 percent of natives thought so.

Over 80 percent of immigrants believe that they strengthen the United States because of their hard work and talents while only 42 percent of natives think so. A majority of natives, 52 percent, believe that immigrants are a burden on the United States because they take their jobs, housing, and health care while predictably only 15 percent of immigrants think that way. Forty-three percent of natives think that immigration has been bad for the country while 56 percent of immigrants think it has been good for the country. Immigrants and natives agree in terms of what kind of country the United States *is:* almost the same percentages stated that the United States is a country with a basic American culture and values that immigrants take on when they arrive (natives, 34 percent; immigrants, 36 percent). Similar percentages see the United States as a country that is made up of many cultures and values, which change as new people arrive (natives, 64 percent; immigrants, 61 percent). However, when asked what kind of country the United States *should* be, the visions diverge dramatically. Sixty-two percent of natives believe that the United States should be a country with a basic American culture and values that immigrants take on when they arrive. This view is only supported by 39 percent of immigrants. Conversely, 57 percent of immigrants believe that the United States should be a country made up of many cultures, with values that change as new people arrive. Not surprisingly, this view is supported by only 33 percent of natives (National Public Radio, Kaiser, Kennedy School Immigration Survey, 2004). These responses reveal a deep-seated uneasiness about the effects of immigration on the economy, as well as on beliefs about what American society should be. Few surveys have been conducted that allow a side by side comparison of native and immigrant sentiments.

Nevertheless, the country's actual immigration policy does not seem to correspond with public opinion. It is true that public sentiments about foreigners tend to be predictably parochial and narrow-minded, with the public having little or no knowledge about the true costs and benefits of immigration. However, governments may pretend to engage in tough policies to protect the borders of the homeland when in reality the backdoor is wide open. According to Cornelius and Tsuda, American immigration policy is nothing but a smoke screen constructed to appease anti-immigrant public opinion. In their words, "Ineffective and 'symbolic' immigration control measures are thus perpetuated because they reduce the potential for a broad public backlash" (Cornelius and Tsuda 2002, 42). In a similar vein, Philip Martin questions whether much of the tough-sounding homeland security rhetoric in terms of border controls with Mexico is real or whether it is "merely symbolic, aimed at public opinion" (Martin 2004, 82).

However, there is evidence that the smoke screen of tough border controls is dissolving. In 2006, the states of Georgia and Colorado have passed the most stringent immigration laws to date, making it harder for illegal immigrants to receive social services and punishing companies that hire undocumented workers. A few hundred so-called American volunteers assembled along the Arizona-Mexico border in April 2005 as part of the "Minuteman Project" to protest the lack of border security and to stem "the massive illegal alien invasion of the United States," according to Jim Gilchrist, the organizer of the project. These armed volunteers, who President Bush called "vigilantes," see themselves "as forward observers for the border patrol" (National Public Radio, March 23,

2005), and as of this writing (April 2005) they are preparing themselves for a showdown with a Central American gang, the MS–13, which has been involved in drugs and weapons smuggling. In this case, nativist resentment has manifested itself in the form of a motley crew of armed, seriously misguided, self-styled defenders of the nation with the potential to do more harm than good.

The issue of immigration tends to bring together a disparate set of interests that usually do not form coalitions. Business interests, religious groups, and immigrant rights groups make strange bedfellows but at the same time highlight the crosscutting nature of this issue. These maneuverings demonstrate the highly politicized character of both immigration and welfare policies. While the Bush administration is certainly not known to be supportive of the most vulnerable in American society, rhetoric notwithstanding, the inability to engage in effective immigration control and to restrict access to welfare benefits by immigrants is mainly driven by four factors.

First, employers' organizations and business interests have a clear interest in keeping the immigration flow from south to north going. Immigrants work long hours, without complaint, for no benefits and a minimal wage. In the words of Wayne Cornelius, "There are literally hundreds of thousands of employers in this country that have a major stake in continued access to this labor" (Cable News Network, *CNN Presents,* November 2004). This hard economic interest is probably more important than "family values" in keeping the backdoor to the United States open.

Second, the very federalist structure of the United States makes a uniform and effective immigration control policy difficult. While border control agents are federal officers, many other elements crucial for immigrants, such as education, welfare benefits, and medical care, are under the purview of the states and differ widely, making it difficult to project a coherent policy of what to do with immigrants once they are on U.S. territory. As the reinstatement of many social benefits to immigrants in 1997 demonstrated, steering immigration policy via welfare policy proved dysfunctional.

Third, immigration-related interest groups and Web sites have grown considerably in the last two decades and, in conjunction with modern means of communication, have a much higher capacity to affect public policy by "moving" votes. As a result, politicians' stances on the immigration issue are very quickly ascertained and disseminated. If his or her voting record on immigration issues is too much out of kilter with public opinion, it can be very costly to the career of a politician. Tom Daschle's loss of his seat and Democratic leadership of the Senate was connected to his history of "proimmigration" votes. Similarly, California's David Dreier saw his majority dwindle sharply after talk radio alleged that he was "soft on immigration" (*Economist,* March 12, 2005).

Fourth, one of the most important reasons why effective immigration control is so difficult to achieve is the "electoral connection." Both parties in the United States court the "Latino vote" before elections. In the 2004 presidential election, around 7 million "Latinos" voted. With very close outcomes having occurred in the last two elections, Latinos are becoming a crucial group—though, of course, so is every other group. However, Latinos' political influence is growing. In the current House of Representatives there are 23 Latino members compared to only 11 two decades ago. Averages in various polls suggest that in the last presidential election 60 percent of Latinos voted for Senator Kerry and around 32 percent voted for President Bush (Leal et al. 2005).

These numbers have not escaped the attention of the architect of President Bush's victory in 2004, Karl Rove. According to the *Economist* (December 11, 2004), Rove has identified immigration reform as a "top priority." He sees immigration liberalization as a "key to his strategy of creating a permanent GOP majority" (*Newsweek,* February, 7, 2005). Immigration has proven to be a remarkably divisive issue within the Republican Party, one that pits liberalizers such as Sen. John McCain of Arizona against conservatives such as Sen. Tom Tancredo of Colorado. Obtaining the support of the Latino community is achieved, of course, by liberalizing immigration reform, by easing entry into the United States; and, once the immigrants have arrived, by making them eligible for all public benefits. Arnold Schwarzenegger, himself an immigrant from Austria and current governor of California, appealed to immigrants: "To my fellow immigrants listening tonight, I want you to know how welcome you are in this party. . . . We encourage your dreams. We believe in your future" (*Economist,* December 11, 2004, 34).

President Bush may disregard the NPR, Kaiser, Kennedy School's survey at his own peril: after the Bush proposal was explained ("As you may know, President Bush has proposed a plan that would allow some illegal immigrants currently in the U.S. to legally stay in this country for several years as long as they hold jobs that no U.S. citizens wants. The plan would require these immigrant workers to return to their countries after their time under this program has expired. Do you favor or oppose this plan?"), 55 percent of native respondents said they opposed the plan while 42 percent favored it. A majority of immigrants (51 percent) supported the plan. In his State of the Union speech on February 2, 2005, Bush described the U.S. immigration system as "unsuited to the needs of our economy and to the values of our country. We should not be content with laws that punish hardworking people who want only to provide for their families, and *deny businesses willing workers*. . . . It is time for an immigration policy that permits temporary guest workers to fill jobs Americans will not take" (emphasis added).

Welfare and immigration, as in the previous two cases of Germany and Sweden, are tightly connected. The United States attempted to steer immigration policy by changing eligibility requirements for immigrants. For institutional and political reasons this policy failed. Germany and Sweden both have managed to gain control over immigration by tightening asylum laws and ensuring that only qualified immigrants are allowed in. Both countries have established integration policies, though Germany was a latecomer. In contrast, the United States does not have an official integration policy, and its immigration control policies have not been effective. While in the United States the "welfare tolerance level" is much lower than in Germany or Sweden, the welfare uptake of immigrants is also much smaller than in the other two countries. The contrast is particularly stark in Sweden, where many immigrants are quickly absorbed into the welfare state and are "trapped" there (Hansen and Lofstrom 2001) while in the United States the much more meager public provisions force migrant labor into more precarious, low-paid, and hazardous work arrangements than in Sweden.

Examining public opinion, while many Americans believe that immigrants do not pay their fair share and are a drain on the economy, there is no evidence to support the charge that the limited welfare state in the United States is undermined *as a result of immigration*. The American welfare state is already a minimal one compared to both Germany and Sweden, and racial heterogeneity may well have been one of the "critical factors explaining the absence of a welfare state in America" (Alesina and Glaeser 2004, 146). However, judging from American public opinion, there is no reason to believe that even that minimal level will be further eroded as a result of immigration-driven diversity. Public attitudes tend to favor stricter border controls rather than a withdrawing from the already minimal schemas of public provision. As figure 7.6 showed, American public opinion is in fact more in favor of redistribution than Swedish public opinion is. The difference is of course the *level* of redistribution achieved. The Swedish level is so high that there is very little enthusiasm for yet more redistribution; the American level is so low that, if anything, there is even more interest in redistribution.

It is highly unlikely that the American governments' proposal of a guest worker program will help control immigration, legal or illegal. If there is anything the government might learn from the German, Swedish, and for that matter Dutch or Austrian experience is that once guest workers have lived in the host country for some time there is no evidence that they will return to their homelands when their work permits expire. Besides, given the economic interest of many businesses in maintaining access to cheap labor combined with the political access to lawmakers that business enjoys in a pluralist society, immigration policy in the foreseeable future will be driven by demography and economics rather than by the desires of the American public.

CHAPTER 8

Conclusions

THE RESURGENCE OF PRIMORDIAL ARGUMENTS in academic discourse on the welfare state is not accidental. Once the dust had settled after the implosion of the Soviet empire the ragged shapes of ethnic conflicts that hid in the shadows of the cold war became visible again. The sudden rise in the relevance of the European Union and the phenomenon of "globalization" have not only instilled diffuse fears but also brought questions of "who are we" into sharper relief. The horrific attacks of 9/11 appeared to give credence to the "clash of civilizations," prompting many social scientists to reexamine the power of primordial attachments and their capacity to shape politics. While the power of primordial attachments cannot be denied, this "essentialist" argument is deeply flawed for it is not ethnic identity that gives meaning to human beings, but rather it is human beings that give meaning to ethnic identity.

And yet the primordial argument is seductive. It is used to explain civil wars, genocide, or ethnic cleansing and is rarely applied to the more refined world of the study of welfare states. With a few exceptions, scholars of the welfare state have not paid much attention to matters of race, ethnicity, or religious diversity as an explanation for the development or viability of the welfare state. This is of course a result of the relative homogeneity of many European welfare states. The one exception in which early warnings have gone out that race and the welfare state may not mix well was produced by scholars who understand these categorical differences to be the main reason why public provision in the United States is comparatively limited. The United States was of course racially diverse from its very beginning and as such provides a laboratory for examining the impact of race on the development of social welfare as compared to many European countries, where diversity appeared later and the welfare state was able to develop under conditions of relative homogeneity. As a result of immigration since the mid-1950s European states have become rather diverse, and only very recently has this issue of growing diversity in Europe appeared on the radar screens of a very few scholars of the European welfare states. If the American experience is any guide, does immigration-driven diversity indeed mean the end of the generous European system of welfare provision? The findings in this book suggest not.

To extrapolate from the American experience with diversity and the welfare state to the European experience is problematic for a number of reasons. Today diversity impinges on European welfare states after they experienced a long period of nation and welfare state building relatively undisturbed by societal heterogeneity. The mostly centralized political institutions prevented a territorial fragmentation of social policy. Proportional representation initially secured pluralities or even majorities for social-democratic parties, cementing the influence of these parties while at the same time allowing broad access for those of different political persuasions to the political process. This has solidified expectations of the role of the state and nurtured large constituencies that are very supportive of the welfare state as opposed to the American experience. Crucially, during this long phase of undisturbed welfare state building some European nations, particularly the Nordic countries, built up a stock of interpersonal trust that functioned as a bulwark against prejudice vis-à-vis immigrants. As a result, as immigration "impinges" on societies with high trust levels, prejudice, hate, and nativist resentment are reduced, putting such countries on a very different policy trajectory than countries that demonstrate strong nativist resentment. Without intending to reify the "welfare state," the point is that the timing of immigration matters: societies that developed welfare states *before* immigration occurred were able to build up a stock of trust with a capacity to reduce nativist resentment, thereby ensuring the continued viability of the welfare state. This provides policymakers much needed room to produce immigration policies that are not only less pressured by virulent anti-immigrant public opinion but are also more "honest" in the sense that fewer policies need to be channeled through venues that are obscured from public view.

This book employed mostly public opinion data to gauge the impact of immigration on the viability of the welfare state. While it is certainly true that public opinion is temperamental, comes with inevitable errors in measurement, and is susceptible to manipulation by various political actors, it is also the only way to estimate where the public stands on crucial issues such as the welfare state and immigration. It is no small wonder that governments, and even supranational organizations, use public opinion polls to measure public sentiments, and it is on the basis of such polls that many policies are enacted. The EU has undertaken three surveys already to measure racism and develop policies to combat racism and xenophobia. More important, public opinion is the first link in the chain between proposed policies and their estimated effects. Any adverse public reactions to immigration and the welfare state should manifest themselves in public sentiments long before aggregate data on public expenditures would show such a connection. In that sense, public opinion is like the proverbial canary in the coal mine that provides warnings that the environment is becoming toxic, allowing the coal miners to flee and policymakers to address problems before a (social) explosion occurs.

On the basis of primordial arguments many observers have claimed that the "public" will "withdraw" or "detach" from systems of public provision because it perceives immigrants to be the main beneficiary of social benefits. As a result, it will have no interest in maintaining the welfare state, or so the primordial argument goes. This book focused on respondents who tend to harbor prejudice and resentment against immigrants and their impact on the viability of the welfare state. This stratum, making up around 13 percent of the population in the 17 modern societies examined here, is generally less educated, has lower incomes, and is generally in a more precarious economic situation than the more educated and well-to-do. The reason for this focus is that any detachment from the welfare state should be most visible in this group, as it is most threatened by immigrants, who compete with it for jobs and scarce social benefits.

The findings suggest that such claims need to be differentiated. There is no evidence for the withdrawal from the welfare state of this most affected of all strata. In terms of the "demand" for welfare programs people with less education and lower incomes are *not* withdrawing from the welfare state insofar as they continue supporting redistribution. This should not be surprising. The most vulnerable in society should be the ones who continue supporting the welfare state, and they do, despite harboring intense prejudices against and hatred of foreigners. Two radical-right wing parties in the fall of 2004 won seats in two German states precisely on the basis of protecting the welfare state against potential cutbacks perceived to be driven by disproportional welfare uptake by foreigners. People who get the short end of the stick, at least in Europe, have no qualms about looking to the state for help. Radical right-wing parties are stylizing themselves increasingly as defenders of the welfare state and virulently agitate against cutbacks, which is precisely why so many are successfully siphoning off votes from the Left.

The situation is different, however, when the "supply" of welfare is examined. Supply of welfare means the willingness of citizens to "pay their fair share" in terms of taxes and not to abuse welfare benefits. This is the location in which the administrative state and the life worlds of citizens intersect. For the welfare state to function, citizens must feel a sense of belonging to a larger community of fate, and if that is the case truthfully paying their taxes and not cheating on welfare benefits are more easily achieved. However, this study finds that people who harbor prejudices against immigrants take a relatively nonchalant view of doing their civic duty. This stratum has a more fractured view of society and is indeed withdrawing from the welfare state, not by not demanding more but by supplying less. Immigration and the attendant sentiments of xenophobia and prejudice among the more vulnerable of society seem to breed attitudes that are incompatible with a welfare state. It is indeed alarming that people harboring attitudes of nativist resentment show few scruples about not paying their taxes or abusing welfare benefits. For them, the cement that unifies society is crumbling. The results presented in this book provide strong evidence that people who are prejudiced against immigrants show little willingness to pay their fair share in taxes. If such attitudes become more widespread, the viability of the welfare state will be put into question.

However, the impact of nativist resentment is tempered by different levels of interpersonal trust. It is not obvious how trust fits into the connection between xenophobia and the welfare state. One of the contributions of this project has been to marry the literatures of immigration and the welfare state to the burgeoning trust literature. Citizens will more likely pay their taxes only if they think that others will do so too. Since they can never be sure that this is indeed the case, they must trust that others will pay their share. If that trust erodes, the welfare state will be in dire straits. Trust in this study is taken as a trait, meaning that it has a rather enduring and relatively unchanging characteristic that has been instilled in people as a result of the socialization process. Hence, trust is taken to be a cause rather than an effect with trust seen as a mediating force between nativist resentments and the propensity of individuals to pay or not pay their taxes and using or abusing welfare benefits.

Taking trust as a trait rather than a state reveals that trust significantly mediates the effect of prejudice on welfare state support. Trust, and particularly its modification, called "universal" trust, generates a very different environment in which "foreigners" are perceived. People who are universal trusters show significantly less nativist resentment than people who are primordial trusters, that is, people who trust those who are like them. In an environment of universal trust that is characterized by openness and interest, and, more important, by concern for the life chances of people who are different from oneself, nativist resentment is drastically reduced. Universal trusters clearly favor a redistributive state by not only demanding welfare but also supplying it. Such trusters have no qualms about paying their fair share. The humble concept of trust, particularly the variant called universal trust, proved to be remarkably powerful in positively affecting public sentiments that are crucial for the future viability of the welfare state.

One of the most striking findings in the empirical analyses is that primordial attachments are no longer strong enough to command allegiance to the maintenance of the welfare state. This stands in stark contrast to a large literature that claims that a welfare state can be built only on common social characteristics. The more primordial the respondents' attitudes the more they tend to withdraw from the welfare state. Their support of the welfare state appears to already rest on weak foundations, and immigration-induced diversity is what breaks the welfare state's back, at least as far as that group of people is concerned. In their perception, increasing diversity leads to the crumbling of the cement of society. This is the most likely interpretation of the findings. Doubts remain, however, as such an argument fundamentally rests on analyses of attitudes over time. However, much of the evidence presented in this book is based on cross-sectional analyses, as standardized questionnaires administered over long periods of time and asking the appropriate questions are simply not available.

Nevertheless, the evidence presented so far tells an intriguing story: in times of massive immigration, the salience of primordial attitudes is heightened, and natives who base their identity on such a narrow sense of morality find themselves on the precarious footing of crumbling remnants of a society that once was able to command their allegiance. As they perceive that their communal sacrifices in the form of taxes are increasingly going to people who are different from themselves, they withdraw from the welfare state by not paying their fair share. This result is incompatible with the widespread assumption that the welfare state can only function if it is built on a sense of community and "fellow feeling" and on shared categorical markers such as race, religion, ethnicity, and language. In the face of immigration, primordialism falls too short to command the allegiance that is necessary for a welfare state to function.

Yet, paradoxically, against much of what the literature claims, this study shows that people with universal trust are the ones who continue funding the welfare state. Citizens with a more expansive attitude of morality, those with a "cosmopolitan" understanding of the relationships between humans, stand ready to engage in the personal sacrifices necessary if a redistributive system is to be maintained. In times of significant immigration, it appears that the welfare state's future does not lie with tightly drawn circles of identity but exactly the opposite, with attitudes that highlight commonalities among humans. The future of the welfare state lies in the outstretched hands of people who believe in a shared "imagined humanity," not in the clenched fists of those who base their identity on narrow in-group characteristics. In this age of massive immigration it is attitudes of "trust beyond borders" that will ensure the future viability of the welfare state, not parochial beliefs in one's own dominance.

If indeed universal trust has the capacity to reduce nativist resentment then the natural question arises as to where such trust comes from. One of the tantalizing findings in this research is the fact that prejudice and xenophobia are lowest in the Scandinavian high-trust societies, which also have the most generous welfare states. Does high trust lead to the development of comprehensive welfare states or do comprehensive welfare states lead to the creation of social trust? Ultimately this is a very difficult question to answer, although many scholars of the welfare state would give priority to institutional conditions combined with the political power wielded by the social-democratic movements that provided the initial impetus to establish comprehensive welfare states. Others may point to the ethnic homogeneity that allowed trust to flourish, which in turn facilitated the creation of encompassing unions and social-democratic parties. This research has revealed that trust flourishes in comprehensive, universal welfare states that do not discriminate among the receivers of social benefits.

The secret as to why trust is higher in more comprehensive welfare states may well lie in the reduction of risk the welfare state provides. Precisely because the social safety net is present, trusting is easier to come by. But this may only be part of the story: by establishing a relative equality of control over one's life and the lives of others, the comprehensive welfare state instills a sense of collective community, a sense of a shared fate, which creates a climate in which trust flourishes. This interpretation seems to be most consistent with the finding that nativist resentment is much more muted in universal welfare states than in corporatist or liberal welfare states.

Just as the welfare state was able to bridge the class divide, so it appears to be able to squash racial and xenophobic impulses. Was it easier to bridge class differences in nineteenth- and early-twentieth-century Europe than it is to bridge today's racial and ethnic differences? Is the rift between natives and newcomers bigger now than it was between the cigar-puffing captains of industry and the impoverished working class in nineteenth-century England or Germany, which was on the verge of revolution? This is difficult to say, but today there certainly are no revolutions in the making as a result of conflicts between natives and newcomers. Bridging the class divide, which was the original purpose of the welfare state in the late nineteenth and early twentieth centuries, proved to be a wrenching process, and yet it was able to douse the fires of revolution. It did so by nurturing a sense of a moral community. It is not unreasonable to argue that the same moral community can mollify the relationships between natives and immigrants.

If policies and institutions can mollify nativist resentment, the limitations of the primordial argument are laid bare. The essentialism of categorical differences runs into the systematic effects of policies that can significantly reduce prejudice and hate. This is also demonstrated in the effects of incorporation regimes and multiculturalism policies. In countries in which it is nearly impossible to become naturalized, a legal barrier separates the in- from the out-group. This is not to say that simply because Turks are becoming German citizens that they will be accepted overnight by the native population. Particularly "visible" minorities will continue to experience occasional discrimination, as hurtful as it is for the person at that time. But it is equally clear that naturalizing them lifts a crucial dividing barrier, a barrier that is not only legal but also emotional. It matters for both immigrants and natives whether newcomers remain inside or outside the national constitutional framework. Endowing them with the same rights and privileges as the native population also allows them to become politically active, which is a crucial step in making them part of the body politic. This research has found strong evidence that those societies that grant citizenship on the basis of jus soli, as opposed to jus sanguinis, display less prejudice and racism.

The findings are similar when multiculturalism policies and their effects on welfare state support are examined. Despite the vitriolic debate over the touchy issue of multiculturalism and claims that such policies erode the welfare state, no evidence to that effect was found. Again the opposite seems to be the case. Using multilevel analysis, those societies with strong multicultural policies engender positive distributional attitudes and less nativist resentment and welfare chauvinism as opposed to those with weak multicultural policies.

Why might this be the case? Multiculturalism policies appear to have three effects: leveling effects, signaling effects, and destigmatizing effects. Although multiculturalism policies tend to highlight differences between the dominant society and immigrant groups, the leveling effect emerges from the affirmative action part of such policies. Such policies tend to reduce the opportunity gap between immigrants and natives, making newcomers less visible as a needy group. This is a lesson that France learned the hard way in the wake of the race riots in November 2005, and it is moving away from a republican model of citizenship toward one that more actively recognizes the material needs of its ethnic minorities through affirmative action policies.

Multiculturalism policies also have a signaling effect, demonstrating to newcomers that their new homeland takes liberal principles seriously. It allows them to practice their customs and traditions, speak their language, and learn about their culture in schools without having to fear persecution. This signaling effect goes in both directions: liberalism not only means natives accepting the lifestyles and cultures of immigrants but also the other way around. It is this mutual acceptance of basic liberal principles out of which a deeper understanding of each other's differences might emerge.

Multiculturalism policies also have destigmatizing effects, which means that they "allow us to see each other as equally worthy of respect" (Banting and Kymlicka 2006, 28). While multiculturalism policies heighten the salience of ethnic differences, they do so in a less prejudicial way. Prejudices against foreigners are present in many societies with or without such policies. Official multiculturalism policies can stave off the development of hatred and prejudice that tend to corrode the relationships between members of the dominant society and newcomers. In that sense, such policies serve an important educational function also.

And yet there are ominous signs that many Western governments are moving away from multiculturalism in the wake of terrorist activities such as the attacks in New York and Washington on September 11, 2001; the bombings in Madrid in March 2004 and London in July 2005; and the political murders of Pim Fortuyn and Theo van Gogh in the Netherlands. This is an understandable impulse, as public sentiments are very strong in the aftermath of such gruesome events and governments do not want to appear weak vis-à-vis terrorist organizations. However, retreating from policies designed to establish a better understanding of other cultures and to reduce the opportunity gap between natives and newcomers can only add to the existing tension. Governments caving in to the rising popularity of radical right-wing parties and taking on a much harsher tone to avoid losing voters to the radical fringes is indeed a worrisome development.

Comparing the immigration and immigrant policies and their effects on the welfare state in Germany, Sweden, and the United States reveals a few intriguing similarities and lots of differences. All three countries, with varying levels of success, are trying to keep out those who are likely to become a public charge, with the exception of political refugees. In all three, the initial opening of borders was influenced by significant global events. Germany's initial liberal asylum law was a direct result of its historical burden, and Sweden's original opening of its borders was a result of its experience with rescue actions of Jews in Denmark and Norway. In the United States the epochal Civil Rights Act of 1964 prompted Congress to end racially restrictive immigration quotas and opened the border to immigrants. In two countries, Germany and Sweden, the belief that rotating manpower that can be shed when it is no longer useful proved to be mistaken. Such arguments ran afoul of international conventions, human rights provisions, and basic common values. On the same basis, family unification could not be prevented, and the number of foreigners grew even though officially there was no more hiring of foreign labor after 1974. The United States might learn a few things by looking at the European experience as it designs its proposed "guest worker" program. Liberal norms proved to be stronger than national interest when it came to the state's inability to expel foreign labor and prevent family unification.

There are more differences than similarities, however. The biggest differences are a direct outflow of the different "national" models of welfare states. The Swedish welfare state has extended its generous protection to all newcomers, generating a massive load on the system of public provision as many immigrants with little human capital took up welfare. This occurred in the early 1990s, when the Swedish economy was reeling with high indigenous unemployment and low economic growth. Yet, overall, few cuts to immigrants' welfare support were made. Instead Sweden tended to attempt to integrate those already in the country and through publicly funded integration programs move them off the unemployment benefit rolls while at the same time tightening asylum laws and accepting only highly qualified new labor migrants. Overall, the Swedish corporate state showed a high capacity to keep the highly popular welfare state largely intact while at the same time responding to the needs of domestic labor markets. What is of crucial importance is that the comprehensive welfare state blunts nativist reactions, thereby avoiding having to engage in restrictive anti-immigrant, populist policies in order to appease virulent public opinion. In such an environment rational public policy is easier to come by.

Germany also demonstrated a high capacity to shape its immigration policy consistent with its statist tradition, although much of it was "reactive" and driven by major events beyond its control. Of all three countries, Germany's model of *soziale Marktwirtschaft* has eroded the most. The reasons are complex, but they cannot be directly linked to immigration. A confluence of factors has contributed to that outcome: German unification, the collapse of the Soviet Union, the extension of the EU into Eastern European countries, and the increased mobility of labor and capital—often referred to as globalization—all of these have put tremendous pressures on public finances. Some of these factors are purely conjunctural, and their unfolding was beyond the ability of any government to control. As a result, Germany was faced with gigantic pressures on its welfare system as it inherited basically overnight millions of East Germans and later ethnic Germans who migrated to their homeland. And yet German policymakers have shown a great capacity to finally extend a welcome to those who have lived in the antechamber of citizenship for many years, integrate them, and selectively choose immigrants on the basis of security and utility considerations. Based on only two time points, allowing only tentative conclusions, it appears that prejudice, nativist resentment, a turning away from multiculturalism, and welfare chauvinism are on the rise in Germany, while the opposite is the case in Sweden and the United States.

The most remarkable observation about American immigration policy is the government's utter inability to change it. Thankfully, liberal norms and civil society groups have gained such strength that earlier policies of quota systems or even race-based "exclusion acts" are a thing of the past. The pluralist model of political economy, of which the United States is the prime representative, provides multiple avenues through which private actors can shape public policy. Many of these actors represent business interests, but they also represent civil rights and religious groups that favor keeping the status quo or even further liberalization of immigration but are generally not in favor of restricting it. There is little evidence that the American public has detached itself from the welfare state as a result of immigrants' welfare uptake. Public provision in the United States is already relatively minimal, and so is public support of such programs. If anything, studies indicate that immigrants, legal and illegal, pay more than their fair share in taxes, at least at the federal level. America's inability to effectively deal with immigration issues is ultimately a direct result of its preference for a weak state and a strong civil society. In such a liberal, laissez-faire environment, the state's ability to shape policies of any kind is limited not for political reasons but for systemic ones.

Overall, there is little evidence that immigration-induced diversity will lead to an "Americanization" of the European welfare state. The conditions under which diversity unfolds in Europe are quite different from the American experience. Institutions, levels of trust, and expectations about the role of the state are significantly different. Nevertheless, prejudices against foreigners are strong in some European countries, and policymakers must take the concerns of local populations seriously rather than caving in to populist rhetoric.

One of the most heartening findings throughout this project is that the more educated people are and the more contact they actually have with immigrants the more positive a view they have of them. Education appears to be the most potent weapon against the seductive claims of demagogues who use identity as a ruse to gain votes for their dubious schemes. It is not surprising that identity comes to the forefront in this post-cold-war era in the time of an ever-expanding EU, globalization, and fears of nightmarish terrorist attacks. This stirring of identity is either a last gasp before it surrenders to the crushing forces of globalization or the beginning of a counterinsurgency of sorts fighting to reclaim "meaning" in an apparently ever-growing sea of uniformity. Whichever it is, it is important to remember that "identity" is built on shifting sands, is malleable, constructed, and not an unchanging essence. This should be humbling to all those who have not yet completely fallen victim to fundamentalism and should remind them that it may be more fruitful to seek common ground than emphasizing what separates us. Diversity is not the enemy of the welfare state—distrust, ignorance, and a parochial view of the world are. The wider people's circle of identity is the more they share an "imagined humanity" and are willing to fund the welfare state. For the welfare state to guard itself against this insidious primordial challenge, what is needed is not trust in one's narrow conception of identity but trust beyond borders.

Notes

Introduction

1. More up-to-date sample sentences for the English writing test can be found at the government Web site http://uscis.gov/graphics/services/natz/natzsamp.htm.

2. This does not mean that countries have not tightened their asylum laws. A case in point is Germany, which after 1993 made it more difficult for asylum seekers to gain admittance.

3. Spiegel OnLine, "The Death of a Muslim Woman: The Whore Lived Like a German," September 2, 2005, http://service.spiegel.de/cache/international/ 0,1518,344374,00.html.

Chapter 2

1. Joane Nagel, in a review essay entitled "The Political Construction of Ethnicity" (1986), summarizes much of the literature. In a remarkable book, Noel Ignatiev (1995, 41) explored the historical construction of "race" among Irish immigrants to the United States, arguing that their race, though outwardly indistinguishable from the accepted English, was a matter of debate: "In the early years, Irish were frequently referred to as 'niggers turned inside out'; the negroes, for their part, were sometimes called 'smoked Irish' an appellation they must have found no more flattering than it was intended to be."

2. Stephan Thernstrom (2004, 57) states, "If there had been a competition for the silliest article published that year, this one would have been hard to beat."

3. This is, of course, precisely the dilemma of multiculturalism: policies driven by the liberal impulse of "leveling the playing field" have the unintended consequence of sharpening the relief among minority groups and between minority groups and native majorities, who complain about "reverse discrimination." This issue will be taken up in chapter 6.

4. Some scholars even go one step farther and argue that primordialism as an organizing concept should be abolished altogether. The terms *primordial* and *construction* are in fact contradictory because if primordial means "from the beginning," "ineffable," "primeval," or "a priori," it, by definition, cannot be constructed and thus is "unsociological, unanalytical, and vacuous. We advocate dropping it from the sociological lexicon" (Eller and Coughlan 1993, 183).

5. For example, the historian Jack Greene argues that British Americans, in the midst

of their revolution, "defined more fully than ever before what made their societies both different from those of the Old World and similar to each other." Greene goes on to state that in "the process of thus elaborating their Americanness, they quickly began to develop an infinitely more favorable sense of collective self" (quoted in Doyle 2002, 20, 21).

6. In such constructivist accounts, it is often difficult to establish who the actors are, and, while it is of course impossible to know who D'Azeglio had in mind when he said "we," we can only presume that he would have mentioned the king of the house of Savoy, Vittorio Emmanuele II, the chancellor Count Camillo Benso di Cavour, the famous revolutionary Giuseppe Garibaldi, his adviser Franceso Crispi, and the Italian army. There is some debate as to whether D'Azeglio actually said it quite that way. Some observers claim that he uttered the phrase after the disastrous defeat in Adua, Ethiopia, in 1896. He explained the defeat as due to a lack of Italian patriotism and, according to Ferdinando Martini, actually said: "Fatta l'Italia bisogna fare gli Italiani," which translates into English as "Having made Italy requires making Italians" (Doyle 2002).

7. Only after a concerted effort by the German president, Richard von Weizsäcker, who appealed to all parties to refrain from such tactics and called for a massive public rally in Berlin, in which all political parties except the Bavarian CSU participated, was there evidence that right-wing radicalism against immigrants was beginning to decline. However, shortly thereafter, on May 29, another bloody arson attack killed five Turkish women and girls in Solingen, Germany. Despite the fact that all the members of the German cabinet joined the funeral services to demonstrate solidarity and sympathy for the victims, the German chancellor, Helmut Kohl, did not attend.

8. Artists also were infected with the fever of nationalism. Arnold Schoenberg, who pioneered *Neu-tonmusik,* joined the Hoch-und Deutschmeister (the official Infantry Marching Band of the monarchy) and started to compose military marches. The famous painter Oskar Kokoschka bought himself a horse, a uniform, and a bronze helmet and joined the cavalry. Thomas Mann, the writer and poet, hoped the war would bring *Reinigung* (cleansing) (Lackner 2004, 41).

9. It has been widely understood to be the case that the American welfare state is "residualist," that is, not as extensive in both scope and depth than the European welfare state. For a more adulterated view of this argument, see Hacker 2002. In addition, the intriguing piece by Skocpol (1992) puts into perspective the widely acknowledged claim that the United States was a laggard in social protection.

10. I would like to thank Eugene Miller, Professor Emeritus at the University of Georgia, for bringing the pertinent literature on cosmopolitanism to my attention.

11. Not all court decisions are inimical to welfare state development. In *Plyler v. Doe,* the U.S. Supreme Court ordered the state of Texas to allow the children of illegal aliens to attend public schools. This is in direct contravention of Proposition 187 in California, which would not extend public schooling to children of illegal aliens in California (Hollifield 1997).

12. Alexander Hamilton, himself an immigrant from the Caribbean, stated that "the safety of the republic depends, essentially on the energy of a common national sentiment . . . and love of country which will almost invariably be found to be closely connected with birth, education and family" (quoted in Bischoff 2002, 120). In 1781, Thomas Jefferson, in his *Notes on the State of Virginia,* also expressed concerns about immigrants from monarchical European regimes: "They will bring them the principles of the governments they have imbibed in early youth . . . [and] it would be a miracle were

they to stop precisely at the point of temperate liberty. . . . In proportion to their number they will share with us in the legislation. They will infuse into it their spirit, warp and bias its direction, and render it a heterogeneous, incoherent, distracted mass" (quoted in Busey 1856, 8).

13. The reasons why the German *Turnvereins* (clubs that promote physical fitness through a combination of gymnastics and calisthenics) and cultural preservation movements eventually declined were twofold. The first was simple expediency. Doing business required learning English, and many Germans simply made cultural sacrifices to take advantage of the economic opportunities open to them in the United States. Second, World War I tarnished the status of the German American cultural organizations, and for reasons of expediency it was no longer advantageous to highlight one's German ancestry.

14. A "welfare backlash" was already visible in the United States in the early 1960s, mostly connected to Ronald Reagan's 1966 campaign, in which he asserted that welfare recipients were on a "prepaid lifetime vacation plan." In the 1970s, after four years in office, Reagan continued to campaign on slogans such as "We are fighting the big spending politicians who advocate a welfare state, the welfare bureaucrats whose jobs depend on expanding the welfare system and the cadres of professional poor who have adopted welfare as a way of life" (Wilensky 1975, 33). The picture of the "welfare queen" driving her "welfare Cadillac" while the middle class was overburdened with work and taxes, which was popularized by Reagan after he became president, became firmly lodged in American political folklore. President Richard Nixon proclaimed, "The current welfare system has become a monstrous, consuming outrage—an outrage against the community, against the taxpayer, and particularly against the children it is supposed to help." Even President Jimmy Carter described welfare as "anti-work, anti-family, inequitable in its treatment of the poor and wasteful of taxpayer's dollars." And of course one of President Bill Clinton's memorable phrases was his pledge to "end welfare as we know it" (quoted in Gilens 1999, 1).

Chapter 3

1. Guiraudon's point is intriguing, though it is hard to believe that right-wing parties are somehow not aware or informed about what they see as the major problems with immigrants and that such "stealth" policies could be crafted under the radar screen of opposition parties and pressure groups. After all, when thousands of French Muslims demonstrated in the streets of Paris on December 21, 2003, protesting Jacques Chirac's call for a law banning the *hijab,* the Muslim head scarf, they were not only carrying signs reading "Don't touch my veil" but also "I vote," reminding the French leadership that the estimated 5 to 7 million Muslims in France constituted a formidable voting bloc with regional elections coming in March (Richburg 2003). While these protesters were either full citizens, or made use of their right to vote at the regional level, it is obvious that such multicultural manifestations would not have escaped the attention of right-wing parties or other radical right-wing groups.

2. *Tages-Anzeiger,* Fernausgabe, February 2, 1993.

3. The speech, entitled "Minister for Immigration and Integration, Verdonk, at a Meeting of EU Press, 30. June 2004 in The Hague," may be accessed at: www.justitie.nl/pers/speeches/archief_2004/08-704verdonk_Pres_EU.asp.

4. According to Gordon Smith (1976), a referendum is uncontrolled if it originates by means of a popular initiative and antihegemonic if its consequences are detrimental to

the regime. It is difficult to empirically investigate the impact of referenda on policy outcomes because of the "extreme unevenness of the incidence of referenda. Switzerland accounts for more than two thirds of the total" (Lijphart 1984, 203) (out of 21 countries).

5. "We shouldn't spend our tax dollars on people who are here illegally" said Wayne
Cashman, a retired business owner who voted for Proposition 200 (*Arizona Daily Star,*
November 3, 2004). Randy Pullen, the chairman of the YES for Proposition 200 campaign, argued that the number of illegal immigrants receiving treatment for diseases such
as HIV underscores the need to "detain and deport" them. "This is why we should get
them out of here as fast as we can" (*Arizona Daily Star,* October 19, 2004).

6. For instance, the race or gender of an interviewer can trigger different responses
in the respondent.

7. Depending on the order in which the questions are asked, respondents may give
different answers.

8. If part of the job of the interviewer is to rate the respondent, halo effects have
been shown to bias the interviewer's judgment. For instance, if an interviewer believes
that the respondent appears unclean, such interviewers tend to rate respondents as having
less intelligence than when interviewers believe they are clean.

9. In May through July of 2002, the Chicago Council on Foreign Relations conducted a poll of the public with about 2,800 respondents and of elites (opinion leaders,
members of Congress and the administration, leaders of church groups, business execu-
tives, union leaders, journalists, academics, and leaders of major interest groups) consisting
of about 400 respondents. Regarding opinions about immigration, comparison of the two
groups revealed a drastic gap: 60 percent of the public regards the present level of immigration as a "critical threat to the vital interests of the United States" compared to only 14
percent of the nation's leaders, indicating a difference of 46 percent (Chicago Council on
Foreign Relations, Worldviews 2002. American Public Opinion and Foreign Policy, 7).

10. While it was the only set of questions asked over all four time periods of the
WVS, the "reject neighbors" battery needs to be used with caution because as different
waves were administered additional groups were added, affecting the choices of groups
the respondents could list as unwanted as neighbors. In the 1981–82 wave, the list from
which respondents could choose was shorter than in the subsequent waves, in which
many more groups were listed. It is possible that the wider range of choices in subsequent waves affected respondents' choice of "immigrants/foreign workers."

11. Of the 64 observations on the independent variable "Who would you rather not
have as neighbors?" 11 had to be estimated since they were not asked in every country
at every time point. These countries and time points are Austria (1981, 1995), Belgium
(1997), Canada (1995), Denmark (1995), France (1995), Italy, (1996), Ireland (1995), the
Netherlands (1981), and Switzerland (1981).

12. The third column in table 3.3 displays "odds ratios" rather than coefficients since
the analysis is of a logit form rather than a regression. Logit coefficients are not intuitively interpretable. The odds ratios indicate the change in percentage in the dependent
variable as a result of a one-unit change in the independent variable. For example, the
odds ratio of .68 for "female" means that females are 32 percent (a reduction from 100
to 68 percent) less likely than males to indicate that they do not want immigrants as
neighbors. The direction of the results using odds ratios is determined depending on
whether the odds ratios are larger than one, in which case the direction is a positive one,
or the odds ratios are smaller than one, in which case the direction is a negative one.

13. This item does not suffer from the problems highlighted earlier when the same question was used across time in WVS, waves 1–3. Since we are not examining responses over time in table 3.5, the lack of diachronic reliability, which became an issue when this item was used across time, does not apply here.

14. There were other groups, such as "people with large families" or "Hindus," that were not included in our principal component factor analysis since some of these questions were asked for only a few countries, or in some cases only one country, reducing the number of observations.

15. Table 3.5 uses the latent construct "nativist resentment" as a predictor variable. However, the results do not change if other questions are used that probe respondents' attitudes about immigration. Virtually the same results obtain when the following two questions are used. Question 1: "How about people from other countries coming here to work. Which one of the following do you think the government should do: a) let anyone come who wants to, b) let people come as long as there are jobs available, c) place strict limits on the amount of foreigners who can come here, d) prohibit people coming here from other countries?" Question 2: "Which of these statements is nearest to your opinion: a) immigrants should maintain distinct customs and traditions, b) take over the customs of the country?"

Chapter 4

1. For 11 of the 16 countries, all four observations using the standard "trust" question were available. The 1990 data point for Australia is not available, nor are the Austrian 1981 and 1995 observations. Belgium 1997, Ireland 1995, and Switzerland 1981 are not available. In other words, five countries did not have all four data points. Austria was missing two, and Australia, Belgium, Ireland, and Switzerland were missing one. In all cases, figure 4.2 consists of the averages across all four data points for 11 countries or averages of those countries that did not have all four observations.

2. Conducting a logit analysis across 11 countries and almost 15,000 respondents in which we used the general trust measure as a dependent variable and the primordial and universal trust types as predictors, we found that universal trust strongly predicts "trust" (odds ratio 1.57, standard error .039, $z = 17.9$, p-value $< .000$) while primordial trust is significantly negatively related to "trust" (odds ratio .76, standard error $-.018$, $z = -11.2$, p-value $< .000$).

3. Nativist resentment and our two forms of trust, primordial and universal, are clearly two separate concepts. For reasons of space we do not show the results of a principal component analysis that combines all the items that make up primordial and universal trust and nativist resentment. The results clearly indicate a sharp separation among the three groups, indicating that these are different latent constructs.

4. Over the last 25 years a massive literature on the decline of public trust in political institutions has developed, starting with the classic work by Michael Crozier, Samuel Huntington and Joji Watanuki (1975) entitled *The Crisis of Democracy*. For its silver anniversary, Susan Pharr and Robert Putnam (2002) published *Disaffected Democracies: What's Troubling the Trilateral Countries?* The underlying message of most of these contributions is that the specter of "civic malaise" is haunting the rich countries. The explanations are many and varied and range from overloaded governments that are unable to respond to the onslaught of waves of new forms of participatory democracy and political action to a general psychological retreat from politics, or what the Germans

call *Politikverdrossenheit,* and the untrustworthiness of presidents, parties, and other political actors.

5. There is no unanimous agreement that more cynicism and discontent are necessarily negative. For Sidney Tarrow, new forms of political activism have arisen, leading to short-lived and shifting coalitions with little likelihood of sustaining high levels of confidence in government (Tarrow 2000). There may in fact be nothing wrong with a more critical and skeptical public that is more vigilant about those in power. The debate about the meaning of declining trust in government goes back at least thirty years, when Jack Citrin (1974) argued that *government* simply means the incumbent and not an institution of government such as the presidency. Changing the people in government might just do the trick and restore confidence in the institutions.

6. There is very little agreement as to the factors that drive this decline in confidence in government and its institutions. Some argue that it may simply have to do with the subpar performance of government and the institutions designed to implement these policies (Alesina and Wacziarg 2000; Newton and Norris 2000); with the decreased need for a state in the first place, which might lead to reduced trust in the state (Hardin 2000); or with a deterioration in the quality of discourse between the elites and masses to such an extent that a chasm has opened up between the desires of the electorate and the capacities of the government (Scharpf 2000). Peter Katzenstein (2000) finds that the small European welfare states are suffering much less from this malaise despite having endured the wrenching process of internationalization and the shock of the end of the cold war. Or maybe it is simply incompetent and corrupt politicians that ruin it for everybody (della-Porta 2000).

7. Of course, not everybody has all of these choices. It is certainly the case that the system of state withholding of taxes for employees reduces dramatically the potential for tax evasion. Still, in most countries even employees have to adjust their taxes on a yearly basis, which allows some potential for creative accounting. Owners of businesses have more control over their accounting and thus more potential for evading the tax man.

8. I am not aware of any surveys that specifically ask respondents whether they are more or less willing to pay for local versus federal taxes.

Chapter 5

1. Interestingly, the United States has developed a very comprehensive welfare state for particular citizens: members of the U.S. military, who enjoy all sorts of benefits (housing, education, and health care among others) that are not means tested. They are simply dispensed as a matter of course to anybody in the military. While many members of the military join for precisely these benefits, they are not stigmatized in any way for using them. In addition, the military is one of the economically more equal organizations in the United States. The income spread between a general and a private stands at a mere 15:1 while in the business world a chief executive officer (CEO) of a large company may make 800 to 1,000 times more than the average worker in his or her company. The universality of benefits and relative economic equality may explain why the U.S. military is one of the most racially integrated institutions in the United States. I am indebted to Michael Jasinski of the University of Georgia's School for Public and International Affairs for some of these reflections on the "universal" welfare state in the military. There is a long tradition of "decommodifying," to use a modern term, the lives of soldiers in the United States.

Theda Skocpol has detailed the origins of benefits, particularly Civil War pensions, in the United States. She highlights the universal character of these policies when she states, "In terms of the large share of the federal budget spent, the hefty proportion of citizens covered, and the relative generosity of the disability and old-age benefits offered, the United States had become a precocious social spending state. Its post–Civil War system of social provision in many respects exceeded what early programs of 'workingmen's insurance' were giving needy old people or superannuated industrial wage earners in fledgling Western welfare states around the turn of the century" (Skocpol 1992, 1, 2).

2. This stands in stark contrast to those who have argued that official social provision leads to the decay of voluntary cooperation and makes citizens increasingly dependent on the state. These views are most strongly expressed by Juergen Habermas (1987) and Michael Taylor (1987, 169), who argues, "The state . . . weakens local communities in favor of the larger national society. In doing so, it relieves individuals of the necessity to cooperate voluntarily amongst themselves on a local basis, making them more dependent on the state. The result is that altruism and cooperative behavior gradually decay." There is also some evidence in the United States indicating that the growth of the welfare state has diminished social capital, as seen in the marginal reduction of private philanthropy that has been connected to state provision (Chambre 1989; Olasky 1992).

3. In April 2005 the United States found itself in a maelstrom of proposals to "reform" Social Security between those who want to keep in a "lockbox" and those who want to create "personal" accounts in which people can invest their Social Security payments. Much of this debate was driven by concerns that Social Security may go "bankrupt" by the third decade of this millennium. However, the war in Iraq and "against terrorism" has overshadowed this issue and as of this writing (August 2006) the idea of privatizing Social Security seems to be a dead letter.

4. Questions of causality have plagued much of the literature on social capital and trust. The latest round of that debate is between Bo Rothstein (2004) and Eric Uslaner (2004). Rothstein argues, in a somewhat Titmussian fashion, that "people with many personal experiences of selective, needs testing welfare institutions will demonstrate lower interpersonal trust than others. Conversely, people with many personal experiences of universal, non needs-testing institutions will evince higher interpersonal trust than others" (2004, 24). For Uslaner (2004, 32) on the other hand, the capacity to trust is dispositional and by definition cannot be created. Trust is there in the first place, and the reason why "Swedes and other Westerners develop strong legal systems is *because people trust each other*" (emphasis in original).

5. I am indebted to Michael Jasinski for some of these thoughts.

6. Estimation procedures in this research were performed using the software HLM V. 6.0 (Bryk et al. 2005).

7. Very few multilevel analyses have been performed in comparative politics so far. The exception that proves the rule is the pioneering work of John Gelissen (2002), who uses multilevel analysis to gauge support for welfare states across different welfare regime contexts. The work by Marcel Lubbers, Merove Gijsberts, and Peer Scheepers (2002) employs such a methodology in analyzing right-wing voting patterns in Europe, as does the work of Robert Rohrschneider (2002), who looks at the quality of national institutions and attendant EU support.

8. The intraclass correlation of the intercept-only model (not shown) was 9 percent, indicating that 9 percent of the variation in welfare chauvinism is explained by level-2 units while 91 percent is explained by individual-level differences. This relatively low percentage of level-2 units is partly the result of the very small number of these units (13 countries) compared to a total of over 16,000 respondents at the individual level. Typically, HLM models are performed in stages, starting with an "intercept-only model," which represents the baseline and captures the overall effects of the level-2 units. This also provides the intraclass correlation (ICC) and the overall variance as contained in the deviance statistic. In the next stage, the individual-level variables are added, and, in addition to seeing the slopes and significance of the variables, it is also possible to measure the reduction in variance that the level-1 variables achieve. Similarly, the next step involves doing the same with level-2 variables only. Finally, the full model, with all the individual- and group-level variables, is added. Comparing the reduction of deviance between the intercept-only and the full model and determining whether this reduction is significant are what can be used to determine overall "fit" of the model.

Chapter 6

1. Kennedy's proposal was driven by a strong belief that immigrants can improve the lives of all Americans. He was not only guided by deep-seated humanitarian values but also by functionalist principles. Kennedy's "Proposal to Liberalize Immigration Statutes," which was sent to Congress on July 23, 1963, was based on three criteria: first, the skills of immigrants and their relationship to America's needs; second, the family relationship between new immigrants and people already in residence, so that the reuniting of families is encouraged; and, third, priority of registration, by which is meant that among people with equal claims the earliest registrant should be the first to be admitted (Kennedy 1964).

2. In order to estimate this nonlinear logit model with population weights, HLM 6.0 was used.

3. The intraclass correlation of the simple intercept only model is 21.

4. Parliamentary and Research Service of Canada, http://www.parl.gc.ca/information/library/PRBpubs/936-e.htm#1.%20The%20Incipient.

5. Ibid.

6. Very similar policies were established in Germany also, where in some *Länder* governments Turkish children were kept out of German classes and were taught in Turkish schools by teachers from Turkey in order to facilitate their integration into Turkey if they returned.

7. The Organization for Economic Cooperation and Development, on whose database this study relies, describes a foreign population as follows: "The population of foreign nationals may represent second and higher generations as well as first-generations of migrants. The characteristics of the population of foreign nationals depend on a number of factors: the history of migration flows, natural increase in the foreign population and naturalisations. Higher generations of immigrants arise in situations where they retain their foreign citizenship even when native-born. The nature of legislation on citizenship and the incentives foreigners have to naturalise both play a role in determining the extent to which this occurs in practice" (OECD 2003, 7). It is important to distinguish between the foreign population and the foreign-born population. The latter tends to generate higher percentages of the total resident population because it also includes

subjects who are foreign born but have attained national citizenship. The OECD describes a foreign-born population as follows: "The foreign-born population can be viewed as representing first-generation migrants, and may consist of both foreign and national citizens" (7).

8. The lead time of two years for the percentage of foreign population is rather arbitrary. How long does it take before a particular percentage of foreign population affects natives' attitudes? This is hard to say. Perhaps a one-year or even a five-year lead time could have been chosen. Overall, however, statistical results would not be drastically affected by different lead times as the percentage of foreign population does not vary dramatically from year to year.

9. Here the term *panel* does not refer to identical individuals who are surveyed over time. Rather, the term is used here to examine identical countries over time.

10. I thank Keith Banting and Will Kymlicka for their insights in the interpretation of the survey results in the Eastern European countries.

11. The law not only prohibits wearing the *hijab* but also yarmulkes for Jewish boys, turbans for Sikh boys, and large Christian crosses.

12. The European Court of Human Rights (ECtHR) in Strasbourg found in *Dahlab v. Switzerland* that the state can limit freedom of expression when it conflicts with the fundamental values of the state, as was seen with the principle of *laïcité*. Riley (2005) makes the point that the French law may end up being challenged on the grounds of religious discrimination as it disallowed head scarves, turbans, and yarmulkes but not "small" Christian crosses. Christians seldom walk into churches wearing large crosses.

Chapter 7

1. May 1981, 416. In some accounts, their blood is drawn and collected in cups, which they exchange and then proceed to drink. The movie version uses the cutting of the palms.

2. Doyle hastens to admit that "this brand of primordialist nationalism was not the dominant mode, and it often coexisted with liberal ideals of nationalism and progress that transcended the past" (2002, 20).

3. However, at the time the law stipulated that at least one of the spouses must have lived in Germany for at least eight years.

4. While it is certainly true that conservative politicians as late as 1996 argued that Germany was not a country of immigration, reformers argued in the early 1970s that the Federal Republic was a country of immigration. For example, the labor minister of North-Rhein Westphalia, Werner Figgin, argued that Germans "must think of ourselves as an immigration country and foster immigration with an appropriate set of policies" (quoted in Triadafilopoulos 2004, 13). Also, leading members of the Social-Liberal government, such as Interior Minister Hans-Dietrich Genscher, went so far as to argue that Germany should accept its status as an immigration country, attempt to integrate long-term foreign residents, and reduce the restrictions in its naturalization requirements (Triadafilopoulos 2004).

5. As is well known, most "foreigners" are Turks who were hired starting in the 1950s on the basis of bilateral agreements between Germany and Turkey, though the first treaty was between Italy and Germany. Germany was in need of additional labor to fuel its *Wirtschaftswunder* (economic miracle) in the 1950s and 1960s. By 1973, as a result of the first oil shock, these bilateral agreements were abandoned. However, immigration

continued as a result of family unification and high fertility rates among foreigners. Their numbers have now reached about 7.3 million. This number has remained stable since about 1996 and represents around 8.9 percent of the German population (Beauftragte der Bundesregierung für Migration, Flüchtlinge und Integration, 2004).

6. And yet, according to *Der Spiegel,* when it comes to the ethnic Germans, the Conservatives in Germany are generally very supportive, an attitude that is quite untypical for this party, which is in general very restrictionist and assimilationist. The reason may lie with the fact that around 75 percent of all ethnic Germans tend to vote for the CDU/CSU. *Der Spiegel* (February 24, 2003) reported that "the Christian Democrats are really bringing thousands of voters into the country, no matter how criminal they are or how little of a chance for integration there is for them."

7. Until 1993, Germany had the most liberal asylum law of any country in the world. This law was influenced by historic guilt. Until 1993, paragraph 16 of the German Grundgesetz (Basic Law) read: "People who are persecuted enjoy the right to asylum." However, after 1989, the number asylum seekers who used this clause in an attempt to gain access to Germany rose dramatically to over 438,000 in 1992. However, only a little more than 4 percent of them were accepted (9,189). There is evidence that many of the applicants were "bogus asylum seekers" (Joppke 1999, 87). After much political wrangling, an asylum law was enacted in 1993 that significantly toughened asylum protection. According to the 1993 law, people from "safe" third countries and "safe countries of origin" are no longer eligible to apply for asylum. In addition, those who land via airplane in a German airport and claim asylum are processed within the confines of the airport. If the asylum application is denied they are not allowed to leave the airport and are deported to their country of origin. By 2002, the number of asylum seekers had dropped to a historic low of 71,127. Of that number, only 1.8 percent were actually granted asylum in Germany, prompting Interior Minister Otto Schily to describe this as a "joyful development" (*Frankfurter Rundschau,* January 9, 2003).

8. One might argue that the *Gastarbeiter* that came in the 1950s and 1960s were needed and served the interests of Germany. During that period, few applicants were denied. What was needed was unskilled labor for jobs, Germans were not willing to perform. Basically everybody who wanted to work was promised a job. Today's situation is different: for people who lack certain qualifications the immigration door remains locked. Such discrimination did not exist in the 1950s, 1960s, and early 1970s.

9. Education is so fundamental to economic success that even natives suffer from the lack of it. In the United States, for example, the unemployment rate of people with a college degree is 2.4 percent. For those who do not have a high school diploma, the unemployment rate is almost 8 percent (National Public Radio, "Jobless with a College Degree: The Numbers Rise," March 19, 2005).

10. It is little known that German governmental agencies and businesses also attempted to recruit young women in Italy and Turkey with the intent to stabilize the low wages for native German women. In addition, it was believed that foreign women would have a greater tendency to return to their homelands, marry, and have children. This turned out not be the case, as young Turkish and Italian women did marry in their homelands but then returned to continue their work, bringing their families with them (Mattes 1999).

11. Part of the reason lies in the curious Swedish confidence in the malleability of society, as exemplified in Hansson's establishment of the welfare state or Alva and Gunnar

Myrdal's reflections in the 1930s on how to increase Swedish birthrates. The debates at that time centered on issues of race and social background as determinants of who should be allowed to have children. Between 1935 and 1975, Sweden engaged in about 63,000 sterilizations, 93 percent of which were performed on women. It is estimated that 40 percent of these sterilizations were involuntary. Persons with inheritable diseases and poor couples were "urged" to undergo such sterilizations, as it was "undesirable" to have handicapped offspring, both physically and socially. In 1975, Sweden abandoned this policy, and in 1999 a law on reparations was passed. Between 1999 and 2002, over 1,600 Swedes were paid 175,000 Swedish kronas (about 20,000 U.S. dollars) by the state as compensation for forced sterilizations. For a good overview of this issue, visit the Humboldt University Web site http://lms.cms.hu-berlin.de/cgi-bin/wohlfahrtsstaat.pl?Eugenik/Schweden.

12. The report is available at http://www.sos.se/FULLTEXT/111/2001-111-3/ Summary.htm.

References

Alesina, Alberto, Reza Baqir, and William Easterly. 1999. Public Goods and Ethnic Divisions. *Quarterly Journal of Economics* 110 (4): 1234–84.

Alesina, Alberto, and Edward L. Glaeser. 2004. *Fighting Poverty in the U.S. and Europe.* Oxford: Oxford University Press.

Alesina, Alberto, Edward Glaeser, and Bruce Sacerdote. 2001. *Why Doesn't the U.S. Have a European Style Welfare State?* Cambridge: Harvard Institute of Economic Research.

Alesina, Alberto, and Eliana LaFerrara. 1999. *Participation in Heterogeneous Communities.* Cambridge: Harvard Institute of Economic Research.

———. 2002. Who Trusts Others? *Journal of Public Economics* 85 (2): 207–34.

Alesina, Alberto, and Romain Wacziarg. 2000. The Economics of Civic Trust. In *Disaffected Democracies. What's Troubling the Trilateral Democracies?* edited by S. Pharr and R. Putnam. Princeton: Princeton University Press.

Allen, Christopher. 2004. Ideas, Institutions, and the Exhaustion of Modell Deutschland? *German Law Journal* 5 (9):1133–54.

Allport, G. 1954. *The Nature of Prejudice.* Cambridge: Addison-Wesley.

Almond, Gabriel A., and Sidney Verba. 1963. *The Civic Culture: Political Attitudes and Democracy in Five Nations.* Princeton: Princeton University Press.

Andersen, Jorgen Goul, and Tor Bjorklund. 2000. Radical Right Wing Populism in Scandinavia: From Tax Revolt to Neo-liberalism and Xenophobia. In *The Politics of the Extreme Right: From the Margins to the Mainstream,* edited by P. Hainsworth. London and New York: Pinter.

Angenendt, Steffen. *Integration geschieht ueber Arbeit.* 2005. http://www.aufenthaltstitel.de/zuwg/0719.html.

Apel, Rainer. 2004. Failing SPD Shocks Germany with Schachtian Cuts. *Executive Intelligence Review* 31 (28).

Arai, Mahmood, and Roger Vilhelmsson. 2001. *Immigrant's and Native's Unemployment Risk: Productivity Differentials or Discrimination.* Stockholm: Trade Union Institute for Economic Research.

Axelrod, Robert. 1984. *The Evolution of Cooperation.* New York: Basic Books.

Banfield, Edward. 1958. *The Moral Basis of a Backward Society.* New York: Free Press.

275

Banting, Keith. 1999. Social Citizenship and the Multicultural Welfare State. In *Citizenship, Diversity, and Pluralism,* edited by A. C. Cairns, J. C. Courtney, P. MacKinnon, H. J. Michelmann, and D. E. Smith. Montreal: McGill-Queens University Press.

———. 2000. Looking in Three Directions: Migration and the European Welfare State in Comparative Perspective. In *Immigration and Welfare: Challenging the Borders of the Welfare State,* edited by M. Bommes and A. Geddes. London and New York: Routledge.

Banting, Keith, and Will Kymlicka. 2003. Do Multiculturalism Policies Erode the Welfare State? Paper presented at the conference New Challenges for Welfare State Research, Toronto, Ontario, August 21–24. Revised version.

Banting, Keith, and Will Kymlicka. 2006. Immigration, Multiculturalism, and the Welfare State. *Ethics and International Affairs.* 20, no. 3: 281–304.

Barry, Brian. 2001. *Culture and Equality.* Cambridge: Harvard University Press.

Bauer, Thomas K., Magnus Lofstrom, and Klaus F. Zimmermann. 2001. Immigration Policy, Assimilation of Immigrants and Natives' Sentiments towards Immigrants: Evidence from Twelve OECD Countries. La Jolla, CA: Center for Comparative Immigration Studies, University of California, San Diego.

Bauer, Thomas K., and Klaus F. Zimmermann. 1997. Unemployment and Wages of Ethnic Germans. *Quarterly Review of Economics and Statistics* 37:361–77.

Beauftragte der Bundesregierung fuer Migration, Flüchtlinge und Integration. 2004. *Migrationsgeschehen.* Berlin: Bundesministerium des Innern.

Becker, Gary. 1957. *The Economics of Discrimination.* Chicago: University of Chicago Press.

Bellaby, Mara. 2005. Blair Proposes Strict Anti-terror Measures. *Washington Post,* August 6.

Bellah, Robert. 1998. Community Properly Understood: A Defense of "Democratic Communitarianism." In *The Essential Communitarian Reader,* edited by E. Amitai. New York: Rowman and Littlefield.

Belseley, D. A., E. Kuh, and R. E. Welsch. 1980. *Regression Diagnostics: Identifying Influential Data and Sources of Collinearity.* New York: Wiley.

Bendor, Jonathon, and Piotr Swistak. 1997. The Evolutionary Stability of Cooperation. *American Political Science Review* 91:290–307.

Betz, Hans Georg. 1994. *Radical Right Wing Populism in Western Europe.* New York: St. Martin's.

Betz, Hans Georg, and Stefan Immerfall. 1998. *The New Politics of the Right.* New York: St. Martin's.

Beyme, Klaus von. 2001. Citizenship and the European Union. In *European Citizenship. National Legacies, and Transnational Projects,* edited by K. Eder and B. Giesen. Oxford: Oxford University Press.

Bianco, William T. 1998. Uncertainty, Appraisal, and Common Interest: The Roots of Constituent Trust. In *Trust and Governance,* edited by V. Braithwaite and M. Levi. New York: Russell Sage Foundation.

Bischoff, Henry. 2002. *Immigration Issues.* Westport, CT: Greenwood.

Bissoondath, Neil. 1994. *Selling Illusions: The Cult of Multiculturalism in Canada.* Toronto: Penguin.

Blackburn, Simon. 1998. Trust, Cooperation, and Human Psychology. In *Trust and Governance,* edited by V. Braithwaite and M. Levi. New York: Russell Sage Foundation.

Blanck, Dag, and Mattias Tyden. 1995. Becoming Multicultural? The Development of a

Swedish Immigrant Policy. In *Welfare States in Trouble: Historical Perspectives on Canada and Sweden,* edited by S. Akerman and J. L. Granatstein. Umea: Swedish Science Press.

Bleich, Erik. 2003. *Race Politics in Britain and France.* Cambridge: Cambridge University Press.

Bok, Sissela. 2002. *Common Values.* London: University of Missouri Press.

Bommes, Michael, and Andrew Geddes. 2000. Conclusion: Defining and Redefining the Community of Legitimate Welfare Receivers. In *Immigration and Welfare: Challenging the Borders of the Welfare State,* edited by M. Bommes and A. Geddes. London: Routledge.

Borjas, George. 1999. *Heaven's Door: Immigration Policy and the American Economy.* Princeton: Princeton University Press.

Borre, Ole, and Elinor Scarborough, eds. 1995. *The Scope of Government.* Oxford: Oxford University Press.

Bourdieu, Pierre. 1979. Public Opinion Does Not Exist. In *Communication and Class Struggle,* edited by A. Mattelart and S. Siegelaub. New York: International General.

Boyer, Robert, and Daniel Drache, eds. 1996. *States against Markets: The Limits of Globalization.* London: Routledge.

Braithwaite, John. 1998. Institutionalizing Distrust, Enculturating Trust. In *Trust and Governance,* edited by V. Braithwaite and M. Levi. New York: Russell Sage Foundation.

Brehm, Sharon S., and Saul M. Kassin. 1990. *Social Psychology.* Boston: Houghton Mifflin.

Brimelow, Peter. 1995. *Alien Nation: Common Sense about America's Immigration Disaster.* New York: Random House.

Brittan, Samuel. 1998. Challenges to the Welfare State. In *Challenges to the Welfare State,* edited by H. Cavanna. Cheltenham: Edward Elgar.

Brochmann, Grete. 2003. Citizens of Multicultural States: Power and Legitimacy. In *The Multicultural Challenge,* edited by G. Brochmann. Amsterdam: Elsevier.

Brubaker, Rogers. 1992. *Citizenship and Nationhood in France and Germany.* Cambridge: Cambridge University Press.

———. 2001. The Return of Assimilation? Changing Perspectives on Immigration and Its Sequels in France, Germany, and the United States. *Ethnic and Racial Studies* 24 (4): 531–48.

———. 2004. *Ethnicity without Groups.* Cambridge: Harvard University Press.

Bruecker, Herber, Gil Epstein, Barry McCormick, Gilles Saint-Paul, Alessandra Venturini, and Klaus Zimmermann. 2002. Managing Migration in the European Welfare State. In *Immigration Policy and the Welfare State,* edited by T. Boeri, G. Hanson, and B. McCormick. Oxford: Oxford University Press.

Buchanan, Patrick J. 2002. *The Death of the West: How Dying Populations and Immigrant Invasions Imperil Our Country and Civilization.* New York: St. Martin's.

Busey, Samuel C. 1856. *Immigration: Its Evils and Consequences.* New York: Dewitt & Davenport.

Butovskaya, Marina, Frank Kemp Salter, Ivan Diakonov, and Alexey Smirnov. 2000. Urban Begging and Ethnic Nepotism in Russia: An Ethological Pilot Study. *Human Nature* 11 (2): 157–82.

Caldwell, Christopher. 2005. A Swedish Dilemma. *Weekly Standard,* February 28.

Cameron, David R. 1984. Social Democracy, Corporatism, Labour Quiescence, and the Representation of Economic Interest in Advanced Capitalist Countries. In *Order and Conflict in Contemporary Capitalism,* edited by J. H. Goldthorpe. Oxford: Oxford University Press.

Castles, Francis G., and Deborah Mitchell. 1993. Worlds of Welfare and Families of Nations. In *Families of Nations: Patterns of Public Policy in Western Democracies,* edited by F. G. Castles. Aldershot: Dartmouth.

Chambre, Susan. 1989. Kindling Points of Light: Volunteering as Public Policy. *Nonprofit and Voluntary Studies Quarterly* 18:249–68.

Chapin, Wesley D. 1997. *Germany for Germans?* Westport, CT: Greenwood.

Chicago Council on Foreign Relations. 2002. Worldviews. American Public Opinion and Foreign Policy.

Citrin, Jack. 1974. Comment: The Political Relevance of Trust in Government. *American Political Science Review* 68:973–88.

Citrin, Jack, and John Sides. 2004. European Immigration in the People's Court: Economic Need or Cultural Threat? Paper presented at the meetings of the American Political Science Association, Chicago, September 2–5.

Cohen, Roger. 2000. Call for "Guiding Culture" Rekindles Political Debate in Germany. *New York Times,* November 5.

Connor, Walker. 1993. Beyond Reason: the Nature of the Ethnonational Bond. *Ethnic and Racial Studies* 16 (3): 373–89.

———. 1994. Beyond Reason: The Nature of the Ethnonational Bond. In *Ethnonationalism: The Quest for Understanding,* edited by W. Conner. Princeton: Princeton University Press.

Converse, Philip. 1964. The Nature of Belief Systems in Mass Publics. In *Public Opinion and Public Policy,* edited by N. Luttberg. Homewood: Dorsey Press.

Cornelius, Wayne A., and Mark R. Rosenblum. 2005. The Neglect of Immigration. American Political Science Association Newsletter for Comparative Politics Section.

Cornelius, Wayne, and Takeyuki Tsuda. 2004. Controlling Immigration: The Limits of Government Immigration. In *Controlling Immigration: A Global Perspective,* edited by W. Cornelius. Stanford: Stanford University Press.

Cornell, Steven, and Douglas Hartmann. 1998. *Ethnicity and Race: Changing Identities in a Changing World.* Thousand Oaks, CA: Pine Forge Press.

Cosmides, Leda, and John Tooby. 1994. Better Than Rational: Evolutionary Psychology and the Invisible Hand. *American Economic Association Papers and Proceedings* 84: 327–32.

Costa, Dora L., and Matthew E. Kahn. 2002. Civic Engagement and Community Heterogeneity: An Economist's Perspective. Paper presented at the conference Social Connectedness and Public Activism, Harvard University.

Coughlin, R. 1980. *Ideology, Public Opinion, and Welfare Policy.* Berkeley: University of California Press.

Cox, Robert H. 2004. The Reconstruction of the Scandinavian Model: Ideas, Institutions, and Welfare Reform. Paper presented at the meetings of the American Political Science Association, Chicago, September 2–5.

Crepaz, Markus M. L. 1992. Corporatism in Decline? An Empirical Analysis of the Impact of Corporatism on Macro-economic Performance and Industrial Disputes in Eighteen Industrialized Democracies. *Comparative Political Studies* 25:139–68.

———. 2002a. Global Constitutional and Partisan Determinants of Redistribution in Fifteen OECD Countries. *Comparative Politics* 34:169–88.

———. 2002b. The Impact of Veto Players, Parties, and Globalization on the Redistributive Capacity of the State: A Panel Study of Fifteen OECD Countries. *Comparative Politics* 34:169–88.

Crozier, Michael, Samuel Huntington, and Joji Watanuki. 1975. *The Crisis of Democracy.* Princeton: Princeton University Press.

Dalton, Russell. 2004. *Democratic Challenges, Democratic Choices: The Erosion of Political Support in Advanced Industrial Democracies.* Oxford: Oxford University Press.

della-Porta, Donatella. 2000. Social Capital, Beliefs in Government, and Political Corruption. In *Disaffected Democracies: What's Troubling the Trilateral Countries?* edited by S. Pharr and R. Putnam. Princeton: Princeton University Press.

Deth, Jan van, and Elinor Scarborough, eds. 1995. *The Impact of Values.* Oxford: Oxford University Press.

Deutsch, Karl W. 1963. *Nation-Building.* New York: Atherton.

Doyle, Don H. 2002. *Nations Divided: America, Italy, and the Southern Question.* Athens: University of Georgia Press.

Durkheim, Émile. 1893. *The Division of Labor in Society.* New York: Free Press.

———. 1961. *Moral Education.* Translated by Everett K. Wilson and Herman Schnurer. New York: Free Press.

Easterly, W., and R. Levine. 1997. Africa's Growth Strategy: Policies and Ethnic Divisions. *Quarterly Journal of Economics* 112 (4):1203–50.

Economist. 2004a. Blokked. November 13, 56.

———. 2004b. Charlemagne: A Civil War on Terrorism. November 27, 56.

———. 2004c. The Kindness of Strangers? February 28, 53.

———. 2005. Which Turkey? March 17, 4.

Edelman, Murray. 1977. *Political Language: Words That Succeed and Politics That Fail.* New York: Academic Press.

El-Deeb, Khaled. 2006. Pakistani Cleric Offers Reward to Kill Cartoonist. Associated Press, February 18, A3.

Eller, Jack David, and Reed M Coughlan. 1993. The Poverty of Primordialism: The Demystification of Ethnic Attachments. *Ethnic and Racial Studies* 16 (2):183–202.

Entzinger, Han. 2003. The Rise and Fall of Multiculturalism: The Case of the Netherlands. In *Toward Assimilation and Citizenship,* edited by C. Joppke and E. Morawska. London: Palgrave Macmillan.

Erikson, Erik. 1963. *Childhood and Society.* New York: Norton.

Erikson, Robert S. 1976. The Relationship between Public Opinion and State Policy: A New Look Based on Some Forgotten Data. *American Journal of Political Science* 20 (1): 511–35.

Esping-Andersen, Gøsta. 1990. *The Three Worlds of Welfare Capitalism.* Princeton: Princeton University Press.

———. 2002. Towards the Good Society, Once Again? In *Why We Need a New Welfare State,* edited by G. E. Andersen. Oxford: Oxford University Press.

Etzioni, Amitai, ed. 1998. *The Essential Communitarian Reader.* New York: Rowman and Littlefield.

Eurobarometer (various studies). Zentralarchiv für Europäische Sozialforschung, Köln, Germany (producer and distributor). ICPSR Inter-university Consortium for Political and Social Research [producer], Ann Arbor, Michigan.

European Social Survey. 2002. R. Jowell and the Central Coordinating Team. European Social Survey 2002/2003. London. Centre for Comparative Social Surveys, City University.

Faist, Thomas. 1994. Immigration, Integration, and the Ethnicization of Politics. *European Journal of Political Research* 25:439–59.

Favell, Adrian. 1998. *Philosophies of Integration.* London: Macmillan.

Fishkin, James S. 1995. *The Voice of the People: Public Opinion and Democracy.* New Haven: Yale University Press.

Flora, Peter, and Arnold J Heidenheimer. 1981. The Historical Core and the Changing Boundaries of the Welfare State. In *The Development of Welfare States in Europe and America,* edited by P. Flora and A. J. Heidenheimer. New Brunswick, NJ: Transaction.

Flora, Peter, and Arnold J. Heidenheimer, eds. 1981. *The Development of Welfare States in Europe and America.* New Brunswick, NJ: Transaction.

Forma, Pauli. 1999. Welfare State Opinions among Citizens, MP Candidates, and Elites. In *The End of the Welfare State?* edited by S. Svallfors and P. Taylor-Gooby. London and New York: Routledge.

Freeman, Gary. 1986. Migration and the Political Economy of the Welfare State. *Annals of the American Academy of Political and Social Science* 485:51–63.

———. 1995. Modes of Immigration Politics in Liberal Democratic States. *International Migration Review* 29 (129): 881–902.

———. 1998. The Decline of Sovereignty? Politics and Immigration Restriction in Liberal States. In *Challenges to the Nation State: Immigration in Western Europe and the United States,* edited by C. Joppke. Oxford: Oxford University Press.

———. 2001. Client Politics or Populism. In *Controlling a New Migration World,* edited by V. Giraudon and C. Joppke. London and New York: Routledge.

Fryklund, Bjorn, and Tomas Peterson. 1992. The Refugee Question: The Touchstone of the Swedish System? In *Encounter with Strangers: Refugees and Cultural Confrontation in Sweden,* edited by G. Rystad. Lund, Sweden: Lund University Press.

Fukuyama, Francis. 1995. *Trust: The Social Virtues and Creation of Prosperity.* London: Hamish Hamilton.

Gans, Herbert J. 2004. The American Kaleidoscope, Then and Now. In *Reinventing the Melting Pot,* edited by T. Jacoby. New York: Basic Books.

Gatzke, Marcus. 2004. Den Sozialstaat gilt es zu schuetzen. *Netzeitung,* June 30.

Geddes, Andrew. 2003. *The Politics of Migration and Immigration in Europe.* London: Sage.

Geertz, Clifford. 1963. The Integrative Revolution. Primordial Sentiments and Civil Politics in the New States. In *Old Societies and New States: The Quest for Modernity in Asia and Africa,* edited by C. Geertz. London: Free Press of Glencoe.

Gelissen, John. 2002. *Worlds of Welfare, Worlds of Consent?* Leiden and Boston: Brill.

Geyer, Georgie Ann. 1996. *Americans No More.* New York: Atlantic Monthly Press.

Gibson, Rachel. 2002. *The Growth of Anti-immigrant Parties in Western Europe.* Lewiston, NY: Edwin Mellen.

Giddens, Anthony. 1971. *Capitalism and Modern Social Theory: An Analysis of the Writings of Marx, Durkheim, and Max Weber.* Cambridge: Cambridge University Press.

Gilens, Martin. 1999. *Why Americans Hate Welfare: Race, Media, and the Politics of Antipoverty Policy.* Chicago: University of Chicago Press.

Gitlin, Todd. 1995. *The Twilight of Common Dreams: Why America Is Wracked by Culture Wars.* New York: Metropolitan Books.

Givens, Terri E. 2002. The Role of Socio-economic Variables in the Success of Radical Right Wing Parties. In *Shadows over Europe: The Development and Impact of the Extreme Right in Western Europe,* edited by M. Schain, A. Zolberg, and P. Hossay. Oxford: Oxford University Press.

Glazer, Nathan. 1998. The American Welfare State: Exceptional No Longer? In *Chal-*

lenges to the Welfare State: Internal and External Dynamics for Change, edited by H. Cavanna. Cheltenham: Edward Elgar.

———. 2004. Assimilation Today. In *Reinventing the Melting Pot,* edited by T. Jacoby. New York: Basic Books.

Glazer, Nathan, and Daniel P. Moynihan. 1970. *Beyond the Melting Pot.* 2d ed. Cambridge: MIT Press.

Goldin, Claudia, and Lawrence F. Katz. 1999. Human Capital and Social Capital: The rise of Secondary Schooling in America, 1910–1940. *Journal of Interdisciplinary History* 29:683–723.

Goodhart, David. 2004. Too Diverse? *Prospect* 95.

Gourevitch, Peter. 1978. The Second Image Reversed: The International Sources of Domestic Politics. *International Organization* 32:881–912.

Granatstein, J. L. 1998. *Who Killed Canadian History?* New York: Harper Collins.

Granovetter, Mark S. 1973. The Strength of Weak Ties. *American Sociological Review* 78:1360–80.

Guiraudon, Virginie. 1998. Citizenship Rights for Non-citizens: France, Germany, and the Netherlands. In *Challenge to the Nation State: Immigration in Western Europe and the United States,* edited by C. Joppke. Oxford: Oxford University Press.

———. 2002a. Including Foreigners in National Welfare States. In *Restructuring the Welfare State,* edited by B. Rothstein and S. Steinmo. New York: Palgrave Macmillan.

———. 2002b. Including Foreigners in National Welfare States: Institutional Venues and Rules of the Game. In *Restructuring the Welfare State: Political Institutions and Policy Change,* edited by B. Rothstein and S. Steinmo. New York: Palgrave Macmillan.

Gwyn, Richard. 1995. *Nationalism without Walls: The Unbearable Lightness of Being Canadian.* Toronto: McClealland and Stewart.

Habermas, Jürgen. 1987. *The Philosophical Discourse of Modernity.* Cambridge: MIT Press.

———. 2001. *The Postnational Constellation.* Cambridge: MIT Press.

Hacker, Jacob. 2002. *The Divided Welfare State.* Cambridge: Cambridge University Press.

Hall, Peter. 2002. Great Britain: The Role of Government and the Distribution of Social Capital. In *Democracies in Flux: The Evolution of Social Capital in Contemporary Society,* edited by R. D. Putnam. Oxford: Oxford University Press.

Hall, Stuart. 2003. Political Belonging in a World of Multiple Identities. In *Conceiving Cosmopolitanism: Theory, Context, and Practice,* edited by S. Vertovec and R. Cohen. Oxford: Oxford University Press.

Hammar, Tomas. 1990. *Democracy and the Nation State: Aliens, Denizens, and Citizens in a World of International Migration.* Aldershot: Avebury.

Hammarstedt, Mats. 2001. Disposable Income Differences between Immigrants and Natives in Sweden. *International Journal for Social Welfare* 10:117–26.

Hansen, Jorgen, and Magnus Lofstrom. 2001. The Dynamics of Immigrant Welfare and Labor Market Behavior. Bonn, Germany: Institute for the Study of Labor.

Hansen, Marcus Lee. 1964. *The Immigrant in American History.* New York: Harper.

Hardin, Russell. 1998. Trust in Government. In *Trust and Governance,* edited by V. Braithwaite and M. Levi. New York: Russell Sage Foundation.

——— 2000. The Public Trust. In *Disaffected Democracies: What's Troubling the Trilateral Countries?* edited by S. Pharr and R. Putnam. Princeton: Princeton University Press.

———. 2001. Conceptions and Explanations of Trust. In *Trust in Society,* edited by K. S. Cook. New York: Russell Sage Foundation.

Harrigan, Steve. 2004. Swedes Reach Muslim Breaking Point. Fox News Channel, November 26.

Harris, Amy R., William N. Evans, and Robert M. Schwab. 2001. Education Spending in an Aging America. *Journal of Public Economics* 81 (3): 449–72.

Helliwell, John F., Stuart Soroka, and Richard Johnston. 2005. Diversity, Social Capital, and the Welfare State. In *Measuring and Modelling Trust,* edited by F. Kay and R. Johnston. Vancouver: University of British Columbia Press.

Hero, Rodney E., and Caroline J. Tolbert. 1996. A Racial/Ethnic Diversity Interpretation of Politics and Policy in the States of the U.S. *American Journal of Political Science* 40 (3): 851–71.

Hicks, Alexander. 1999. *Social Democracy and Welfare Capitalism: A Century of Income Security Politics.* Ithaca: Cornell University Press.

Hirst, Paul, and Grahame Thompson, eds. 1996. *Globalization in Question: The International Economy and the Possibilities of Governance.* Cambridge: Cambridge University Press.

Hobsbawn, Eric J. 1987. *The Age of Empire, 1875–1914.* New York: Pantheon.

Hoge, Warren. 1998a. Swedes Yearn for the Good Old Times as Election Nears. *Herald Tribune,* August 12.

———. 1998b. Swedish Party Pledging Expanded Welfare Gains Slim Victory. *New York Times,* September 21.

Hollifield, James F. 1997. Immigration and Integration in Western Europe: A Comparative Analysis. In *Immigration into Western Societies,* edited by E. M. Ucarer and D. J. Puchala. London and Washington, DC: Pinter.

———. 2000. Immigration and the Politics of Rights: The French Case in Comparative Perspective. In *Immigration and Welfare: Challenging the Borders of the Welfare State,* edited by M. Bommes and A. Geddes. London and New York: Routledge.

Holmberg, Soren. 1999. Down and Down We Go: Political Trust in Sweden. In *Critical Citizens: Global Support for Democratic Government,* edited by P. Norris. Oxford: Oxford University Press.

Horowitz, Donald. 1985. *Ethnic Groups in Conflict.* Berkeley: University of California Press.

Huddle, Donald. 1993. *The Costs of Immigration.* Washington, DC: Carrying Capacity Network.

Huntington, Samuel P. 1968. *Political Order in Changing Societies.* New Haven: Yale University Press.

———. 1996. *The Clash of Civilizations and the Remaking of the World Order.* New York: Simon and Schuster.

———. 2004. *Who Are We? The Challenges to America's National Identity.* New York: Simon and Schuster.

Husbands, Christopher T. 1988. The Dynamics of Racial Exclusion and Expulsion: Racist Politics in Western Europe. *European Journal of Political Research* 16:701–20.

———. 2002. How to Tame the Dragon; or What Goes Around Comes Around: A Critical Review of Some Major Contemporary Attempts to Account for Extreme-Right Racist Politics in Western Europe. In *Shadows over Europe: The Development and Impact of the Extreme Right in Western Europe,* edited by M. Schain, A. Zolbert, and P. Hossay. Oxford: Oxford University Press.

Ignatieff, Michael. 1993. *Blood and Belonging.* New York: Farrar, Straus and Giroux.

Ignatiev, Noel. 1995. *How the Irish Became White.* New York: Routledge.

Inglehart, Ronald. 1990. *Culture Shift in Advanced Industrial Society.* Princeton: Princeton University Press.

———. 1997. *Modernization and Postmodernization.* Princeton: Princeton University Press.

———. 1999. Postmodernization Erodes Respect for Authority, but Increases Support for Democracy. In *Critical Citizens: Global Support for Democratic Government,* edited by P. Norris. Oxford: Oxford University Press.

Inglehart, Ronald, Miguel Basanez, Jaime Diez-Medrano, Loek Halman, and Ruud Luijkx. 2004. Human Beliefs and Values. World Values Survey.

International Social Survey Program. National Identity Module I (1995) and II (2003). Zentralarchiv für Europäische Sozialforschung, Köln, Germany.

Ireland, Patrick. 2004. *Becoming Europe: Immigration, Integration, and the Welfare State.* Pittsburgh: University of Pittsburgh Press.

Iverson, Torben. 2001. The Dynamics of Welfare State Expansion: Trade-Openness, De-industrialization, and Partisan Politics. In *The New Politics of the Welfare State,* edited by P. Pierson. Oxford: Oxford University Press.

Jäntti, Markus, Knut Reed, Robin Naylor, Anders Björklund, Bernt Bratsberg, Oddbjørn Raaum, Eva Österbacka and Tor Eriksson. 2006. American Exceptionalism in a New Light: A Comparison of Intergenerational Earnings Mobility in the Nordic Countries, the United Kingdom and the United States. Discussion Paper No. 1938. Forschungsinstitut zur Zukunft der Arbeit.

Jederlund, Lars. 1998. From Immigration to Integration Policy. Stockholm: Swedish Institute.

Jennings, Kent M. 1998. Political Trust and the Roots of Evolution. In *Trust and Governance,* edited by V. Braithwaite and M. Levi. New York: Russell Sage Foundation.

Joppke, Christian. 1998. Immigration Challenges to the Nation State. In *Challenges to the Nation State,* edited by C. Joppke. Oxford: Oxford University Press.

———. 1999. *Immigration and the Nation State.* Oxford: Oxford University Press.

Joppke, Christian, and Ewa Morawska. 2003. Integrating Immigrants in Liberal Nation States: Policies and Practices. In *Toward Assimilation and Citizenship.* London: Palgrave Macmillan.

Kaase, Max, and Kenneth Newton, eds. 1995. *Beliefs in Government.* Oxford: Oxford University Press.

Kanchan, Chandra. 2001. Cumulative Findings in the Study of Ethnic Politics. *American Political Science Association Comparative Politics Newsletter* 12, no. 1 (winter).

Kangas, Olli E. 1997. Self Interest and the Common Good: The Impact of Norms, Selfishness, and Context in Social Policy Opinions. *Journal of Socio-Economics* 26 (5): 475–95.

Katzenstein, Peter J. 1985. *Small States in World Markets.* Ithaca: Cornell University Press.

———. 2000. Confidence, Trust, International Relations, and Lessons from Smaller Democracies. In *Disaffected Democracies: What's Troubling the Trilateral Countries?* edited by S. Pharr and R. Putnam. Princeton: Princeton University Press.

Kelly, June. 2001. Summer of Discontent. BBC News. July 12.

Kennedy, John F. 1964. *A Nation of Immigrants.* New York: Harper and Row.

Keohane, Robert, and Helen Milner, eds. 1996. *Internationalization and Domestic Politics.* Cambridge: Cambridge University Press.

Kitschelt, Herbert. 1995. *The Radical Right in Western Europe.* Ann Arbor: University of Michigan Press.

Klingemann, Hans Dieter, and Dieter Fuchs, eds. 1995. *Citizens and the State.* Oxford: Oxford University Press.

Klingholz, Reiner. 2004. Demographie: Was Deutschland erwartet. *GEO Magazin* (May).

Knight, Jack. 2001. Social Norms and the Rule of Law. In *Trust and Society,* edited by K. S. Cook. New York: Russell Sage Foundation.

Korpi, Walter. 1983. *The Democratic Class Struggle.* London: Routledge.

Korpi, Walter, and Joakim Palme. 1998. The Paradox of Redistribution and Strategies of Equality: Welfare State Institutions, Inequality, and Poverty in the Western Countries. *American Sociological Review* 63 (5): 661–87.

Kotlikoff, Laurence J., and Scott Burns. 2004. *The Coming Generational Storm: What You Need to Know about America's Economic Future.* Cambridge: MIT Press.

Kumlin, Staffan. 2002. Institutions—Experiences—Preferences: How Welfare State Design Affects Political Trust and Ideology. In *Restructuring the Welfare State,* edited by R. Rothstein and S. Steinmo. New York: Palgrave Macmillan.

Kymlicka, Will. 1996. *Multicultural Citizenship: A Liberal Theory of Minority Rights.* Oxford: Clarendon.

———. 2001. *Politics in the Vernacular: Nationalism, Multiculturalism, and Citizenship.* Oxford: Oxford University Press.

Lackner, Herbert. 2004. Als ein Reich zerfiel. *Profil,* June, 34–41.

Lahav, Gallya. 2004. *Immigration and Politics in the New Europe.* Cambridge: Cambridge University Press.

Leal, David L., Matt A. Barreto, Jongho Lee, and Rodolfo O. de la Garza. 2005. The Latino Vote in the 2004 Election. *Political Science and Politics* 38 (1): 41–49.

Lehmbruch, Gerhard. 1967. *Proporzdemokratie: Politisches System und Politische Kultur in der Schweiz und in Oesterreich.* Tübingen: Mohr Siebeck.

Leibfried, Stephan. 1992. Towards a European Welfare State? On Integrating Poverty Regimes into the European Community. In *Social Policy in a Changing Europe,* edited by Z. Ferge and J. E. Kolberg. Frankfurt am Main: Campus Verlag.

Lessenich, S., and I. Ostner. 1998. *Welten des Wohlfahrtskapitalismus: Der Sozialstaat in vergleichender Perspektive.* Frankfurt am Main: Campus Verlag.

Levi, Margaret. 1998. A State of Trust. In *Trust and Governance,* edited by V. Braithwaite and M. Levi. New York: Russell Sage Foundation.

Leyton-Henry, Zig. 1990. *The Political Rights of Migrant Workers in Western Europe.* London: Sage.

Liberman, Robert C. 2002. Political Institutions and the Politics of Race in the Development of the Modern Welfare State. In *Restructuring the Welfare State,* edited by B. Rothstein and S. Steinmo. New York: Palgrave Macmillan.

Lijphart, Arend. 1968. *The Politics of Accommodation: Pluralism and Democracy in the Netherlands.* Berkeley: University of California Press.

———. 1969. "Consociational Democracy." *World Politics* 21 (2): 207–25.

———. 1977. *Democracy in Plural Societies: A Comparative Exploration.* New Haven: Yale University Press.

———. 1984. *Democracies: Patterns of Majoritarian and Consensus Government in Twenty-one Democracies.* New Haven: Yale University Press.

———. 1999a. About Peripheries, Centres, and Other Autobiographical Reflections. In *Comparative European Politics,* edited by H. Daalder. London: Pinter.

———. 1999b. *Patterns of Democracy: Government Forms and Performance in Thirty-six Countries.* New Haven: Yale University Press.

Lijphart, Arend, and Markus M. L. Crepaz. 1991. Corporatism and Consensus Democracy in Eighteen Countries: Conceptual and Empirical Linkages. *British Journal of Political Science* 21:235–56.

Lindert, Peter H. 2004. *Growing Public: Social Spending and Economic Growth since the Eighteenth Century.* Cambridge: Cambridge University Press.

Lipset, Seymour M. 1960. *Political Man.* Garden City, NY: Doubleday.

Lipset, Seymour M., and Gary Marks. 2000. *It Didn't Happen Here: Why Socialism Failed in the United States.* New York: Norton.

Lubbers, Marcel, Merove Gijsberts, and Peer Scheepers. 2002. Extreme Right Wing Voting in Western Europe. *European Journal of Political Research* 41:345–78.

Luhmann, Niklas. 1988. Familiarity, Confidence, Trust: Problems and Alternatives. In *Trust: Making and Breaking Cooperative Relations,* edited by D. Gambetta. Oxford: Oxford University Press and Basil Blackwell.

Luttmer, Erzo. 2001. Group loyalty and the taste for redistribution. *Journal of Political Economy* 109 (3):500–528.

Magnusson, David. 1990. Personality Development from an Interactional Perspective. In *Handbook of Personality: Theory and Research,* edited by L. A. Pervin. New York: Guilford.

Mansbridge, Jane. 1999. Altruistic Trust. In *Democracy and Trust,* edited by M. Warren. Cambridge: Cambridge University Press.

Marriott, McKim. 1963. Cultural Policy in the New States. In *Old Societies and New States: The Quest for Modernity in Asia and Africa,* edited by C. Geertz. London: Free Press of Glencoe.

Marshall, Barbara. 2000. *The New Germany and Migration in Europe.* Manchester: Manchester University Press.

Marshall, T. H. 1950. Citizenship and Social Class. In *Citizenship and Social Class,* edited by T. H. Marshall and T. Bottomore. London: Pluto Press.

Martin, Philip L. 1999. Germany: Migration Policies for the Twenty-first Century. Institute on Global Conflict and Cooperation.

———. 2004. The United States: The Continuing Immigration Debate. In *Controlling Immigration: A Global Perspective,* edited by W. Cornelius, T. Tsuda, P. L. Martin, and J. F. Hollifield. Stanford: Stanford University Press.

Mattes, Monika. 1999. Zum Verhaeltnis von Migration und Geschlecht: Anwerbung und Beschaeftigung von "Gastarbeiterinnen" in der Bundesrepublik 1960 bis 1973. In *50 Jahre Bundesrepublik: 50 Jahre Einwanderung. Nachkriegsgeschichte als Migrationsgeschichte,* edited by J. Motte, R. Ohliger and A. v. Oswald. Frankfurt am Main: Campus Verlag.

May, Karl. 1981. Winnetou III (1909). Heyne Verlag.

McCarty, Therese. 1993. Democratic Diversity and the Size of the Public Sector. *Kyklos* 46:225–40.

Mercer, Jonathan. 2005. Rationality and Psychology in International Politics. *International Organization* 59:77–106.

Messick, David M., and Roderick M. Kramer. 2001. Trust as a Form of Shallow Morality. In *Trust in Society,* edited by K. Cook. New York: Russell Sage Foundation.

Meyers, Eytan. 2004. *International Immigration Policy: A Theoretical and Comparative Analysis.* London: Palgrave Macmillan.

Mill, John Stuart. 1968. *Considerations on Representative Government.* Chicago: Regnery.

———. 1991. *Considerations on Representative Government.* Buffalo: Prometheus.

Miller, David. 2000. *Citizenship and National Identity.* Cambridge: Polity.

Miller, Gary. 2001. Why Is Trust Necessary in Organizations? The Moral Hazard of Profit Maximization. In *Trust in Society,* edited by K. S. Cook. New York: Russell Sage Foundation.

Mommsen, W. J., ed. 1981. *The Emergence of the Welfare State in Britain and Germany.* Beckenham: Croom Helm London.

Monroe, Alan D. 1979. Consistency between Public Preferences and National Policy. *American Politics Quarterly* 7 (1): 3–19.

Moon, J. Donald. 1988. The Moral Basis of the Democratic Welfare State. In *Democracy and the Welfare State,* edited by A. Gutmann. Princeton: Princeton University Press.

Myrdal, Gunnar. 1960. *Beyond the Welfare State.* New Haven: Yale University Press.

Nagel, Joane. 1986. The Political Construction of Ethnicity. In *Competitive Ethnic Relations,* edited by S. Olzak and J. Nagel. Orlando, FL: Academic Press.

Nee, Victor, and Jimy Sanders. 2001. Trust in Ethnic Ties: Social Capital and Immigrants. In *Trust in Society,* edited by K. Cook. New York: Russell Sage Foundation.

Neumayer, Eric. 2004. Asylum Destination Choice. *European Union Politics* 5 (2):155–80.

Newton, Kenneth. 1999a. Social and Political Trust in Established Democracies. In *Critical Citizens: Global Support for Democratic Government,* edited by P. Norris. Oxford: Oxford University Press.

Newton, Kenneth, and Pippa Norris. 2000. Confidence in Public Institutions: Faith, Culture, or Performance. In *Disaffected Democracies: What's Troubling the Trilateral Countries?* edited by S. Pharr and R. Putnam. Princeton: Princeton University Press.

Niedermayer, Oskar, and Richard Sinnott, eds. 1995. *Public Opinion and Internationalized Governance.* Oxford: Oxford University Press.

Noble, Charles. 1997. *Welfare as We Knew It: A Political History of the American Welfare State.* Oxford: Oxford University Press.

Norris, Pippa. 2004. From the Civic Culture to the Afrobarometer. *APSA-CP Newsletter,* 15, no. 2 (summer): 6–10.

Nunnally, Jum C. 1978. *Psychometric Theory.* New York: McGraw-Hill.

Nussbaum, Martha, ed. 1996. *For Love of Country: Debating the Limits of Patriotism.* Boston: Beacon.

Nye, Joseph S. 1997. Introduction: The Decline of Confidence in Government. In *Why People Don't Trust Government ,* edited by J. S. Nye, P. D. Zelikow, and D. C. King. Cambridge: Harvard University Press.

Nye, J. S., P. D. Zelikow, and D. C. King, eds. 1997. *Why People Don't Trust Government.* Cambridge: Harvard University Press.

OECD. (various years). *Trends in International Migration.* Paris.

OECD. 2004. Organization for Economic Cooperation and Development. *Social Expenditures Database.* Paris.

Offe, Claus, and Susanne Fuchs. 2002. A Decline of Social Capital? The German Case. In *Democracies in Flux,* edited by R. Putnam. Oxford: Oxford University Press.

Olasky, Marvin. 1992. *The Tragedy of American Compassion.* Washington, DC: Regnery Gateway.

Orbell, John M., and Robyn M. Dawes. 1991. A Cognitive "Miser" Theory of Cooperators. *American Political Science Review* 85:515–28.

Pagden, Anthony. 1988. The Destruction of Trust and Its Economic Consequences in the Case of Eighteenth Century Naples. In *Trust: Making and Breaking Cooperative Relations,* edited by D. Gambetta. New York: Basil Blackwell.

Papadakis, Elim. 1992. Public Opinion, Public Policy, and the Welfare State. *Political Studies* 40:21–37.

Papadakis, Elim, and Clive Bean. 1993. Popular Support for the Welfare State: A Comparison between Institutional Regimes. *Journal of Public Policy* 13 (3): 227–54.

Parsons, Talcott. 1951. *The Social System.* Glencoe, IL: Free Press.

Passel, Jeffrey S., and Rebecca L. Clark. 1994. How Much Do Immigrants Really Cost? A Reappraisal of Huddle's "The Costs of Immigration." Washington, DC: Urban Institute.

Pateman, Carole. 1988. The Patriarchal Welfare State. In *Democracy and the Welfare State,* edited by A. Gutmann. Princeton: Princeton University Press.

Peel, Mark. 1998. Trusting Disadvantaged Citizens. In *Trust and Governance,* edited by V. Braithwaite and M. Levi. New York: Russell Sage Foundation.

Pettersen, Per A. 1995. The Welfare State: The Security Dimension. In *The Scope of Government,* edited by O. Borre and E. Scarborough. Oxford: Oxford University Press.

Pettit, Philip. 1998. Republican Theory and Political Trust. In *Trust and Governance,* edited by V. Braithwaite and M. Levi. New York: Russell Sage Foundation.

Pharr, Susan, and Robert Putnam. 2000. *Disaffected Democracies: What's Troubling the Trilateral Countries?* Princeton: Princeton University Press.

Pierson, Paul. 2001a. Postindustrial Pressures on the Mature Welfare States. In *The New Politics of the Welfare State,* edited by P. Pierson. Oxford: Oxford University Press.

Pierson, Paul, ed. 2001b. *The New Politics of the Welfare State.* Oxford: Oxford University Press.

Portillo, Michael. 2005. Multiculturalism Has Failed but Tolerance Can Save Us. *Times Online,* July 17, 2005.

Poterba, James. 1997. Demographic Structure and the Political Economy of Public Education. *Journal of Policy Analysis and Management* 16 (1): 46–66.

Preuss, Ulrich K. 1999. National, Supranational, and International Solidarity. In *Solidarity,* edited by K. Bayertz. Dordrecht: Kluwer.

Putnam, Robert D. 1993. *Making Democracy Work: Civic Traditions in Modern Italy.* Princeton: Princeton University Press.

———. 2000. *Bowling Alone: The Collapse and Revival of American Community.* New York: Simon and Schuster.

Putnam, Robert D., ed. 2002. *Democracies in Flux.* Oxford: Oxford University Press.

Rae, Douglas W. 1967. *The Political Consequences of Electoral Laws.* New Haven: Yale University Press.

Raudenbush, Stephen W., and Anthony S. Bryk. 2002. *Hierarchical Linear Models: Applications and Data Analysis Methods.* London: Sage.

Reisman, David. 2001. *Richard Titmuss.* London: Palgrave Macmillan.

Richburg, Keith B. 2003. Veiled Opposition Comes Out in Force. *Washington Post,* December 22, A19.

Riley, Alan. 2005. *The Headscarf Ban: Is France Risking European Court Action?* http://www.ceps.be/wp.php?article_id=328.

Rimlinger, G. 1971. *Welfare Policy and Industrialization in Europe.* New York: Wiley.

Rodrik, Dani. 1997. *Has Globalization Gone Too Far?* Washington, DC: Institute for International Economics.

Roepke, W. 1960. *A Humane Economy: The Social Framework of the Free Market.* Chicago: Regnery.

Rohrschneider, Robert. 2002. The Democracy Deficit and Mass Support for an EU-Wide Government. *American Journal of Political Science* 46 (2): 463–75.

Rokkan, Stein. 1977. Towards a General Concept of Verzuiling. *Political Studies* 25:563–70.

Roller, Edeltraud. 1995. The Welfare State: The Equality Dimension. In *The Scope of Government,* edited by O. Borre and E. Scarborough. Oxford: Oxford University Press.

Room, Graham J. 1981. The End of the Welfare State? In *The Emergence of the Welfare State in Britain and Germany,* edited by W. J. Mommsen. London: Croom Helm.

Rothstein, Bo. 1998. *Just Institutions Matter.* Cambridge: Cambridge University Press.

———. 2002. Social Capital in the Social Democratic State. In *Democracies in Flux,* edited by R. Putnam. Oxford: Oxford University Press.

———. 2004. Social Trust and Honesty in Government: A Causal Mechanism Approach. In *Creating Social Trust in Post-socialist Transition,* edited by J. Kornai, B. Rothstein, and S. Rose-Ackerman. New York: Palgrave Macmillan.

Rothstein, Bo, and Eric Uslaner. 2004. All for All: Equality and Social Trust. Manuscript.

Runblom, Harald. 1994. Swedish Multiculturalism in a Comparative European Perspective. *Sociological Forum* 9 (4): 623–40.

Ruth, Arne. 1986. The Second New Nation: The Mythology of Modern Sweden. In *Economics and Values,* edited by L. Arvedson, I. Haegg, M. Loennroth, and B. Ryden. Stockholm: Almqvist and Wiksell.

Salter, Frank K., ed. 2004. *Welfare, Ethnicity, and Altruism.* London: Frank Cass.

Sanderson, Stephen K. 2004. Ethnic Heterogeneity and Public Spending: Testing the Evolutionary Theory of Ethnicity with Cross National Data. In *Welfare, Ethnicity, and Altruism,* edited by F. K. Salter. London: Frank Cass.

Sassen, Saskia. 1998. Transnationalizing Immigration Policy. In *Challenge to the Nation State,* edited by C. Joppke. Oxford: Oxford University Press.

———. 1999. *Guests and Aliens.* New York: New Press.

———. 2004. Diversity Consumers. http://www.prospect-magazine.co.uk/start.asp?P_Article=12394.

Schain, Martin, Aristide Zolberg, and Patrick Hossay. 2002. *Shadows over Europe: The Development and Impact of the Extreme Right in Western Europe.* New York: Palgrave Macmillan.

Scharpf, Fritz. 2000. Interdependence and Democratic Legitimation. In *Disaffected Democracies: What's Troubling the Trilateral Countries?* edited by S. Pharr and R. Putnam. Princeton: Princeton University Press.

Schily, Otto. 2005. Zuwanderung—das Neue Gesetz. Vorwort des Bundesinneministers. Bundesministerium des Innern.

Schirmer, Dietmar. 2004. Closing the Nation: Nationalism and Statism in Nineteenth and Twentieth Century Germany. In *The Shifting Foundations of Modern Nation States,* edited by S. Godrey and F. Unger. Toronto: University of Toronto Press.

Schlesinger, Arthur M. 1998. *The Disuniting of America: Reflections on a Multicultural Society.* New York: Norton.

Schmidt, Manfred G. 1986. Politische Bedingungen erfolgreicher Wirtschaftspolitik: Eine vergleichende Analyse westlicher Industrielaender. *Journal fuer Sozialforschung* 26:251–73.

Schneider, Anne L., and Helen Ingram. 1997. *Policy Design for Democracy.* Lawrence: University Press of Kansas.

Schneider, Friedrich, and Dominik H. Enste. 2003. *The Shadow Economy: An International Survey.* Cambridge: Cambridge University Press.

Scholz, John T. 1998. Trust, Taxes, and Compliance. In *Trust and Governance,* edited by V. Braithwaite and M. Levi. New York: Russell Sage Foundation.

Scholz, John T., and Mark Lubell. 1998. Trust and Taxpaying: Testing the Heuristic Approach to Collective Action. *American Journal of Political Science* 42 (2): 398–417.

Schwartz, Herman V. 2001. Round up the Usual Suspects. Globalization, Domestic Politics, and Welfare State Change. In *The New Politics of the Welfare State,* edited by P. Pierson. Oxford: Oxford University Press.

Scruggs, Lyle. 2004. Welfare State Entitlements Data Set: A Comparative Institutional Analysis of Eighteen Welfare States, Version 1.0.

Scruggs, Lyle, and James Allen. 2004. Welfare State Decommodification in Eighteen OECD Countries: A Replication and Revision. Paper presented at the Department of Social and Political Studies, University of Edinburgh, University of Kent, and University of York.

Seligman, Adam B. 1997. *The Problem of Trust.* Princeton: Princeton University Press.

Shalev, Michael. 2002. Limits and Alternatives to Multiple Regressions in Comparative Political Economy. Manuscript.

Shiller, Robert J. 2003. Learning Economic Dynamism: Project Syndicate. Institute for Economic Research, Munich. October.

Shils, Edward. 1957. Primordial, Personal, Sacred, and Civil Ties: Some Particular Observations on the Relationships of Sociological Research and Theory. *British Journal of Sociology* 8 (2):130–45.

Shonfield, Andrew. 1965. *Modern Capitalism: The Changing Balance of Public and Private Power.* Oxford: Oxford University Press.

Singer, Peter. 2004. *One World.* 2d ed. New Haven: Yale University Press.

Sinn, Hans Werner. 2004. *Ist Deutschland noch zu retten?* 8th ed. Munich: Econ Verlag.

Skocpol, Theda. 1992. *Protecting Mothers and Soldiers: The Political Origins of Social Policy in the United States.* Cambridge: Belknap Press of Harvard University Press.

———. 1997. The GI Bill and US Social Policy: Past and Future. In *The Welfare State,* edited by E. F. Paul, F. D. Miller, and J. Paul. Cambridge: Cambridge University Press.

Smith, Craig S. 2004. In Mourning Slain Filmmaker, Dutch Confront Limitation of Their Tolerance. *New York Times,* November 11.

Smith, Gordon. 1976. The Functional Properties of the Referendum. *European Journal of Political Research* 4 (1): 1–16.

Smith, James P., and Barry Edmonston. 1997. *The New Americans: Economic, Demographic, and Fiscal Effects of Immigration.* Washington, DC: National Academy Press.

Sombart, Werner. 1976. *Why Is There No Socialism in the United States?* White Plains, NY: International Arts and Sciences Press. First published in German in 1906.

Soroka, Stuart, Keith Banting, and Richard Johnston. 2002. Ethnicity, Trust, and the Welfare State. In *Diversity, Social Capital, and the Welfare State,* edited by F. Kay and R. Johnston. Vancouver: University of British Columbia Press.

Soysal, Yasemin. 1994. *Limits of Citizenship.* Chicago: University of Chicago Press.

Spencer, Sarah. 2003. Introduction. *Political Quarterly* 74:1–24. Special issue on immigration.

Spira, Thomas. 1999. *Nationalism and Ethnicity Terminologies: An Encyclopedic Dictionary and Research Guide.* Gulf Breeze, FL: Academic International Press.

Steiner, Jürg. 1970. *Gewaltlose Politik und Kulturelle Vielfalt: Hypothese entwickelt am Beispiel der Schweiz.* Berne: Paul Haupt.

Steinmo, Sven, Kathleen Thelen, and Frank Longstreth, eds. 1992. *Structuring Politics: Historical Institutionalism in Comparative Analysis.* Cambridge: Cambridge University Press.

Stepan, Alfred, and Ezra Suleiman. 2005. French Republican Model Fuels Alienation Rather than Integration. *Taipei Times,* November 18.

Stephens, John D. 1980. *The Transition from Capitalism to Socialism.* Atlantic Highlands, NJ: Humanities Press.

Stolle, Dietlind. 2001. Clubs and Congregations. The Benefits of Joining an Association. In *Trust in Society,* edited by K. Cook. New York: Russell Sage Foundation.

Strange, Susan. 1995. The Limits of Politics. *Government and Opposition* 30: 291–311.

Suny, Ronald Grigor. 2001. Constructing Primordialism: Old Histories for New Nations. *Journal of Modern History* 73:862–96.

Svallfors, Stefan. 1997. Worlds of Welfare and Attitudes to Redistribution: A Comparison of Eight Western Nations. *European Sociological Review* 13 (3): 283–304.

———. 2002. Political Trust and Support for the Welfare State. Unpacking a Supposed Relationship. In *Restructuring the Welfare State,* edited by B. Rothstein and S. Steinmo. London: Palgrave Macmillan.

Svallfors, Stefan, and Peter Taylor-Gooby. 1999. *The End of the Welfare State?* New York: Routledge.

Swank, Duane. 2001. Mobile Capital, Democratic Institutions, and the Public Economy in Advanced Industrial Societies. *Journal of Comparative Policy Analysis: Research and Practice* 3:133–62.

———. 2002. *Global Capital, Political Institutions, and Policy Change in Developed Welfare States.* Cambridge: Cambridge University Press.

Swank, Duane, and Hans Georg Betz. 2003. Globalization, the Welfare State, and Right-Wing Populism in Western Europe. *Socio-Economic Review* 1:215–45.

Sztompka, Piotr. 1999. *Trust: A Sociological Theory.* Cambridge: Cambridge University Press.

Tajfel, Henri. 1981. *Human Groups and Social Categories.* Cambridge: Cambridge University Press.

———. 1982. *Social Identity and Group Relations.* Cambridge: Cambridge University Press.

Tan, Kok-Chor. 2004. *Justice without Borders.* Cambridge: Cambridge University Press.

Tarrow, Sidney. 2000. Mad Cows and Social Activists. In *Disaffected Democracies: What's Troubling the Trilateral Countries?* edited by S. Pharr and R. Putnam. Princeton: Princeton University Press.

Taylor, A. J. P. 1955. *Bismarck: The Man and the Statesman.* New York: Knopf.

Taylor, Charles. 2003. No Community, No Democracy. *The Responsive Community* 13, no. 4 (fall): 17–27.

Taylor, Michael. 1987. *The Possibility of Cooperation.* Cambridge: Cambridge University Press.

Taylor-Gooby, Peter. 1985. *Public Opinion, Ideology, and State Welfare.* London: Routledge.

Taz, die Tageszeitung. 2002. "Global oder Lokal." Interview with Emmanuel Todd. August 19.

Thernstrom, Stephan. 2004a. Rediscovering the Melting Pot. In *Reinventing the Melting Pot,* edited by T. Jacoby. New York: Basic Books.

Thompson, Michael, Richard Ellis, and Aaron Wildavsky. 1990. *Cultural Theory.* San Francisco: Westview.

Thraenhardt, Dietrich. 1997. The Political Uses of Xenophobia in England, France, and Germany. In *Immigration into Western Societies,* edited by E. M. Ucarer and D. J. Puchala. London and Washington, DC: Pinter.

Tilly, Charles. 1975. Reflections on the History of European State-Making. In *The Formation of National States in Western Europe,* edited by C. Tilly. Princeton: Princeton University Press.

———. 1998. *Durable Inequality.* Berkeley: University of California Press.

Titmuss, Richard. 1965. Goals of Today's Welfare State. In *Towards Socialism,* edited by P. Anderson and R. Blackburn. London: Fontana.

———. 1968. *Commitment to Welfare.* London: George Allen and Unwin.

Tocqueville, Alexis. 1994. *Democracy in America.* New York: Knopf.

Togman, Jeffrey M. 2002. *The Ramparts of Nations.* Westport, CT: Praeger.

Tönnies, Ferdinand. 1988. *Community and Society.* New Brunswick, NJ: Transaction.

Traynor, Ian. 2004. Extremist Parties Exploit German Anxiety. *Guardian,* September 20.

Triadafilopoulos, Triadafilos. 2004. Guest Workers into Germans? The Politics of Citizenship in the Federal Republic of Germany, 1960–2000. Paper presented at the meetings of the American Political Science Association, Chicago, September 2–5.

Tsebelis, George. 2002. *Veto Players: How Institutions Work.* Princeton: Princeton University Press.

Tyler, Tom R. 1998. Trust and Democratic Governance. In *Trust and Governance,* edited by V. Braithwaite and M. Levi. New York: Russell Sage Foundation.

Uddmann, Paula. 1992. Democracy and Refugee Policy. In *Encounters with Strangers: Refugees and Cultural Confrontation in Sweden,* edited by G. Rystad. Lund, Sweden: Lund University Press.

Uslaner, Eric M. 2002. *The Moral Foundations of Trust.* Cambridge: Cambridge University Press.

———. 2003. Tax Evasion, Trust, and the Strong Arm of the Law. Paper presented at the conference Tax Evasion, Trust, and State Capacity, University of Saint Gallen, Saint Gallen, Switzerland, October 17–19.

———. 2004. Honesty, Trust, and Legal Norms in the Transition to Democracy: Why Bo Rothstein Is Better Able to Explain Sweden than Romania. In *Creating Social Trust in Post-socialist Transition,* edited by J. Kornai, B. Rothstein, and S. Rose-Ackerman. New York: Palgrave Macmillan.

Van den Berghe, Pierre. 1981. *The Ethnic Phenomenon.* New York: Elsevier.

VanEvera, Stephen. 2001. Primordialism Lives! *American Political Science Association Comparative Politics Newsletter* 29 (1): 20–22.

Vertovec, Steven, and Robin Cohen, eds. 2002. *Conceiving Cosmopolitanism.* Oxford: Oxford University Press.

Voland, Eckart. 1999. On the Nature of Solidarity. In *Solidarity,* edited by K. Bayertz. Amsterdam: Kluwer.

Waldrauch, Harald. 2001. *Die Integration von Einwanderern.* Frankfurt am Main: Campus Verlag.

———. 2003. Electoral Rights for Foreign Nationals: A Comparative Overview of Regulations in Thirty-six Countries. Paper presented at the conference The Challenges of Immigration and Integration in the European Union and Australia, University of Sydney, February 18–20.

Waldrauch, Harald, and Christoph Hofinger. 1997. An Index to Measure the Legal Obstacles to the Integration of Immigrants. *New Community* 23 (2): 271–85.

Waldron, Jeremy. 1992. Minority Cultures and the Cosmopolitan Alternative. *University of Michigan Journal of Law Reform* 25 (3): 751–93.

Wallace, Charles P. 2004. Driven to Extremes. *Time Europe,* November 24.

Walzer, Michael. 1983. *Spheres of Justice.* New York: Basic Books.

Wandruszka, Adam. 1954. Oesterreichs Politische Kultur. In *Geschichte der Republik Oesterreich,* edited by H. Benedikt. Vienna: Verlag fuer Geschichte und Politik.

Weber, Max. 1978. *Economy and Society.* Berkeley: University of California Press.

Westerloo, Gerard van. 2004. *Niet spreken met de bestuurder.* Amsterdam: De Bezige Bij.

Whiteley, Peter. 1981. Public Opinion and the Demand for Social Welfare in Britain. *Journal of Social Policy* 10 (4): 453–70.

Whiting, Susan H. 1998. The Mobilization of Private Investment as a Problem of Trust in Local Governance Structures. In *Trust and Governance,* edited by V. Braithwaite and M. Levi. New York: Russell Sage Foundation.

Wilensky, Harold. 1965. The Problems and Prospects of the Welfare State. In *Industrial Society and Welfare,* edited by H. Wilensky and C. N. Lebeaux. Glencoe, IL: Free Press.

———. 1975. *The Welfare State and Equality: Structural and Ideological Roots of Public Expenditures.* Berkeley: University of California Press.

———. 1981. Democratic Corporatism, Consensus and Social Policy: Reflections on Changing Values and "Crisis" of the Welfare State. In *Welfare State in Crisis,* edited by H. Wilensky. Paris: OECD.

Wilensky, Harold L. 2002. *Rich Democracies: Political Economy, Public Policy, and Performance.* Berkeley: University of California Press.

Wilensky, Harold L., and Charles N. Lebeaux. 1965. *Industrial Society and Social Welfare.* New York: Free Press.

Williams, Bernard. 1988. Formal Structures and Social Reality. In *Trust,* edited by D. Gambetta. Oxford. Basil Blackwell and Oxford University Press.

Wintrobe, Ronald, and Klarita Gerxhani. N.d. Tax Evasion and Trust: A Comparative Analysis. Amsterdam.

Wolfe, Alan, and Jytte Klausen. 1997. Identity Politics and the Welfare State. *Social Philosophy and Policy* 14 (2): 213–55.

World Values Survey (WVS). Various waves. ICPSR Inter-university Consortium for Political and Social Research [producer], Ann Arbor Michigan.

Wrong, Dennis. 1994. *The Problem of Order: What Unites and Divides Society.* New York: Free Press.

Wüst, Andreas, M. 1995. Vorbild USA? Deutsche Einwanderungspolitik auf dem Prüfstand. M.A. thesis. University of Heidelberg, Germany.

Young, Iris. 1990. *Justice and the Politics of Difference.* Princeton: Princeton University Press.

Zimmermann, Klaus F., Thomas K. Bauer, Holger Bonin, Rene Fahr, and Holger Hinte. 2001. *Fachkraeftebedarf by hoher Arbeitslosigkeit: Gutachten im Auftrag der Unabhaengigen Kommission Zuwanderung der Bundesregierung.* Bonn: IZA.

Zolberg, Aristide. 1987. Wanted but Not Welcome: Alien Labor in Western Development. In *Population in an Interacting World,* edited by W. Alonso. Cambridge: Harvard University Press.

Index

claim, 11
concepts, 2
differences, 24, 153
fears, 92
group, 13, 115
impulses, 50
literature, 41
nationalism, 271
sentiments, 30, 41, 45, 92, 103, 134
story, 20
theory, 50
trust, 12, 110, 111, 114, 115, 117, 121, 122, 125, 130, 132, 134, 267
view, 19, 32, 49
Progressive Party, 89
Progress Party, 55
Prophet Muhammad, 7
Proportional representation, 43, 44, 136, 137, 251
Protection of the Constitution (*Verfassungsschutz*), 206
Protestants, 23, 135
Public pension, 5
Putnam, Robert D., 94, 96, 97, 100–103, 105, 106, 108, 124, 140, 267

Race frames, 166
Racialization, 20
Racial profiling, 22
Racists, 13, 22, 37
Regional elections (*Landtagswahlen*), 211
Religious
    affiliation, 36
    cleavages, 33, 136
    community, 19
    conflicts, 152
    discrimination, 271
    diversity, 78, 250
    fundamentalism, 24
    groups, 246, 260
    identity, 16
    symbols, 194, 195
    tension, 58
Republikaner, 25
Revolutionary War, 28
Richburg, Keith, 265
Right-wing parties, 3, 4, 25, 53–55, 61,

71, 75, 85, 86, 89, 151, 216, 217, 253, 258, 264, 265, 269
Roepke, Wilhelm, 104
Roller, Edeltraud, 79, 86
Rosenblum, Mark, 4
Rothstein, Bo, 42, 124, 145, 151, 269
Runblom, Harald, 224

Sassen, Saskia, 25, 46, 210
Scarborough, Elinor, 78
Scharpf, Fritz, 268
Schirmer, Dietmar, 206, 207
Schmidt, Manfred G., 238
Scholz, John T., 94, 98, 126
Schwartz, Herman V., 15
Scruggs, Lyle, 141–45, 147, 153, 156, 178, 230
separation of church and state (*laïcité*), 194, 195, 271
Shils, Edward, 19
Skocpol, Theda, 43, 139, 265, 269
Social
    affinity, 34
    assimilation, 45
    capital, 94, 97, 98, 100–104, 114, 115, 140, 269
    chasms, 29
    class, 167
    cleavages, 137
    conflict, 6
    construction, 30
    diversity, 47
    expenditure, 72, 74, 80, 164, 178, 205, 223, 241
    fabric, 4, 58
    harmony, 136, 137, 153
    heterogeneity, 15, 16, 29, 32–37, 42
    homogeneity, 2, 3
    identity theory, 35, 171
    insurance, 15
    integration, 170
    mobility, 32, 79
    networks, 104
    policy, 27
    practices, 19
    security, 5
    sociobiological, 27, 32, 135